JOSEPHINE TEY

Jennifer Morag Henderson grew up and lives in Inverness. She is an author, playwright and editor, whose writing has been published in magazines, newspapers and anthologies, and has featured on BBC radio and television. Recent work includes a short play for the National Theatre of Scotland. She edited *Random Acts of Writing* from 2008 – 2011. She is a graduate of the University of Glasgow, has a graduate degree from Dalhousie University (Canada), and further qualifications in proofreading, languages and teaching.

'A much needed biography of one of the great mystery writers of the twentieth century. 'Josephine Tey' is also a well-kept secret in Scottish Literature: a forensic stylist and the most elegant of minds.'
– Professor Gerard Carruthers, University of Glasgow

'This biography by Jennifer Morag Henderson is to be warmly welcomed and will be read eagerly by anyone curious about Josephine Tey, modern theatre, crime genre fiction, women's writing, or Scottish literature, in all its multi-faceted complexity.'
– Professor Alan Riach, Scottish Literature, University of Glasgow

'It strips away a lot of the myth surrounding Mackintosh; and it also tells the moving story of a major leading Scots writer for whom the detective novel became "a medium as disciplined as any sonnet".'
– *The Observer*, Best Biographies of 2015

'The life of one of the great golden age crime writers is granted a forensic examination in Josephine Tey.'
– *The Independent*, Best Crime Books of 2015

'In Henderson's loving, meticulously-researched book we have a first and vital account of that life...hugely valuable to anyone who cares about the story of writing in Scotland, what it has been, how it has changed, and where it may go next.'
– *The Scotsman*

'This is the image of Josephine Tey which Henderson leaves us: not a closeted introvert forever scuttling back to Inverness out of shyness, but a strong woman who put her duty to her family and her work before everything else. '
– *The Telegraph*

JOSEPHINE TEY

A life

Jennifer Morag Henderson

Foreword by Val McDermid

SANDSTONEPRESS
HIGHLAND | SCOTLAND

First published in Great Britain and the United States of America
Sandstone Press Ltd
Dochcarty Road
Dingwall
Ross-shire
IV15 9UG
Scotland.

www.sandstonepress.com

Editor: Moira Forsyth

The publisher acknowledges support from
Creative Scotland towards publication of this volume.

ISBN: 978-1-910985-37-3
ISBNe: 978-1-910124-71-0

Jacket design and photo sections by Raspberry Creative Type, Edinburgh
Typeset by Iolaire Typesetting, Newtonmore.
Printed and bound by CPI Group (UK) Ltd, Croydon CR0 4YY.

This book is dedicated to my mum Christine,
who first introduced me to Josephine Tey.

'Her life was much more than I ever imagined. My life expanded in the writing of hers.'

Valerie Lawson, *Mary Poppins, She Wrote: The Life of P. L. Travers*
(New York: Simon & Schuster, 2013)

Contents

List of Illustrations

14. Anstey Physical Training College; with thanks to the Anstey Association.
15. Beth, in her Anstey sports kit; with thanks to Colin Stokes.
16. Rhoda Anstey; with thanks to the Anstey Association.
17. Gordon Barber.
18. Colin and Josephine MacKintosh; with thanks to Colin Stokes.
19. Colin MacKintosh; with thanks to Colin Stokes.
20. Beth, interwar summer holidays; with thanks to Colin Stokes.
21. The letterhead from Colin's shop; with thanks to Colin Stokes.
22. Castle Street in Inverness today: the site of Colin's shop; from the author's collection © Jennifer Morag Henderson.
23. The arrival of the London sleeper train at Inverness Railway station, early 20th century; with thanks to the Highland Railway Society.
24. Hugh McIntosh's house in London (on the left); from the author's collection © Jennifer Morag Henderson.
25. Hugh's grave in Tomnahurich; from the author's collection © Jennifer Morag Henderson.
26. Captain Murdoch Beaton, the inspiration for the fictional Murray Heaton; with thanks to Iain Beaton.
27. Elizabeth MacKintosh's first 'author photo' – never used: 'Josephine Tey, December 1928/January 1929' © Andrew Paterson Collection.
28. The New Theatre, London (now the Noel Coward); from the author's collection © Jennifer Morag Henderson.
29. Gordon Daviot's own copy of *Richard of Bordeaux*, signed by the cast; with thanks to Colin Stokes.
30. Magazines featuring Gordon Daviot's first three plays; from the author's collection © Jennifer Morag Henderson.
31. Peggy, Marda, Gwen and Gordon, Portmeirion, 1934; with thanks to Colin Stokes.
32. Gwen, Gordon and Peggy, Portmeirion, 1934; with thanks to Colin Stokes.
33. Tagley Cottage today; from the author's collection © Jennifer Morag Henderson.

Acknowledgements

Full references and acknowledgements are given in the endnotes to the main text. Every effort has been made to trace copyright holders.

Thank you first of all to Mr Colin Stokes for generously sharing family papers, photographs and memories.

Thanks to the National Trust, David Higham Associates and Mr Colin Stokes for permission to quote from Elizabeth MacKintosh's published and unpublished writings.

Quotes from John Gielgud are by kind permission of the trustees of the Sir John Gielgud Charitable Trust.

Use of the Gwen Ffrangcon-Davies archive was made possible by kind permission of Margaret Westwood.

Acknowledgements and thanks go to: the Dodie Smith Collection, Howard Gotlieb Archival Research Center at Boston University; the National Library of Scotland; the British Library; the Scottish Theatre Archive at the University of Glasgow; and Argyll & Bute Council Archives. Thank you to Dr Ida Webb, Prof Tansin Benn and the Anstey Association – particularly the Scottish section of the Association, for the invitation to their biannual meeting where they shared many stories of their Anstey experiences. I am grateful to Charles Bannerman for his help in accessing and understanding the Inverness Royal Academy archive, and thanks go to Academy archivist Robert Preece, particularly for his help with photos. Thank you also to the Highland Railway Society, to Iain Beaton, and to the Harvard Theatre Collection at the Houghton Library, Harvard University for further assistance with photos. Thank you to Valerie Lawson for allowing me to quote from her work.

I should also like to acknowledge the following institutions and organizations, and their staff: Inverness Museum and Art Gallery (and Cait McCullagh); the Highland Archive Centre; Am Baile (and Jamie Gaukroger); the Paterson Collection (and Adrian Harvey); the National Archives of Scotland; Inverness Central Library; Malvern Theatres; the Applecross Heritage Centre (and Gordon Cameron); the Mitchell Library, Glasgow; the Highlander Museum at Fort George; the Inverness Local History Forum; and the Richard III Society.

Researching and writing this biography took several years, and during that process I was lucky to meet many interesting people who shared their enthusiasm and expertise, and I should like to express my thanks to all of them. Many people replied to emails and took time to talk to me about Tey and about writing, including Judith Braid, Prof Ian Brown, Prof Gerry Carruthers, Catherine Deveney, Jane Dunn, Maureen Kenyon, Val McDermid, Shona MacLean, Tinch Minter, Donald Murray and Prof Alan Riach. Dr Helen Grime of the University of Winchester helped me navigate Gwen Ffrangcon-Davies' archive and world; Patrick Watt answered questions about the army and generously helped me with research into Tey's soldiers; former librarian Norman Newton was the first to invite me to give a talk about Tey and has shared his wealth of local history knowledge; and my friends Stuart Wildig and Helen Young showed me how a Highlander could learn to like England and the English, and didn't mind their holidays being taken up by visits to graveyards, strange houses and old theatres.

Thank you also to Robert Davidson and Moira Forsyth of Sandstone Press.

Finally, I should like to thank my family for supporting me and putting up with me: my mum Christine Henderson, whose fault it all is, and especially my husband Andrew Thomson and our son Alec. I could have done it without you, but I wouldn't have wanted to.

Val McDermid

In 1990, the Crime Writers' Association voted *The Daughter of Time* the best crime novel ever written. I can't say I was surprised. I can still remember the excitement of my first encounter with Josephine Tey more than forty years ago. It was a battered, second-hand paperback of *Miss Pym Disposes*. I hadn't read a crime novel like this before. It was the opposite of formulaic; it explored relationships and character in a nuanced way that made it feel much more modern than most other genre novels I'd read; and the ending was far from the usual cut-and-dried resolution of its era.

It left me hungry for more. I soon discovered that Tey had produced a handful of novels that were still fascinatingly readable decades after their first publication. But more than that, they were all startlingly different from their contemporaries, cracking open the door that made possible the work of successors such as Patricia Highsmith, Ruth Rendell and Gillian Flynn.

That's a significant achievement in itself, but the truth behind Josephine Tey's pseudonym is so much more than that. Biographical information has always been scant, mostly because that's the way this most private of authors wanted it. The brief details on her book jackets reveal that Tey was born Elizabeth MacKintosh and that she also enjoyed success under another pseudonym – Gordon Daviot, author of the West End hit *Richard of Bordeaux*, the springboard that launched John Gielgud to stardom.

Sometimes they mention that she was a native of Inverness who lived most of her life there. But until now, Josephine Tey was herself the greatest mystery at the heart of her fiction.

But at last, with Jennifer Morag Henderson's biography, we can fill in the colours and bring animation to the sketchy outline of the life of one of our most significant crime writers, an author who provides a unique bridge between the Golden Age and the modern genre, a woman who characterized the detective novel as 'a medium as disciplined as any sonnet'.

With her access to family papers and previously unpublished material, a picture emerges of a writer with several strings to her bow. Acclaim as a playwright in London and with the pioneering Glasgow Citizens Theatre; success as a radio dramatist; a fledgling career as a Hollywood scriptwriter; a writer of short stories, historical biography and literary fiction. All of this has faded from public consciousness, but it sheds light on what shaped her.

With this illumination of the life, the work becomes clearer. It's hard to resist the sense of a life divided, and not just in the practical sense of the gap between the life Beth MacKintosh might have expected and the two she had. She left her native Inverness for Birmingham in her late teens to train as a PE teacher but the career she'd just begun to enjoy was cut short by the death of her mother and she returned to Inverness to take care of her father. Her emergence as a writer meant she spent a few weeks every year in London, giving an almost schizophrenic aspect to her life.

In Inverness, she was the self-contained daughter of the local fruiterer who went to the cinema on her own; in London, she was a fêted playwright who moved in theatrical circles and attended glittering parties. She was a straight woman whose strongest friendships were with a group of lesbians that included actresses, artists and directors. She was a proud Highlander who left the bulk of her estate to the National Trust in England at a time when most of the Scottish literary establishment espoused Scottish nationalism. Yet somehow as a writer she was enriched by these contradictions, creating characters in her fiction who struggle constantly with the idea of identity.

Jennifer Morag Henderson's meticulous biography gives us the chance to understand what shaped Beth MacKintosh into the writer she became. It's a revealing journey that makes sense of one of crime fiction's most intriguing mysteries. Finally, we can feel we have come to know the crime writer's crime writer.

Val McDermid

A Mystery Writer

Mystery writer Josephine Tey's work has never been out of print since her first book was published, over eighty years ago. Never backed by any publicity campaign, the books' popularity has spread by word of mouth, and Tey is ranked among the best of the Golden Age crime writers, number Five to the Big Four of Agatha Christie, Dorothy L. Sayers, Ngaio Marsh and Margery Allingham. Tey's extraordinary novel *The Daughter of Time*, with its unique mix of contemporary detective work with the historical mystery of Richard III, was selected by the Crime Writers' Association as the greatest mystery novel of all time. Josephine Tey's novels have been adapted for radio, television and film – most notably by Alfred Hitchcock – and they have been cited as inspiration by many modern writers, including Ian Rankin. And yet, Josephine Tey herself is a mystery.

There has never been a full-length biography of Tey, and most readers' knowledge of her is limited to the brief blurb on the back of her books. That blurb only raises more questions, for all it says is that 'Josephine Tey' was a pen-name for a woman called Elizabeth MacKintosh from Inverness in the Scottish Highlands, who was once a PE teacher, and who, after her death at the early age of 55 in 1952, left her fortune and the copyright to her books to the National Trust in England.

A little more digging reveals the information that, before Elizabeth MacKintosh wrote the 'Josephine Tey' crime novels, she had another 'life' as an extremely successful novelist and play-wright under a different pen-name – 'Gordon Daviot'. Gordon Daviot's first play *Richard of Bordeaux* launched the career of a young John Gielgud, and she worked, and was friends with, the best stage actors of the 1930s, including Laurence Olivier and Gwen Ffrangcon-Davies.

Despite her popularity, however, information on 'Gordon Daviot' seems almost as scarce as information on 'Josephine Tey'. Two short biographical essays written by her near-contemporaries talk about an 'enigma', 'a lone wolf', 'a strange character' – a mysterious woman writer from the Highlands with a secret life, possibly a secret past, perhaps even a tragic romantic past.

Elizabeth MacKintosh was a mystery to those around her because she inhabited more than one world, and lived more than one life. Yet she is a writer whose work and life should be understood. A brief snapshot of Elizabeth MacKintosh's life in the late 1940s gives an idea of the very different worlds that she inhabited, a glimpse of the sort of woman she was – and an idea of just how important her work was, and how highly it was rated by the influential and important names of the literary and theatrical worlds.

By late 1949, Elizabeth had re-established some routine in her life after the disruption of the Second World War. She was at the height of her writing powers, completing *The Franchise Affair*, *Brat Farrar* and *To Love and Be Wise*, and publishing at least one new work a year. Most of the time she was settled in Crown Cottage, her father Colin's home, situated in a good area of Inverness, in the north of Scotland. Elizabeth was needed at Crown Cottage as housekeeper, organizing the chores in the large house with only occasional help. She and her father Colin took pride in their beautiful garden, growing roses admired by their neighbours. Inverness was still a small town of around 20,000 people, and almost everyone knew everyone else. Elizabeth was surrounded by people she had gone to school with, their children and families, but she held herself slightly aloof from them. With no children herself, she was no longer involved with teaching or the local schools, or the friendly chats over tea that other women, mothers and grandmothers her age, indulged in. Instead, Elizabeth settled into a routine that allowed her enough time to care for Colin and the house, enough time for her hobbies, such as walking – but plenty of time to focus on her writing career.

Her father Colin was in his eighties and beginning to need more and more care. He and Elizabeth had now lived together for over twenty years as adults, and had managed to find ways to co-exist harmoniously. Colin, a hard-working and ambitious man who had spent his childhood caring first for his parents, then his siblings, then his nephews and nieces – in addition to his wife and daughters – could be demanding. He had dedicated his life to his family, and was proud of his three daughters and what they had achieved. Now that they were all grown up, he sometimes wished that they had not been so ambitious and that their work had not taken them so far from Inverness. His middle daughter didn't write to him as often as he would have liked, and he rarely saw his youngest daughter and his new grandson, who were based in London. He respected Elizabeth's work, and was glad that she stayed in Inverness with him, but he and Elizabeth were too close in character to have an entirely peaceable relationship. Elizabeth's love of literature and learning came from both her parents, but, despite her attachment to her beloved mother, it was her father that she most resembled in character: they had the same drive and ability; they were both dedicated to hard work, with a similar sensible, practical outlook – which could sometimes seem unfeeling, sarcastic or even harsh to outsiders, but which was born, at least in Colin's case, from a true understanding of what poverty was, and what could happen only too easily if you didn't work hard.

Despite his age, Colin was relatively fit and healthy, a dedicated angler who was proud of his career as a fruiterer. He still went down to his fruit shop on the town's Castle Street every morning, though he now employed one or two shop assistants to help out. Elizabeth was left alone in Crown Cottage and could settle down to work. She wrote whenever she was able, bashing out her novels on a typewriter which she either set on the kitchen table, or took out to a little writing shed at the bottom of the garden. This was the life of Beth MacKintosh, dutiful daughter in Inverness.

However, at least twice a year Beth hired a housekeeper to look after Colin, and would set off on holiday. Because of Colin's age, her holiday time was now limited, but she aimed to recapture the freedom of her early twenties and thirties. Her usual destination was London, and she could easily walk the ten minutes down the hill from her house to Inverness station, where she caught the London sleeper train that features so memorably in many of her stories.

Always smartly dressed, for her trips to London Beth would wear a tweed suit, with smart yet practical brogues, gloves, and, of course, a hat to finish off the ensemble. No beauty – her youngest sister Moire was the belle of the family – Beth was, however, striking. Always interested in fashion, she knew how to dress to her advantage. The famous costume and set designers the Motleys, who made their name working on Beth's first play *Richard of Bordeaux*, always remembered Beth by her clothes: interviewed much later in life they were shaky on her real name and her former profession, but had a vivid memory of what she was wearing. A petite woman, Beth favoured classic, well-cut tweeds matched with soft blouses in the epitome of 1930s chic, the masculine form of dressing popularised by Coco Chanel, which suggested a literary and artistic sensibility. A journalist friend once commented that, surrounded by actresses whose job it was to look beautiful, Beth, with her dark, west-coast-of-Scotland colouring and big eyes, more than held her own. In fact, Beth's charm attracted the strong attention of one charismatic and aristocratic lesbian actress, an unasked-for and almost certainly unrequited romance that Beth at first found almost incomprehensible, and which, although she treated it with remarkable tolerance, did cause her real problems.

In the late 1940s, Beth was confident in her London friends. This was a trip that she had taken many, many times since she first left home aged nineteen, and, even though she had to stay in Inverness to look after Colin, she also regularly took short train journeys on day trips to escape into the hills. The first part of the journey south was achingly familiar, yet the incongruity of the Highland landscape she was leaving, and the London town life she was going to, struck Beth anew each time.

When the train finally pulled into Euston station in the early morning, Beth made her way to her Club. She had been a member of the Cowdray Club for professional women – mostly nurses and teachers – for many years, and its Cavendish Square location, in a grand building formerly owned by Prime Minister Asquith, was an ideal base both for heading out into town and a grand surrounding in which to hold any business or social meetings she might want to arrange. Before Beth went to meet anyone, she had one more stop to make to finish her ensemble: she would go to Debenhams on Oxford Street and collect her fur coat from the cold storage department. Now, she was Josephine Tey the writer, as at home in London as Beth was in Inverness.

Walking past one of the larger bookshops, Josephine Tey could see large displays of her new book – something that gave her just as much pride as seeing her name in lights in the West End had before the War. Knowing that she was in London, Tey's publisher and friend Nico Davies would take her out to lunch; as one of their bestselling authors, Josephine Tey got the best treatment. Nico, of course, was steeped in the literary world. The former ward of J. M. Barrie, he worked for his brother's publishing firm Peter Davies – Peter being the inspiration for *Peter Pan*, and another good friend of Tey's. Other authors on the Peter Davies roster included Nico's cousin Daphne du Maurier. Josephine Tey never knew Daphne well, but did know her sister, Angela du Maurier.

Josephine Tey would also meet her literary agent, David Higham. She had been with Higham since he was first employed at the Curtis Brown agency – and both Curtis Brown and David Higham remain among the largest and most important agencies in Britain even now, representing a formidable array of talent, including other crime writers such as Dorothy L. Sayers.

As well as her literary agent, Beth was also represented by a theatrical agent, who dealt with enquiries about her 'Gordon Daviot' plays, and, when she was in London, it was the friends she had made as 'Gordon Daviot' that Beth still contacted. When she had written her first play, it had been many months before the producer and actors realized that the script they were dealing with had been written by a woman, and many of her friends from this time habitually called her 'Gordon'. The artist, socialite and writer Caroline (or Lena) Ramsden wrote later of the joy she always felt when a phone call from 'Gordon' came out of the blue – Lena instantly recognized the soft Highland accent, and knew that the phone call was coming from the Cowdray Club. Lena and Gordon had become closer after the Second World War as, despite her privileged background, and unlike many of their other friends, Lena had opted not only to remain in London as the bombs fell, but also to work long and difficult hours in a factory making aircraft parts. The two women had a mutual love of horse racing. Lena was an accomplished rider and the proud owner of a racehorse, whose father was Chairman of the Manchester Racecourse Company, and Gordon was a real enthusiast, whose descriptions of horses and horse racing occur and reoccur throughout her writing.

Lena had a wide circle of theatrical and artistic friends, many of whom Gordon also knew. Gwen Ffrangcon-Davies, star of two of Gordon's 1930s plays, had returned to London after the Second World War, though her stormy partner Marda Vanne remained tied to her home of South Africa. Others, like Peggy Webster, flitted back and forth between London and America, depending where the work was. Peggy had gone from bit parts in Gordon's plays to being lauded as one of the first female directors of Shakespeare on Broadway; courted by Hollywood. Dodie Smith, another 1930s playwright and friend of Gordon, was also in America, where she had spent the war years obsessively rewriting her masterpiece, the novel *I Capture the Castle*. Dodie was soon to return to her beloved country home in Essex, to start work on her best-known work *The 101 Dalmatians*, and Gordon would often visit Essex, where not only Dodie, but also Gwen and John Gielgud had houses, the latter two having bought their homes with the proceeds made when they starred in Gordon's first play.

As Josephine Tey and Gordon Daviot enjoyed themselves immensely in London, Beth made a reappearance as well, visiting her sister and her new nephew, who lived near London. However, the different worlds – family, and theatrical and literary – did not overlap, and when the two weeks of parties and visits and meetings and theatre and culture were over, Beth returned by sleeper train back to Inverness, to Colin, and to days of writing.

Always alive to nature, Beth often remembered how, after one memorable trip down south, she arrived at her sleeper compartment to find it filled with flowers; yellow roses, frangipani and orchids, all picked from the garden at the country cottage of her actress friends Gwen and Marda. 'I feel like a film star,' Beth had written to them in her thank-you note. To the people around Beth in Inverness, film stars were people they saw on screen at the cinema. To the people Beth knew in London, film stars were their friends – were themselves – while to Beth herself, film stars were the people paid to say her words: in the course of her career, she had written for various acclaimed screen actors, including not only John Gielgud and Laurence Olivier, but also James Mason and James Stewart. Beth lived in an extraordinary space between completely different worlds. It was no wonder that so many of her friends, from both Inverness and from London, and so many of her later readers, found her something of a mystery.

Elizabeth MacKintosh was one of the most successful writers to ever come out of the Highlands. In her lifetime she was lauded as the greatest Scottish playwright. And yet her story is almost completely unknown, surrounded by myths and misconceptions. Even people in her home town of Inverness don't always recognize her name or realize how much she achieved. Her full body of work, her writing as Gordon Daviot and Josephine Tey – as well as under a third, almost completely secret pen-name – has not been acknowledged, and she has not received the critical attention, respect and credit that she deserves. Elizabeth MacKintosh achieved everything from her home in the north of Scotland, where, as the eldest, unmarried MacKintosh daughter, she kept house for her widowed father. She never moved to London, and was rarely interviewed by the press, despite such notable successes as having plays on simultaneously in the West End and on Broadway. She focused on her writing – and her writing was so good that Hollywood literally came north to find her.

The story of Elizabeth MacKintosh is not only the story of a fascinating and complex woman, but provides an entirely new way of looking at the Scottish Literary Renaissance – and at Scotland itself. Her writing directly engaged with the rise in Scottish nationalism that came out of Inverness in the 1930s and the formation of the Scottish National Party. Her literary relationship with her contemporary and fellow Inverness resident, Scottish nationalist Neil Gunn, is of particular interest. Elizabeth's writing can provide a new understanding of the situation in Scotland – and Britain – today.

So why is such a popular and influential writer as Elizabeth MacKintosh still a mystery? Partly it's because she had such a diverse body of work – fans of her Alan Grant mystery novels don't always know about her plays – and that's before taking into account her other literary fiction, short stories and serious biography. But partly it is because Elizabeth MacKintosh chose to hide behind pen-names, and almost never publicized her work. She was a genuinely modest person, whose reticence has sometimes been misunderstood. An inspiring, yet sometimes difficult woman, she successfully balanced very different lifestyles – at the same time a Highland housewife and an attendee of the brightest London theatre parties – though neither of these different societies that she moved in fully understood her. Elizabeth achieved what she did through pure talent. She didn't have influential parents or an easy route into the literary and theatrical worlds, and many of the people around her struggled to understand her because she did not fit the mould. Privately-educated thespians like Laurence Olivier could not fully appreciate that Elizabeth's family had come from a background of crofting and domestic service in some of the most isolated parts of the north of Scotland. Elizabeth was the granddaughter, on one side, of illiterate Gaelic-speaking crofters. However, as a writer whose strength lay in her observational skills, Elizabeth was able to take these differences and put them to good use in her writing. She had great – and justified – confidence in her own abilities and experiences, and did not try to assimilate into the new literary and theatrical worlds that were opened up to her, instead sticking to her own path, not compromising on what she wanted from life and from her writing. As a result, she produced an extraordinary body of work, shot through with experiences and imaginative situations drawn from real life and supplemented by her wide reading and interest in history and research. The only common feature of all her writing is its sometimes stunning originality.

This biography aims to present the story of Beth's life – of her many different lives – and also to show just how good, and how important a writer she was, setting her full body of work – her plays, her mystery novels and her other writings – in both the context of her life, and in the context of the literary canon.

Beginning with original documents like birth, death and marriage certificates, and visiting libraries and archives across the country – from a tiny one-room family history centre on the remote Applecross Peninsula, to the archives of her schooldays at Inverness Royal Academy to the British Library in London – I have traced Beth's story from her family origins onwards. Born in 1896, the daughter of a fruiterer and the eldest of three sisters, she was eighteen years old when the First World War broke out, and was deeply affected by her experiences, something that was later to come out in her writing, but which originally influenced her choice of further education.

After being accepted to the prestigious Anstey College near Birmingham – an incredible journey for a young girl to make away from the Scottish Highlands during wartime – Elizabeth worked as a PE teacher in several different places after the war was over. She had a difficult start to her teaching career, including at least one serious accident in the gymnasium, but eventually established herself happily in England, teaching in an all-girls private school. Living through the war and the ensuing Depression meant that Elizabeth had her fair share of challenges and disappointments, but she managed to create a good life for herself in the south of the country. However, a dark period in her twenties saw the early – and, to Elizabeth, shocking – death of her beloved mother, Elizabeth's return to the Highlands, and then a period that was marred by the death and loss of family members and friends. Out of this dark time grew Elizabeth's new career as a writer, which was marked by steady and growing success. She was to achieve publication, critical acclaim and considerable financial reward.

I have rediscovered Gordon Daviot's short stories, written at the same time as much of her most well-known work. I have visited the London theatre that showed Gordon Daviot's major plays, stood where John Gielgud stood, seen the photographs of the performances, heard from Dame Judi Dench about her memories of Gordon Daviot's contemporaries, and collected rare magazines and souvenirs from Gordon Daviot's productions. I have also discovered the third pen-name she kept secret until her death. Beth's romantic life has been the subject of some speculation, and I have untangled the separate stories of the officer in the First World War who meant so much to her, and her later, lasting friendship with another soldier, a tragic forgotten poet. This latter search took me from Tomnahurich cemetery in Inverness to a church in south-east London.

Having worked so hard to build up her writing and create the life she wanted within the family constraints she felt obliged to honour, Elizabeth's life changed all over again with the advent of the Second World War. Once again, Elizabeth came back stronger than ever: she developed her writing in new ways, and worked with the artistic challenges she was facing to create new and better work. After the war was over, she entered a remarkable period of creativity, writing most of the Josephine Tey novels that remain so beloved today and responding thoughtfully to the changing world around her – all while caring for her now elderly father, and dealing with the beginnings of her own final illness.

I have read the original manuscripts of Josephine Tey's novels, and deciphered her almost indecipherable handwriting, and, finally, I have met with Beth's surviving relatives, who have given me their full support and opened up to me their own family papers: personal letters, photographs, memories – and even unpublished manuscripts.

For me, Josephine Tey, Gordon Daviot and Elizabeth MacKintosh are an inspiration, not just because their writing has brought me hours of enjoyment, but because the story of Elizabeth's life showed me a new version of what was possible for a Highland woman. Her family came from a background of crofting and domestic service, and, through hard work and a belief in education, supported their daughters and encouraged them to aim high. Elizabeth went from Inverness Royal Academy to London's West End, to Broadway, to Hollywood – and back again, to my home, to the small town of Inverness. Her biography paints a vivid picture of the society that she lived in, particularly in the north of Scotland, but also further afield. In a time of political change, which foreshadows the time we live in now, an examination of Elizabeth's writing shows a different Scotland, a different history, and a new way of looking at the world, which can help us to understand where we are now.

Elizabeth MacKintosh is a writer whose work is worthy of critical appreciation, not just a genre writer who produced excellent crime fiction. Of course, she was that too. The main reason Josephine Tey's work has stayed in print is that her books are really good. Every new generation of readers rediscovers them, and, having read one, reads them all – and recommends them. Josephine Tey's novel *The Daughter of Time* recently received a lot of attention, dealing as it does with the mystery of Richard III, the king whose remains were so dramatically discovered under a car park. The book was read on BBC Radio 4, and programmes celebrating it were re-broadcast. In one of these programmes, a reader said that *The Daughter of Time* was possibly the most important book ever written. There was a moment of realization as he heard the sweeping statement he had made. Then he took out the qualifier: *The Daughter of Time*, he said, was simply the most important book he had ever read. That is the sort of devotion that Josephine Tey, that Beth MacKintosh, inspires in her readers.

This is Beth MacKintosh's story, the biography of the mystery writer who was once such a mystery herself: a mystery solved.

PART ONE

Elizabeth MacKintosh
1896–1923

CHAPTER ONE

'With Mr & Mrs MacKintosh's Compliments'

Elizabeth MacKintosh was born in Inverness on 25th July 1896.[1]
Her parents, Colin and Josephine, were not writers, and there
was no family history of writing or involvement in the theatre.
Colin and Josephine ran a fruit shop, and, on both sides of her
family, Elizabeth's grandmothers had been in domestic service.
The thing that really made the difference to the MacKintoshes
was the Education Act of 1872, which had provided free state
education for all children until the age of fourteen. This was what
gave Elizabeth's father, Colin, a love of literature. School was
where Colin learned to speak English, and it provided him with the
education that enabled him, the child of illiterate Gaelic-speaking
crofters, to survive and build a business in Inverness. The demand
for more education gave Elizabeth's mother Josephine her job
before marriage, as a pupil-teacher. It was their love of learning
that brought Colin and Josephine together, and they passed on
their respect for education, particularly reading and literature, to
their daughters, starting Elizabeth on her route to becoming a
writer.

One of the few facts about Elizabeth's mystery life which seems
to be well known is her love for her mother Josephine, who was
sadly to die young, and whose name Elizabeth preserved when
she chose to write as 'Josephine Tey'. Growing up, Elizabeth
and her two sisters were close to their mother. And, contrary to
the received view that Elizabeth was a loner, she was actually

born into a large extended family. Josephine was the fourth of seven children, and Elizabeth had one aunt and five uncles on her mother's side of the family, and was to have many cousins.

Josephine Horne had grown up in Inverness, though her family roots were from Aberdeenshire, Perthshire and England. These roots, and the stories from her mother's side of the family, were very important to Elizabeth, particularly the link with England, which, as an adult, she identified with more and more. Josephine's mother, Elizabeth's grandmother Jane, was a strong matriarchal figure who lived into her 90s. She was present for all of Elizabeth's childhood, as well as being around when Elizabeth returned to Inverness in her twenties, and it was Josephine and Jane's stories that Elizabeth absorbed.

Elizabeth's grandmother was born Jane Ellis in 1837 in the small village of Forgandenny in Perthshire. One of the easiest ways to trace Elizabeth's relatives has been to look for Jane's surname 'Ellis' – it was preserved as the middle name of not only Elizabeth's sister but also several of her cousins. Jane meant a lot to the whole family. Elizabeth even used the surname Ellis for the fictional family in her second novel, *The Expensive Halo*.

By the time Elizabeth's grandmother Jane Ellis was fourteen years old she was working as one of three female servants in a big house called the Barracks in Kinloch Rannoch, as a tablemaid. While she was working there, Jane met Peter Horne, a young carpenter from Aberdeenshire. Jane and Peter married in Kinloch Rannoch, before moving back up north to Inverness. Inverness was a rapidly expanding town with many new buildings being erected after the expansion of the railways had made travel to the Highlands easier for tourists and workers alike, and there were many opportunities for a well-qualified and time-served craftsman like Peter. The young Horne family rented a flat in Shore Street, but after a few years they did well enough to buy a house – a significant achievement for the time – in a better part of town, at 53 Crown Street, where Josephine and her brothers and sister were brought up.

Jane Ellis told her seven children about her childhood working in the big house in Perthshire, but she also told them stories going much further back: her father Robert had been a hedger, or gardener, and had originally come from Suffolk. Robert had travelled for work, making his way north before meeting a Scotswoman and finally settling in Perthshire. Jane passed on to her daughter Josephine and her granddaughter Elizabeth a sense of difference, a connection with the south of England, so far away and exotic-sounding to an Invernessian. But as well as this 'Englishness', Jane also identified strongly with her husband Peter and his family, and they too imparted something of that sense of difference to first Josephine, and then Elizabeth MacKintosh.

Peter Horne was from an even more numerous family: one of at least sixteen children, he was born in Aberdeenshire. Peter, and several of his siblings, left their home village to look for work, spreading out to other parts of Scotland and down to England. Peter followed his father's profession when he became a carpenter, but others of his siblings took different routes, with his younger brother Joseph being one of the notable successes of the family after he emigrated to Australia and became involved in land management and real estate, founding a business that is still thriving today. This became one of the family stories, passed down to Elizabeth and encouraging her to believe that moving on, aiming high and succeeding was possible.

Peter Horne's other legacy to his family was his strong religious belief. His birthplace of Forgue in rural Aberdeenshire is in an area still known for its strong Protestant faith, and glimpses of this can be seen in Elizabeth MacKintosh's writing. Elizabeth's father's family were Free Church of Scotland, and it is perhaps saying something to state that the Free Church side of the family was the less religious side. Although Elizabeth was later to stop attending church, her childhood included religious instruction, and she was to go on to write a series of religious plays. Other glimpses of Peter Horne's religious beliefs appear in Elizabeth's early novels, such as the references in *The Expensive Halo* to 'a sect which were a kind of superior Plymouth Brethren. A very greatly superior kind, of course.'[2] Peter's children continued this religious upbringing to different degrees. Josephine took the Protestant emphasis on education and literacy into her first career as a pupil-teacher, but softened her attitude to fit in with her husband Colin's, so their daughter Elizabeth was given a less strict upbringing than some of her cousins. Elizabeth's later plays took religious figures and humanized them, in a reaction to the strict and sober religion of Peter Horne, but the Horne family's strong sense of morality and the Protestant insistence on education and literacy was definitely something which influenced Elizabeth's life choices as well as her writing.

Although Elizabeth always emphasized her closeness to her mother's side of the family, and her identification with her English ancestors, her father's side of the family had just as important an influence on her – arguably, in fact, even more influence, whether Elizabeth liked that or not.

Colin MacKintosh was the eldest son – though not the eldest child – in a family of five. Unlike his wife and daughters, he was not born in Inverness. The MacKintosh family came from Applecross, on the west coast of Scotland, where they had lived for generations in Shieldaig, a tiny, remote crofting community. Colin and his siblings grew up speaking Gaelic; they had no English until they went to school, and their parents never learned English to full fluency. Elizabeth's mother Josephine grew up a town girl: although Inverness was small, it was the largest town of any size for miles, it had all the amenities, and counted itself as the capital of the Highlands. Shieldaig, on the other hand, was a totally different proposition, and Colin's upbringing would have been almost foreign to Elizabeth, and it was not something that she learned to value in the same way as she valued Josephine's and Jane Ellis's stories of England and big houses.

Shieldaig in Applecross is exceptionally remote, while the Applecross peninsula is famously accessible by the treacherous and torturously slow trip over the mountain road known as Bealach na Ba (the Pass of the Cattle), which is clearly signposted as being unsuitable for inexperienced drivers, impassable for large vehicles, and totally useless in bad weather. Readers of Josephine Tey's first mystery novel *The Man in the Queue* might start to get an idea of where Alan Grant's tortuous journey into the Highlands came from. Shieldaig itself is a tiny collection of houses alongside the shore, but Colin and his family actually came from settlements even smaller than that, on the top of a hill behind Shieldaig: Camus na Leum and Camus na Tira. These settlements were literally one or two houses, surrounded by small areas of cultivated land where the family could grow vegetables or raise a few animals. Many of the MacKintosh men were also fishermen, while Colin's mother Elizabeth (known as Betsey) supplemented their income by doing domestic service work at the local big house, Courthill. The MacKintosh family had been there for many generations: the earliest records for the area which I have found are lists of able-bodied men made in 1715, after the first Jacobite rebellions, with the MacKintoshes of Shieldaig clearly noted.

However, it was not an easy life. It goes some way to giving an impression of the area when it's explained that Shieldaig was not included in the Highland Clearances: it was one of the areas of poorer grazing land that people were cleared *to*, rather than *from*. Both Camus na Leum and Camus na Tira are completely abandoned now, with only a few stones showing where the walls of the houses once were. Walking up the track from Shieldaig into the mountains, with steep cliffs going down on one side to the water, it is easy to see that just a few winters of bad weather could be enough to encourage a family to clear out, and the MacKintosh family endured further hardship when two of Colin's fishermen uncles were lost at sea.[3] Colin's father John MacKintosh decided to make the long walk down to Lochcarron and take the train to Inverness to look for work. Attracted to the town for the same reasons as Colin's future wife's family, John found a job amongst the building work going on in Inverness, mostly as a general labourer, though sometimes specializing as a mason's labourer.

Many years later, Colin wrote to one of his daughters about this time in his life, describing how in 1877, when he was fourteen, he remembered walking from his home in Shieldaig to the train station in Lochcarron to pick up a parcel that his father had sent home from Inverness. This was a round trip of about forty miles, and Colin described how he, small for his age, set off alone at daybreak, which would have been around 4 or 5 am in summer. He walked all day, armed only with the address of a relative in

Lochcarron who could give him some food. On the way he met the local doctor, who was astonished at how far he had come, and on the way home he met the coachman for the big house, who refused to give him a lift. Colin made it home just before dark – which, in summer, would have been around 11 pm – perhaps a full nineteen hours after setting out. 'Think of it. It makes me sad,' Colin wrote.[4] His daughters kept the letter as a curiosity, but could barely understand their father's upbringing, it was so different from their own. Unlike Josephine and Jane Ellis's English roots, her father's poverty in Applecross was not something Elizabeth MacKintosh talked of with pride to her friends.

Colin's father's job as a labourer was less specialized than Peter Horne's trade as a carpenter, and less well paid, but it was enough to eventually move the rest of his family out from Shieldaig to Inverness. By 1881 the whole MacKintosh family – mother, father, daughter and four sons – were living in the Maggot in Inverness. Although the name 'the Maggot' was actually a corruption of 'Margaret' (the area being dedicated to the saint), the more evocative name perhaps gives a better idea of the type of area it had become. Thatched cottages sat on a rather damp piece of land, parts of which had been reclaimed from the river, or had been a sort of island. It was not an attractive part of town, though it is sometimes fondly remembered for its community spirit – rare photos of the area show the communal green festooned with families' washing. The MacKintoshes lived in a flat in Friar's Court, alongside a couple of other large families. Colin MacKintosh was actually quite close to his future wife Josephine in Shore Street, but Josephine's family was always just a slight step up and one street along on the social scale from the MacKintoshes.

The Maggot was also close to the Gaelic church. There was no Gaelic enclave in Inverness; Gaelic speakers were widely spread throughout the town, but newcomers tended to gravitate towards areas where something was familiar, or where they knew someone. Colin MacKintosh had relatives in Inverness already. As well as his father, his uncle Roderick, or Rory, Maclennan (his mother's brother) was living in the town, and had got married there in 1877. Rory Maclennan was to be a big help to Colin and his family, because Colin's father John was still not earning enough to keep everyone.

By the 1881 census, Colin's trade was listed as 'grocer's apprentice'. He was eighteen years old, and his older sister Mary was also already out working as a domestic servant, though his younger three brothers, being under fourteen years old, were still at school. Colin's job was an important part of the family income, and was to become even more important. Census records give a snapshot of the MacKintosh's family life every ten years, but their fortunes seem to have fluctuated rather more than the steady life of Josephine Horne and her family. The move from Applecross to Inverness was not easy, and the whole family had to work hard.

There were other challenges to face as well. At the very end of 1882, Colin's older sister Mary gave birth to an illegitimate son, whom she named Donald. Donald's father's name is not listed on his birth certificate, but he was born at an address in Rose Street in Inverness. Mary had been working as a domestic servant, and Rose Street was not the sort of address where one might expect servants to be employed, so it's reasonable to assume that a pregnant Mary had lost her job, and was staying with the father of her child. However, a search through the records to find the owner of the Rose Street address does not make it clear who that father might have been. Mary gave her son Donald her own surname, and moved back into the family home. Whatever her Free Church family might have thought of Mary's actions, they welcomed her and her son, and supported them.[5]

Colin's mother Betsey turned to her brother Rory for help. Perhaps drawing on her experience as a crofter growing her own food, and using her son Colin's expertise gained as a grocer's apprentice, Betsey decided to set up a shop, selling fruit and flowers.[6] The shop opened around 1887, staffed by Betsey, Rory and Colin. It's not entirely clear just how and where the shop started, but two years down the line, in 1889, it was based at 50 Castle Street, on the right-hand side of a narrow street leading up a hill, directly underneath Inverness Castle walls. At that time, Castle Street had buildings on either side, and was much darker than it is now, when one side of the street is open. Little alleys, now all blocked off or demolished, ran between the shops and houses, and the flats above the shops had small private courtyards and drying greens to the back of what we would now consider the main street. The shops were all small stores, selling things like food or furniture. Many west coast Highlanders lived and worked on the street, and Betsey would have been able to speak to them in Gaelic, but, since her English was not good, Colin's role in the shop (and in the MacKintosh family) was becoming something more than an apprentice.

Soon the fruit shop was doing well enough to move to larger premises. A big advert in the centre of the front page in the local paper the *Scottish Highlander and North of Scotland Advertiser* on 4th June 1891 gave

NOTICE OF REMOVAL for E. MACKINTOSH, FRUITERER AND FLORIST, In returning thanks to his Customers and the Public in general for their liberal support during the past four years, takes this opportunity of intimating that he has now REMOVED from 50 CASTLE STREET, to those more commodious Premises, No. 55 CASTLE STREET, (DIRECTLY OPPOSITE) where he hopes by strict attention to Business, and keeping only the best quality of Goods, to merit a continuance of their kind support.

The mixing of pronouns in the advert – E. MacKintosh, the owner, was a 'she' of course – reflects Colin's growing role in the day-to-day running of the shop. By the 1891 census, Colin's occupation is given as 'fruiterer', the title he would proudly bear for the rest of his life. He is no longer an apprentice, and, in fact, was training his two youngest brothers, Murdoch (Murdo) and Donald (Dan). Colin and his family had also moved to one of the flats on Castle Street, to be closer to their shop. The whole family, including Mary and her illegitimate son, were at number 67; seven adults and one child in a three-roomed flat.

The tenement houses of Castle Street were known for their overcrowding after the Second World War, but even by the end of the nineteenth century the houses here were holding very large families. However, despite what seems to modern eyes to be cramped conditions, the flat on Castle Street was actually larger than the MacKintosh's old home in Friar's Court: that had only two rooms. Number 67 Castle Street was owned by the Sutherland family from Broadstone Lodge on Kingsmills Road in the Crown area of Inverness, who also owned the new, larger shop premises at number 55, simplifying Colin's rental arrangements. They were now Colin's rental arrangements, as he, not his father John, was listed as the named tenant. The income from the fruit shop had obviously become more important than John's wage as a labourer, and since John was now in his early sixties, it is easy to see that hard physical labour might have become more difficult for him.

Colin's oldest sister Mary was also contributing, having gone back to work as a domestic servant, but this meant that her son needed care. Perhaps this job fell to Colin's mother, leaving Colin in charge at the shop. Colin's brother John, the closest to him in age, did not help at the shop. John had been apprenticed to a butcher, but was currently unemployed. Over time, Colin found that working with his two youngest brothers, Murdo and Dan, was to become difficult, and John perhaps anticipated this: perhaps he did not want to do what Colin told him, and maybe he disliked the move away from a crofting lifestyle to the town, because John decided to look elsewhere for work.[7] In the 1890s there was a recruitment drive for Highlanders to become shepherds in Patagonia in South America: Highlanders were thought to have the right temperament and skills, and John took up this opportunity, emigrating from Scotland, where he was not to return for twenty years.

Not all of this family history would have been known to the young Elizabeth MacKintosh, though she may have learned more of it as she grew older, particularly when she returned to Inverness as an adult. There are glimpses in her novels of her knowledge of the West Highlands and Gaelic, but these are always spoken of in a derogatory tone. There is little indication that she came from a family whose beginnings in Inverness were fuelled by poverty and relentless hard work, and certainly no mention of a cousin who was illegitimate (though perhaps Brat Farrar's experiences abroad are reminiscent of her uncle, the Patagonian shepherd).

The general perception is that Elizabeth MacKintosh and her father Colin did not have a very easy or close relationship, but I think that Colin has had a particularly bad press. If he was a strict father, it was because he knew what his own childhood had been like, and did not want his daughters to have the same experience – he wanted them to live in a nice house, and have good jobs, and he certainly did not want them to have children out of marriage like his sister Mary. Colin took on the financial responsibility for his family – his mother, father and siblings – at an early age, and he continued to support them all for many years. This shaped his character and influenced the way he chose to bring up his own children. Colin's experience of his mother setting up the shop also shows another side to his character. He certainly never treated his daughters as second-class because they were not sons – in his family, the women worked just as hard, and were given just as much respect, as the men. It is perhaps significant that Colin chose to name his eldest daughter Elizabeth after his mother. Colin also gave to his daughters his own ambition: he was living proof that if you worked hard and aimed high, you would be rewarded.

Colin MacKintosh and Josephine Horne married on 1st February 1894. Josephine was twenty-three, and Colin almost eight years older, about to turn thirty-one. Colin had been working in the family fruit shop now for about seven years, was well known to his customers, and was making enough money to start supporting a family of his own. He had already expanded his business into bigger premises, renting number 57 Castle Street as well as number 55.[8] Josephine was working as a teacher. She had worked her way up as a pupil-teacher, beginning her training aged thirteen or fourteen, first receiving extra coaching at school and teaching elementary work to other pupils under supervision, before continuing an apprenticeship over about five years.[9] The apprenticeship of a pupil-teacher had rigorous standards, with regular assessment from school inspectors, and was one way into the teaching profession. Josephine's attitude to hard work mirrored Colin's, and, like him, she had an interest in and love of education and reading. They were well matched, and their marriage was to be a happy one.

Photographs of Colin and Josephine taken around the time of their marriage show a serious young couple. Josephine was held to be very like her eldest daughter Elizabeth, but in the photos of her as a young woman, the likeness is not so marked: she appears less dark than Elizabeth, with a resemblance to her own mother, the redoubtable Jane Ellis. Josephine is dressed as befits a teacher, with her hair up and the demure clothes of the day: a long skirt and a top with long sleeves, buttoned up to the neck. Colin, despite the ten years he could give Josephine, almost looks younger: there is still a glimpse of the child, small for his age, who made that long walk from his home in Shieldaig to Lochcarron. Colin and Josephine were neither of them tall, and Colin still has some of the gangliness of a young man, with his ears just a little prominent. He was not yet the secure businessman of photos of later middle age. For a posed portrait of the young couple, however, Colin wore all the trappings of a successful man: a dark suit, handkerchief tucked into his top pocket, watch chain just seen going into his other pocket, and a white collar. Colin's hair and small moustache were as dark as his daughter Elizabeth's hair was to be – that west coast of Scotland look that Elizabeth sometimes described in her stories. She even used the phrase 'black man' in its old Scottish sense of meaning someone very dark.[10] As was the fashion in photography, the couple gaze into the distance, not looking at each other or the camera. One can almost sense the hopefulness of a young married couple, together for the first time.

A charming souvenir of the marriage has been passed down the generations: the beautifully designed wedding invitation cards which Josephine and Colin sent out. Small pieces of card, rectangles of less than 10x6 cm when folded up, they are decorated on the front with the initials of the couples' surnames: M & H. Inside, the text reads 'Mr & Mrs Horne request the pleasure of [your] company at the marriage of their Daughter Josephine to Colin MacKintosh'. The Hornes were delighted to see their spinster daughter married to a man with prospects, and both families wanted it to be a memorable occasion. Little matching thank-you cards were also made up for any gifts the couple might receive, 'With Mr & Mrs MacKintosh's Compliments'. The wedding was held at the Palace Hotel, on the banks of the River Ness in Inverness. The Palace, still an impressive building, looks over the water to Inverness Castle, and had been built only four years earlier, in 1890. It was the new and fashionable place in town to marry, and the ornate lettering on the delicate, tiny invitation cards reflects that sense of occasion. The impressive dining room would have looked very spacious to the Hornes and MacKintoshes, used to their small houses. Holding the wedding in a hotel, rather than a church, also avoided any concern over the Horne's strong religious beliefs – Colin and Josephine were married by a minister from the United Presbyterian Church. Interestingly, both Colin and Josephine chose friends to be witnesses, rather than any of their numerous siblings. Donald Gill, an apprentice grocer, probably knew Colin through work, and Christine Gibb lived close to Josephine, so it's easy to speculate that they were school friends. This inclusion in the ceremony of friends as well as family was a first indication that the young couple wanted to set up on their own. Although Elizabeth was born into a large, extended family, Colin and Josephine gradually drew away from their relatives. Friendships, as well as family ties, were always very important, not only to Colin and Josephine, but also to their daughter Elizabeth.

Colin and Josephine MacKintosh moved into Norwood Villa, on Midmills Road. It was close to both Josephine's family on Crown Street, and Colin's family and business on Castle Street, but Colin and Josephine gradually moved on to larger houses in better neighbourhoods. Biographical sketches of Josephine Tey have emphasized the fact that she and her family lived in the Crown, a pleasant, middle-class part of Inverness on a slight hill (the name comes from the fact that it was originally Crown land, not that it is on the crown of a hill). In fact the real picture is a little more complex. The big Victorian mansions in Crown, where the MacKintoshes did eventually move, are not quite the same as the little cottages on narrow streets where Josephine had grown up. Although Josephine's family home on Crown Street is linked to the best area of town by its name alone, Invernessians sometimes refer to this area as the Hill. It is Crown, but not quite Crown. It's all a matter of how the families living there want to present themselves. Colin and Josephine definitely wanted to emphasize their aspirations.

Josephine left her work as a teacher to help in the fruit shop, work that she particularly enjoyed. A near-contemporary description exists of the MacKintoshes, which describes how Josephine worked together with her husband; Colin's chatty, friendly demeanour with his customers; and Colin's accent, which still retained its Gaelic inflections:

> [T]he mouth-watering fruit shop owned by the parents of the late Gordon Daviot, the playwright. Here on occasion Gordon's mother – not unlike her illustrious daughter, but rather smaller – attended to one's wants, a running commentary coming from her husband all the time. I always felt I travelled the world in this shop – for no sooner were apples chosen, than Mr MacKintosh's husky voice regaled us with – 'All the way from Canada, these'; oranges 'from sunny Spain'; bananas 'from the Tropics'; dates 'from Africa'; and glorious melons 'from Salonika'.

The same customer insisted that the fruit Colin's shop sold was exceptional: 'Often after I grew up, I met people who insisted that no fruiterer in Britain could vie with Mr MacKintosh for quality and selection.'[11] In fact, Colin got some of his fruit from local growers, while some of it was sent up to Inverness on the night train from the markets in Covent Garden, London.

Josephine, after growing up with five brothers, had been a bit of a tomboy, and she loved the challenge of working in a new place and the process of the young couple establishing themselves. She was less keen on the housekeeping and domesticity that came with married life, but, after a year or so, she was pleased to fall pregnant with her first child. When they found out Josephine was pregnant, Colin and his wife moved to a new rented flat at 2 Crown Terrace, on the east side of Ardconnel Street. With four rooms, this was a bigger place than either of them was used to, and shows how well the fruit shop was doing.

Ardconnel Street is above Castle Street, and it's easy to imagine Colin walking to his shop down the little side streets and narrow steps of Raining's Stairs. Both sets of parents, the Hornes and the MacKintoshes, were nearby, and Colin and Josephine's brothers and sisters also lived within easy walking distance. Of particular comfort to Josephine was the fact that her older sister Mary – there were four years between them – was living close by at 4 Crown Street and was also pregnant. Mary was married to a man called Robert Jeans, who worked alongside her brother Peter, and it was to be Mary and Robert's fifth child. It must have been a very happy time for the two sisters Mary and Josephine. They were both married to men who were doing well in their careers, living close to a supportive family network, and they were going through the exciting experience of pregnancy with each other's support. It is a measure of not only how close the sisters were, but also how happy Josephine was in her marriage and how Colin had been accepted by the Horne family, that when Mary's child was born in December 1895 she called her 'Josephine MacKintosh Jeans', using her sister's new married name.

Josephine gave birth the following year, and Elizabeth MacKintosh was born on the 25th July 1896.

CHAPTER TWO

Bessie

Colin and Josephine MacKintosh settled into married life with their new baby. Two years after Elizabeth was born, Josephine was pregnant again. Her sister Mary was again pregnant at the same time – though this was now Mary's eighth child, as she had had a son the year before. Elizabeth MacKintosh's new baby sister was born on 8ᵗʰ September 1898, again at the family home on Crown Terrace.[1] She was named Jane Ellis MacKintosh, after Josephine's mother. It was also important to Mary to preserve her mother's maiden name, and she called her child Elizabeth Ellis Jeans. With so much repetition of names, the cousins became used to using nicknames and short pet names to distinguish between everyone, and perhaps Elizabeth MacKintosh's love of pseudonyms and different pen-names began here. Colin and Josephine began to call their eldest daughter Bessie, while their second daughter was known as Jean.[2]

Bessie was part of a large extended family, with many Horne and MacKintosh cousins across town. Her mother Josephine was close to Mary, and the strong relationship between cousins is something that is frequently mentioned in Josephine Tey's novels, while large families are a feature of much more of her writing than people assume. Josephine Tey is often remembered for her portrayal of strong, independent, single women, but she also wrote about the large Ellis family in *The Expensive Halo*, and the convincing family arguments over breakfast that open

Brat Farrar. There were some differences opening up in the family though, the beginning of the process that would see the young Bessie grow into the 'lone wolf' that the adult Beth MacKintosh was perceived to be.[3]

However close Josephine was to her family, Colin had begun to make choices that would emphasize the difference between him and his siblings. His two younger brothers, Murdo and Dan, no longer worked with him as his assistants in the fruit shop. Across town, his brother Murdo was finding a new path in life. He married a woman called Jane, and had two daughters (also called Elizabeth and Mary). Murdo and his family lived on the other side of the river on Tanner's Lane, near the cathedral (and the Ragged Boys School), and he had found work as a cab driver, meaning, of course, that he drove a horse and cab.[4] Pictures of Inverness cabmen of the time show serious men with flat caps or bowler hats, and fancy moustaches. The normal method of getting around Inverness at this time was walking, but cabmen could earn a living working for local businesses, and, particularly, from waiting at the train station to collect visitors. Murdo, by choosing to work in this different profession and live across town on the other side of the River Ness, showed that there were many different choices available to Colin and his siblings. Murdo was younger than Colin when the MacKintosh family moved to Inverness and perhaps, as the younger sibling, he felt less of the ambition and family responsibility that drove Colin on. On the side of the river where Murdo lived, people were poorer, and there was more Gaelic spoken. Colin, by moving further and further into the upmarket Crown district, and staying close to his wife Josephine's English-speaking family, and not raising his daughters to speak Gaelic, was making conscious choices. There was a significant Gaelic-speaking population in Inverness at the time, but they were never the elite: English was the language of education, and, as Colin saw it, the key to success. Even his sister Mary's illegitimate son Donald was encouraged to always speak English.[5] As Colin prospered, the contrast between him and his siblings became greater, and relations became more strained. Colin's daughters remembered their uncles Murdo and Dan as the relatives who bothered their father, trying to borrow money and, on one memorable occasion, coming to blows with Colin, fighting in the back of the shop.

Colin wanted to improve his station in life, and to have the best for his family. One of the very real and pressing reasons for this was the state of medical care at the end of the nineteenth century. Disease was more prevalent, cures were not as advanced, and healthcare was not free. Common childhood ailments could be fatal. On 7th August 1899, Bessie MacKintosh's cousin, her mother's namesake the little Josephine MacKintosh Jeans, died of bronchitis.[6] She was only three years old. Colin wanted the best for his daughters because he knew exactly what the worst could be. More bereavement was to follow.

About a year later, on 19th July 1900, Colin's father John died. There are almost no surviving photographs of Colin's family, and a family myth grew up that Colin's parents John and Betsey had disliked having their photograph taken for the old superstitious reason that a photograph might have trapped their soul, but this perhaps says less about John and Betsey than it does about the way Colin presented his family to his daughters. Nevertheless, one photograph of a very elderly John MacKintosh does survive. It looks as though it is taken straight out of a book about the west coast and its heritage, showing a man in a rough jacket and trousers with a traditional working-class round bowler hat on his head, a cane in his hand, and his feet planted squarely in front of him as he sits and faces the camera with a challenging expression.[7] Between the hat and a long white flowing beard, his eyes are just visible. John was seventy-two when he died, and had worked as a manual labourer. He had managed to move his family from Applecross to Inverness for better prospects, and had seen his four sons and his daughter Mary grow up, find work, marry and give him grandchildren.

For his final years, Colin had been supporting his father, paying the rent on his home. After John's death, Colin continued to support his mother, his sister Mary and his nephew Donald by paying the rent on their flat in Castle Street, but he was also able to expand his business. Colin now started renting number 53 Castle Street, as well as numbers 55 and 57. Number 53 had previously been a baker's shop, and it was owned by a different landlord to numbers 55 and 57, making Colin's business dealings more complicated.[8] Castle Street was still peopled with little shops, like a baker's, confectioner's and a spirit merchant, all with flats above them, packed with tenants. There were plenty of people around to buy fruit, and Colin's business was becoming an important landmark on the street. He also aimed for the top end of the market, selling high-quality fruit to the big houses in town, to landed gentry, and to their visitors who came to stay on the big Highland estates. The shops on Castle Street have now changed considerably, and out-of-town supermarkets mean there are far fewer small food shops. The building that used to house numbers 55 and 57 has been demolished, with a pool hall and bar now standing in the spot where they once were. However, there are some shops in town that represent the world that Bessie MacKintosh grew up in: Duncan Chisholm and Sons, Highland Dress Outfitters, now based on Castle Street, has been an established business since the 1800s, providing a link with the retail world the MacKintoshes knew, while the indoor Victorian Market hasn't changed out of all recognition from its heyday. A number of other family businesses still exist in town, such as Duncan Fraser's the butcher, which the MacKintoshes would have known. The traditional markets of Colin and Josephine's time, where Nairn fishwives sold their wares wearing long skirts, Shetland shawls and knitting needles in a special pouch around their waist, are long gone.

While Colin was working hard expanding the fruit shop, Josephine's family was hit by fresh tragedy. Only five months after Colin's father died, on 13th November 1900, Josephine's niece, Mary's daughter Elizabeth Ellis Jeans, died aged two. She was buried alongside her sister Josephine, and a sad gravestone in Tomnahurich cemetery records the resting place of Bessie's two little cousins. It must have been very hard for the sisters Josephine and Mary, who had gone through their pregnancies together. Both Mary's daughters had died, while Josephine's had lived. Mary must have felt the unfairness and the loss, while Josephine must have felt fear for her own children. As an adult, Elizabeth

MacKintosh was to say that life was for living, as death could come at any time. Many years later, a schoolfellow remembered her saying, 'If there's anything you want to do, do it now. We shall all be in little boxes soon enough'.[9] The phrase about 'little boxes' was often repeated, and this fear of time running out was almost an obsession. Elizabeth was to live through two World Wars and to suffer her own share of bereavement as she grew older, but her outlook was also shaped by her early childhood and by her mother's experiences.

By 1904 Josephine was pregnant for the third time. She, Colin, and their two daughters Bessie and Jean had moved house, again staying in the same area, but renting something bigger. They were now on Greenhill Terrace, close to Norwood Villa where they had lived when they first married. It's an address that, thanks to development, no longer exists, but valuation rolls show that the houses here had around five rooms, while newspaper adverts of the time list houses for sale on the street as having 'coalyard and stabling'. In addition to paying the rent on his own house, Colin was still the named tenant at his old family home at 67 Castle Street, where his mother Elizabeth, widowed and now almost seventy, and his sister Mary and her illegitimate son Donald, were living. Mary was now working as a cook, and Donald had also found work in service, as a footman.[10] It is a measure of Colin's success and upward social mobility that while his sister and nephew were working in service, Colin was moving into an area where his neighbours were hiring servants of their own, as Colin was eventually to do. When the MacKintosh's third daughter, Mary Henrietta, was born, she was born into a family that was settled and doing well.

Mary Henrietta was born on 21st June 1904. She was to be the MacKintosh's last child. Etta, as she was soon known, was almost eight years younger than Bessie. Bessie had started school a couple of years before, and Jean was getting ready to start. The two older girls called their new baby sister 'The Kid', a nickname that stuck, half-joking, half-teasing, until Etta was an adult.[11] Over time, Etta was to become the sister Bessie was closest to, though Etta's outlook on life and her view of her place in the world was slightly

---

different to her elder sister's. Bessie had been growing up in a large extended family, with many cousins, and had memories of the houses they had previously lived in. Etta, by contrast, knew only one house, and was brought up with very little contact with her family on the MacKintosh side.

Relations between Colin and his brothers had deteriorated until they could no longer work side by side in the shop. Colin's mother was elderly, and his sister's and nephew's jobs in service were not what he wanted for his own children. Many years later, Etta told her own son that neither she, her sisters, nor her mother Josephine had contact with her father's family. Etta told her son that her MacKintosh grandparents were from Applecross, and gave the impression that they had never lived in Inverness. When Colin went to visit his mother, climbing the stairs to her flat up the street from his shop and conversing in Gaelic, he went alone.

In pre-war society, class was a constant preoccupation, and Inverness, a very small town, was particularly divided. The awareness of class is constant in Elizabeth MacKintosh's writing, from her bitter early short story, 'His Own Country', where people in a small town cannot let go of the idea that 'they knew his father', therefore can judge the man whatever his achievements, to the uncharacteristic lapse of confidence Sara shows in *The Expensive Halo* when she first visits the races in the company of her aristocratic boyfriend. In Josephine Tey's novels social standing is the key to *The Franchise Affair*, on view everywhere in the village of Salcott St Mary in *To Love and Be Wise*, and part of the world that Brat Farrar needs to learn. In classic crime, with its country house settings, its butlers and the introduction of criminal low lifes, class and social standing are part of the plot. The entire genre of crime writing has a focus on class – on the disruption of the order of things, and then its reordering with the solution to the crimes. 'Josephine Tey' had such varied experiences of the class system in her life that it is perhaps no surprise that she ended up as a crime writer. By the time she started school she had already experienced her family's social mobility, and a changing place in the class system was to be one of the themes of her life, and one of the reasons that she ended up living different 'lives', creating this image of her as a mystery.

The MacKintoshes choice of school for their daughters was a clear indication of what they hoped they could achieve. The Inverness Royal Academy was a fee-paying school with an excellent reputation. The Academy was very close to their home in Crown, but it was not the only school nearby: there was also the High School, which was free, and which was considered more of a technical school, for children who were not so academic. Colin and Josephine had passed their love and respect for learning on to their daughters, and were determined that they would continue to better themselves. Elizabeth's attendance at the Academy is one of the facts about her that is well known – and her relationship with the school has been given added importance because one of the few supposed authoritative biographical sketches of her was written by one of her schoolfellows, Mairi MacDonald. This article, entitled 'The Enigma of Gordon Daviot', was first published in the *Scots Magazine* not long after Elizabeth's death, and then anthologized in a collection of Mairi's work. Because there is so little written information about Elizabeth's life, the sources that are available tend to assume greater importance than they might actually deserve, and Mairi's article, with its assertions that Elizabeth was a loner, who didn't like school and didn't mix with the community, is quoted in almost every biographical source about Elizabeth, particularly on the internet. However, although Mairi did know Elizabeth, she was actually two years below Jean at school – that is, she was several years younger than Elizabeth. Much of Mairi's article is actually based on secondary sources rather than personal knowledge, and Mairi's assessment of 'Gordon Daviot' can't be understood without an awareness of the class system of Inverness and where Mairi believed she and Elizabeth stood in that system.

The Inverness Royal Academy, known locally as the IRA, still exists, though it's rather different now. In Elizabeth's day it was a prestigious private school situated in a grand building, noted for its strong academic reputation and stellar cast of Old Boys and Girls, tracing back its origins to 1792 (if not earlier). In the early twentieth century, when Elizabeth was a pupil, it took primary and secondary pupils, both boys and girls. The Education Acts that had made schooling compulsory had not made it entirely free. Although the IRA was still a fee-paying establishment, a crisis in its funding meant that in 1908 it was taken over by the burgh school board, the start of the process which was to see it become free to everyone, as it is today. Although the IRA was in the process of becoming a local authority school, it was still only taking the best students, the ones who were preparing for university or further study and doing exams. Elizabeth's schoolmates would have been the children of doctors or teachers and of the leading families of the town, and there wouldn't necessarily have been many other shopkeeper's children there. Contemporary pictures of younger pupils of the era show serious-looking infants, unused to being photographed, the girls with white, full-length pinafores (even some very old-fashioned pinafores with sleeves) over their clothes, while little boys are in shorts, suit jackets and smart white shirt collars. The school building itself, as it was in Elizabeth's day, still exists. A large, impressive building in its own grounds, it is a focal point of the area. The IRA remained there until 1977, and it was for many years after that the Midmills campus of Inverness College. During Elizabeth's time the school had a roll of around 350 pupils.

Given the relatively recent change from private to burgh school, there was likely separation between the pupils whose richer parents had attended the Academy, and those, like Bessie, whose parents had only been able to benefit from schooling up to the age of fourteen. Bessie, by the time she started school, would already have been steeped in her own family history, well aware of the strength of Jane Ellis, her grandmother and a former servant, and, of course, loving and respecting her hard-working parents. In contrast, fellow pupils like Mairi MacDonald had families that had been well established in the area for generations, who were the town's doctors and lawyers and elected officials – not people who had lived in the Maggot in recent memory. Colin and Josephine may have been able to send their daughters to a 'better' school, but they could not make Elizabeth feel part of it. As Mairi

MacDonald makes clear in her writing, many Invernessians saw the class divisions in their town as an excellent and necessary way of ordering society, which should not be disturbed by social mobility. Any discord between Bessie and her contemporaries would be a fault Mairi would attribute to Bessie herself, as an individual, not to the society she lived in, because she was completely happy with the way society was organized, and saw no reason to change it. Mairi was readier to see Bessie as someone 'different' than to acknowledge that there could be people of different backgrounds within her social group. 'Inverness', wrote Mairi,

> was a very Highland, very residential town – two facts of which its inhabitants were highly conscious. Socially, it acknowledged four distinct strata. There were the "county" families, usually of long Highland pedigree; the professionals – doctors, lawyers, accountants and the like, and if any of those could claim descent from good Highland family, they mixed freely with the "county"; next came the trades folk and shopkeepers, many of whom were substantially well-to-do, but thought to be lacking in the social graces and culture of the other classes; and lastly, the "working class" and labourers. Social climbing was considered an ignorant vanity.[12]

Even Mairi's attitude to Gaelic was significantly different to the MacKintosh family: whereas Colin saw it as a backward language that he had to drop in order to get on in life, Mairi's father was a major figure in the Gaelic Society of Inverness and an organizer of the Mod. For Mairi, Gaelic was a romantic, ancient language of poetry which was recited in concert halls; for Bessie it was the living language her relatives spoke in the poor part of town. Mairi's romanticizing of Gaelic reflected the views of those around her, who wanted the positive cultural aspects of Celtic culture, with none of the perceived negative qualities. Alexander MacEwen, later a provost of Inverness and a significant figure in Bessie's later writing life, wrote a polemic on Gaelic, Highland and Scottish culture entitled *The Thistle and the Rose*, where he expounded at length on the qualities of Gaelic and the Gaels, but simultaneously criticized 'west coast' characteristics: 'Is there something in the climate and soil of the West which envelops the inhabitants with a miasma of lethargy and timelessness?'[13] These were the attitudes that Colin was working hard to overcome; this was why he chose to raise his daughters separately from their MacKintosh grandmother and cousins.

Whatever attitudes Colin was fighting against, and whatever decisions he and Josephine made about child-rearing, Bessie herself was relatively unaware of them in her early childhood. She remembered a happy, loving upbringing, and unposed family snapshots show the three MacKintosh girls with their mother in sunlit gardens, playing on swings, in front of deckchairs and lounging outside on the grass, wearing Victorian straw boater hats and clothes as relaxed as the demure long-skirted fashions would allow. These are the photographic memories of childhood summer holidays, and Bessie was later to commemorate these happy times in her first pen-name. The surname she first chose to write under, 'Daviot', was picked in remembrance of happy childhood holidays spent at Daviot, just outside Inverness, where the MacKintoshes had family friends. Bessie's childhood was happy, and her writing is peopled with intelligent, happy children in loving families. Although remembered for her portrayal of independent, single, childless women (like Miss Pym), they are never women with a 'secret sorrow'. They may not be women who have found love or had children, but this is presented as a choice, not something they were forced into or chose to avoid because of demons in their own upbringing. They were never women with unhappy childhoods.

Colin and Josephine took their three daughters to professional photographers for posed family group shots, and the pictures show very proud parents with beautifully turned-out children: Bessie's shy smile is mirrored by her younger sisters', and her long hair, not yet as dark as in later photos, is brushed out and tied with a large bow. Jean's hair is shorter, and she, like Bessie, has the strong features of her mother's family, while Etta, blonde and pretty, holds a large doll. The three of them wear white, frilly dresses festooned with lace.

Many of Bessie's aunts and uncles had several children, giving her many cousins, but they did not join her as she went up the primary school at the IRA. Bessie remained closer to her mother's side of the family, and Josephine kept in touch not only with her own siblings but also with Horne cousins in Aberdeenshire.[14]

Even these family ties were weakening, though: in 1907, when Bessie was eleven and coming to the end of her primary schooling, her maternal grandfather, Josephine's father Peter Horne, died. Like Colin's father, he was in his seventies and had worked in a manual profession, moving across Scotland for work. A studio photograph of Peter and his wife Jane shows a more formally dressed man than John MacKintosh had been: a stern-looking figure with a long white beard, a very much neater beard than the wild MacKintosh look, teamed with hair neatly brushed back from the forehead and wearing a dark jacket, trousers and waistcoat.[15] Peter Horne's wife, Bessie's grandmother Jane Ellis, stands behind her husband, with her hand supportively on his shoulder. While Peter looks directly at the camera, every inch the upright religious man of strong moral principles, Jane, in her turban-style hat, scarf and gloved hands, looks more reflective. When she was widowed, Jane was also in her seventies, but she continued to live independently in their house at 53 Crown Street, supported by her family.

Peter and Jane's six children, including Josephine, were now established in work and marriage. Their professions give a glimpse of a world that has now died: alongside Peter jnr, the Printer Compositor, eldest son George was a Coach Painter, while younger son Alexander started out as a Gunsmith's Messenger Boy.[16] When Peter Horne died, it seemed to end not only a link to Bessie's wider family, but a link to the past. The world he had known was going to be swept away by the events of the twentieth century, and Josephine, Colin and their three daughters were now looking firmly towards the future. The move to Inverness had been a good one for both the Horne and MacKintosh families: the town was thriving, with the wide new streets and tall buildings representing prosperity and possibilities, and Colin and Josephine were taking full advantage of what was open to them. Bessie MacKintosh was to have a very different life to her mother and father, and a vastly different life to that of her grandparents.

CHAPTER THREE

Secondary Schooldays, up until 1914

In 1909, Bessie MacKintosh was thirteen years old, and going into the secondary stage of her education. Another family photograph taken around this time shows a change from the early childhood photos.[1] Bessie is taller, with the gangly look of a teenager. The strong features, especially the large nose, of her mother's family seem almost too big for her face (as an adult, she broke her nose in an accident, which explains some of the difference in how she looks as a child). Standing close behind Josephine in the photo, the similarity between mother and daughter is very strong, especially around the eyes. Bessie the teenager, who hated getting her photo taken, has rather sad-looking eyes, while Josephine, very smartly dressed in a sailor-style blouse with a bouffant hairdo, is clearly looking at the photographer with pride in her little family. At some point in her schooling, Bessie, or Beth, as she started to be called, discovered that she needed to wear glasses because she was short-sighted. She never wore the glasses for any posed photo, and they were a source of some resentment as they nearly spoilt her career choice.

On the other side of the photo, Jean too has something of a teenage, sulky look, and stands almost apart from her family. She comes across as a sometimes difficult middle child who didn't always fit in with her two sisters or her parents and went her own way, though, unlike Bessie, there is never any hint of sadness about her expression; she, like Etta, always shines with confidence. Etta is still very much 'The Kid', standing in front of her father's knee, with Colin's arm around her. There is little left of the earnest young man in Colin; he is very much a successful businessman, with his shirt and tie, waistcoat and chain.

By 1909 the IRA had completed the process of becoming a burgh school, open to anyone, but the fees were still in place.[2] With three daughters now at school, Colin and Josephine had to make some adjustments.[3] Colin moved his fruiterer business again. He had originally rented both his living accommodation (the flat at number 67) and shop (at numbers 55 and 57) from a family called Sutherland. The odd numbers ran down one side of Castle Street, with some relating to flats above the shops, so 55 and 57 were next door to each other. Colin had then expanded next door to 53, which, with a higher rental value of £24, was larger than 55 and 57 (which came in at £18). Number 53 was owned by a John Mackay, so Colin was now renting business premises from two separate people. However, by 1909 Colin's original landlord Duncan Sutherland had died, and Colin moved, for the same rent, into another of John Mackay's properties: the shop just one door down at number 49 – so Colin was now renting numbers 49 and 53 Castle Street. This was not to be his last move.

Family circumstances also changed again for the MacKintosh family, as Colin's mother, his eldest daughter's namesake Elizabeth (Betsey) Maclennan, died on 31st January 1910.[4] Whatever his relationship had been with his mother before she died, after her death Colin paid for a handsome memorial to both his parents in Tomnahurich cemetery. If he couldn't establish the Gaelic-speaking former crofters creditably in Inverness society in life, he was certainly going to make sure they had their rightful place in death. A tall column with an urn on top, the memorial is situated almost opposite the headstone for Elizabeth's other grandfather, Peter Horne, and very close to the headstone for Elizabeth's little cousins, Josephine and Elizabeth Jeans. Colin wished to stay close to his wife's family even in death, showing how much he had been accepted into the slightly wealthier Horne family's lives. There may also have been an element of Colin wishing to show people how well he had done: the first name on his parents'

41

memorial is not theirs, but his: 'Erected by Colin MacKintosh, Fruit Merchant, Inverness,' it proclaims in large letters. Colin, like his daughter Bessie, was not immune to the snobbery and class division he encountered as he made more money. The memorial is then dedicated to the memory of his parents John MacKintosh and Elizabeth Maclennan, and Colin made sure to reference their original home: 'Both natives of Shieldaig of Applecross'.

Josephine's family was also hit by tragedy, as in March 1910 her unlucky sister Mary, who had lost two daughters in infancy, died of a heart attack.[5] She was in her early forties. Mary and her husband Robert had had ten children, though not all had survived infancy. Josephine and Mary had been close, and it must have been hard for Josephine to lose her older sister. She may have done what she could to help Robert, but the widower found consolation a year later, remarrying to a Jessie Gillie Dunlop. Keeping close to a brother-in-law who has remarried is more difficult than staying in touch with a sister and brother-in-law, and family bonds between Bessie and her cousins loosened as well, though Josephine and her daughters did make an effort to keep in touch with Mary's children.

Another of Beth's cousins was to die in infancy in 1910. Beth's aunt Mary died only one day after Beth's cousin, Robert Ellis Horne, aged only five-and-a-half. Robert Ellis was the son of Mary Dewar Macdonald and Josephine's younger brother Peter, the Printer Compositor. Peter worked with Robert Jeans, the recent widower, so it must have been tough at their workplace at the *Northern Chronicle*, with two of the workforce suffering bereavements so close together. On the official register of deaths in Inverness, the death of Mary Jeans (née Horne) is recorded on the same page as her nephew's. It was a difficult time for Beth's mother Josephine, to lose a sister and a young nephew in such a short space of time, and it strengthened Josephine and Colin's resolve to do their best for their own young daughters as they progressed through their school years.

The new rector of the IRA in 1909 was Gilbert Watson.[6] He only lasted a year, and was replaced quickly by George Morrison, so Beth's time in the school saw her work under three headmasters (the first was William J. Watson). George Morrison, who was rector for most of Beth's senior school years, had previously been senior Classics master at Robert Gordon's College in Aberdeen, and was, several years later, to return to that institution as rector. Classics was one of the subjects Beth was good at, and Morrison made sure the standard of teaching was high in his specialist subject. Morrison was also a keen musician, and music was offered as an extra at the school (for a cost). Beth and her sisters took music, learning the piano, while in 1909 Beth was awarded a 'Very Good' mark (the highest the IRA awarded) for her singing.[7] Her background in music was to surface in an unusual, and little known, way when Beth first started writing, but, although she was obviously well-grounded in the technicalities, she wasn't an outstanding musician. There are numerous well-informed references in her writing to music, from early short stories to the island concert (with its comments on the singing) in *The Singing Sands,* but music is generally shown as being more of a background activity, or concerts seen as a good social meeting place.

Rector George Morrison's interest in quality teaching is shown by his later appointment as MP for Scottish Universities, a post he held after his retirement from teaching.[8] The circumstance of having three rectors in quick succession may have unsettled the school staff – it wasn't typical of the time – but many of the teachers were popular local figures, whose names are still remembered today, such as the PE teacher Donald Dallas, who was also a local Highland Games competitor. The teachers were mainly male, though female teachers increased in numbers after the First World War began, another general change which mirrors Beth MacKintosh's own life experience, as she became a teacher. Although the school was co-educational, girls and boys were not taught together in every subject (PE was not mixed, for example, and needlework was girls only). Education was compulsory for all in Scotland up to the age of fourteen, and academic children could stay at school longer if they wished – free places and bursaries were available for those whose work was of a high standard.

Daughter of Josephine MacKintosh, the former teacher, and Colin, lover of literature, Beth always maintained that she 'began to write very soon after she began to walk', and literacy and learning were highly praised by her parents.[9] She was an academic child, winning several prizes during her time at school, but she does not seem to have left much impression on her teachers and classmates, and neither do they seem to have impressed her much. Beth had a talent for making and keeping friends and was to keep in touch with performers and backroom staff from her later plays for years, even when she wasn't able to live nearby them – but she was also selective in her friendships. Once she was your friend, she was a friend for life, but it took time for her to get to know people.

Mairi MacDonald's biographical essay on Gordon Daviot has its faults, but it is generally fair and well-researched, and it does provide a unique picture of what Beth was like at school. Mairi remembered 'Bessie MacK', particularly good at PE, especially gymnastics, though not necessarily always interested in other lessons, a 'happy, very active young person, trim in her sailor suit with its braided collar; her light brown hair always smoothly brushed – and ever ready to break into a most attractive, lively smile'. Mairi also tells the story of how, when asked by the rector of her former school if anything from her schooldays had helped her to become a writer, Beth had replied 'with a bright smile, "Oh, I have no doubt whatsoever that the four-leaved clovers I so often found at interval-time, in the playground, were responsible for my great good luck"'.[10] Although this has to be taken with some reservations, it's true that Beth doesn't seem to have loved school, and certainly never referred to any particular teacher as having inspired her. Since no one at the school picked up on her writing talent, there seems no reason why she should credit them with any inspiration. Beth, with her 'humble' origins and quiet demeanour, was exactly the sort of child who could easily be overlooked: she wouldn't cause a teacher any trouble, and could be relied on to work without much supervision or interference.

There is a persistent idea, perhaps based on a too-literal reading of Mairi's writings coupled with Beth's later choice of PE as a specialist subject, that Beth wasn't terribly academic. To anyone who has read her books carefully – not only the mystery novels but also her historical work – this is clearly not true. The attitude that a 'games teacher', as Beth was to become, could not write plays is another version of snobbery: people, especially girls, are often 'supposed' to be good at either sport or intellectual pursuits, an artificial split between the body and mind. This attitude would not have endeared Beth's teachers and schoolmates to her, but she did keep up links with her old school, making a later contribution to the school magazine, for example. At school, Beth won prizes and merit in Art, and in Music, which she took as an extra subject. She had consistently high marks for English and French. Beth's command of and interest in English is clearly shown by her writing career, while she developed her knowledge of France and French in her teens and twenties, and features French characters and settings in short stories and novels. Beth's Drawing was 'quite good', and other arts and crafts, like Needlework, 'very good'. In Physics she had notably lower marks, though she later successfully worked hard on science subjects, particularly Biology, in order to pass her college course. Her Maths marks were steady, if not brilliant. She was a hard-working good all-rounder, probably among the smarter students, with a definite leaning towards English and the Arts, but not standing out. She was at that level of ability where she was good enough not to need help and so suffered from a lack of attention from teachers. Her talents for research and writing were never picked up.

The education given at the IRA was rigorous and to a high standard and there is evidence throughout all of Beth's later writing of this excellent academic grounding, from her thorough knowledge of history and religious education to her use of French and her wide-ranging and open-minded interest in a variety of subjects. When she is interested in a topic, she explores it thoroughly, reading up on its background and asking for help from those who know more. In *The Singing Sands* when Grant wants to know more about the Hebrides, he immediately goes to a library, where he peruses a selection of books and asks the librarian for advice. In *The Daughter of Time*, Grant sifts through historical evidence using both primary and secondary sources, and is able to argue from cause to effect, rather than repeating a series of facts. Girls like Beth MacKintosh and Mairi MacDonald expected this sort of education – questioning, rigorous and encouraging private study – as standard, and the image of the ill-educated Highland girl – or the exception fighting against the rule – shown in some contemporary early twentieth-century literature (e.g. by Lewis Grassic Gibbon) is just plain wrong. It was a stereotype Beth MacKintosh would fight in both her private life and in her writing. The popular idea that in the 1900s girls maybe learnt a bit of drawing, French and music was simply not true in Scotland.

Beth's interests changed as she went through the school. She always loved writing, but she also enjoyed and gained prizes and merit in drawing, and in later life she said that she had considered art school, though had eventually decided that her work was not of a high enough standard. Her knowledge of art is shown in her writing, with her second full-length West End play, *The Laughing Woman,* being based on the life of an artist and sculptor. Other artists feature prominently in her books, such as Lee in *To Love and Be Wise.* The IRA gained a new art department in 1912, and publicity photos of the new department show serious female pupils with long skirts, long-sleeved white shirts and neatly pinned-up hair, drawing at easels, while the walls of the classroom are covered with framed paintings, and fruit, vases and busts for still-life drawing are all around.

Beth's high marks in English and History are particularly notable given her later career as a writer. English literature was well-taught at the IRA, with the English teacher an Oxford graduate with a particular interest in Shakespeare, but the real interest lies in the linking of the two subjects. The fact that History and English were taught together at the IRA reveals one source of Elizabeth's working methods. Her first breakthrough play was a historical drama, and for her it must have been natural to consider a historical topic suitable for writing – the modern day speech rhythms which she used in *Richard of Bordeaux,* which were so revolutionary at the time, could be traced back to this early association of History as a creative subject. The history that she was taught at school was also different from today's Scottish curriculum in that it focused heavily on British and Empire history.

When Elizabeth came to write her plays and novels, it was the English kings Richard II and III who had captured her imagination. Her interest in Scottish figures, such as Claverhouse (subject of her only full-length factual biography) and local figure Duncan Forbes, was heavily weighted towards a view of them within a British context. Now, even referring to kings by their Scottish or English numbering (i.e., James I or VI, or Elizabeth I or II) is a political issue. This has the effect of making some of Beth's historical ideas – especially in her biography of Claverhouse, or in *The Singing Sands* – seem not only dated but also even anti-Scottish.

Another subject held particular interest for Beth: Physical Education, or PE. A new gym (as well as the new art block) was opened at the IRA in 1912, when Beth was in her final years of senior school – the age when she was starting to think about her future career.[11] PE was an important part of the curriculum in the early twentieth century, and took a slightly different form than it would today, developing quickly from the old-fashioned 'drill', where pupils were marched up and down like soldiers. There are some posed photos of the gym opening, showing girls of around Beth's age in the PE kit of the day: a long dark pinafore sort of garment, with wide knee-length skirts for easy movement, a long-sleeved white shirt underneath, and comfortable gym shoes. Long hair is neatly tied back, and the girls demonstrate the new gym equipment: parallel bars, a horse, beam and mats. This is the same sort of equipment Beth was later to describe in her book *Miss Pym Disposes*. Other sports popular at the IRA at the time were football and cricket. Nowadays, football is still played, of course, but rugby is also popular, while the idea of a Scottish school playing a lot of cricket seems strange, since this is now a very English sport. But at the beginning of the twentieth century there was a real games cult – the Boer War had highlighted the poor physical condition of many potential soldiers due to bad diet and overwork, and, as the First World War approached, the need to train the next generation became ever more imperative.

With schooling compulsory for all, this idea of PE as an integral part of school life had grown, and this is the time when many popular girls' school stories were written, with authors like Angela Brazil creating the idea of the hockey-playing schoolgirl, who always 'played the game'. Games, or PE, were not just about physical education, they were a moral training ground, a particularly British idea, where pupils learnt to 'play the game', following the rules of sportsmanship. The lessons themselves would have been different from today not only in their theory but also in practice, as gym teachers were concerned also with, for example, their pupils' posture and any physiotherapy needs. A physical training teacher had to have a broad academic background and their work was taken very seriously; they were not just the people who led sports.

In the academic session of 1912–1913, when she was sixteen, Beth was awarded a final year's bursary as a result of her good academic marks. This financial award helped with school fees for her last three years of school. As Jean was also in secondary school, and their youngest sister Etta was now eight years old and making her way through primary school, this helped Colin and Josephine MacKintosh to pay for their daughters' education. The award was made solely on academic merit not family circumstance; Jean, who left school after her fifth year, did not receive a similar bursary.

The final years of Beth's secondary education, however, were coloured for her not just by her progress in studying, but also by a significant change in family circumstances, and by the lead up to and the outbreak of World War I.

In summer 1914, Beth was getting ready to go into Class VI, her final year of school. She turned eighteen on 25th July 1914, and war was declared three days later, a few weeks before the end of the summer holiday. The IRA had a longer break than most schools, a legacy of its days as a private institution, and those first days of war were mixed up for Beth with her birthday, the long summer, and the romance of patriotism. The outbreak of the First World War was met with a huge outpouring of patriotism, and young men from Inverness joined others across the country in rushing to sign up to join the armed services in what became known as the 'August Madness'. Many of the young men Beth knew from the year ahead of her at the IRA left school and went straight to volunteer and sign up to help the war effort.

Newspapers from the time show how the rhetoric around war has changed. In 1914, with no knowledge of what was to come in the trenches, it was all stirring speeches and Britishness, and an image of a short glorious war. Inverness then, as now, was an army town, with troops permanently stationed at Cameron Barracks and at Fort George, just along the coast, so the world of soldiers would not have been unknown to Beth – but even if she had been aware of some of the realities of war, at eighteen she didn't fully appreciate them. For her, war initially meant great change in her home town, as the whole local area became an important military training ground, and it must also have meant the romance of her classmates and cousins signing up and parading through town in their new uniforms – kilts, of course, for the Highland regiments. Throughout her life, Beth was always greatly moved by regimental display, and her writing, particularly her early poems and her first novel, but also many of her later writing choices, was heavily influenced by the war.[12]

There were large contingents of soldiers stationed at Cameron Barracks in Inverness, while the Seaforth Highlanders were based nearby at Fort George.[13] These were not only local Invernessians who had signed up, but also men who had come in from the surrounding areas; regular career Army men; and, as time went on, soldiers from other areas including (after 1917) Americans. Boats were also stationed in the Cromarty Firth. In the 'August Madness', that first patriotic rush of enthusiasm for the Great War, hundreds of young men signed up. One of the units particularly associated with Inverness is the Cameron Highlanders. The first and second battalions of the Queen's Own Cameron Highlanders were the regular army units who operated even during peacetime. The 1st Camerons were based just north of Inverness at Invergordon, and within a month of the declaration of war, they marched through town, cheered on by a crowd, and got onto a train heading south through Scotland, England and onto France. These were the soldiers who were already trained, who were theoretically ready for war. These professional soldiers were to be joined by the 4th Cameron Highlanders, the Territorial Army, and by the volunteers who had joined the TA and who were also being formed into new units. The 4th Cameron Highlanders was the battalion that most Invernessians were associated with. It was the battalion that Beth's friends from school joined, and the battalion that her cousin Peter Horne joined. The Inverness Royal Academy and the local paper the *Inverness Courier* closely followed the progress of the 4th Camerons, and Beth followed it as avidly as everyone else. Her first novel, *Kif*, is in many ways a novel of the 4th Camerons.

The 4th Camerons, at the start of the war, had about a thousand men, organized into different companies, each of which were based in different parts of the Highlands, from Inverness and Nairn right over to Fort William, Broadford and Portree. As part of the Territorial Army, men in the 4th Camerons had work outside the army, and volunteered in their spare time. An unusual characteristic of the battalion was that two-thirds of both the officers and men were Gaelic-speaking, probably the highest percentage of any battalion in the British Army. Officers were generally middle-class, from professions such as teaching, in contrast to the private-school educated English officers of the 'regular' army, such as the 1st Camerons. The popular Captain of 'A' Company in Inverness was Murdoch Beaton, whose name may seem familiar to those who know Gordon Daviot's early work.

Although the 4th Camerons were theoretically at full strength of a thousand men, in reality there were only about six to seven hundred ready to go, which meant they needed more volunteers before they could set out. It was not hard to find young men eager to join up: around a hundred volunteered in Inverness in the first two weeks of the war while in London two hundred and fifty men signed up with the proviso that they be assigned to a Scottish regiment. In Inverness, the 4th Camerons paraded through Bell's Park, and the commanding officer, Lieutenant-Colonel Ewen Campbell, made a stirring speech asking for volunteers. Bell's Park is now known as Farraline Park: stripped of the bus stances which now take up the space there, it is an open square in front of an imposing, columned building (now the Library, but formerly a school). Beth was surely among the crowds who watched the kilted 4th Camerons marching to the sound of pipes and drums in this impressive setting. During the first few months there were briefly six thousand troops stationed in Inverness, a very large number for a town of only 20,000 people. The war must have seemed very close for Beth.

The 4th Camerons, now up to full strength, were sent down to Bedford for extra training by the end of August 1914. Dressed in their kilts – and the majority of them speaking Gaelic – they made a formidable impression on the English town where they did their training. A short film, *The Highlanders at Bedford*, was made about them, which was then shown as a recruiting tool in Inverness in November 1914. Advertisements were printed every week in the local press to raise even more recruits, and the local papers also carried letters from the men who went away. Beth was among the many who devoured every scrap of information.

The first indication that things were not going to go well, however, arose out of the unique character of the 4th Camerons. The regiment was made up of volunteers from the Highlands who had often never travelled far from their homes. They did a bit of soldiering on the weekends, but had never seen active service. Their trip to Bedford was their first trip out of their region – and their first exposure to large groups of people. The Bedford camp was crowded with men, and a measles epidemic swept through the camp. The Highlanders in the Cameron and Seaforth regiments, particularly those from the more remote villages, had never come into contact with measles and had no immunity. Fourteen men died. Twelve other men died from other infectious diseases. The measles epidemic delayed the 4th Camerons' departure out to France, but they eventually left in February. While the early months of the war maintained some of the camaraderie and patriotic fervour of the 'August Madness', it was not long before trench warfare became embedded in earnest, and the families of those who died of the measles may have begun to think that their sons might have been the lucky ones.

For those staying in the Highlands, travel, especially north (where troops and boats were stationed) was restricted and all

Invernessians had to carry ID (a Local Pass). This wasn't just a temporary or minor inconvenience. The rush of soldiers in 1914 began a process that, by 1917, had given the armed forces almost complete control over the north of Scotland and thoroughly militarized the landscape. The First World War was the beginning of a total change in the way of life, and in the Highlands this was particularly visible and long-lasting, with military bases and jobs still a feature of the landscape across the north and Moray today. Beth was used to spending family holidays at Daviot, near Inverness, a place that she loved so much that she used it in her later pen-name, but the First World War stopped this link to her childhood.

However, while his daughter was watching the soldiers, in 1914 Colin MacKintosh was concerned with two changes closer to home. First of all his business: until 1914, his shop seems to have done particularly well, and he saw no reason to think that the war would make any difference.[14] With such large numbers of troops moved suddenly into the area, it seems reasonable to assume that large amounts of food were suddenly needed, and Colin was there to supply fruit. Colin's business had aimed for the top of the market, and he had been selling to the big houses, these same houses whose sons were now officers. These officers must have had to organize food for their troops, and Colin's business was perfectly situated to serve the army barracks. In about 1914, Colin had saved up enough to move himself, his wife Josephine and their three daughters from rented accommodation to a bought house, costing around £42, at 4 Victoria Circus (later renamed Crown Circus). 'Crown Cottage', as it came to be known, was not a cottage at all, but a large Victorian villa in the best part of the Crown area. This was a significant step up for the MacKintosh family.

Colin also had a family problem to deal with. His brothers Murdo and Dan he considered troublesome, people he could no longer work with, who had tried to tap him for money, and who had even tried to fight him in the back shop. He still paid the rent for his sister Mary and her son Donald. His other brother John, closest to him in age, he had considered settled: he had emigrated to Patagonia twenty years before, where he was working as a shepherd. But in summer 1914 John reappeared, in dire circumstances. John had been sacked from his job and deported to Britain, sailing into Liverpool and somehow making his way back to Inverness. When he arrived, he was in a terrible state. Previously a teetotaller, for the past two years John had been drinking heavily, had become moody, neglected his work and finally 'became silly', leading to his deportation. He was filthy, yet apparently happy and unaware of the state he was in. John was taken in by his brother Murdo and his wife, but they struggled with him as he wandered aimlessly and forgetfully around, not recognizing them, staring wildly and laughing and behaving with no sense of propriety. They were also concerned that John continued to insist that he was a wealthy man who had somehow been done out of all his money. With no money for medical care, and a family of their own to look after, drastic measures were necessary. Murdo and his wife arranged to have their brother John sectioned, and he was admitted into Craig Dunain District Asylum.[15]

John's case notes from Craig Dunain are detailed, and show that he was suffering from a number of physical ailments, including persistent rheumatism which had troubled him for years. It was noted that he was not always lucid, but that he was able to give clear descriptions of life on a ranch in Patagonia. The theme of the money in the bank which had somehow disappeared recurred. John's condition deteriorated fast, and he died on 15th July 1914, aged forty-seven. The final cause of death was pneumonia, but it had been preceded by a 'General Paralysis'. Colin registered his brother's death.

Emigration to Patagonia was not uncommon in the Highlands, and, sadly, John's story was not uncommon either. The climate in Patagonia did not always agree with Highlanders, and there were a number of diseases that John would have been exposed to that Highland doctors may not have recognized, or known how to treat. His symptoms, while clearly involving a mental element, also had a physical component, which may have had a deeper underlying cause. John's complaint about money may not have been the ravings of a madman: there are several well-documented cases of Highlanders who had emigrated to Patagonia finding, on their return, that money that had been promised to their accounts on completion of their contracts was not forthcoming.[16] Whatever the truth, John's illness and death was a distressing experience for Colin, Murdo and the wider MacKintosh family. John was married, with children, but despite extensive searches I have not found out what happened to his widow and her family.

John's death was only ten days before Beth MacKintosh's eighteenth birthday. As Colin kept his family at a distance, Beth was probably unaware of the finer details, just as Colin was distracted and unaware of what Beth was experiencing. It was a strange time: the war was about to change everything.

Much has been made in biographical sketches of Beth's attachment to a soldier who was killed in the First World War, and it is easy to see how she would have been caught up in the atmosphere of the 'August Madness' and the rush to volunteer, and in the romance of the young boy soldiers. It is also easy to see that Colin would not have approved of any serious romance: John's death must have reinforced his determination to offer his daughters the best future possible, and, for Colin, a good future was inextricably linked to hard work. His daughters were going to work hard at school, go on to further education, and only marry at some unspecified date in the future. He would want them to have a marriage like his own and Josephine's, built on hard work and mutual trust, and, crucially, with a solid financial foundation. Colin was keeping family secrets from his daughters, perhaps making it harder for them to bridge the gap between them. Because of this, Beth kept many of her thoughts to herself, not even sharing them with friends. Her romance in the Great War is one of the areas of her life that was the hardest to research, it was so shrouded in mystery, but she was clearly entering a new stage of her personal and emotional development.

CHAPTER FOUR

War, and first year at Anstey

After the 'August Madness' and the crazy rush to sign up, the reality of war did not take long to assert itself. In a small town like Inverness, everyone was aware of losses. The first former pupil of the Academy to die was Albert Corner, in March 1915. Ironically, Albert's mother was German.[1] The son of the owner of the *Inverness Courier*, James Barron, was killed at Loos in 1915. George, the son of the IRA's former rector Dr Watson, volunteered to join the army when he was only sixteen, and was killed by a sniper before he was eighteen. Hugh Melven, son of a well-known local bookseller, died in 1916, three weeks after spending time home on leave. His younger brother was already dead, killed the year before.[2] Murdoch Beaton, rapidly promoted after several deaths to be in charge of the 4th Camerons, had the difficult task of writing home to families he knew well, to let them know that their sons had been killed. He wrote extraordinarily frank letters home to his own family, describing in detail the bloody attacks in the trenches.[3] Private letters from relatives were routinely sent in and published in the *Inverness Courier*, giving the ordinary people in Inverness a realistic idea of life in the trenches.[4] To modern eyes it is difficult to understand why men still volunteered, but for the first couple of years of the war there was still a strong belief that, however hard it was, it was the right thing to do. In descriptions written after the war there is a great deal of bitterness, but the contemporary quotes from the early years still emphasize patriotism. It wasn't until later, when the stalemate and conditions in the trenches was exacerbated by the invention of new weaponry such as trench mortars, that notes of dissent began to creep in.

Within Beth MacKintosh's own family, there were radical differences in the experience of the war and it played its part in dividing the once-close Horne and MacKintosh families. As the father of three daughters, perhaps Colin saw the First World War differently to his brothers and brothers-in-law, fathers of sons. There was moral pressure from the beginning of the Great War for all men of the right age (between nineteen and forty) to enlist, which included most of Beth's male cousins. Two of Beth's cousins, both called Peter Horne after their grandfather, had very different experiences of the First World War, illustrating the different ways it affected the family.[5]

The first Peter Horne was the son of Josephine's older brother Robert and his wife Margaret. Robert was older than Josephine, and Peter was his second son, his firstborn, James, having died in infancy. Robert worked as a janitor at Farraline Park School in the centre of Inverness, and, as a member of the Territorial Army, was called up only a month after the Great War started. His son Peter was a couple of years younger than Elizabeth, and took over his father's job – but went on to join the 4th Camerons as soon as he was able, in 1915.[6] Peter was sent to France in September 1915, where he fought through the end of the Battle of the Somme. The Somme is notorious now for the huge number of lives lost, and the Camerons were particularly badly hit. In July 1916, the 1st Camerons were at full strength of around a thousand men. They were the regular army who, as professional trained soldiers, were given attacking assignments at the Somme. Two months later, at a roll call on the third of September, this battalion had only 132 men: a less than 15 per cent survival rate. Many of the 4th Camerons were sent to reinforce the 1st Camerons, and eventually the 4th Camerons were so depleted in numbers that they were disbanded altogether, and all the men deployed to different units. Peter Horne was posted to the 6th Camerons in August 1916. He was killed during the Battle of Arras on 24th April 1917. He is commemorated on a memorial in Arras, and also on a Horne family headstone in Tomnahurich cemetery in Inverness.

Beth's other cousin, Peter John Horne, was the son of Josephine's younger brother, Peter, who worked as the printer-compositor at the *Northern Chronicle*. He was just one year younger than Beth. Unlike Beth, Peter had already left school, and had started training alongside his father as a Compositor Apprentice when war broke out. In 1916 he too enrolled in the army, but his enrolment form is clearly marked 'Exemption from combatant service has been granted'. Peter John Horne was a conscientious objector. While the first Peter Horne was posted to France, Peter John was posted to a non-combatant corps in Hamilton, Lanarkshire, refusing to fight because of his deeply-held religious beliefs. Conscientious objectors were very uncommon during the Great War, and were treated as near outcasts from society. Josephine and her siblings had been brought up in a religious household, and, although neither Josephine nor her brother Robert seem to have held to this, Peter John's branch of the family felt that they could not countenance sending their sons to war. One can only imagine how two brothers would feel, when the son of one was killed fighting in a war, while the son of the other was a conscientious objector. Peter John survived the war with his religious beliefs strengthened by his experiences. In later life he was an evangelist, ending up in Bolivia.

It wasn't just men who were actively involved in service over-seas: although women did not fight, many of them volunteered to help, doing nursing work for example. The IRA kept its pupils informed of what their former classmates were doing, and the 1916 school magazine had a particularly striking description of the work of two female former pupils, Dr Anna Muncaster and Mrs Green, who found themselves in Serbia.[7] Anna Muncaster was ten years older than Elizabeth. After leaving the IRA she had gone to Edinburgh University, where she had gained a first class honours degree in medicine and had gone on to work in lunatic asylums. In 1915 she volunteered to join with the work being done in Serbia by Mrs Mabel St Clair Stobart, who had set up a field hospital for soldiers and various dispensaries providing medical aid to civilians. Serbia was one of the major theatres of the First World War and was well known as an area that welcomed Scottish nurses, providing also the base for Dr Elsie Inglis, who had gone abroad when her offers to help in the UK were rejected. In Serbia, Dr Anna Muncaster worked first as a sort of basic GP, giving aid as required to the Serbian people, but as German troops started to invade the country, including an aerial bombing campaign, Anna was sent to work in military hospitals. The German advance eventually meant she had to flee Serbia. In effect she became a refugee, forced to walk over the mountains in extremely cold weather, with little food, trying to find sanctuary. After a few false starts, Anna and her colleagues ended up in Montenegro, got down to Albania, and finally escaped by boat to Italy. From there, she went by way of Switzerland and France back to England. This forced evacuation took two months. In the matter of fact way in which participants in the First World War reported their journeys, Anna remarked in a letter to a friend that she had not had a bath during those two months, but at least she had managed to buy a hat and gloves in Paris! She survived the war, and was decorated by the King of Serbia. After 1918 she worked in England for a few years, then emigrated to South Africa, where she worked again in asylums.

Beth, at eighteen, was one of the oldest in her year at school. She was well aware of what other people her age were doing, fighting in France and serving as doctors and nurses in Serbia, and this influenced her decisions about her future. In 1915 she left the IRA, gaining her Leaving Certificate (a group award across a range of subjects, examined nationally) and 'proxime accessit' (second prize) in Art. This second prize was the source of some disappointment as Beth had originally believed she was going to be placed first: an experience that she later used as inspiration when writing the scenes in *Miss Pym Disposes* where Mary Innes loses out on the prize of the job at Arlinghurst. The disappointment also helped to convince Beth that art school was not for her.[8]

Beth still loved writing, and wrote in her spare time, but, unencouraged at school, and aware that she needed to earn a living, she wanted her private and favourite hobby kept separate from her working life. 'When [I] was old enough to choose a profession,' Beth said later, '[I] took care that it was one as far removed from writing as possible [... I] wanted a life of many facets.'[9]

Her parents Colin and Josephine wished Beth to go to university, and she had also considered art college before the disappointment of the lost first prize in art, but instead she made the decision to apply to physical training colleges. Physical training was popular at the time, and the curriculum at a PT college would have included not only gymnastics and dance, but also academic book-based study such as medicine, biology, theories of teaching, and 'physical therapy', or basic treatment of injuries – all things which would have appealed to an intelligent, active girl like Beth who saw her fellow classmates working in military medicine. *Miss Pym Disposes*, the Josephine Tey mystery novel set in a physical training establishment, makes clear just how rigorous and highly regarded this type of training was.

Specialist colleges for training girls in PE were still relatively rare, particularly those operating at the high academic level Beth expected. There was one PT college in Scotland, based in Dunfermline; previous students from the IRA had attended here, and Beth did apply, but was rejected because she wore glasses. However, Beth's eyesight did not prevent her pursuing her chosen career, as she gained an acceptance to Anstey Physical Training College near Birmingham. Anstey had established itself as one of the premier girls PT colleges since its foundation nineteen years previously, and it maintained strong links with Scotland through its teaching staff and former pupils – supplying, for example, the Physical Training Instructress for the district of Ross-shire.[10]

Anstey College had been begun by a woman called Rhoda Anstey in about 1895, gradually building up from what was originally billed as a 'health centre' called 'The Hygienic Home for Ladies' in Bristol, to offering academic, accredited courses, taught by a number of specialists, and based in a large house with gardens in Worcestershire, near Birmingham. In 1907, the school made one final move to similar premises nearby in Erdington (Sutton Coldfield), the location it was in when Beth MacKintosh attended. Rhoda Anstey, originally from Devon, was a formidable woman:

an active feminist and suffragist, sometimes seen as unconventional, who, with the support of her family, was able to create a school where she could teach girls the physical training principles she had herself learnt at college. In 1915, when Beth MacKintosh started her course there, Rhoda Anstey was fifty years old, and the actual teaching of physical work was by then done by others, but Rhoda still remained as the principal and continued to be involved in her school even after her retirement, and right up until her death in 1936 at the age of seventy-one. One of Rhoda Anstey's particular talents was the hiring of staff. Although the school bore her name and propagated many of her ideas, it was never a one-woman show, but always strived for good quality academic and practical achievement, with demonstrable results. Rhoda was well aware that she was fighting against received ideas about women and, despite some eccentric ideas of her own, always encouraged her teachers and pupils to aim for the highest standards. Anstey was a prestigious institution, which accepted only the very best students, carefully screening all applicants to make sure they were young ladies with suitable (i.e. middle-class) values. The school continued for many years, until it was finally incorporated into Birmingham City University.

Anstey College continued the high educational standards that Beth MacKintosh had been used to at the IRA, and in later life she was to say that she never regretted her choice of further education. In the Josephine Tey novel *Miss Pym Disposes*, Lucy Pym, sitting with the gathered staff of the Physical Training College, reflects on the breadth and depth of education offered to PT students of the time:

> If this were any other kind of college that gathering would have been homogenous. If it were a college of science, the gathering would consist of scientists; if it were a college of divinity, of theologians. But [...] in this one room many worlds met.
>
> [...] All these worlds had gone to make the finished article that was a Leaving Student; it was at least not the training that was narrow.[11]

This is an excellent refutation to anyone who queries how a woman who was trained as a PE teacher could go on to write plays and novels.

Anstey was fee-paying, and cost Beth and her parents approximately 35 guineas a term, or just over £100 a year. Colin and Josephine MacKintosh were committed to seeing that their daughters got the best education possible, but it must have been particularly hard to see their eldest daughter leave home and go to college so far away in war time.[12] The journey down to Birmingham was arduous and difficult to contemplate, given the wartime restrictions on travel: at times the train to the Highlands was almost taken over by military transportation of troops.

Beth did not make the long journey from home alone, as a fellow IRA pupil attended Anstey with her.[13] In the new house in Crown, Beth's next-door neighbour was Marjorie Davidson, an IRA pupil from the year below her. Marjorie left after Fifth Year to attend Anstey College, and the two girls went through their two-year training at Anstey together, and kept in touch for many years afterwards. Colin and Josephine could not have travelled down to see their daughter, but at least Marjorie meant she had company. Although Beth came home for the summer, she would probably not have been able to travel home for shorter holiday periods. Leaving home really meant leaving home.

Their time at Anstey – and the period of war they lived through – made Beth and Marjorie very close. Beth remembered their wartime journeys vividly, writing beautifully evocative descriptions of them over several pages to Marjorie years later. 'Do you remember,' Beth said, 'the atmosphere of our shared miseries – the blackened stations and overcrowded trains and the swarming services [...] the long nights sitting up four a side with fat snoring men collapsing onto our shoulders every three minutes, and what Crewe looked like at four in the morning.'[14] Marjorie Davidson and Beth MacKintosh shared a room together at Anstey, where college custom was for girls to be referred to by their surnames. The room-mates became known as 'Mac' and 'Dave'.

There was another major threat from the war. We think of the First World War as being fought mainly on the battlefields in

Europe, but there were also air raids on Britain. Only a few months after Beth started college at Anstey, there was a Zeppelin bombing raid in the Birmingham area – two German airships, which had been aiming for Liverpool, drifted around Birmingham on the evening of the 31st January and through the night to February 1st 1916.[15] The black-out that was in force confused their pilots, but they eventually dropped their bombs towards the north-west of Birmingham (Elizabeth's college was situated in the north-east of the city). Thirty-five local people died. Both of the German Zeppelins escaped England, though one only made it back to its base in Nordholz in Germany, as the other crashed into the North Sea after being shot at by Dutch sentries. The black-out was even more strictly enforced after this. British air defences improved, but there was another Zeppelin bombing over the Birmingham area in the autumn of the following year. Blackouts and travel problems affected Beth daily at Anstey as she travelled across Birmingham to take classes. During term time, the MacKintoshes could communicate regularly by letter, and they also sent Beth copies of the *Inverness Courier*, the traditional gift for the Invernessian in exile. Beth was an excellent correspondent, who wrote chatty, readable letters all through her life, with descriptions that bring alive her day-to-day activities, but it must have been horrifying for Colin and Josephine to read about Zeppelins in the papers and then have to wait for a letter from Beth to find out whether she or anyone she knew had been affected.

In the long summer holidays of 1916 and 1917 Beth contributed to the war effort through her work as a VAD (Voluntary Aid Detachment member). VADs were trained by the Red Cross to provide first aid and nursing help where needed, such as in nursing homes, thus freeing up other medical staff to join the military – Anstey students, including Beth, did VAD work in convalescent homes near the college, and in their home towns. There were three convalescent homes in Inverness during the First World War: Inverness Military Hospital, Hedgefield Auxiliary Hospital, and Leys Castle Auxiliary Hospital.[16] All three were within walking distance of Beth's home in Crown – at least, for an active walker – but given her choice of name for her fictional training college in *Miss Pym Disposes*, it seems likely that Beth spent some time at Leys, which opened in summer 1917.

Leys Castle is a large house which is now located near new housing developments and a supermarket, about three miles from Inverness city centre. In Beth's time it was rural and isolated. It operates now as an exclusive hotel (the Dalai Lama stayed there when he visited Inverness), but was originally a private family residence and was commandeered for war work. As a hospital it had fifty beds. Beth had some medical knowledge from her college coursework, and she also went on to work in hospitals and private clinics after graduation. Her VAD work was encouraged by Anstey as contributing not only to the war effort but also to her education. Beth's experiences in hospitals are briefly mentioned in some of her writing, such as the descriptions of the girls' career plans in *Miss Pym Disposes* or the short plays *The Staff-Room* or even *Sweet Coz*. However, although doctors and nurses are sharply drawn in these works, as in all her excellent character descriptions, there are no detailed descriptions of hospital life. Beth's time as a VAD was not extensive, and her time doing medical work after college was interspersed with, and finally superseded by, teaching. Nursing was not a vocation for her, though Beth's respect for the medical profession is clear throughout her work.

Beth's time as a VAD was motivated less by a desire to be a nurse than by a wish to contribute to, and be involved in, the war effort. The glamour of young men in uniform is easy to imagine. Beth and her female friends, like most of their contemporaries, were very enthusiastic about the soldiers they met, particularly the men of the US Navy who were stationed in Inverness towards the end of the war. It would have taken a while for the horrors of the trenches, and the lasting psychological damage of the war, to become apparent, and, at the beginning of the war all the sacrifices still seemed worthwhile, even glorious.

At first, for Beth, the Great War was all about growing up, and her first romance. Sometime after the outbreak of war, before going into her second year at Anstey, Beth met and became romantically attached to a young officer in a Highland regiment. There has been a lot of speculation about Beth's romantic life:

she kept her personal feelings very close. She never mentioned the name of her First World War soldier to her friends, and never described their romance. However, Beth's sisters did know about it, and Etta, in particular, believed that it was an important turning point in her sister's life.[17]

Many of Beth's friends did speculate that she had lost someone important to her, being aware, for example, that she made visits to First World War gravesites in France to see where her young man had died. Beth's later acquaintances, such as John Gielgud, felt that she was bitter about a love lost in the First World War, without knowing any details.[18] I believe that this bitterness was not about one man, but about two very different men, whom Beth met at different stages in her life, as well as having its root in a wider understanding of the vast changes that the Great War brought about in society, but her first romance with the Highland officer was a brutal introduction to the frailty of relationships.

It seems from what Beth said – and, more often, from what she didn't say – that her first romantic experience in about 1915–16, in the middle of the First World War, was more of a crush than a serious engagement, but it was one that, because of the dramatic and abrupt nature of romance in war time, had important consequences for her both personally and professionally. From circumstantial evidence, it's possible to guess who Beth's young man was, and knowledge about the lives of typical Highland officers of the time reveals a little more about the background to Beth's life, the society she lived in and her own personal values.

At the age of eighteen, Beth couldn't know that she was going to become a career woman. All the women around her – her beloved mother, her aunts and grandmothers – were primarily wives and mothers, and that was probably the future that Beth imagined for herself as well. Her family later recalled that she was interested in a young man at the IRA, a musician who went on to play for the London Philharmonic, but she had not had any serious romantic crushes before that.[19] She was aware that her family didn't 'fit' completely at the IRA, and she had inherited her father's ambition – she was going to move on and up. Not for her the son of an Invernessian shopkeeper; she was going to find someone further up the social scale. This may have been a completely unconscious decision, but one that was understandable given her upbringing. Her romantic attachment in the First World War was to an officer – and he was not from Inverness. Beth had seen from her father and grandmother's experience that the way for an ambitious person to get on in life was to move around for work, and by the end of her school career she was looking out beyond Inverness to the wider world.

Beth worked as a VAD in both Birmingham and in Inverness, giving her many opportunities to meet soldiers.[20] In her last year at school, Beth had made plenty of connections with the 4th Cameron Highlanders, through schoolmates who had joined up, and her family members in the army. Entertaining the troops was practically considered a patriotic duty – and was enormous fun for the girls of Inverness. They used to make 'autograph books', asking the soldiers to sign their names and say where they were from, and many of the signees gave their addresses and asked for letters.[21] Soldiers from all over the country were sent to the Highlands for training, and there were numerous social events, such as dances, church events, and fundraisers for the war effort, at any of which Beth could have met and pursued a friendship with her young officer – and the same sort of events were equally as important in her college town.

The other known fact about Beth's officer is that he died at the Battle of the Somme, in July 1916.[22] There was not a lot of time for Beth to get to know him, and not very much time for the romance to develop into something serious enough to be recognized by many people. It was more in the nature of a crush, or a private, tentative beginning to a romance. This is the main reason that information about Beth's officer is hard to come by: the relationship was a brief, intense, wartime experience.

Troops moved around the UK quickly as they were trained up. Once Beth had met her officer, though, she would have been able to follow his progress quite easily, particularly if he was in a 'local' Highland regiment. The Highland papers gave as much coverage as censorship would allow to the exploits of local regiments, particularly the 4th battalion Cameron Highlanders, which was one of the earlier battalions raised from Inverness, and which had attracted many of the first volunteers, including many former IRA pupils. Officers were regularly mentioned by name, and deaths and injuries were listed as fully as possible, while private letters from soldiers published in the correspondence pages gave more information to relatives and friends waiting anxiously for news.

Using the information that Beth's young man was an officer in a Highland regiment, and putting this together with the knowledge that he was killed at the Somme, I made extensive searches through the lists of Commonwealth War Graves, and searched the history of local regiments, in an attempt to identify Beth's officer.

Several small pieces of anecdotal evidence, coupled with clues in Beth's writing, such as the mention of Becourt military cemetery in a dedication, helped to narrow the search. Beth said, later in life, that her officer died on the same day and near the same place as the poet Robert Graves was seriously wounded.[23] This would make it the 20th July 1916 at High Wood, during the Battle of the Somme – although Beth might have exaggerated this connection to a writer she admired: poetic licence, as it were.

It is dangerous to put too much emphasis on what Beth wrote in her fiction – it wouldn't have been typical for her to have simply fictionalized a real person, she was a more complex writer than that – but there are little touches in her novels, particularly in her choice of names, that often link to real people, whilst the beginning of *Kif*, her first novel, is full of information that directly links back to the real 4th Cameron Highlanders.

Alfred Trevanion Powell was an officer of the 4th Cameron Highlanders.[24] An Englishman, born in Camden Town, London, he was only three years older than Beth, but, educated at a private school called Edward Alleyn's, he was, as befitted a man of his class, already commissioned as an officer, in charge of a group of men and ready to lead them to the Front. He was a volunteer, and had left his job as a banking clerk with Thomas Cook and Son to join a cavalry regiment, the Royal Bucks Hussars, in April 1915. Along with his brother Charles Sydney, Alfred had been transferred to the 3rd/4th Cameron Highlanders as a reserve officer, and sent up to Inverness for training. Alfred had the opportunity to meet

Beth, and had many of the qualities that would have attracted her: his English background, his class, his education. He was typical of the sort of officer Beth would have met. There is nothing to definitively prove that he was Beth's soldier, but the thing that stands out to me is Alfred's unusual middle name: Trevanion. In Beth's first novel, *Kif*, which deals with the First World War, there is a small cameo of a soldier called Travenna. Travenna, a Cameron Highlander, meets the hero on a train going south, shows him London, sparks the hero's interest in horse racing – and then is never heard of again. Beth, travelling regularly by train down to Anstey, retained a life-long love of England, particularly London, and an equally long-lived love of horse racing. Did Beth's officer spark these two loves? Trevanion to Travenna is not too great a leap, and Beth always had an interest in names: it would be consistent with other links with real people's names. Was Alfred Beth's lost World War I soldier?

Alfred, however, did not die at the Somme in High Wood exactly as Beth said her soldier did: he died nearby, at Vimy Ridge, two days later. The 4th Camerons were so heavily depleted by 1915 that the regiment ceased to exist, and Alfred was reassigned to the London Scottish – a regiment made up of men who had enlisted in London, but who had specifically requested to be assigned to a Scottish unit. He went out to France on 6th July 1916, but only lasted 16 days. He was killed on 22nd July 1916 at Vimy Ridge near Arras. He is commemorated at the Maroeuil British Cemetery in France.

Was Beth's officer Alfred? I have considered other possibilities, including the tall and dashing Gordon Barber, a young officer of the 1st Cameron Highlanders.[25] In favour of this theory are the date of his death, the place of his burial (Becourt Cemetery, which Beth was known to have visited) and his connections with Inverness. Beth was petite; a tall man like Gordon would have stood out as he led his men on parade, and the difference in their heights may well have been an attraction. His interest in history; his well-educated background; his interest in writing; his interest in horses – all these things would have appealed to Beth as they chimed with her own interests. This young, English officer would have epitomized her ideas about the quality of education and the possibilities open to young people in England as opposed to Inverness. Finally, his name, 'Gordon' stands out: why did Beth choose the pen-name 'Gordon Daviot' to publish her first writings under? Was it a homage to her first love?

Gordon Barber's posthumously published diary tells the story of this period of the First World War in a way that gives a sense of immediacy not found in later history books. This was the war as Beth and her contemporaries experienced it. Gordon's diary paints a vivid picture of a popular, boyish young man, who wanted to join an army of glorious, patriotic professionals, wearing colourful uniforms, trained to fight at close quarters as well as shoot, led from the front by officers on horseback; the sort of romantic, active young man who would have appealed to a teenage Beth.

Gordon was wounded at Ypres, and, after a short period back in England recovering, the Boys' Own capers and constant descriptions of food in his diary are replaced by an entirely different tone. The trenches have become semi-permanent, conditions are worsening, with the countryside all cut-up round about, earthworks and barbed wire everywhere. He remarks that each day is becoming like the last; that there seems to be no change or advancement. The ground in front of his position in the trenches is littered with dead bodies. There is no truce at Christmas in 1915, as there had been the year before. Gordon laments this, as a truce would have been an occasion to gather up and bury decently the bodies of the dead. New weapons have been invented: trench mortars, rifle grenades and bombs, and he gets an idea of what gas attacks can be like. 'War is now a much more undesirable profession than it used to be', he writes.

Gordon was a popular officer, and he felt an enormous responsibility to the men he commanded. He knew their personal lives intimately as he was responsible for censoring their letters home, and knew exactly who would not be getting a letter after they were dead, who would be mourning a son, a brother, or a husband. He describes burying his men by moonlight as shells light up the night sky. One of the final entries in his diary states that at least going 'over the top' of the trenches would be a change from the daily monotony.

Gordon's published diary ends a little while before the Somme. An introduction explains that he had not had time, before his death, to send home the latest portion, but quotes from a letter he had left to be opened in the event of his death:

> Whatever be my fate, I have no fear; for the God who has watched over me from infancy will care for me still [...] if I fall it is God's will, and is best for me. Don't think of me as dead, but rather as living the great and glorious life of that happy band of warriors who have fought the good fight and fallen in the Faith. After all, death is only the key to life everlasting. So think of me rather as supremely happy in the arms whose protection is sure and whose care is infinite. I die happy – glorying indeed in the manner of my death.

One hopes that the letter gave some comfort to his grieving parents, John and Jane. His mother, Jane Muir Barber, donated a copy of Gordon's published diary to a Scottish collection, inscribing in it by hand 'with much gratitude from Gordon's mother'. It's hard not to feel, though, with hindsight, that the sentiments of Gordon's final letter match more closely with the first half of the diary than with the impressions of the second half. Gordon had written this letter some time in advance of his death. Did he still hold the same sentiments when he died in the chaos of the Somme, crossing the no-man's-land strewn with bodies?

Beth had been brought up in a religious family, but, in common with many of her generation, although her later writing shows her continuing interest in religion, she was not known as a regular churchgoer – her absence from church was remarked on in Inverness. Her generation was brought to question their fundamental beliefs by the events of the First World War. Many of them started in 1914 believing like Gordon, but the survivors, such as women who were never able to marry or men who were permanently disabled, began to question everything they had been brought up with. The post-war years were also the Roaring

Twenties, when people partied desperately, trying to ignore the Depression and live for the moment, since they had seen what happened when men followed orders blindly for what they thought was the greater good.

Against the theory that Gordon Barber was Beth's officer is the fact that Beth's name is never mentioned in his diary. Gordon spent very little time in Inverness and so had little opportunity to meet Beth there, though there is the chance that they could have met in England, when Beth was working as a VAD. Either way, the window of time when Beth and her officer could have met is very small indeed: Beth's first experience of love was a high-pressure wartime romance.

I have considered other possibilities when trying to identify Beth's soldier by name, such as other Cameron Highlanders buried at Becourt, an Australian soldier met by chance on the train to Anstey (Travenna in *Kif* is Australian), or even one of Beth's cousins. In each case there is no definite link. Gordon and Alfred are the most likely candidates, but it could equally be someone I have not yet come across. Young officers like Gordon and Alfred were a breed that was virtually wiped out by the war. Graduates of public schools, feeling a deep devotion to those schools, their family and their country, their average life expectancy on the Western Front was six weeks. They led their men from the front, and were usually first over the top of the trenches and running out into no-man's-land, to be shot down almost instantly. The death toll for the British Army on the first day at the Somme *alone* was 60,000 men. Beth's home town of Inverness at that time had a population of around 20,000. When the battle of the Somme was over, with a total Allied loss of anything between 400,000 and 500,000 men, and a similar number from the German side, it wasn't entirely clear which side had won. Whoever Beth's officer was, for Beth it was very meaningful, and the conditions in which it took place, and the way in which it ended affected her deeply. It was her first experience of love, and one which was not allowed to develop due to the artificial, heightened wartime atmosphere.

The death of Beth's officer came to symbolize for her the death of one possible route her life could have taken: instead of being allowed to develop a relationship and marry, like so many of her generation Beth's life took a completely different track because of the devastation of the First World War. In later life, Beth was to make more than one journey to see both the spot where her officer fell and the cemetery where he was commemorated. In her writing, she refers to the Somme in passing more than once, even in unlikely contexts, such as in her biography of seventeenth-century figure Claverhouse. Her second major play, *The Laughing Woman*, set partly in France and featuring a character whose potential is wasted and whose friend's life is devastated after he is killed in the war, is dedicated 'FOR—— /BECAUSE OF THE HYACINTHS AT BECOURT'. Whose name could fill in the blank space? Gordon Barber? Alfred Trevanion Powell? (Or, alternatively, Beth's sister's name, since it was Etta and Jean who made the journey to France with Beth to visit the battlefields). Did Beth pay homage to her first love in her first choice of pseudonym when she chose to call herself 'Gordon Daviot' – the 'Daviot' part referring to a place near Inverness where she had enjoyed happy pre-war family holidays as a child, and 'Gordon' after a young soldier? Her first pseudonym as an evocation of her lost childhood and lost young womanhood, a summation of the different paths that led her to her writing.

CHAPTER FIVE

Anstey's second year, and teaching

After the summer of 1916 which saw the devastation of the Somme, Beth returned to Anstey College for her second year.[1] The long train journey south was becoming familiar – throughout her entire body of writing are detailed descriptions of the journey south from Inverness, from the winter trip described in her early short story, 'Madame Ville d'Aubiers', to the night train in *The Singing Sands*. However, the familiar journey was also different each time: the trains were still full of soldiers, but now Beth saw them less romantically, as men who would face death. Beth was moving through a changing landscape in many ways: after the Battle of the Somme, if not before, people could no longer kid themselves that this was a glorious war that would be over quickly. The scale of loss of life was immense, almost unimaginable, and the men who were dying now were not only young, but also conscripts: people who had not chosen to volunteer to fight. The air raids over Birmingham had brought war home in another fashion. However, Beth was starting now to think about staying in England, not returning home to the Highlands for every holiday but instead planning a new future for herself, embracing the change. In the final year at Anstey, preparation for work was important. The curriculum at Anstey was mentally and physically demanding, and by absorbing herself in her studies Beth could put feelings of loss after her officer's death to the back of her mind.

Rhoda Anstey, who was still principal of the college she had set up, was an enthusiast, passionately interested in a wide variety of subjects and dedicated to teaching her students. She had done her initial training at the college of a Madame Bergman Österberg in London, the premier, original and most respected of the new breed of women's physical training institutes.[2] Before Madame Österberg started to teach in Britain, the main sort of physical training taught in schools was military drill. Madame Österberg, a Scandinavian, had been unimpressed, and set up her college to establish the Swedish system of gymnastics, in which students practised a carefully-worked-out system of movements, designed to improve and encourage natural movement and posture. It has elements in it of physiotherapy or the Alexander Technique, where practitioners try to understand the body and work with it, rather than forcing it into unnatural positions. There were no similar institutions for men at the time Madame Österberg began her work, and the net result was that women's physical training became far superior. The students who trained under this system saw it almost as a vocation; it was their duty to spread the word and improve women's health. Rhoda Anstey was a total convert to Madame Österberg's cause, but also continued to cast around for other new ideas, enthusiastically sharing with her students her thoughts on subjects as varied as vegetarianism, vaccination, the benefits of sunbathing, clairvoyance, horoscopes, or her own brand of practical Christianity.

Rhoda was also an active campaigner for Women's Suffrage. In 1910 she had taken Anstey students with her on Christabel Pankhurst's march through London to demand the vote for women. She had also been taken to court for non-payment of taxes after being part of the campaign where women refused to pay the government money if they were denied the vote. The First World War had stopped suffragist activity, as women concentrated on the war effort, but Beth was in an institution where women's talents and abilities were highly valued. Beth wrote later that she never considered herself a 'feminist', but she came from a background where women were equals whose work and opinions were valued, and she was educated in institutions where that was the norm.

Although the Anstey curriculum had become more formal and professional over the years, with training for Anstey students in Anatomy and Dissection taking place at Birmingham University, Rhoda's strong personality still had a lot of influence. In pictures of the staff and students of Anstey, Rhoda stands out as a big, formidable-looking woman, with fair, rather untamed hair standing out around her face. Described as a 'countrywoman' by her colleagues, she was quite at home in Anstey's rural surroundings. She was strong and capable, stood no nonsense and was quite single-minded when it came to doing the best for her students (or her patients, in the early years when Anstey had been more of a health retreat than a training ground), regardless of how this affected her long-suffering staff. Rhoda Anstey was clear about what needed done and who was to do it – and what she herself was willing and able to do. One of Rhoda's particular talents was to hire as teachers women who were as competent as herself, who were passionate about their subjects and dedicated to aiming to the highest possible standards. Although Rhoda's eccentricities could have made her a difficult person to work with, her ability to hire professionals, and the confidence she was then able to place in her staff, made Anstey an excellent college. It was, by the time Beth attended, well established, and in the process of expansion: a new gallery and cloakroom were added onto the existing gymnasium in 1915.

At Anstey, Beth was exposed to women of different cultures far more than in Inverness: in addition to having pupils from all over the UK, Swedish teachers were also employed. There are Swedish characters in Beth's later writing, including a gym teacher in *Miss Pym Disposes*, and the main female character in *The Laughing Woman*. 'Ingrid', the Swede in *The Laughing Woman*, is based on the real-life Sophie Brzeska, who was Polish. With large quantities of dialogue given to Ingrid, Beth made the decision to change her nationality to one she was familiar with, and whose speech patterns she could more easily replicate. As well as exposure to different students and staff at Anstey, Beth met people in Birmingham, as Anstey students were encouraged to take gymnastic classes in the local community (another thing described in *Miss Pym Disposes*).

Beth herself taught keep-fit classes at the local Cadbury factory, travelling around Birmingham by tram, and returning on foot in the dark to college to save money.[3] In addition, students continued to do similar work to VADs, using their nursing and physiotherapy skills to help out in local hospitals or medical practices. Local people, at first resistant to this strange community in their midst, had, by Beth's time at the college, accepted them, and were regular attendees at the annual Demonstration of students' skills at the end of the year. This Demonstration forms a key part of the plot of *Miss Pym Disposes*. Beth's later writing is also foreshadowed in Anstey students' extracurricular interest in drama.

Anstey women went on to many and varied career paths, including setting up private practices, physiotherapy, teaching, housewifery in extremely varied settings from English farms to overseas, war work and government work. The mixture of body and mind that was an integral part of Anstey's training meant that Beth was being exposed to myriad new ideas and influences, being shown through example that women could have fulfilling careers in many different areas. With so many men away fighting in the war, women around her were doing jobs that had previously been men's work.

As well as this mental stimulation Beth was physically tired from the work she was doing as an Anstey student. A typical day started with that early rising bell Miss Pym was so horrified by, with early lectures sometimes before breakfast. An assembly or prayers was held at the start of the day, marking a more traditional, Christian sensibility than would be found in a similar establishment today. Beth's later religious plays are less accessible to the modern reader than her historical or modern works, but to her contemporaries they would have been a natural expression of interest in a subject that was far more pervasive than religion is in our lives today. More lectures were then followed by 'remedials' or practice (that is, exercises), then lunch. Afternoons were devoted to team sports like hockey, netball or cricket, and there was even more activity in the evening, with dancing before dinner. Remedials were given higher priority than team sports, as the small number of students at Anstey meant there was not always the right numbers for teams.

The emphasis in the team games was on how the Anstey girls would teach games like hockey or cricket to their future students. Netball had actually been invented by Madame Österberg (from the American sport of basketball) and remained very popular within physical training colleges. Occasionally, Anstey students were able to play away games against school, university or local teams – cricket matches against the workers from the local Cadbury / Bournville factory (where Beth took keep-fit classes) were particularly popular as chocolate was served at half-time. The model village built for Bournville workers had an Anstey Old Girl as its resident PT teacher.

Dance was an important part of the curriculum at Anstey. There were two forms taught: artistic dancing, and folk dancing. The high standard of dance teaching is commented on in *Miss Pym Disposes*, and the main teacher, Mrs Ida Bridgeman (who later became principal when Rhoda Anstey retired), was a modern dance specialist. She was acknowledged to be different to many of the physical training teachers, as she was interested in a more aesthetic ideal. She was tall, dark and handsome, a physically striking woman, with a commanding presence, demanding strict attention from the girls in her classes. The modern, interpretive dance she taught was based on a precise system of movement, and even girls who did not have the essential artistic temperament necessary to fully express themselves through dance were expected to be able to follow the movements precisely. 'Miss Pym' comments on the difference between the students who went through the movements and the character of Desterro, who is a real dancer, showing that Mrs Bridgeman managed to impress upon Beth some of the real artistry of dance. English folk dancing was at that time undergoing something of a revival, though English and Scottish country dancing are slightly different, and the forms that Beth was used to might have hindered her. The main difference is that in Scottish country dancing the dancers point their toes, whereas this is not done in English folk dancing.

For dancing, a special outfit was worn, of a long green silk skirt or dress for Juniors, and a similar black dress for Seniors. Dress reform was one of Rhoda Anstey's hobby horses, and she was clear that it was not possible for women to practise physical training properly if they were hobbled by restrictive fashions. She believed that these restrictive fashions, such as tight lacing and high heels, could actually damage women's bodies, and this was emphasized in physiotherapy classes at Anstey. Beth had a life-long interest in clothes, favouring a country look with smart tweeds, and the occasional nod to fashion such as the sheer pussy-bow blouses of the nineteen-thirties, but her clothes were always practical. She loved walking in the Highlands, and dressed accordingly. During Beth's time at Anstey, students wore a navy blue, loosely fitting tunic, which was cut just above the knee. Compared with the long skirts and white blouses of daily wear in the photographs of IRA students in their final year, this gave Beth and her fellow students much greater freedom of movement, and this tunic was worn for all classroom-based lessons as well as practical work. The Anstey uniform went completely against prevailing fashion for tight-laced tops and long skirts, and several students found that, when they had their first job, their new employers were shocked by their PE kit. Out of school, when walking into Birmingham for example, Anstey students were expected to create a good impression of the college by being smartly dressed at all times. On these occasions they wore a navy full-length skirt, a three-quarter-length coat, a straw boater with College band, a white blouse, and a College tie.

Presentation was also a big part of 'Commanding' classes. These were basically lessons on how to be a teacher and give instructions, especially the loud shouted 'commands' necessary for drill and gym. As a quiet, reserved person, Beth struggled with these classes at first. Dress and presentation were part of the 'Commanding' classes, but the accents students used were also criticized, and, as a Highlander, Beth's accent was something her later students and friends in England particularly remembered. As the Inverness accent is not as distinctive as, for example, the Glasgow accent, it's generally regarded as clear and pure, but it is usually soft-voiced. In a later letter Beth wrote, 'I have vivid recollections of these dark days when we first faltered forth our feeble utterances under Mrs Bridgeman's pitiless eye, and wondered vaguely why suicide was considered a sin!'[4]

In their free time, depending on the seasons, Anstey students also went sledging, skating or walking in the extensive and beautiful college grounds. It was a small, close-knit community, with the thirteen students of Beth's year being a typical class size. There was plenty of opportunity for classmates to form a strong bond, while outside interests and the emphasis on vocational training meant the community wasn't stiflingly isolated. It is easy to see how Beth, a good but overlooked student at the IRA, would have thrived in this more adult, yet still academic, environment. The detailed descriptions in *Miss Pym Disposes* are testament to Beth's absorption in Anstey, and she remained proud and positive about her experiences there throughout her life. Amongst the scant biographical details she allowed her publishers to put on her books, Anstey was specifically mentioned. Beth spoke highly of Anstey to her family and friends as well, and was a direct example to one of her little sister's friends: Mary-Anne Symington, a classmate of Beth's sister Etta, followed Beth from the IRA to Anstey College, graduating in 1925.[5]

Beth graduated from Anstey in 1917. Back in Inverness, her sister Jean finished school in 1917, after her fifth year.[6] Jean was eighteen, and that summer Beth was twenty-one. Their younger sister Etta was thirteen. Their home in Inverness had been very much affected by the war. In addition to the loss of so many young men, the large number of soldiers stationed in the Highlands and the training taking up the landscape made the town Beth returned to after graduation very different to the one she had left. There were practice trenches dug in the surrounding countryside, and the whole area was militarized, with citizens' movement curtailed. If people had still hoped that things would return to 'normal' after the war ended in November 1918, they were soon to discover their mistake. In the Highlands, as elsewhere, the whole way of life was changed by the war: from being a relatively stable, hierarchical society, the idea of change and the progress of technology was pervasive, even if the reality of change and progress took longer to arrive. Beth was to become very aware of how Britain was not the 'home for heroes' that the returning troops and their families wanted it to be, and her first full-length novel, *Kif*, was to deal particularly with the effects of economic depression and the difficulties that people, especially returning soldiers, faced after the end of the First World War.

Beth did not return to Inverness to live, though she spent the summer there before she started work, spending some time probably as a VAD at Leys Castle hospital.[7] In *Miss Pym Disposes* there is a vivid description of the students' plans for the future, with each of them 'assigned' to a placement by their eccentric headmistress. A number of Anstey students down the years worked not just as PE teachers, but as teacher trainers, and, as universities began to admit more women, even went on to work in academia, studying the theory and development of physical training. Anstey students were highly regarded by employers. Beth was not the only writer to come from the college (though the other writers tended to specialise in non-fiction, such as technical writing on physical education), while the strong emphasis on vocation at Anstey seems also to have appealed to girls with other callings in life: the college produced more than one missionary. Beth herself worked a number of short-term placements in a variety of settings after graduating from college, both as a physiotherapist and as a teacher. In the six years following her graduation, she worked in at least seven different settings. It took her some time to find a place where she was happy to live and work. The end of the war meant that women were now competing with men for jobs, affecting physiotherapy and medical positions though not, of course, female PE teaching positions. The number of short-term placements that Beth went through was influenced by this, but the general impression is of restlessness and constant movement when Beth was in her twenties. '[Y]our wandering life', her mother Josephine called it, in a letter she wrote to Beth for her twenty-fifth birthday, saying she would keep her present (a ring) safe in Inverness until next time she came home.[8] The lack of many concrete details about Beth's life at this time adds to the impression that she was, if not yet an enigmatic woman, at least restless and unsettled.

Immediately after graduation, Beth stayed in the Midlands, near Anstey. She took the trouble to write to her former college to let them know how she was getting on. Many Anstey students kept in touch in this way, with letters often published in the school's magazine.[9] As a member of the Old Girls' Association, Beth kept up to date with her college, and received copies of the magazine. Interestingly, Beth's letter to her old college was singled out when a history of Anstey was written. Although the compiler of the college history had no idea that Beth had become an author, her talent for expressing herself in writing was already clear. Beth said in the letter that she had found work, essentially three part-time jobs at centres in Nottingham, Newark and Hucknall. This meant her working week involved a fair amount of travelling, but she had a lot of variety and plenty of chance to learn more and build on what she had learnt at Anstey. The first two places were girls' schools, while the Hucknall Centre was a Pupil Teacher Training Centre, for both boys and girls. Unlike other students at Anstey, Beth had experience of co-educational teaching from her years at the IRA, and throughout her career worked with both sexes. She enjoyed working at the Hucknall Centre most, where she taught pupils aged from thirteen to around seventeen. She was teaching subjects as varied as Theory and Practice of Teaching Drill, Folk Dancing, and 'Commanding' – and after her own struggles with 'Commanding' she noted that she was very gentle with the students of the latter.

Beth also wrote to her old college room-mate, 'Dave', who had found work in the far north of Scotland; a cheerful letter that masks what seems to be homesickness. Her general impression of Nottingham was 'red-brick – soot – fog'. 'On the whole it's a lovely life – till I get bored!' Beth joked, describing the disparate group of people she shared lodgings with (a list that is rather familiar to readers of her novel *The Expensive Halo*).[10]

Back in Inverness, Beth's middle sister Jean was also thinking about her career. Like Beth, Jean had her sight set on further education, and she too wanted to travel and wanted the best. Leaving school after fifth year – one year early – she had opted for secretarial college, but chose to move to London for her studies.[11] She enrolled as a pupil at Kensington College, run by a James Munford and specializing in shorthand and business work. It was a one-year course, against Beth's two-year period of study, so she was catching up with her elder sister, able to travel south with her and thinking too about moving on to the world of work. Beth and Jean met up in England, particularly for holidays, and continued to do so over the next few years as Jean moved around.

The MacKintoshes financial situation had changed considerably. They could afford to send their two eldest daughters to fee-paying colleges, and were happy to see them both starting good careers. Towards the end of the war Colin made a significant purchase, when he bought the shops that he had been renting for the last few years.[12] In addition to his fruiterer's shop at number 53 Castle Street, Colin was now the landlord for the flats at number 51. There were nine properties of different sizes; some may just have been rooms, while others accommodated families, and Colin charged different rents accordingly. His tenants ranged from the spinster Miss Christina Macdonald, to John Diack, a warehouseman, and his family. Some of Colin's tenants, like the Diacks and Alexander Thomson, clerk, were to remain in the flats for many years, with their rents fairly stable during that time. Unlike his work as a 'Fruiterer', which Colin mentioned proudly on every official form, he never described himself as a 'Landlord'. In his will, it wasn't even clear that he owned the flats, they were just included with his other assets, while, in contrast, he left detailed instructions for what was to happen with his shop. The landlord side of his business did not engage his interest as much, and was not so successful. Colin had also bought 47 Castle Street, which had room for a shop downstairs and rented flats above, and, although these (comprising seven individual flats or rooms) had been occupied when they were owned by the previous landlord, by 1918 they were all vacant, listed in the valuation rolls of Inverness as 'to be reconstructed', while the flats' value is recorded starkly as 'nil'. The space under the flats was not suitable for a shop, though Colin used it as a store, along with neighbouring number 49. Castle Street, with its tall tenement flats going up each side of the hill, was an area that was going downhill. Over the next couple of decades, the buildings deteriorated structurally, and the flats were to get a bad name for overcrowding and slum-like conditions.

Although Colin and Josephine never struggled for money, their purchase of the Castle Street buildings was not necessarily the bargain they thought it was. Even the fruiterer's business did not do so well after the First World War, as the Depression took hold, and Colin's upmarket clientele in the big houses of the Highlands ordered less as their circumstances changed. There was no question for Colin that his daughters would have to keep working.

After probably only one academic year in Nottingham, Beth moved on. She is variously noted as working for a physiotherapist in London, as a physical therapist at a private clinic in Leeds, and as a PE teacher in a school near Liverpool. By focusing on physiotherapy as well as PE teaching, Beth was following a national trend which saw Anstey and other physical-college-trained gymnasts in much demand for work in rehabilitation. Anstey had emphasized the medical and scientific background to gymnastics, with students trained in anatomy, and this knowledge was particularly useful for helping injured and disabled war veterans. Beth also had the added practical training of her VAD work. Her later playwriting draws on her knowledge of medicine and hospitals, but nursing was never a vocation for her, and her main focus is always the relationships between staff, or their social lives.

The exact chronology is unclear, but one move is of particular interest. In January 1920, two and a half years after graduating, Beth, despite her later reputation as an Anglophile, chose to return to Scotland, to work as a PE teacher at Oban High School.[13] It was an important choice, though a part of her career that she later wished to forget: 'I never worked in Scotland, by the way', she wrote in the 1930s to someone wishing to write a profile of her career. 'I went straight from school to England, and spent all my working years there.'[14] This wasn't true. She did work in Scotland – her identification with England, and her love of that country had not yet taken hold. This was to come later. In another letter written many years later, Beth said that in her twenties she felt almost unbearably homesick:

[O]f all the major emotions [homesickness is] by far the most all-pervading. Grief rolls you over in waves, like surf [...] love has climax and anti-climax, but homesickness blackens everything, day and night, in one constant fog [...]. There is no rising to a new day, no new point of view. You go to bed with the thing, and it is there when your eyes open again. I haven't known it since I was in my first few "twenties", but I shall remember till I die what it was like.[15]

Even this small extract from one of Beth's letters shows her developing writing skill: grief doesn't 'roll over you' it 'rolls you over' – providing a vivid image of just how strong the feeling was. Whatever Beth's day job, she continued to write in her spare time, and her experience of homesickness was used to great effect later in her play *Valerius*. It was something that had affected her deeply and inspired this brief return to Scotland.

Beth started work at Oban on 12th January 1920. Oban High School was a co-educational secondary, taking pupils from a wide surrounding area, some coming in each day by train, and some weekly boarders, including Gaelic-speakers from the islands (boys boarding with families in town and girls living in a residential hostel). School life for a teacher in the small town was all-consuming, with extra-curricular activities for the boarders encouraged, particularly in Beth's area of sport. Boys played shinty and football; there was hockey, athletics and cricket for all; and swimming and rowing were promoted in the warmer terms. A new rector, Mr Angus Macleod, had started just three months before Beth was appointed, and he was in the process of making several changes to the curriculum and employing new teachers.

Qualified in Mathematics, Angus Macleod's real interest lay in Gaelic. A noted Gaelic scholar, he promoted the study of Gaelic language and culture at Oban, and the school was to become significant to both Gaelic and Scottish literature, and to Scottish nationalism: later teachers employed at Oban included Sorley Maclean's brother John, Iain Crichton Smith and SNP politician Iain MacCormick (son of leading nationalist John MacCormick). Beth was in the first influx of new teachers, but there were also many long-established staff members and customs. In her later play, *The Staff-Room*, Gordon Daviot gave a vivid picture of a young, enthusiastic female gym teacher who 'teaches because she likes the children', and her relations with the older, jaded schoolmistresses. The play is not entirely a success, partly because the real observation lies in the descriptions given of the teachers, written only to be read, rather than in the play's dialogue: '*MISS HINCH [the English mistress ...] is tall, thin and weary, and her ash-fair hair is always on the verge of falling from its insecure knot at her neck. She likes that knot, however. It suggests art and literary coteries, and most of MISS HINCH'S life is suggestion.*' [16]

The experiment of returning to Scotland to cure her homesickness was not a success. The small-town atmosphere of Oban did not appeal, and neither did the Gaelic revival. There was also an accident in the gym, less than a month after she arrived. It was not Beth's first sporting accident – she had also broken her nose riding in London some time in those first 'wandering' years after she graduated from Anstey – but it was a serious one. On the 30th January 1920, the school log book dryly records, 'Miss McIntosh [sic.] met with an accident in the Hall – the heavy bar striking her head. The Rector took class IV'. It was the spark that provided the murder method in *Miss Pym Disposes* many years later, but in 1920 it was the result of trying to control a difficult class, in a school setting that Beth was not finding congenial. As a petite, rather quiet young woman, she might not have had the easiest time controlling large mixed classes – particularly given her attitude to 'Commanding' class at Anstey. Two months later, on the 31st March, 'Miss Elizabeth MacKintosh demitted office of Physical Instructress today'. She had not even lasted a term.

To go back to Inverness was to return to the house that her parents had bought only in her last year of school; it wasn't returning to her childhood home. Neither would Colin and Josephine have encouraged her to stay. Jean was doing well in her chosen career, first having been employed in London by the college she had trained in, and then securing an excellent post working in France, first for the Ministere Britannique des Munitions, and then following her boss, with whom she got on well, to move on to the British Scientific Apparatus Manufacturers. The IRA's excellent teaching was shown in Jean's employer's testimonials about her 'sound knowledge of commercial French', and she was also 'quite at home with French Shorthand'. With her younger sister setting an example, Beth tried again down south. She secured new positions, including at a school in Eastbourne, but also focused on extracurricular work: her growing interest in writing, and the experiences she could gain in the long school holidays.

Beth was mixing with writers and other artistic people outwith school hours. In a letter written many years later, she described her social group around this time as 'entirely "intellectual" [...] scholastic, literary and what-you-will'.[17] She made the most of social opportunities, and spent little time at home; she was not a particularly domesticated person.

> I've an encyclopediac experience of digs, boarding houses, hotels, and other people's homes. But [...] I've never made a home in my life [...]. Never wanted to, of course – I could have had a flat when I was working, but I always preferred the appalling ugliness of rooms to doing anything for myself.[18]

There are descriptions of the sort of flats Beth knew, and their formidable landladies, in *The Man in the Queue*, where a mousy teacher creeps in and out of the sitting-room while Mrs Everett plots to help her tenant Lamont to escape the police. Beth's contemporary Dodie Smith, whom she was later to encounter when they were both successful playwrights, gives long and vivid descriptions of renting rooms in her autobiographies, evoking a lost world where young career women had a different sort of independence. Life in lodgings lacked privacy, but housework duties were smaller as there was only the one room to look after, and meals were often provided.

Beth's salary as a teacher – around £100 a year at Oban, for example – was quite enough for her to be able to travel in the summer.[19] She visited Jean in France, and travelled extensively by train and bus throughout Britain and Europe. When Etta was older, she too joined the sisters on their travels. Beth's early short stories and plays show particular familiarity with France, though she was always at her best when writing about England or Scotland – her view of France was always rather romantic.

One important journey which Beth made more than once was the pilgrimage to view the battlefields and graveyards of the Great War. After the war was over, many mothers and widows – those who could afford it – made the journey to Europe to try and find their loved ones' graves. Perhaps they felt that if they could see where they lay, they could come to terms with what had happened, and gain some understanding of it. At first, these visits were informal; the towns and villages around the trenches were flattened, with few places to stay and large swathes of countryside covered in black mud, still full of unexploded shells. Surprisingly quickly, these mud-plains were seeded over with grass and flowers, the formal cemeteries were laid out with the rows upon rows of little crosses that we know today, and the battlefield tours became organized events. Beth visited both the site of the Battle of the Somme itself, and the cemetery where her young officer was buried. She found the battlefield most affecting, rejecting the formality of the official cemetery. Her first novel, *Kif*, has a fairly realistic picture of the landscape the troops knew in France, but, given the lack of description in her writing, and the pastoral view of France in her short stories, Beth probably only saw the battlefields once they had been cleaned up.

Although it may not have been ideal, after her years working in the English Midlands, and the brief spell back in Scotland in Oban, Beth had managed to establish a teaching career for herself. She accepted a new post, as PE teacher in the High School in Tunbridge Wells, Kent. Here, she was happy. She loved the surrounding countryside and, much later, wrote to Marjorie, her Anstey room-mate, 'I never really felt at home in England until I went south of London, and now for me it is like going home. Over the hill south of Sevenoaks, and there is "my" country stretching in front of me. Each time I go back and I am surprised anew by the shattering beauty of the Weald.'[20] Her Tunbridge Wells pupils remembered her fondly as well – particularly her lovely accent – and Beth must have kept in touch with someone at the school because, almost a decade later when she had her hit play

Richard of Bordeaux, a party of schoolchildren from Tunbridge Wells High School travelled up to see the former teacher's play.

It was not as a student that Beth fell in love with England, but as a young working woman. She had overcome the difficulties of starting her career, had put behind her the loss of her young officer in the war, and had managed to create for herself a fulfilling and happy life as a teacher in the south of England. However, this hard-won contentment was not to last, as bad news was coming to her from Inverness.

PART TWO

Gordon Daviot
1924–1945

CHAPTER SIX

Josephine, and Hugh Patrick Fraser

In the early 1920s, Beth's mother Josephine became ill. Colin and Josephine did not tell their daughters at first, but by 1923 things had become so bad that Colin wrote to Beth, asking her to come home.[1]

Josephine's illness was already far advanced, and it was a shock to Beth to see the change in her mother since her last visit. Josephine had been being treated for breast cancer for two years, but the cancer spread to her liver six months before she died.[2] With her basic medical training from Anstey, Beth would have had some knowledge to assist her to understand her mother's condition and be able to help care for her, but it was still incredibly difficult for the family to watch Josephine die.

Josephine MacKintosh died on the morning of 24th June, 1923, about a month before Beth's twenty-seventh birthday. The final cause of death was cardiac failure. Her death was to change Beth's life, not just because of the emotional impact, but also because of the practical consequences. Beth was close to her mother, and for Josephine to die at the relatively young age of fifty-two was a shock. Beth's youngest sister Etta was only nineteen, just leaving school. Josephine's mother, Jane Horne, was still alive, and Beth had probably imagined her own mother living as long as her grandmother, telling stories about their family for many years to come.

Colin MacKintosh was bereft. He had been married to Josephine for twenty-nine years, and they had worked together to build up their business and raise their three daughters. Colin was close to his wife's family, living near them and embracing their English-speaking heritage. Now, just as they could finally relax together in their lovely house in Crown, with the war over, and their three daughters becoming established in their own lives – he was alone. The day after Josephine died, Colin registered her death, and he and his daughters began to make arrangements for this new life he would face as a widower.

Josephine was buried in Tomnahurich cemetery, not far from her father, sister and Colin's parents. Unlike the large monument he chose to mark his parents' passing, Colin chose a simpler marker for Josephine's grave: a raised kerbstone marking out the plot, inscribed with only their names – 'Josephine Horne Wife of Colin MacKintosh' – and the date of her death. Since the colossal loss of life in the First World War, fashions in gravestones had changed. Perhaps Colin also hoped to make this a family plot, and put up a larger headstone in later years, but this was not to be. Nowadays, the grave is difficult to find, and the names hard to read, particularly as the letters are raised, rather than engraved, and are slowly wearing away as the grave is forgotten. During his lifetime however, Colin visited Josephine's resting place with fresh flowers every week.

Colin was named joint executor in his wife's will, along with his two eldest daughters, Beth and Jean.[3] Josephine had made her will a couple of years before her illness took hold, and had made sure, the year before she died, that it was lodged with the family solicitors, Stewart, Rule & Co. She left all her money and property to her family, with personal items of jewellery bequeathed to each of her daughters.

It was decided that Beth would remain with Colin in Inverness, to keep house for him. In the same way that Colin had cared for his parents, so his daughter cared for him. As the eldest, Beth took most of the responsibility. Jean had left her job in France after some ill-health, and had recently started a new job as a secretary at St James School, West Malvern, and Etta was just starting domestic science college in Edinburgh.[4] Beth was ambiguous about teaching and had other interests, such as writing, that could be continued in Inverness. The situation may have been temporary to begin with, but, as things turned out, Beth was able to make her career based in Inverness. She was to remain the only daughter unmarried, so the responsibility for their father always stayed with her.

The house in Crown was large. After living in lodgings for eight years as a student and a teacher, learning how to run the household was an all-consuming task at first. She had only moved into this house a couple of years before leaving to go to college, and had seen her home as being the place she had created for herself as a teacher in the south of England. She had to relearn how to live in Inverness. There were many practical things she had to learn about Crown Cottage. 'Keeping a house' in the 1920s meant something different than it does today; without the benefit of modern technology, all household tasks, such as washing, cooking and cleaning, took a lot longer. The pace of life necessarily had to be slower: food had to be bought or ordered every day, from many different little shops; no fridge meant that food was prepared and kept differently; no washing machine meant washing was either done by hand or sent out to a laundry; no central heating meant fires had to be laid and maintained; and so on. Beth had some domestic help, and in later letters mentions someone doing tasks like cooking. There was some help with cleaning and washing went out to a laundry, but these were all people she had to speak to and arrange work rotas with.[5] This was not a grand house with servants, it was a normal middle-class household, but domestic help was routine in most similar households. It had become more difficult to fill these sorts of positions after the Great War as the women who had previously been domestic servants now had other opportunities opening up to them.

The Depression in the 1920s and 30s may also have affected Colin and Beth's ability to pay for domestic help – and, of course, Beth was no longer drawing her regular teacher's salary. There is some suggestion that Beth did a little teaching work – perhaps tutoring? –after returning to Inverness, but she did not go back to work full-time.[6] She was relying once more on her father's money, although, like most Scottish women of her class, it is likely that the family's finances had been managed by Josephine, and this job may now have fallen to Beth. Colin doesn't seem to have been fully aware of his daughter's financial position once she started earning from her writing (as shown by the provisions he makes for her in his will), but Beth was probably in charge of not only the household accounts, but also the accounts from the shops. Despite this, Beth was no longer an independent woman in the same way, but once more her father's daughter. She had to learn how to keep house, and also how to adjust to living in Inverness as an adult; to start thinking of a career other than teaching; and learn how to live with her father now that she was an adult.

Some of Beth's early writing – particularly her short story 'His Own Country' – betrays a deep sense of bitterness and isolation about her return to her home town. She felt that there was no one she could relate to – and no one she wanted to relate to. After her experiences as a teacher and in hospitals, meeting people from all walks of life, Beth did not feel stimulated by the people she was returning to in Inverness. She also felt keenly the snobbery of the small town, as shown by the obsession with class in her second novel, *The Expensive Halo*. Beth made a deliberate decision when she first returned to the town not to get involved in the usual society rounds, a decision that affected her reputation greatly. She never re-joined Inverness 'society' fully: 'I found that the "going out to tea" business would leave me no life of my own at all if I didn't do something drastic,' she wrote in a letter. 'So I decided to go nowhere […]. This was held to be slightly queer – in those days no one knew that I "wrote" and so I had no right to be queer – but it has worked out very well in practice.'[7] Many people began to see her as a little odd or different – even arrogant – because of this. Beth did keep in touch with all of her close friends, and was to make friends with people in the local area such as the schoolteacher known as 'Miss Mac' at her old holiday destination of Daviot, and she was always a regular, chatty correspondent, but after her mother's death she did not make much effort to become part of her neighbours' world.

She did not totally isolate herself. Although there is some bitterness in some of her early short stories, there are also several stories which tell of happy Highland upbringings, little portraits of happy family life, describing quirky situations and the attraction of the rural settings Beth was familiar with in Inverness and on the west coast, where her MacKintosh relatives were from. This is an important strand of her work, though it is sometimes overlooked as it is mainly expressed through the less well-known short stories and one-act plays such as *The Balwhinnie Bomb*. On her mother's side of the family, Beth's grandmother, Jane Horne, was still living close to her son-in-law and granddaughter in her little house in Crown. Now in her eighties, she was physically and mentally frail, needing daily help at home. Jane Horne was the great matriarch of the family, telling the stories that gave Beth her extensive knowledge of her maternal antecedents and her English ancestors. Beth was sometimes considered to like the company of the elderly more than that of her own generation, but perhaps her mother's illness had made her more sensitive to the needs of those who were housebound: 'She often asserted with a quick smile – "I won't go to anyone's house until they're bedridden. Then I'll go and see them as often as they like" – and she did, showing a kindness, thoughtfulness, and tenderness which surprised many of her contemporaries.' [8]

Beth was a great walker, and her walks around town grew longer and longer the more time she spent in Inverness, as she re-explored the area. Though her family were no longer so close, her uncles and aunts were scattered around town, all within walking distance. She also shared two key interests with her father: reading and fishing. Beth and Colin may have been too alike always to get on, but they each took great pleasure in their hobbies, and these were pastimes that could be carried out side by side, in companionable silence, allowing them to spend time with each other but also time with their own thoughts.

All this time, Beth was thinking about and looking for something else. She wanted to develop her writing, and started to search out the literary communities in Inverness, a search that would shape her work and also bring her into contact with the man who was the real love of her life; the man whose story has been lost until now, confused with that of the First World War soldier. As with that first romance, her feelings for this man were not a part of her life that Beth shared with her friends, but, of course, her family were aware of the relationship. Etta later passed on some of the story of this second, important romantic friendship, while I have uncovered the rest through research.[9]

Inverness had a thriving cultural scene. Then, as now, there was plenty of music, including outdoor concerts on the Ness Islands. This, along with the music she played at home, influenced Beth's early writing. She had access to lending libraries and read widely, and the literary community in Inverness was strong enough to have several distinct groups. Mairi MacDonald, who was later to write the biographical sketch of Gordon Daviot, left school and stepped into a writing community made up of her parents and parents' friends, well-established townspeople with a keen interest in the Gaelic revival, writing short essays about Highland culture, joining and creating societies, and with a strong interest in folk music. Beth lampooned their meetings mercilessly in her early short story 'The Find'.

Neil Gunn, the future author of *The Silver Darlings*, was living just across the river, only fifteen minutes' walk from Beth. Gunn, newly married, was, in 1923, at exactly the same stage in his writing career as Beth – making a start and hopefully sending out short stories to magazines. He was to become well known and successful, producing novels about Highland history and culture with a strong Scottish nationalist bent, and he was at the heart of the Scottish Literary Renaissance. Given just how different the writings of Neil Gunn and Josephine Tey are, it is startling to realize that Elizabeth MacKintosh and Gunn are almost exact contemporaries. Their work has never been discussed in any detail in the same context, but they were aware of each other and reacted to each other's writing. Placing Gordon Daviot/Josephine Tey in the context of the Scottish literary scene sheds new light on her work, and shows Gunn's work and attitudes in a new light as well. Realising Tey's place in relation to her contemporaries of Scottish literature and the accepted Scottish literary canon is like reading *The Daughter of Time*: it makes the reader question what they have been taught and taken for granted. Her exclusion from a mainly male group of writers is understandable in the context of the time. However, given her success and lasting influence, her continued exclusion from later assessment of twentieth century Scottish literature is something that should be challenged.

Neither Gunn's personality nor his politics were of the type to appeal to Beth, but she was fortunate enough to meet one young man whose literary aspirations and attitudes more closely mirrored her own.[10] Hugh Patrick Fraser McIntosh was to have a lasting influence on Beth's writing. Not only did they start out sending work to magazines together, but his life and stories were to be reflected in her novels right up until her death, and their relationship had a lasting effect on her. Hugh is the man whose story has become tangled with the story of Beth's First World War soldier; he is the man who really captured her heart, the real relationship-that-could-have-been.

Hugh Patrick Fraser McIntosh moved to Inverness in October 1924, a year and a half after Beth had moved back.[11] The first shock of Josephine's death was over, and she was trying to build her new life. Despite their similar surnames, Hugh and Beth were not related, and Hugh had actually been brought up in London – though always with an awareness of his Scottish identity. A couple of years older than Beth, he was a mix of Highlander and Englishman, perfectly placed to understand how much Beth missed the south of England, whilst still understanding her Highland background. They were drawn together through their shared interest in writing.

Hugh's father, also Hugh, had been born in Culloden, just outside Inverness.[12] From a humble background, Hugh Senior had been swept up in the religious fervour that accompanied the Disruption of 1843 and the establishment of the Free Church of Scotland, and had trained as a minister in Aberdeen, gaining his MA. He was posted to various places before eventually ending up as the minister of the Presbyterian Church in Brockley, London, where his son Hugh was born and brought up. Described as a 'well-known and charismatic preacher', the Rev McIntosh, already used to success after his establishment of a large church in Glasgow, oversaw the expansion of his new church in London, raising membership from under 200 to around 700 people.[13] He did much work amongst the poor in the Deptford area of his parish, raising money for his parishioners by giving well-received lectures on 'The Highlands and Islands of Bonnie Scotland', often accompanied by musicians.[14] He was also popular in the more affluent area of Brockley directly beside his church, where he and his family lived, and his congregation gifted his wife a diamond ring in celebration of his long service. The only picture I have been able to track down of Hugh Senior is rather surprising. Instead of an austere, bearded Highland minister, it shows a man with a kind, open face and neatly clipped sideburns.[15] He is not the dark type of Highlander that Beth so often described in her writing, but has sandy, fairer hair. There are no surviving pictures of Hugh Patrick Fraser, his only son and third child of his second wife, but in Josephine Tey's fiction a sandy-haired Scotsman is one of the 'types' she sometimes describes – never the hero, like dark-haired Grant, but always a complex, sometimes irritating though appealing character.

After the Free Church joined with the United Presbyterian Church to form the United Free Church, Hugh McIntosh moved back to Scotland with his son and two of his youngest daughters. Described, when he was in London, as a 'typical Scotchman'[16] who could entrance his listeners with descriptions of his native home, Hugh Senior was pleased to move his family back, even if the changes within the church structure had been difficult for him. They were initially posted to the west coast of Scotland, not too far from Colin MacKintosh's home of Applecross.

A literary man, Hugh Senior published several religious books, and gifted his love of writing and education, as well as his love of Scotland, to his son, who was in the second year of an arts degree at Edinburgh University when the First World War broke out.[17] In addition to their interest in literature and their shared knowledge of both England and some of the more remote parts of Scotland, Hugh Patrick Fraser also had the attraction for Beth of having been a military man. Hugh had been an early volunteer, first with the RAMC (Royal Army Medical Corps), signing up to the Black Watch in 1914. By 1915 he had been promoted to the rank of officer in the Argyll and Sutherland Highlanders, where he served with the 9th, and later the 8th battalion – a promotion and changes in regiment which reflected not only his education and ability, but also the heavy losses that were suffered in the trenches. Hugh was involved in some of the worst battles of the war, and was wounded and gassed several times. In November 1917, over a year after Gordon Barber was killed at the Somme and Alfred Trevanion Powell killed at Arras, Hugh Patrick Fraser was awarded the Military Cross for the part he took in action at Polcapelle.

Polcapelle (or Poelcappelle), near Ypres, was part of the Battle of Passchendaele, where Allied forces attacked the German trenches in Belgium. It was one of the slow, muddy, horrific trench battles typical of the First World War, with little gain in land and large loss of life. The British front line was in a terrible position, slightly lower down than the German front line, and thus extremely difficult to defend from direct fire. The wet weather also played a major part in the battle, with rain churning up the ground. It has been said that there were few wounded from Passchendaele, only those who made it through and those who did not. Anyone who fell from wounds slipped into the atrocious conditions underfoot, where they were literally drowned in mud. Hugh must have been both brave and lucky.

His experience in the trenches did not stop Hugh from re-joining the army when the First World War was over. When he was demobilized from the Argyll and Sutherland Highlanders, he chose not to return to university, but went to his parents' home village of Culloden near Inverness, where he decided to re-enlist in the Cameron Highlanders. With the army no longer looking to recruit so many men, Hugh was not reinstated at the same rank he had held in wartime, but re-joined the army as a private. He rapidly worked his way up through the ranks again to Sergeant, but his progression would always have been limited, and, having chosen not to finish his degree, he would effectively never have been able to regain the rank he had held during the war. Popular amongst his colleagues, Hugh was remembered in the Camerons as an entertaining and outstanding musician, who played the piano at Hogmanay and recited the 'Immortal Memory' at a Burns Supper.[18] He had a particularly unusual army career. Sent to Ireland in 1921 with the 2nd Cameron Highlanders, he was stationed in Queenstown, fighting against Sinn Fein in the Irish War of Independence, an unpopular posting. Notes from the Camerons' regimental magazine say that this situation was considered by many to be worse than war service, due to the violence and complicated loyalties and politics involved. Hugh's later writing about the army focuses mainly on moments of beauty and nature amongst the fighting, but the only real notes of bitterness are in his poems about Ireland.

He then managed to be transferred on secondment to the Palestine Gendarmerie, an elite police force set up by Churchill to help control the new British mandate of Palestine. Much of the recruiting for the Palestine Gendarmerie was done in Ireland. Hugh briefly returned to England and the Camerons, before joining the West African Frontier Force in 1923, working in Nigeria. By October 1924 he was back in Inverness, invalided out of active service, adjusting, like Beth, to life in the Highlands and writing both about that adjustment, and poetry based on his military experiences.

Hugh shared his literary taste with Beth, enjoying some of the First World War poets like Rupert Brooke, and the English literary scene, and when Hugh and Beth sent out their first pieces of writing it was to a magazine based in London.

The *Weekly Westminster Gazette* ran features and stories, featuring, over the years, authors of the quality and reputation of Rupert Brooke, Raymond Chandler, D. H. Lawrence, Arthur Ransome and Katherine Mansfield. Beth and Hugh had their first work published in this paper, and it was something Beth was particularly proud of, mentioning it many years later in her entry for *Who's Who*. Like many new writers, Beth and Hugh began their writing careers by focusing on shorter pieces, particularly poetry. Beth was published first, with a short 'Triolet' poem appearing on 29th August 1925.[19] It was a clever piece, written in a form that was popular in the magazine. She had chosen to submit work under a pen-name, Gordon Daviot, as work by a male author often found a more ready audience. Her pleasure at seeing her work in print was slightly marred by the spelling error in her new name (poem by 'Gordon Davitt'), but she was encouraged by the quality of the other pieces her poem kept company with: other authors published that week included Graham Greene.

Hugh's submission to the *Weekly Westminster Gazette* was also accepted, and his short story 'Innocence' was published a couple of weeks later, on 12th September 1925. 'Gordon' may have been masquerading as a man, but 'Innocence' has a subtle male earthiness that her writing never had – it's an accomplished piece that evocatively immerses the reader in both its landscape and characters. Gordon Daviot was to become well known for her longer writing, and Hugh was to achieve most in poetry, but for these first publications their roles were reversed. Hugh's longer piece meant that his biography was also featured, and the editor of the *Weekly Westminster Gazette* noted that Hugh McIntosh was already known to the magazine as a reader who regularly entered the crosswords and competitions: 'one of the more gifted competitors of the Problems Page'. Hugh and Gordon had thoroughly researched the magazines they sent their first pieces to, they were magazines they read and enjoyed, and they were aiming to be like the writers they read and admired.

Gordon Daviot always said that she had begun her writing career by having poetry published. In addition to the Triolet in the *Weekly Westminster Gazette*, the following year, in 1926, she had poetry published in the *Saturday Review* – though these poems were mainly short comic efforts, submitted as competition entries. Like Hugh, Gordon was a regular entrant to competitions, using them as a form of writing exercise. For example, she won prizes in the *Saturday Review* for inventing six new proverbs and a Latin motto, and composing a new nursery rhyme.[20] There is at least one example of what must be her poetry in her Josephine Tey books (in *To Love and Be Wise*, where Inspector Grant quotes a poem that was printed 'to fill up the spaces'), though I have not found any other published work.[21] However, in the small Josephine Tey archive in the National Library of Scotland is an intriguing collection of handwritten poems, some with 1920s dates, which shed light on Daviot's development as a writer – and also on how much music meant to her.

The small collection in the NLS comprises around ten poems, or fragments, each handwritten on music manuscript paper, with musical notation handwritten alongside it. Some of the poems are Gordon Daviot's own, while others are poems she liked, such as 'The Skylark' by James Hogg and several by Rudyard Kipling.[22] Her own poems, as with all her writing, draw on her own experiences. She always grounded her work in reality, and, although they share a more traditional structure with the poets she admired, she never attempted to copy other poets' subject matter – something which always gave her writing its own power, and shows the beginning of that individuality which makes her Josephine Tey novels such a joy to read. However, the particularly interesting thing is that the music the poems are set to also appears to be of Beth's own composition.

Beth had studied music at school, as had her sisters, and her later writing shows an interest in and appreciation of music, with many memorable scenes, such as the folk singers in her short stories, or the Gaelic singing in *The Singing Sands*.[23] Beth is always very decided in her views on music – she really doesn't think much of the Gaelic singing. The only other documents by Elizabeth MacKintosh kept by the NLS are final drafts of some of her final published works – *The Singing Sands, Valerius* and *Dickon* – so this sheet music from her very early days as a writer must have been important enough for Beth to have kept all her life, and for her sister and the other executors of her will to have saved instead of throwing away.

The music itself is pleasant, if basic. It's obviously the work of an amateur, although a talented and enthusiastic amateur. If the music was meant to be played on the piano, then there is only notation for one hand – that is, there are no chords or left-hand part – though it would be easy enough to work with the key and create these. There are some errors in timing and notation (Beth's writing of musical notation is as messy and illegible as her handwriting), but the tunes are playable, and work well with the lyrics. The general impression is of someone amusing themselves

– though in a serious and committed way – but the words are more important than the tunes.

Amongst the Kipling poems – 'Boots – Infantry Column of March', 'Mounted Infantry', 'The Last Chantey' – are Gordon Daviot's own pieces. Several deal with homesickness, or the consolation of nature: 'Treasure' tries to find beauty in a grey day; 'Home-going' is also a little grey but happy about going home; 'South Away' gives a good indication of where home is; 'Youth' looks at nature; 'Spring' speaks for itself. 'A Song of Racing' stands out as the first written declaration of Gordon Daviot's love for horse racing – 'Epsom downs, Newmarket spaces [...] Goodwood graces, Kempton fun and York sobriety, Oh the lovely dear variety!' – something that she explored more fully in two of her first three novels: *Kif* and *The Expensive Halo*. 'Old Vin Rouge' stands out as being the only poem that attempts to copy the military images in Kipling, but also probably puts in something of what Beth herself had seen in France. The images are a precursor to Gordon Daviot's French-set short stories, or the scenes in *Kif* when Kif himself is sent to the Western Front, with the same sort of stereotypical French bohemian bonhomie: 'Old vin rouge in a cracked old cup, Old vin rouge oh drink it all up, for you won't have the chance tomorrow morning!'

Gordon Daviot was always interested in poetry and it is something she wrote, mainly for her own pleasure, throughout her life. She wrote short, funny verses for her friends in her letters, and, as mentioned above, the Josephine Tey mystery novel *To Love and Be Wise* contains an unattributed poem which is surely her own.[24] As the brief extracts from her poetry – and her taste in poets – show, she was interested in more traditional verse forms, and a discussion between two characters in *To Love and Be Wise* makes that clear.[25] This was the time of T.S. Eliot, but Beth and Hugh were still far more interested in the poetry of the First World War than anything else. Although Hugh, with the romantic ideas of Scotland given to him by his father, had more of an interest in Scottish identity than Beth, his experiences in the military in Ireland, and later in the Palestine Gendarmerie where many of his colleagues were former 'Black and Tans', coloured his view of Celtic nationalism. The 'British' poetry of people like Kipling spoke more strongly to Hugh's and Beth's own experiences and their own lives than the literary work done in Inverness by Scottish nationalists and Gaelic revivalists. When Beth moved her work forward, she did so by taking her own path: not by ignoring what was going on around her, but by taking what she liked and was interested in, and what she felt was relevant to her. Her interests coincided with Hugh's, and both of them were starting to find an interested audience in the literary magazines as well.

So, if Hugh Patrick Fraser McIntosh was such a perfect fit for Beth, and their writing was progressing so well, why did their romance not develop? The answer lies in the reason that Hugh was in Inverness: he had been invalided out of the army, and he was dying.

Hugh had tuberculosis.[26] This contagious disease is often associated with poverty and poor living conditions. It could have been caught at any point in Hugh Patrick Fraser's army service, as he was living and working in often appalling conditions from the time he had first joined the army ten years before and been sent to the Western Front. He had a long and painful death. The image of the poet with consumption, or tuberculosis, is a romantic cliché, and, at first, the illness would not have been apparent. Hugh would have been pale and interesting, a little thinner than normal, perhaps with a slight cough. As the illness progressed, any idea that it was romantic evaporated, as a hacking, uncontrollable coughing would have racked his frame and brought up blood; the paleness of his skin would have been offset with red cheeks; and bright eyes would have looked less glittering and more manic. He would have been in considerable pain.

A search through the records revealed that Hugh Patrick Fraser MacKintosh (the different spelling is used), a (retired) Sergeant in the Cameron Highlanders, died of pulmonary tuberculosis (affecting his lungs) in the TB hospital in Culduthel, Inverness on August 14th 1927, at the age of only 33. He was single, and his death was registered by his sister, Mamie (Marianne) McIntosh, who, although she was in Inverness for Hugh's last days, gave as her usual address St George's Square, Regent's Park, London. A corresponding notice in local paper the *Inverness Courier* gives notice of Hugh's death, mentioning his Military Cross, and also his father, the Reverend Hugh McIntosh, MA, of London, suggesting that this was a name known to local readers of the paper. A further notice a week later on Friday 19th August 1927, inserted by his relatives, thanks friends, the RSM (Regimental Sergeant Major) and Sergeants of the Cameron Highlanders for their sympathy and flowers, as well as thanking the staff of Culduthel hospital.

Hugh and Beth had worked hard on their writing in the time that had been left to Hugh. They had begun writing longer pieces, with Beth focusing on short stories while Hugh concentrated on poetry. Working from notes that he had made, and from remembered impressions of his time in the army, by 1927 Hugh had the nucleus of a poetry collection. Writing is a solitary activity, particularly in the beginning, when there is a lot of work for very little reward, and it must have been sustaining for both Hugh and Beth to have someone to bounce ideas off, and to know that someone else was working towards similar goals, and also believed it to be worthwhile and achievable. It's particularly interesting to see that Gordon Daviot, who was later thought to be always working in isolation, in fact associated with other writers from the start of her writing career.

Some of Hugh's early work was also published in the magazine of a group called the Panton Arts Club; an English group supporting literature and the arts. This group then advertised a competition, for the best unpublished collection of poems by a new author, and it was to this competition that Hugh sent his small book. Like Gordon Daviot, Hugh was to find his first success through a competition, as his collection won the first prize of publication, but Hugh never knew that he had won the Panton Arts Competition, as the result was announced a week after his death. The publication of his winning entry was overseen by his family. A biographical note at the start of Hugh's only book was provided by 'R. M.' – his other sister, Robina McIntosh – and a foreword, lamenting the passing of a new talent, was provided by Ernest Rhys, the well-known English writer and editor who founded the Everyman's Library series of affordable classic books, and who had been a judge in the competition. Rhys rated the poems very highly, saying that, of all the competition entries, 'this one, brief, psychic, born out of the war, had a different quality from the others: it touched reality'.[27] He goes on to praise the 'characteristic mixture of grimness and prettiness in some of the succeeding lyrics' and concludes, 'for me, hardened critic that I am, they have a convincing individuality, a perfect sincerity, and a curious power of bringing to life the actual sensation of these terrible war-days as confronted by a soldier who at heart was a true poet'.

A Soldier Looks at Beauty is a charming collection, now virtually impossible to find second-hand. It is a short book, containing only 31 poems. In traditional verse-forms, the poet focuses mainly on moments of beauty in nature. Although *A Soldier Looks at Beauty* is hard to come by, two of Hugh P. F. McIntosh's poems were anthologized in a popular collection called *Holyrood: a Garland of Modern Scots Poems*, showing that his work was admired by contemporary readers – and, as the anthology included authors such as MacDiarmid, that Hugh's work could have been seen in the context of the Scottish Literary Renaissance, unlike Beth's. One of the poems included was a tale of a soldier on guard duty, while the other describes the Highlands with aching homesickness. Ironically, although Hugh's poetry is forgotten, his father Hugh Senior's dry religious writing is still in print: *Is Christ Infallible and the Bible True?* is a Christian classic.

If Hugh had not been terminally ill from their first meeting, he and Beth could have developed their friendship along more romantic lines – but what use were 'what ifs' to Beth? If Hugh hadn't been ill, he would never have come to Inverness, and they would never have met. For Beth, as the years went on, Hugh's death, even more than that of her First World War officer, came to symbolize the lost opportunities that war had made in her life. This intelligent, unusual man, with a shared interest in writing and a similar outlook on life, had been a good match for her. There is an awareness of Hugh, a memory of his writing and of the man himself, scattered throughout Beth's work. Not only did she talk about the quality of his poems and their reception, but she also engaged with Hugh's strong feelings about Scotland. If he had lived, Hugh had stood more chance than Beth of acceptance to the Scottish literary establishment, as shown by his poems' inclusion in the anthology *Holyrood*. Beth's writing, even when she was very successful, was never viewed as particularly 'Scottish' in content, and she was not part of the Scottish literary scene. Hugh, in contrast, embraced a more romantic image of Scotland in some of his poetry. Beth did not idealize Hugh, and her challenges to Hugh's romantic images of Scotland throughout her work, and her realistic and not always complimentary descriptions of poets, point to a level of maturity in this relationship that is not necessarily there in her feelings about her First World War soldier. Beth was aware of Hugh's flaws and their differences; this was not a perfect first romance, but a friendship that could have had a real future.

One of Hugh's poems, 'A Flooded Field', is prominently featured and quoted in the Josephine Tey mystery novel *To Love and be Wise* (published in the 1950s), and it is primarily from here that I was able to begin tracing back Hugh's story. However, there is another thread running through Beth's writing which refers to Hugh: her use of the name 'Patrick'.

Hugh Patrick Fraser was given his first name after his father, and his second middle name after his mother's maiden name: Patrick is his own. Beth MacKintosh gives the name 'Patrick' or 'Pat' to a character in one of her early short stories, published in the *Glasgow Herald* – and then uses the same name, same character and same incident, in her last book, *The Singing Sands*. Pat, in this early short story, sits on a fence making a flute – exactly the same image as Hugh used in his short story 'Innocence'.

This same character Pat also gets a mention in *The Daughter of Time*. Although Beth reused some ideas (the play *Dickon*, for example, is a forerunner to *The Daughter of Time*) the striking similarity between the early short story and the incident in her last, best book, stands out. *The Singing Sands* is too sophisticated to be an early unpublished work – Beth's development as a writer is clear when comparing this to *The Man in the Queue* – so it is safe to say that the character of Patrick is one she went back to:

a character based on someone she knew. In *The Singing Sands*, Patrick is the son of Laura, the woman Grant once thought of marrying. Patrick is also the name of a major character (albeit one we never meet) in *Brat Farrar*. Finally, in *Claverhouse*, there is the following line: 'Perhaps if he had been a "character", they would say: "Patrick. He was the one who flung his bonnet at the Commissioner" .'[28] The 'he' in this sentence is Claverhouse, and there are no Patricks anywhere near this sentence – it's just a 'random' name – but its repeated use throughout Gordon Daviot's work suggests it's something other than random. Perhaps Hugh Patrick Fraser did once fling his bonnet at the Commissioner. He must have had a strong personality, to survive the trenches and decide to sign up again, and then, when he was too ill to continue, to decide instead to emulate his heroes, the First World War poets. A soldier who had seen active service in many different fields, a gifted poet, and the son of a charismatic and successful preacher, I imagine that Hugh was indeed a 'character' – if he and Beth had had a romance, it could have been a stormy one, with so much talent and ambition thrown into the mix.

Hugh Patrick Fraser was buried in Tomnahurich cemetery, where his headstone reads 'In Loving Memory of Hugh P. F. McIntosh, MC, only son of the late Rev Hugh McIntosh, MA. Born at Brockley, London, died at Inverness [...] aged 33. "May God be thanked who has matched us with His hour"'. The last quotation is not a religious one, but is from Rupert Brooke, the First World War poet, from a 1914 poem written when the war and soldiering still seemed glorious. Hugh's work would have slipped into obscurity if it wasn't for Josephine Tey, but it seems that Hugh's family never knew Beth. Hugh and Beth's relationship was officially one of friendship, and Beth was left with no claim over him when he was dead. Almost no one knew of their shared interest in writing, and Hugh's life story, and his part in Beth's life, has never before been written about. It was almost as if their friendship ceased to exist after his death. If Beth had been Hugh Patrick Fraser's fiancée or wife, she would have been able to mourn him in a different way, but, as a friend, she was almost forgotten. Their relationship did not have a chance to develop, because of Hugh's illness. Beth was well aware that her choices had effectively been limited by the war, and she retained a bitterness about this. For Beth, a new reality of her life was brought home to her by Hugh's death: as one of the post-war generation where women now outnumbered men, living in a small town where she already knew most people, having already lost two relationships as a direct or indirect result of the First World War, and now thirty-one years old, Beth was probably never going to marry and have children.

CHAPTER SEVEN

Short Stories and First Two Novels

The earliest Gordon Daviot story I have found is 'Pat', published in the *Glasgow Herald* on 2nd April 1927. It features the young boy, the Pat of the title, who reminds me of Hugh Patrick Fraser McIntosh, recalling the same imagery that was in Hugh's story, 'Innocence'. 'Pat', this first published creation of Daviot's, goes on to reappear in another *Glasgow Herald* short story, and then, again, over twenty years later, in the Josephine Tey novels *The Daughter of Time* and Beth's final published work *The Singing Sands*. The striking thing about Daviot's early short stories is their confidence. Her style develops over time, but she focused on many of the same themes throughout her life, looking at them with increasing maturity and writing expertise.

There is a gap of over ten months between 'Pat' and the next published short story I have found. In the interim, Beth had a number of short pieces published in the *Saturday Review*.[1] Each of these short pieces was a competition entry. Some of the competitions were on general themes (for example, write a poem about July), but others were very prescriptive (for example, make a list of typical Hollywood sub-titles on set topics). Most of them were meant to be funny ('We offer a First Prize of One Guinea... for the most forcible letter writer to 'The Times' either for or against a proposed tax on Beards').[2] Beth used these competitions as writing exercises: they gave her practise in writing to a deadline and allowed her to experiment with different forms – and they gave her feedback on her work, as each week the results were printed with extensive comments. Beth continued to enter these competitions until 1929, when her first book was published – though with decreasing frequency. She was a frequent winner, and a regular enough entrant that, when she didn't send in writing, the *Saturday Review* took the time to say that "The competition was the poorer from the absence of any contributions by Gordon Daviot", and later asked her to both set and judge the competition entries one week. It was a gratifying early sign for Beth that her writing could attract attention, and that her expertise was acknowledged by a community of fellow writers.[3]

It's possible that Beth wrote and published other, as yet undiscovered work, but there were also changes in her personal life that affected her writing. Hugh was in the final stages of his illness, and died four months after her short story 'Pat' was published. And Beth's grandmother, the ninety-year old Jane Horne, died the day after 'Pat' was published, on 3rd April 1927.[4] The death of her maternal grandmother, who had told her so many family stories, was the loss of another connection to Beth's mother Josephine and her happy childhood. Even in an era where loss was widespread, Beth was unlucky enough to have several people die at meaningful periods in her life. Beth was always left behind to pick up the pieces as people died and left her increasingly alone. She poured her feelings into her writing, creating in some of her first short stories pictures of happy family life, with carefree children.

'Pat' had been well received, and Gordon Daviot went on to have four more short stories published in the *Glasgow Herald* between 1927 and 1929. Observational pieces featuring 'characters' and quirky situations, they were well-tailored to the readership of the paper's 'Weekend Page'. They also, surprisingly, given Daviot's later novels and Anglophile attitude, have Scottish settings and feature a number of Scots words, such as scunnered, aye, haivers and bubblyjock. Generally, though, they are specifically 'Highland' stories, rather than 'Scottish' stories. Beth herself always made that distinction, recognizing the vast differences in language and culture between the north and south of the country. 'When I came home to live,' she wrote for a short biographical sketch, 'I knew nothing of Scotland except the Highlands'.[5] It's an important distinction. Beth felt that 'Scotland' could mean many different things. Later, she did not fit easily into a 'Scottish' literary world that she felt did not include her own experiences, and she continued to feel a close connection to the south of England.

In 'Pat's' second appearance, in the short story 'Haivers' in February 1928, the character of Pat, like his later incarnation in *The Singing Sands*, speaks in a broad brogue, which is semi-put-on – reserving his best 'English' accent for when he is displeased. Pat is also described in his kilt as having 'a grace worthy of his ancestors'. There is little yet of the cynicism of *The Singing Sands* – or even of *The Man in the Queue*, with its pejorative descriptions of Gaelic. It is starting to creep in, though, in 'The Find' (June 1928) which pours scorn on the celebration of couthy, idyllic rural settings.

In terms of style, rather than subject, the stories are closer to Daviot's literary novels, *Kif* and *The Expensive Halo*, than her more popular Josephine Tey mysteries. There are some nice turns of phrase: 'Agnew's rooms are full of bright primitive colour and wood ornaments and queer mats and a general lack of comfort and upholstery' ('The Find') and pithy descriptions, as of the folk-song enthusiasts: 'Two of the women had untidy hair and the hair of the third hadn't enough life to get untidy; it just hung' ('The Find'), but occasionally Daviot's style can seem particularly convoluted and rather old-fashioned because of this. 'The surgeon [the child Pat] glanced indifferently at his parent as she came, and continued his torturous explorations, to the accompaniment of much heavy breathing' ('Pat'). Daviot doesn't use a simple word when a fancier explanation can be used instead, and, without the driving force of the readable plots of her mysteries, this is one of the things that can make her short stories, and her literary novels, hard going.

The plots, as well, are not entirely straightforward. Tortuous plotting was one of Daviot's hallmarks, and what makes her mysteries (and plays) so effective. She manages to fit rather a lot of plot into a short space. For example, in 'Pat', which is just over 1200 words long, we hear about the cowman, Pat's uncles, a dispute with Pat's mother, a visit from one uncle, a trip to a different farm, a week in a new place, his cousin, a discussion of his uncle's personality, an argument between Pat and his uncle, and the final denouement. That is rather a lot for a very short story, yet Daviot manages to make it flow and keep the reader's interest. The only thing that does not quite work is perhaps the denouement itself: both in 'Pat' and in 'The Exquis' the ending doesn't quite live up to the build-up, or perhaps the moral points they were trying to make are no longer so relevant in the twenty-first century. 'A Three-Ha'Penny Stamp' (November 1928) also suffers from this, with the distinction between the Wee Free and the United Free Church no longer being so meaningful, and the idea of raffles being sinful (even if Daviot is making the point that Carninnish is backward) is old-fashioned now. The 'point' of the story is lost to the modern reader.

Characters and places are strongly drawn, from Carninnish (the setting which was re-used in *The Man in the Queue*) to the French café where the hall is bordered with 'four minute tables where only a Frenchman would have thought of finding room for them' ('The Exquis', January 1929). In this last, her final story for the *Glasgow Herald*, Daviot moves the setting away from Scotland for the first time.

Gordon Daviot was carefully targeting her writing, however. As well as the short stories based in Scotland which she sent to the *Glasgow Herald*, she was also writing stories on quite different subjects, which she sent out to the *English Review*. In later life, Gordon Daviot was particularly proud of the *English Review* stories, mentioning them alongside her biggest success, *Richard of Bordeaux*, in her *Who's Who* entry.

The *English Review* ran from 1908 until 1937, and published many leading authors, particularly in its early days, including Thomas Hardy, H. G. Wells, Joseph Conrad and Katherine Mansfield. The magazine's tone was resolutely highbrow, with political and cultural commentary in the editorial and letters pages. Major books were reviewed, and reviews and factual articles appear under the sort of pseudonyms that people find amusing if they have had a classical education. Advertisements were kept to a minimum. The first Gordon Daviot story to appear was 'His Own Country', in July 1928, almost a year after Hugh's death. It doesn't have a specifically Scottish setting, unlike the short stories in the *Glasgow Herald*, though the characters' names do have a Scottish tinge (Willie Rawson or Meikle for example) – and the place name of 'Feriton' is a clear nod to the Ferry district in Inverness. It is a remarkably bitter story, and the first real indication that Beth was not happy in Inverness. 'His Own Country' concerns the return of army man Willie Rawson to his home town. A huge success in the wider world, at home he is regarded as something of a joke, by townspeople who are too stupid to understand what he has achieved. It is easy to read into the story something of Gordon Daviot's own attitude and frustration at returning home to the small town of Inverness after living and working successfully in England – and it is possible also to see her friendship with either – or both – Hugh McIntosh and her First World War officer reflected in the story.

Both were successful soldiers, and Hugh, in particular, made a return to the family home, like Willie Rawson in this story. It is tempting to see Beth in the woman who defends Willie Rawson, puncturing Anderson of the Furniture Emporium's speech by retorting, '"There isn't anything Willie Rawson couldn't do. He would beat you all at your own jobs, if he were interested enough." Anderson thought it very bad taste on her part not to smile and agree, like everyone else. But she was queer, of course. Or perhaps she thought that she was going to get off with the so-called colonel.' The attitude of the Feriton people is sharply drawn, and the depiction of the characters and the small town gossip are very true to life: the taxi-man complaining of an over-large tip; the woman who used to do the Rawsons' washing not wanting to see them get above themselves. They all remember where Rawson came from, they all know that his father was just a dancing teacher, and they are not going to let him forget it. He may have won over strangers, but he's not going to fool them. Gordon Daviot, daughter of Colin, was no stranger to this sort of jealous attitude.

However, it's worth remembering that the Gordon Daviot who

wrote 'His Own Country' is not yet the Gordon Daviot who was a success on the West End and whose plays were performed across the country. It is as if she has taken her own situation – look how they treat me, my family and friends – and magnified it several times to create fiction. Her description is accurate. Many people have experienced that sort of jealousy, and, in the Highlands, where to succeed almost inevitably involves leaving home, it can be prevalent. However, the story is so relentless in its description that Rawson becomes a less sympathetic character. Younger people – Daviot was thirty-two when she wrote this – don't always realize that academic and work achievements in themselves are not always as valuable as learning to live with others. University graduates, full of their achievements, return home regularly to irritate those around them, full of ideas on how to change everything and how little towns are full of people who are too stupid to understand the brilliant concepts emanating from the university cities. Rawson does sound rather irritating, as in conversation he

caught a phrase almost before the judge had dropped it, twisted it, juggled with it, made it into something quite different with a skill that no law court could have bettered; told a story as illustration and mimicked the hero of it with such a faithfulness tinged with burlesque, that, when he had finished, they shouted with laughter, and the ambassador lifted his glass in a little gesture of congratulation.

He is too good to be true. Daviot is not trying in her story to understand more about the townspeople's view; she is solely on Rawson's side. However, whatever its flaws, it is certainly a compelling story. The description of an awkward homecoming is universal enough to appeal to many people, and the passion in it, as well as its well-crafted style, show unmistakable promise.

The editors of the *English Review* agreed, as they followed up the publication of 'His Own Country' with 'Deborah' (in March 1929). This slightly anti-climactic but beautifully evocative ghost story was the longest of Daviot's short pieces, at almost 3,000 words, showing that she was already turning away from the genre.

Intriguingly, the manuscript of 'Deborah' has the first indication that Daviot was already considering another pen-name, as it is signed 'Josephine Tey'.[6] However, 'Gordon Daviot' was still a name worth keeping, as Daviot was now the published author of a novel. In 1929, four years after the publication of her first poem, and six years after her return to Inverness, Gordon Daviot had not one, but two novels published.

Gordon Daviot's first novel was *Kif*. Several years later she advised a friend on how to get published: 'did you ever send poems or novels round the publishers – and go on sending them? Or try them on an agent?'[7] Beth had no particular connection with any literary agent or publisher, and was published through persistence and talent. Her first agent was Curtis Brown, one of the largest literary and talent agencies in the country, whose clients have included Kenneth Grahame, A. A. Milne, Samuel Beckett and D. H. Lawrence, and her first publisher was Ernest Benn. *Kif* was published in both the UK and, a year later, in the US, and was widely and positively reviewed. For the daughter of a fruiterer, Beth had broken into an exclusive literary world.

When her copies of the hardback version of *Kif* arrived at her house in Crown, Beth inscribed one to her father: 'Colin MacKintosh / from / Gordon Daviot / 1st February 1929'.[8] She wanted her family to share in her success. The printed dedication in the book is a little mysterious, as most of Beth's dedications were. It read, 'TO M—— / WHO MIGHT HAVE LIKED IT / OR MIGHT NOT / BUT IN ANY CASE / WOULD HAVE BEEN PLEASED'. I have always thought that, instead of 'M' being a name, it stood for 'Mother', and was a private dedication to the late Josephine MacKintosh.

Kif was very definitely an attempt at serious literature. The title character (Kif is a nickname – his real name is Archibald Vicar), is a boy from a farm in Scotland, who joins the army at the outbreak of the Great War. He does well enough in the army, but his story really begins when the war is over, and he returns to London. He has fallen in love with that city, and tries to make his way there, but the harsh post-war conditions – and his own inability to make the right choices – lead him eventually into a life of crime, and the book ends with him on trial, where his crimes are judged serious enough to invoke the death penalty. He has been unable to find love, but the only true women in his life – the sister of his best friend, and an old woman from the farm where he grew up – lament his passing and show the reader that Kif was not completely responsible for his downfall, but only a victim of the times he lived in.

One of the striking things about the book is that, for a first novel, it is remarkably polished: too often a first novel is thinly disguised autobiography, but Gordon Daviot chose a male protagonist – and one of her strengths as a writer is that her characters always seem alive. They aren't mouthpieces for Beth's opinions, but fully formed. Kif's choices interest Daviot, she writes about his motivations, but he is independent of Daviot, and makes choices she never would. She was a born storyteller and novelist, not writing about her own life, but interested in other people, particularly different characters and what motivates them. It is what gives her detective novels, in particular, such enduring appeal, but it is also one of the contributing factors in making Beth herself such a mystery. To the modern reader, there is an extra layer of both mystery and an understanding of the extra layer of finely crafted writing, as we know that 'Gordon Daviot' is the assumed name of a Highland housewife, not a man who could have experienced the war.

Daviot, however, although not writing autobiographically, always wrote from knowledge and experience. *Kif* is in many ways an Inverness novel; it is a novel of the 4th Cameron Highlanders. The geography of the novel is the invented geography familiar to Daviot's short stories, with Kif signing up in 'Feriton' to the fictional regiment 'Carnshires' – but the Carnshires follow the path of the 4th Camerons throughout the war, and they are led by the admirable 'Murray Heaton', a homage to the 4th Camerons' real leader 'Murdoch Beaton'. Like the real Beaton, Heaton is loved and respected by his men – and ends the book promoted and married to Ann, a VAD and one of the few sympathetic female characters. The real-life Beaton survived and prospered, going on to have a fascinating career, involving work for the Dewar

Report, which foreshadowed the NHS.[9] A photograph of Beaton in his army kilt shows a neat, dark man with a tidy moustache: an almost Alan Grant-like figure. Incidents throughout the novel, such as the fight when the Highland regiment reach their training camp at Bedford, echo real life. And, of course, the one Cameron Highlander who is mentioned, Travenna, is perhaps a cameo of Beth's real-life soldier boyfriend.

Beth had kept the writing of *Kif* a secret from many of her friends – her college room-mate 'Dave' was surprised when it was published, and Beth wrote apologizing for not discussing it before, explaining that she'd felt it would have been strange to suddenly say 'I've written a book' before it had been accepted for publication.[10] Now it was published, though, Beth was happy to talk about it, and about her next novel, *The Man in the Queue*.

The Man in the Queue, Beth explained to Dave, was being held back from publication at her request until *Kif*'s reviews had a chance to take. In the meantime, *Kif* was being prepared for the US market. This brought Beth face-to-face with Gordon Daviot for the first time: she had never told her publishers that 'Daviot' was a pseudonym, or, indeed, that she was a woman. Benn, the publisher, wrote asking for a biography and photo to put on the back of the US edition of *Kif*, as was standard American practice. Unsure how to explain herself, and unwilling to supply the biography and photo, Beth took the train down to London and went to see her publisher. The trip was worth it, Beth told Dave, if only to see the look on her publishers' faces when 'Gordon Daviot' was announced at their office and Beth walked into the room! Beth went to Inverness photographer Andrew Paterson to have her portrait taken, but was unhappy with the result.[11] She generally disliked having her photograph taken and was self-deprecating about her appearance. *Kif*'s author stayed anonymous a little longer.

In 1929, the First World War still hung over everything. *Kif* was published around the same time as the classics *A Farewell to Arms* and *All Quiet on the Western Front*. *Kif* was Gordon Daviot's attempt to make sense of the changes the Great War had wrought – Kif himself sees the war as a series of experiences, not all bad, but he is not able to see the wider picture and see how the war has irrevocably changed both him and the society he lives in. Daviot's portrayal of post-war London and the struggle for soldiers to find their place and find work is sensitive and well-drawn.

The cleverness and humour of Josephine Tey's detective novels is not so apparent in *Kif*, which has a very serious tone in places, but, although *Kif* approaches the war directly, *The Man in the Queue* is also influenced by it. Detective fiction generally shows a deviation from the norm that is then fixed; the moral code of society is challenged but then returned to – a rather post-war attitude, and something that is recognized as being a common thread in Golden Age detective fiction. Beth later made a distinction between her literary writing as 'Gordon Daviot' and her mystery novels by 'Josephine Tey', but it gives a clearer view of her work to know that *The Man in the Queue* was first published as being by 'Gordon Daviot'. Beth was interested in the same themes in her first 'literary' and 'mystery' novels, they just express them in different ways.

Kif had been sweated over for months and years. Beth had written it and sent it out repeatedly before it was accepted for publication. *The Man in the Queue*, published just three months later, in May 1929, had a very different genesis. Detective fiction – the thing Beth is best known for today – was almost an accident. Frustrated by her progress in getting her work published, Beth had been attracted by a competition. She later wrote to a friend that *The Man in the Queue* 'wouldn't have been written at all if Methuen hadn't offered £250 for a detective novel. Even then I had no intention of writing one but one night an idea struck with such force that it hurt.'[12] She sat down at her typewriter and bashed out what became the first Alan Grant novel, completing the manuscript in only two or three weeks. *The Man in the Queue* is far freer in style than *Kif*, and far more enjoyable to read. It doesn't have the ponderous feel of a first novel and its story has stood the test of time (despite some outdated language). In keeping with the lighter tone, the novel is dedicated 'To Brisena, who actually wrote it'. Brisena was the nickname Beth had given her typewriter. Despite the claim that it was written in only a fortnight, the reason it could be completed in such a short time was that Beth had already dedicated considerable time and effort into writing other long works, and had learnt a lot about structure, storytelling and technique, which she was then able to apply to the framework of a detective novel. This framework was always the best showcase for Beth's original ideas and style: by taking something familiar to the reader (the detective genre) and adding her own unique spin, she was able to take the reader into her own world, and her own original way of thinking and mix of experiences. Beth told her college friend Marjorie that she thought *The Man in the Queue* was a much greater achievement than *Kif*.

The Man in the Queue was the most successful of Beth's early novels, and has never been out of print since it first appeared in 1929. Although it was originally published under her pseudonym 'Gordon Daviot', it is now published under the name 'Josephine Tey'. It is generally thought that the Tey name did not appear until the publication of *A Shilling for Candles* in 1936, but it seems that it may have actually been 1929 when Tey made her first appearance. Orlando, the well respected reference database on women's writing, literature and cultural history, states that *The Man in the Queue* was repackaged for the US market later in 1929, and appeared in two editions. "The Man in the Queue" by Gordon Daviot was published by E.P.Dutton of New York, while an abridged version was also published by Mercury under the title "Killer in the Crowd" – and the name Josephine Tey. It was previously thought that Mercury's abridged edition and alternative title first appeared in 1954, but editions listed in library catalogues and for sale online do appear to exist with the 1929 publication date. When coupled with the 'Josephine Tey' name on the manuscript of 1929 story 'Deborah', and with the knowledge that it was at this time that Beth revealed to her publisher her real identity, it does seem likely that the Tey name was first considered in 1929, for the American publication of her first mystery. Her US publishers had wanted an author photo and biography for Gordon Daviot, and, when shown the photo of a young woman, they may have suggested that a female pen name would be more acceptable to them.[13] Since then, the book has been through numerous editions, with various different publishers and very varied cover art.[14] It won a second award, the Dutton Mystery Prize, on its publication in the US, has been adapted for radio and was translated into French not long after its first publication, published by Librarie Plon under another new title as *Le Monogramme de Perles* in 1932.[15]

The 1920s and 30s became known as the Golden Age of crime fiction, an era when the genre was phenomenally popular, and when several masters of the form were writing. The 'Big Four' were all writing at this time – the authors whose names have become synonymous with the crime fiction of the era, whose work has stood the test of time, and who are familiar to modern readers: Agatha Christie, Dorothy L. Sayers, Ngaio Marsh and Margery Allingham. Other popular detective fiction published around the time of *The Man in the Queue* included Georgette Heyer's detective novels.

The Man in the Queue was originally written and entered by Beth for a competition run by the publisher Methuen, who presumably wanted to capitalise on the popularity of detective fiction.[16] It must have been thrilling for the judges to realize the sheer quality of Gordon Daviot's entry, and to receive such an assured book from an unknown writer. From the opening chapter of *The Man in the Queue*, the reader knows they are in safe hands. Chapter 1 describes the queue waiting to get into a theatre performance. The anticipation and build-up is palpable – as readers we can't wait to get in to the theatre. And then, the build-up leads instead to the amazing discovery of the dead man's body in the lively queue. It is a perfect opening chapter. Beth's inspiration came partly from a discussion with a friend who had argued that dying in a solitary place would be horrific – Beth countered with this shocking description of death in public – where everyone should be able to stop it and no one does.[17]

Chapter 2 is the first introduction to Inspector Alan Grant, and the reader knows instantly that this is a sympathetic character; this is the hero. Daviot even switches to second person when introducing him: 'if you can visualize a dapperness that is not of the tailor's dummy type, then that is Grant.'[18] This is not a narrative device that is used in her later books, and it is a sty-listic trick that is often associated with less experienced or less confident writers, who feel they cannot let their story stand on its own without giving the reader extra information. However, in this, Daviot's first mystery novel, it works, inviting the reader into the world of the story. There are some aspects of Grant that don't seem to fit with the later books in which he is featured (for example, it is hard – though not impossible – to reconcile the idea that he was born in the Midlands, as mentioned here, with Grant returning to the Scotland of his childhood in *The Singing Sands*) but generally he remains a consistent character. His traits are well formed here, particularly his logical approach to crime solving and interest in people and places. Grant follows the trail of the suspicious character seen arguing in the queue, chasing him round London and up to the Highlands, before the plot twist is revealed at the end.

Like *Kif*, *The Man in the Queue* has moments where its 1920s date is too apparent for the modern reader, particularly when characters talk about 'Dago' stereotypes. Indeed, Beth even con-sidered titling the book *The Dago* at one point, though changed her mind when she found out another book had recently come out with this name.[19] However, Grant's interest in the character of his villains, rather than judgement on them, is what saves *The Man in the Queue* from outdated racism. Grant is always prepared to admit that the opposite of what he thinks might be true: it is inte-gral to his crime-solving approach and shows Daviot's genuine interest in people, a defining characteristic of a good writer. In *Kif*, too, there is a startlingly large range of characters, drawn without judgement, from Kif himself, to the middle-class friend he makes in the army, to boxers, 'Pinkie' the black servant, Scots on the make in London, criminals, betting men, jockeys – it is clear from what she writes about that when Beth moved away from Inverness she went around with her eyes open, seeing the many different cultures in London, for example, and drawing her own conclusions.

One of the attractions of *The Man in the Queue* is the action: the section where Grant careers off to the Highlands makes the

Beth, smartly dressed for London

John MacKintosh, Beth's grandfather

Near Shieldaig today, site of Colin's family croft

Beth's maternal grandparents, Peter Horne & Jane Ellis

Josephine Horne and Colin MacKintosh

Beth, Etta and Jean MacKintosh

Summer holidays: Jean, Josephine and Beth

MacKintosh family portrait: Jean, Colin, Etta, Beth, Josephine

Jean, Beth, Etta, circa 1914

The monument to Colin's parents

Pupils outside the Inverness Royal Academy, 1905

The new art room at the IRA, 1912

The new gym at the IRA, 1912

Anstey Physical Training College

Beth, in her Anstey sports kit

Rhoda Anstey

Gordon Barber

Top: Colin and Josephine MacKintosh

Left: Colin MacKintosh

Beth, inter-war summer holidays

The letterhead from Colin's shop

Castle Street in Inverness today: the site of Colin's shop

The arrival of the London sleeper train at Inverness Railway station,
early 20th century

Hugh McIntosh's house in London (on the left)

Hugh's grave in Tomnahurich

book like a more sedate Buchan (or a chaste Fleming), and one of its strengths is that Daviot knows all the places she describes. The place names, including Carninnish and Garnie, are fictional, and Grant is travelling across the fictional landscape that Daviot had already laid out in her short stories – but they are clearly based on a real place: the west coast home of her father Colin MacKintosh. Colin visited and kept up links with his home of Shieldaig not only in the 1920s but right up until the 1940s, and Beth must have accompanied him on some of his trips west.[20] The geography may be slightly rearranged to suit the story, but when Grant takes the train up from London to Inverness, then transfers onto a railway heading west – 'a little local affair that for the rest of the morning trundled from the green countryside back into a brown desolation [...] West and still farther west they trailed, stopping inexplicably at stations set down equally inexplicably in the middle of vast moors devoid of human habitation'– that must be the Kyle line.[21] The trains are more modern now, but the journey, as you pass through request stop stations like Achnashellach, is still recognizable. The unnamed station Grant gets out at is probably Strathcarron. Even in the 1980s and 90s, you still had to get the postbus from the station down to Loch Carron and on to the other villages, sitting in amongst the German hikers and mailbags, though it wasn't quite such a rattly old contraption as Grant endures. In the 1920s, there was only one road from Strathcarron to Shieldaig, Beth's father's home on the Applecross Peninsula, and it was certainly in the terrible condition that Grant describes. Twisting and turning until it eventually headed north to the coast, it would have taken, with stops to drop off the mail, roughly the thirty-six miles and five hours that Josephine Tey gives to Grant's journey. Shieldaig is still very isolated, but in the 1920s, when Beth seems to have first made the journey, it really was a trip as epic and basic as she describes in *The Man in the Queue*.

Arriving at Garnie (which has a real-life near-namesake in nearby Dornie), there is a little confusion between real places and imagined, as Garnie, with its sandy beach, seems to bear more than a resemblance to Applecross itself, rather than Shieldaig, where the beach is stony. There are islands visible off the coast at both Applecross and Shieldaig, and Beth was familiar with several west-coast beaches, after her time working in Oban. The fishing lochs so important to the story are matched with fishing lochs in the hills around Shieldaig – there's no 'Loch Finley', but there are other places with similar names, like Loch Lundie. There is a choice of manse and other houses in the area which could have been models for Mr Logan the minister's house, since, as described in the book, there are both Free and United Free churches. Walking up from Shieldaig to the site of Colin's family croft at Camus na Leum, I passed several large stone houses which reminded me of Mr Drysdale's.

Despite the Highland links, neither *Kif* nor *The Man in the Queue* were recognized as 'Scottish' novels. Beth's pen-name was widely known locally in Inverness, but she was not fêted as a local celebrity. She did not court the local press, but, under the heading 'Novel by Inverness Author', *The Man in the Queue* was very positively reviewed in the *Inverness Courier* on its publication, in June 1930. This is the first local press cutting I have found for Gordon Daviot.[22]

Neil Gunn, now a full-time writer who had made enough from the proceeds of his novel *The Grey Coast* to build his house Larachan on Dochfour Drive, and who certainly did enjoy being fêted as 'our local author', noted the *Courier* review of this 'Inverness lady who has already contributed an excellent novel to the literature of the day, and who bids fair to become well-known as a writer of fiction'. Gunn's concerns as a writer were focused on his national identity, and 1929 was the year he officially joined John MacCormick's National Party of Scotland, the forerunner of the SNP. In his published correspondence, a letter from the exact same time, dated May 1929 and addressed to publishers Hodder and Stoughton, expounds at length on what Gunn saw as the impossibility of any Scottish writer getting published.[23] Gunn's latest novel had been rejected. Privately, at the same time, Neil Gunn also sent his rejected novel to Gordon Daviot's publisher, Ernest Benn. Benn rejected it as well.[24] A few months later, Gunn wrote to another friend and writer, Nan Shepherd, concluding that perhaps the reason his novels were being rejected was that they were too political.[25] *Kif*, in its criticism of the way former soldiers were left to fend for themselves, and its analysis of class division, has a strong political message – though not, of course, the area of politics that Gunn was keen to discuss. Gordon Daviot's disassociation from Gunn, and the writers he considered his contemporaries, had begun, and was to increase over the years, particularly as their views on Scottish nationalism developed.

In some ways, Gordon Daviot's work sits more easily with British writers of her time than it does with those of her Scottish contemporaries who were explicitly concerned with a 'Scottish literary renaissance', like Gunn, MacDiarmid or Grassic Gibbon. Another way to contextualise *Kif* is to compare it with contemporary literary novels such as those of Elizabeth Bowen, who published *The Last September* in 1929, and who shared the same literary agency as Gordon Daviot. Bowen was an Anglo-Irish writer, and, although her Irish background is central to some of her plots, she is very interested in characterization and her novels are very British. For example, *The Heat of the Day* is a novel about the Second World War first, then about betrayal, and then a London book. Beth MacKintosh's books, even the genre mystery novels, are similarly concerned with character. They also share the obsession with London.

After her earliest short stories, Beth never again wrote about Scotland in quite the same way. She no longer deliberately used specifically Scottish words, and her descriptions of Scotland often came with qualifying statements or comments from her characters about what they thought of the country. As she became more and more fixed in Inverness, she wrote more longingly about the England she would no longer live in, and both *Kif* and *The Man in the Queue* are full of joyful descriptions of London's attractions. Beth's sister Jean, in autumn 1929, moved to London to work for a solicitor, while their youngest sister had left both college and her baby nickname behind her and had also headed for the capital. Mary Henrietta had ditched the name Etta, which she had never liked, and now called herself Moire, the Gaelic version of her first name.[26] After leaving domestic science college, Moire found an excellent job working in London for the Gas Board, as a demonstrator and tester of gas cookers. Moire enjoyed London life immensely, and Beth was able to visit both her sisters on holidays, indulging her interest in theatre and horse racing. It is amazing to think that *The Man in the Queue* was published four years before Gordon Daviot's massive theatrical success *Richard of Bordeaux* – Ray Marcable's show presages the extraordinary turn Daviot's career was to take over the next few years. Daviot was creating in her imagination and writing the life that she wanted in London, and she was almost able to write it into being – but not quite. As she proved to her family that she was able to write and look after Colin, Beth wrote herself into a corner. There was no reason now why she shouldn't stay in Inverness, as she could work from there. Beth's next writing projects began to take a different turn.

CHAPTER EIGHT

The Expensive Halo, 'Ellis' and Invergordon

After her first two novels, the next publication of Gordon Daviot's was actually another short story: 'Madame Ville d'Aubier' in the *English Review*. It could have been written and sent off before her two books came out, particularly since the attached biography makes no mention of either novel, but Beth did continue to write and publish short stories throughout her career. 'Madame Ville d'Aubier', although it's not really a mystery, does feature another murder. With the same character names and similar setting to the *Glasgow Herald* story 'The Exquis', Daviot was continuing to build up her world, and the theme of artists in France was something she was to return to again in her playwriting. However, the thing that stands out in 'Madame Ville d'Aubier' is the opening description of the Scottish countryside, which is among the best things that Daviot wrote. The cold wintry landscape contrasts nicely with the descriptions of France, while the maturity expressed in the sentiments is already a world away from the jealous traders in the short story 'His Own Country', published two years before:

> Outside, the white dead moors stared blankly back at me as the train trailed its slow length across the Grampians. The hills stood withdrawn and cold and magnificent. Even the winter sunlight that lit them to beauty could not make them less aloof, less symbolic of eternity. And suddenly the chugging train with its load of little mortals, each busy with his own futilities, was somehow

heart-breakingly pathetic. If we were to count so little, it was surely unfair that we should suffer so much.[1]

Daviot obviously realized the power of this image, as she refers back to it in the closing sentence, giving it one of the more satisfying conclusions of her short stories: 'And we went to luncheon, watched by the staring indifferent hills'. This haunting closing image, set on the train, shows that Beth was an already powerful writer – and it shows a snapshot of her life, as that train journey south from Inverness was so well known to her, and was to continue to feature throughout her life.

With an agent and publisher in London, and her sisters based there too, Beth took many trips south. *The Man in the Queue* was serialised in the *Evening Telegraph* in 1930, and, although these sort of spin-offs from her work could be organized by letter, Beth took pleasure in her visits.[2] The colourless, grim, post-war landscape of *Kif* was not the only reality. This was the time of the Scottish Colourists, whose vivid paintings show an altogether different side of Scotland, and, for some sections of society, the post-war years were gay and bright. Those who had made it through alive wanted to celebrate their lives, not endlessly commemorate death. It was the time of the Bright Young Things of the twenties. Evelyn Waugh published *Vile Bodies* in 1930, and Nancy Mitford's *Highland Fling* came out the following year. All in work, and with money to spend, the three MacKintosh sisters could enjoy London: the parties of the original aristocratic 'Bright Young People' had, by the early 1930s, become a widespread youth movement that everyone was aware of, chronicled and mythologized in literature.

The Expensive Halo, Gordon Daviot's third novel, is her contribution to this world; an alternative view of the post-war years that stands in contrast to *Kif* and gives a glimpse into an upper-class world of parties, privilege and boredom – balanced by a contrasting story about the children of a greengrocer. Obsessed with class, the novel shows that talent and money can't buy happiness, or entry to a closed society – it is a cynical take on romantic relationships, firmly a novel of youth. *The Expensive*

Halo is probably Gordon Daviot's least-known book today, but it is one that deserves proper attention because of what it tells us about her development as a writer, and also what it tells us about her development as a person.

The Expensive Halo features as one of its main characters a stern father who runs a shop selling fruit and vegetables. This fictional fruiterer is called Mr Ellis – the maiden name of Beth's grandmother Jane. Little incidents in the book bring the fiction uncomfortably close to the reality. Mr Ellis is as strict and religious as Jane's real-life husband, Beth's grandfather Peter Horne. The fictional fruiterer 'Alfred Ellis' used to work with his younger brothers, as Colin MacKintosh had done, but buys his brothers out of the business because he doesn't like to defer to other family members.[3] Colin and his brothers had clashed too, though not for these reasons.

It's hard to see quite what Beth thought she was doing with this mixture of fact and fiction. Beth's connection with the surname 'Ellis' was not well known outwith her own family, but many of her cousins (and her own sister) had been given Ellis for a middle name, as Josephine and her siblings had honoured their mother. In contrast to the extended family of her babyhood, Beth and Colin had now lost touch with many of their cousins, but they still lived in the same small town. Beth's pen-name of Daviot was widely known in Inverness and further afield: one of the first articles I have found 'revealing' her real identity was in 1931 in the *Chicago Tribune*, following the US publication of *The Expensive Halo*.[4]

Colin's upbringing had made him a strict, though loving father. Whether 'Alfred Ellis' was meant to be a portrayal of Peter Horne, or an amalgamation of many people, there are passages in the book that must have worried Colin and strained his relationship with Beth. Beth had proudly dedicated a personal copy of *Kif* to him, and Colin was an avid reader, though neither he, nor Beth's sisters, shared her passion for literature in quite the same way. Perhaps *The Expensive Halo* was some sort of challenge, to see if any of Beth's family or acquaintances were actually reading her books. Perhaps she thought they weren't reading, and so it would slip under the radar. Perhaps it was a deliberate attempt at provocation, as she found herself living in a town where she did not want to be, looking after her father instead of being allowed to live independently as either a teacher or a full-time writer. Perhaps it was naivety, or an over-commitment to her fictional world – Beth was often known as a sharp person, whose first consideration was not necessarily other people's feelings. Perhaps she felt it was essential to express her feelings somehow, and safer to do so in writing.

Knowledge of Beth's real life changes the experience of *The Expensive Halo* for the modern reader, but it is perhaps worth saying that in a town as small and as gossipy as Inverness, there has never been any suggestion that Beth put her family into her writing. However it may seem at this distance, and with extra knowledge of her background, to their contemporaries there was never any suggestion that Alfred Ellis was Colin MacKintosh – and the connection to Peter Horne was not even mentioned. Colin and Beth were already at a distance from that side of the family, and Colin's own reputation was established. The novel may have harmed relations with her father, but it did not do Beth any harm with anyone else.

The Expensive Halo turns firmly away from Scotland, and is set in London, telling the story of two sets of siblings: a rich girl, Ursula, falls in love with a poor boy; whilst unknown to them the poor boy's sister falls in love with Ursula's brother. The novel is narrated from the point of view of both Ursula, the rich girl, and Sara, the poor girl, and one of the strengths of the novel is that each voice is distinct: whoever is narrating is the person the reader understands and feels sympathy for. Gordon Daviot was always excellent at writing in different 'voices', and it is one of the aspects of her novels that most strongly recalls her skills as a playwright. Some of the dialogue has a dry humour that matches the way her friends described Beth herself, while there are some biting comments:

'Darling, *did* you see her at Raoul's last night with Freddie Owen?' Julie said. 'In a frock that looked like a telephone cover that someone had sat on.'

'What does she spend her money on?' someone asked.
'Cocaine,' Lola said.
'Oh, is she trying *that* now?'[5]

However, there are parts of the dialogue that don't ring true, particularly the romantic scenes. The blurb for the novel describes it as a 'sparkling comedy of topsy-turvy London in the hectic Twenties' – but I wouldn't say that 'sparkling comedy' is the description that comes first to my mind, however her publisher wished to market it. I think Gordon Daviot was trying to write a more serious literary work, but one of her starting points may have been a rather theatrical or cinematic, artificially heightened version of English life – something like a Noel Coward play.

The Expensive Halo in fact started out life as a play script.[6] Beth had made clear her interest in the theatre in *The Man in the Queue*, and she continued to attend the theatre with her sisters when she visited London. It was her aim to write a stage play. She made several attempts that she was not quite happy with, and *The Expensive Halo* seems to have grown out of one of these abortive attempts. Perhaps the transposition of genre accounts for some of the slightly off-kilter feel of the book, but again, the fault seems to come back to the character of Alfred Ellis. As with most of Daviot's work, observed characters are her speciality, but this central character is not fully rounded. There are some beautifully descriptive passages, such as the incident with Mr Ellis's attitude over the lodger Dastur bringing flowers to Mrs Ellis, but there is a lack of understanding at the heart of Mr Ellis that makes him too much of a caricature. The father has no redeeming characteristics, and there is little attempt to understand why he is the way he is, and why Mrs Ellis may have loved him. Mrs Ellis herself is a more rounded character, as Sara can see her faults, and see that she encourages her husband, but Mr Ellis remains a one-dimensional villain. When Sara comes home from the party, and suddenly finds her father's anger at her funny, I think this is meant to be more of a climactic scene than it actually is. Because the reader has never understood him properly, his undoing is not the relief it should have been.

131

Perhaps Beth, who, along with her father Colin, seemed to have followed a policy of not seeing family that she didn't like, didn't really understand her religious grandfather, or whoever had been the inspiration for 'Alfred Ellis'. Perhaps Beth was not as grown-up and sophisticated and clever as she thought – perhaps this, too, explains why she thought she could get away with writing nasty characters with the same name as her family. It's almost a step back from *The Man in the Queue* which, for all its dismissal of Gaelic and west coasters, seems to have more of a genuine understanding of Colin's family background. Something has gone wrong here – Beth is no longer trying to understand and fit in with her family; *The Expensive Halo* is a novel of youth, where family only holds back the heroine. It is a novel of fashion; a novel of Bright Young Things, and the Highlands have little place in that.

The people that Sara meets are far from the Highlanders Grant met in *The Man in the Queue*, and the biggest preoccupation is always with class. Gordon Daviot tries to express that inexpressible class feeling: 'Why *should* she [Sara] expect to feel at home with these people? And (the next moment) why *shouldn't* she? They were just human beings like herself.'[7] It is at the races, at Kempton Park, that we get the first explicit sense that Sara feels she is out of her depth with her upper-class boyfriend and his associates. It's worth comparing the Kempton scene in *The Expensive Halo* with the similar scene in *Kif* – in *Kif* there is less of the nuance of class that Sara is aware of, though this, to me, says more about Gordon Daviot's ability to write from different points of view: the young boy Kif would not have been aware of the people around him in the same way that the young girl in love, Sara, was aware.

Sara's prospective father-in-law is a Blandings-like pig-owning aristocrat, a character that recurs in Daviot's writing, appearing again in her posthumously published play *Mrs Charing is Cross*. Was he too based on a real person? There does seem to be slight evidence for Beth, at some point in her teaching career in England, having perhaps had a third significant romance, with an upper-class man. Then again, as a teacher in both private and comprehensive schools, and during her time as a VAD, Beth would have had plenty of opportunities for meeting people from many different classes and social groups.

The main interest of the racing scene is perhaps the rhapsodic description, both of the event itself – horse racing was a particular interest of Beth's, and something she enjoyed on her visits south – but also of the England that horse racing represented for her. Following on from her Scottish-set short stories, and the Highland scenes in *Kif* and *The Man in the Queue*, *The Expensive Halo* more obviously reflects the Anglophilia that Beth was to foster, which was to become a major part of her reputation. The first enjoyment of moving back to Scotland was wearing off, and Beth was beginning to realize that, in choosing to stay and look after her father Colin, she was missing out on the independent lives her sisters Moire and Jean were enjoying down south. *The Expensive Halo*, with its declaration that family is not always right and that England is wonderful, is a defiant book. It has something of the short story 'His Own Country' in its tone, but there is genuine feeling – and more subtle nuance and understanding of the age she was living in – in Gordon Daviot's uncharacteristically long description of England as personified in Kempton Park, which follows on from pages of dialogue:

[B]efore them, in the October sunlight, spread a little bit of the England one remembers with affection in distant places; a bit of the England which not wars, nor the ridicule of the intellectual, nor the fanaticism of the reformer can destroy [...].

Everything that was England was down there between the stands and the far trees; and every type of man that made her was down there in the crowd: saint and scallywag; and all the courage, optimism, and philosophy which are common to both [...].

Kempton Park. But it might have been any English racecourse on a Saturday afternoon.[8]

This is not a completely rosy picture of England; it is a clear-sighted vision of a society riddled with class bias. Beth did love England, but she was not blind to all its faults, and much of the inspiration for *The Expensive Halo* actually came from closer to home. The plot hinges on an orchestra and a talented fiddle player, and this was partly inspired by the musical culture in Inverness. Beth didn't see the culture in Inverness as inferior in any way, and she took what she had access to and applied the same standards and imagination to it as she did to any show she might see in London. In the summer, Inverness played host to a German orchestra led by a 'Herr Meny'.[9] Mr Philippe R. Meny's band, dressed in green military uniform, played the summer season at the Ness Islands, a tiny group of islands in the middle of the River Ness, linked to the banks by a series of footbridges. The islands are just slightly downriver from the town – five or ten minutes leisurely walk – and are still one of the nicest parts of Inverness. There was an open-air bandstand on the islands in the 1930s, and the summer musical season had been run there for over twenty years. Tea was served, and in fine weather it was an ideal concert venue. Nowadays there is still a small seating area, and the islands still play host to musical events and other entertainments. The tradition of Invernessians taking a stroll down through town and along Ladies' Walk to listen to music there on summer afternoons is a long one. Mr Meny's band returned every summer for several years, and attracted large crowds – delighting not only Invernessians, but also tourists.

Tourism is still a major industry in Inverness, and the town takes on a different atmosphere in summer, that heady feeling of meeting strangers and seeing people you know turn out differently to what you expect that is captured so well in *The Expensive Halo*. In the late 1920s, the *Inverness Courier* reported that there were 235 enquiries at the tourist office, from visitors from such diverse countries as Japan, Australia, Argentina, America and England.[10] Beth and her sisters joined this throng walking through town and down to hear Herr Meny. Meny and his band were reportedly excellent, and were very popular, particularly with the ladies of the town, who found their 'continental' manners particularly charming. The concerts on the islands were the thing to see and the place to be seen. Beth went there with one of her sisters, and was inspired, apparently by the band's excellent cellist, to create the band and the violinist Gareth Ellis in *The Expensive*

Halo. Another glimpse of Beth's private life, which supports the theory that the romances in *The Expensive Halo* had some basis in reality, was given by her family, who remembered that her love of music was connected to romance, as she had admired a young man from her school, who had gone on to play violin in the London Philharmonic Orchestra.[11]

Beth made use of her trips to London to soak up the culture – music and theatre being high on the list. *The Expensive Halo* as a script, rather than a novel, was to go on to further life, but at the moment Gordon Daviot was focused on writing something new. On one of her trips south she took two outings that remained particularly strong in her memory, and which she carefully recorded in her journal.[12] The first was to see the Cameron Highlanders at Aldershot. The memory of the Cameron Highlanders during the First World War, and her personal connections with the regiment, was very dear to her, and Beth was always moved by the sight and sound of the military. 'I'll be dead when a column-of-four doesn't give me a kick any more', she wrote to a friend, describing the London trip many years later.[13] The second visit Beth made in London was to the Old Vic Theatre.

The Old Vic was an extraordinary theatre. Located outwith the fashionable West End theatre district, it had a temperance history, with a mission to try and engage its local audience with entertainment that would distract them away from drink and expose them instead to high culture. Its manager was Lilian Bayliss, who had inherited control of the theatre from her aunt, Emma Cons, the original instigator of its temperance principles. Lilian upheld these formidably. In 1914, Lilian had decided that the best way to engage her audience was by providing the best quality theatre, and she had embarked on an ambitious project to have every single Shakespeare play performed. She did this in her own inimitable way, always insistent on keeping production costs as low as possible, always with an eye on the box office and profits. This had the effect of making the acting the focus of every performance, and, despite Bayliss's notoriously low wages, actors became desperate to star at her theatre, not only for the opportunity to play the great Shakespearian roles, but also to prove themselves in front of what had become an extremely educated, demanding and loyal audience. The complete Shakespeare cycle took almost ten years, and established the theatre's reputation. The Old Vic audience had become fiercely loyal, returning week after week no matter what was on, safe in the knowledge that they were guaranteed a good night out. They were also fiercely possessive, loudly and vocally criticizing actors' performances, and following with great enthusiasm the career of anyone they approved of. Inevitably, the audience now consisted not only of the locals the theatre had originally set out to attract, but also anyone who considered themselves interested in theatre – or interested in whatever was popular. This audience was to become very important to Gordon Daviot, but, in 1930, she was just one among the crowd, filing in to see the up-and-coming young actor John Gielgud star in *Hamlet*.

Gielgud was born in 1904 and died in 2000, outliving most of his contemporaries, and it can be difficult to imagine him as he appeared to Beth when she first saw him act, rather than as he is remembered now.[14] Born into a family with strong links to the theatre, a relative of the revered stage actress Ellen Terry, Gielgud was interested in and exposed to theatrical life from an early age. He had decided to go to drama school instead of university, and his family connections had helped him to gain a place, and to then start getting walk-on and later speaking parts in the London theatres and on regional tours. He slowly built up a track record in the theatre, and by the 1930s was beginning to focus on Shakespeare and more classical work, though his passion for the theatre was wide-ranging and all-consuming, and he was interested in directing, production, set design, and all the technicalities of acting. His season of Shakespeare plays at the Old Vic, where Beth saw him play, was generally well received, with critics saying that he was one to watch, and theatrical magazines beginning to print photos and profiles of the slim young actor. Gielgud's performance made a big impression on Beth.

In her will, Beth asked for some of her possessions to be donated to Inverness Library and Museum. Included in this was 'the original script of *Richard of Bordeaux*' – but in fact, what was given to the museum was not only the script, but all her notes, giving a fairly comprehensive overview of the entire creative process that went into the writing of her most famous play.[15] During her lifetime, after the play was produced, Beth had stored these documents in a safe deposit at the North of Scotland bank, at the Eastgate in Inverness, and she obviously felt they were important documents, worthy of being securely stored and later seen by the public.

After Gielgud's portrayal of *Hamlet* had sparked her interest, Beth looked out for other information about the young actor and the season of plays he was involved in at the Old Vic. One of his next performances was in *Richard II*. Beth had already studied this period of history at school, so knew a little bit about it, and the popularity of Gielgud's Old Vic season meant that there were other people interested as well. In Inverness Museum's collection, newspaper clippings from the *Daily Express*, dated 11th March 1931, give an idea of where the original research for what was to become *Richard of Bordeaux* began. Reacting to Gielgud's portrayal of the Shakespearian king, the articles focus on the real life of Richard and his queens, Anne and Isabella. The focus on Richard's domestic life gave a new dimension to his character and sparked further interest for Beth. Back in Inverness and unable to see Gielgud's London performances as Richard II, she tried to imagine how he might portray this king. Interested in the discrepancies between Shakespeare's account and the historical reality, Beth began to reimagine Richard, and started to write her own play.

In some ways it is significant that Beth saw Gielgud as Hamlet, not Shakespeare's Richard II. In *Richard of Bordeaux*, Richard is very definitely the romantic hero, whereas in *Richard II*, Richard is sometimes an ambiguous figure. In the recent 2012 BBC production of *The Hollow Crown* series of Shakespeare history plays, for example, Ben Whishaw played Richard as a slightly camp, delicate figure – standing in contrast to the future Henry IV. The history of the play is bound up in Shakespeare and his contemporaries' understanding of the outcome for the Tudors in the Wars of the Roses. It is a very English play, with the speeches about English men, English soil, and 'this sceptred isle' – but this was lost on Scot Elizabeth MacKintosh, who sees only the man, Richard, and his relationship with his queen. She was more interested in historical fact than English national propaganda. *Richard of Bordeaux* was a reaction to what was happening in the cultural world around her, but, like all her work, it came out of her own reactions to it: she took her own tangent and her own original thoughts. That is what makes her work simultaneously universally appealing and unique. It is the root of what sets her apart from both the London-based literary scene, and the Scottish literary scene, and the root of what created the image of her as an enigma. She wanted to be part of the London theatrical world, but, up in Inverness, she was isolated from it. To take part, she would have to do it in her own way.

One of the reasons that *Richard of Bordeaux* was such a success, and struck such a chord with its audience, was that they read into the historical play parallels with their modern-day problems, and responded to the themes of war and appeasement. Although it might seem that Beth was more isolated from the centres of power by living in the Highlands, this ignores the fact that the north of Scotland was the base for much of the British army, and Beth's awareness of the politics of the day must have been heightened by the fact that she was coincidentally in Invergordon on the day of the Invergordon Mutiny, one of the major post-war incidents in Britain.[16]

In September 1931, the British government was attempting to deal with the Depression by reducing public spending. One of the ways they tried to do this was by reducing military pay. The cut in pay, in real terms, worked out at something between 10 per cent and one-quarter of sailors' pay packets, much more than the reductions in other public servants' wages. Those earning the least were the most affected. Just north of Inverness, at Invergordon, there were about a dozen fully staffed warships. Beth often escaped Colin and her housekeeping duties to take day trips on the train from Inverness, and in mid-September 1931, at the time she was writing the first drafts of *Richard of Bordeaux*, she decided to visit Invergordon. The sailors there had been hearing rumours about the pay cuts, which suggested they would be even worse than they were, and they were disbelieving when their senior officers tried to explain, particularly when these officers had to admit that it was true that some people really would be losing 25 per cent of their next salary. The men believed that the news had been held back until they were far away from home and so would not have the support of friends and family to protest. A crowd of people met in the canteen to decide what to do, but so many tried to attend that it spilled out onto the navy football field. The sailors decided to refuse to carry out their duties, and mutinied. They remained in port, cheering, singing and shouting from one ship to another, and wouldn't go to sea.

Although the protests were well mannered and well founded, the British government was seriously worried. The Depression and post-war conditions were making life extremely difficult for a large number of people, and morale was very low. They were genuinely afraid of a Russian-style revolution, and now thousands of military personnel on armed warships were refusing to obey orders. The King was in Scotland at the time, and was placed under armed guard at Balmoral, while the government updated him on the situation by messages that were sent by private aeroplane as they were so afraid that the telephone exchanges were being manned by Bolshevists. One MP suggested the problem was so severe that it should be resolved by force, and that the rest of the army should be sent to open fire on the men in the boats in Invergordon.

In the event, the action ended peacefully after only a couple of days, though it was to have lasting consequences for many of the navy personnel involved. The government backed down and, although pay was reduced, it was cut by only 10 per cent. Beth was probably more aware of the situation from the papers than from her time in Invergordon on the day of the mutiny itself, but the effects of the mutiny were serious for the British economy, with widespread panic on the Stock Exchange, which ultimately meant that Britain had to withdraw from the Gold Standard. A General Election was held in 1931, with the Tories elected back to power, taking over from the Labour party and their National Government coalition which, it had been thought, had handled the Invergordon crisis badly.

Beth was not always happy in Inverness, and, after the modern-day setting of *The Expensive Halo*, with its potential to upset her family, she turned to the far-away history of *Richard of Bordeaux*. Her escapist, romantic description of politics which were removed from her audience's lives by several centuries, but which the modern language meant they could still identify with, was part of what made the play the success it was. All around them, the theatrical audience could see a political mess, which had led to one world war where all of them had lost loved ones, and they could see their government pursuing policies they did not agree with. *Richard of Bordeaux,* written by a woman who knew the value of escapism and reinvention, offered the audience something it desperately wanted – and changed everything for Elizabeth MacKintosh.

CHAPTER NINE

Richard of Bordeaux

Many years later, Beth wrote to a friend that in her diary she had written of a trip to London in the 1930s, 'The two things that gave me the greatest kick were Gielgud's Hamlet and the Camerons at Aldershot; but the Camerons had it'.[1] She added two exclamation marks for emphasis, but whatever nostalgic appeal the army regiment had for her, it was that trip to *Hamlet* that would change everything.

Richard of Bordeaux, written with Gielgud in mind after watching his Hamlet, was Elizabeth MacKintosh's breakthrough play. Published and performed under her chosen pseudonym of Gordon Daviot, it was a huge success, and the piece of writing for which she was best known in her lifetime. Her Josephine Tey mysteries have stood the test of time better than her Gordon Daviot plays, but *Richard of Bordeaux* was the game changer, the piece that brought her fame on London's West End, opened up doors and opportunities for her, brought her into contact with people who were to become her friends for life and shaped her future writing career. It also destroyed her anonymity, changing the way she wrote, affecting her personal relationships, and shaping how we see her reputation today.

The files in the Inverness Museum archive give a complete picture of how *Richard of Bordeaux* was written. After her interest had been sparked by Gielgud's London Shakespeare performances, and the newspaper publicity surrounding them, Beth scrawled out a basic outline of the different acts of her play as she first imagined it, in chronological order, carefully working out how old Richard would be in each Act. She then wrote a more formal essay, typewritten and then annotated by hand, sketching out the historical background to Richard's life, stating why she felt he was interesting – and misunderstood. 'No sovereign was ever so entirely the author of his own destruction,' she wrote.[2] *Richard of Bordeaux* was a romantic chronicle play, showing scenes from the king's life as he first fought for true control of his country, and then saw his beloved queen die and his power taken from him. Notes from other books show that Beth read widely on the historical background before starting to write her play, writing short biographies for many of the characters, such as De Vert. The museum collection also includes a hand-drawn map of the London of the period, as Beth visualized the scene.

There is not only a script of the finished play in the Museum, but three complete rough drafts, as well as a few loose scenes. As discussed, part of the reason *Richard of Bordeaux* was to become so successful was that Beth chose to write it in modern language, something which was relatively new in theatre at the time. Instead of the stately Shakespearian Richard, who spoke a language his audience had to work to understand, Beth's Richard spoke as her audience did. Historical phrases such as 'moony tire' (a pejorative description of one of Anne's elaborate headdresses, taken from the Bible) and descriptions of the extravagant fashions worn at the time occur in the newspaper articles Beth had read, and reoccur in the drafts of the play, but as she reworked it, the language became more and more like the speech patterns of the 1930s.[3] Beth also included short scenes throughout the play that featured Richard's subjects – the common people of the time, rather than royalty – people her audience could identify with. The drafts of the play show the care and attention Beth put into this, with scenes and stage directions changed and cut from one draft to the next, while her attention to the modern speech rhythms that made her play so accessible to audiences is highlighted in the colour coding she chose to use in one draft: all the speech is typed in red, while stage directions are in black. Dates and annotations are pencilled in, showing that Beth went back to her notes to confirm details before making changes to fit historical accuracy or to help the 'flow' of the play.

By late 1931 /early 1932 *Richard* was finished, and Beth sent it, via her agent Curtis Brown, direct to the actor who had inspired her: John Gielgud. Gielgud told the story many times of how he received the script, and always acknowledged the debt he owed to Gordon Daviot, as he always called Beth.[4] As a rising star, Gielgud was receiving many scripts from people anxious to work with him, and he read *Richard of Bordeaux* backstage in the interval of another play he was working on. He liked it, but was concerned about some scenes which he found confusing, particularly the political discussions with a large number of characters. He wrote back to Gordon Daviot, suggesting a number of changes. In the meantime, he started work on another play which had been sent to him unsolicited: what was to become *Musical Chairs*.

At this stage in his career, Gielgud carefully read all the scripts that were sent to him. The story of *Musical Chairs*, produced just before *Richard of Bordeaux* shows both that it was possible for an author to have a script performed in the West End with no prior experience – and that it was extremely unlikely for that to happen to Gordon Daviot.[5] The script for *Musical Chairs* arrived in the same post as *Richard of Bordeaux*, but it came with a more personal covering letter. The playwright, Ronald A. Mackenzie, had been at prep school with John Gielgud. Gordon Daviot was writing under cover of her agent, but she had no links with the theatre world at all. After writing back to suggest the changes to *Richard of Bordeaux*, Gielgud forgot all about that play, and went on to produce *Musical Chairs*, backed by manager Bronson Albery, for a trial run of two performances at the Arts Theatre, starring Gielgud and directed by a Russian whom Gielgud admired greatly, Theodore Komisarjevsky. It was successful enough to then go on to a longer run at the Criterion Theatre in 1931.

While Gielgud was working on *Musical Chairs*, he received another letter from 'Gordon Daviot', but he did not meet the author and had no idea that it was a woman living in the Highlands. Although Gielgud had almost forgotten the play since sending back his criticisms, he was pleased and interested to read that the unknown author had taken all his comments into account, and had carefully altered and improved the play. He was flattered by the idea that the play had been written specially for him, and interested in reprising the role of Richard in a different way. Following on from the success of *Musical Chairs*, Gielgud was keen to repeat the experiment of staging a new play and decided to move forward with planning a production of *Richard of Bordeaux*.

Despite the similarities in the way the plays were picked up, the writer of *Musical Chairs*, the spiky Ronald Mackenzie, disliked *Richard of Bordeaux* intensely, according to Gielgud, finding it too romantic.[6] Mackenzie, a complicated character, showed great promise as a playwright, but never fulfilled his potential, as he was tragically killed in a car accident just after *Musical Chairs* finished its run.

Gielgud started work on *Richard of Bordeaux* while *Musical Chairs* was still running. Originally, he wanted to work again with the same director on both plays, but Komisarjevsky was abroad and declined. Gielgud decided to co-direct with Harcourt Williams, but they used the same backer as with *Musical Chairs*, Bronson Albery. With the backing in place, Gielgud then assembled the rest of his cast. For the other main part, Richard's Queen Anne, Gielgud wanted the actress Gwen Ffrangcon-Davies. Gwen was an established theatre actress with an excellent reputation, and she was to go on to become one of Gordon Daviot's dearest friends. Gwen had made her stage debut in 1911 at the age of twenty, working initially as a singer as well as an actress. Although she is not such a well-known name today as her near-contemporaries Gielgud and Laurence Olivier, in her day she was an extremely famous and well-respected theatre actress, known for her beauty, her commitment to her profession, her appealing personality and her moving acting. While I was researching this book, I read and heard many things about Gwen, and not one person had anything negative to say about her.[7] She was an absolutely charming woman, dedicated to her craft and generous to her friends. Gwen was particularly well known for her interpretation of Juliet, which she had played to great acclaim opposite Gielgud's Romeo. It had been one of John Gielgud's first major Shakespearian parts, and he had never forgotten the help and encouragement the older actress had given him – and he knew that the public had enjoyed their pairing and would want to see them play another romantic couple together.

The same attention was paid to casting each of the numerous parts in the play, and, for all of these decisions, Gielgud acted without the input of the playwright. 'Gordon Daviot' did not appear in the theatre or meet the actors until the dress rehearsal of the play, and many of the cast, including Gielgud, were initially surprised to discover that she was a woman. This decision on Gordon's part not to be involved in the minutiae of casting, rehearsing and backstage decisions wasn't necessarily typical for a playwright. Many other writers preferred to be intricately involved in every stage of the process, desperate to protect their vision and their words from any potential changes. By contrast, Gordon, although happy to work on her writing, did not feel her personal presence was necessary in the theatre every day. A playwright whom Gordon Daviot was to become friendly with, Dodie Smith, whose first play *Autumn Crocus* had opened in 1931 and was still running a year later, had, when she discovered her play was going to be staged, immediately asked for a sabbatical from her day job, and had been on set from the very first day, challenging the director, choosing the actors, directing their movements and explaining nuances to them, and vocally expressing her opinion at every opportunity.[8] Gordon Daviot's more back seat approach was very popular with her director and star, as it gave him creative control – and Gordon appeared to be very pleased with the results herself. She never changed her way of working: once a play was written, she always handed it over with the confidence that her writing was strong enough that her vision would come through any changes or interpretation that a director or actor might choose to make. Her experiences with her first play influenced this working method considerably, and, although this confidence was perhaps misplaced with some of her later plays, with *Richard of Bordeaux* it was eminently successful. Since she had written *Richard of Bordeaux* specifically with Gielgud in mind, he played it exactly as she wanted.

The completed play was staged for two nights at the Arts Theatre Club in London, on two consecutive Sundays in June 1931. These 'semi-staged' performances were a common test, to show backers how audiences and critics would react before the commitment of a longer run at a bigger theatre. The two test performances at the Arts Club were deemed successful enough for *Richard of Bordeaux* to be booked to play at the New Theatre in London from February 1933 onwards. The New Theatre was owned by Bronson Albery, who had backed the initial two test performances. Albery worked closely with Gielgud at this time, continuing the family tradition of supporting actors whose work could bring in audiences to their two theatres. The Wyndham-Albery theatre dynasty is still going today; Gordon Daviot was being backed by some of the best people in the business.[9] She was stepping effortlessly into the heart of theatre world.

Added to this background of respectable theatre royalty, Gielgud brought in a swathe of new talent. Gielgud decided that *Richard of Bordeaux* was going to be a Full Production, with stunning scenery, elaborate costumes and spectacular set pieces on stage. In addition to deciding to direct and produce the play himself – something he was not an expert on – and working with a script by a new and untested playwright, Gielgud also insisted on hiring new costume and set designers, his friends The Motleys. The whole production of *Richard of Bordeaux* was filled with new, untried and enthusiastic talent, backed up with established and seasoned actors, and playing in a well-respected theatre. It was to be a winning combination.

The new designers John Gielgud hired for *Richard of Bordeaux* contributed in no little way to its success. 'The Motleys' were three women: sisters Margaret and Sophia Harris, and their friend Elizabeth Montgomery, whom Gielgud had met in 1932 when he was involved in a production of *Romeo and Juliet* at Oxford University. The name 'Motley' came from a line in *As You Like It*: 'Motley's the only wear', and the women specialized in elaborate costumes, which was perfect for *Richard of Bordeaux*. The outlandish fashions of the day are frequently mentioned in the text of *Richard of Bordeaux* and play an important part in establishing the characters and their background. It is difficult to imagine the play being effective if it had to be done as a 'bare bones' text-only production, and it is not the sort of play that could easily be revived in modern dress – unless there were outlandish modern versions of, for example, Anne's enormous headgear.

John Gielgud came to the Motleys initially only for the Sunday performances at the Arts Club, with some vague ideas about making the costumes in bright, primary colours, inspired by heraldic designs. The Motleys drove a hard bargain, saying that they would only be involved if they could design both the costumes and the sets, and making sure that they would be involved if *Richard of Bordeaux* went on to a longer run. They also dismissed the idea of bright colours, presenting John instead with a design featuring very little colour: an oatmeal, white, gold, and dusty blue palette, based on medieval tapestries.[10] Gielgud loved it, and wrote enthusiastically to his leading lady Gwen Ffrangcon-Davies describing in detail the pale pink dress she would wear for her death scene, the colour co-ordination with the simple white background scenery, and his ideas for including a dramatic burning scene.[11] Gielgud was never short of ideas, and Gordon Daviot, who had not been deeply involved in previous decisions, but was now working more closely with Gielgud on rewrites of the play, was not the only person to find him exasperating and difficult to work with.[12] His continual new ideas could be difficult to assimilate into the normal routine of rehearsal. Gielgud wanted to include several tableaux scenes to show off the costumes and scenery, and only abandoned his idea of the scene with the burning down of Sheen Palace in a catastrophic dress rehearsal when the theatre nearly burnt down.[13]

He was persuaded to drop the tableaux as well, when it was found in rehearsal that they slowed the pace of the story. It was at this rehearsal that Gordon Daviot made an appearance, surprising the cast and finally making her voice heard – though only to support Gielgud in his decisions.[14] Gielgud had by this time dropped correspondence with Daviot's agent, and was communicating with her directly. They worked together on some adaptation of the script after the Arts Club performances. He was always impressed by her professionalism, and a real friendship was starting to build. However, he did struggle to completely understand this quietly spoken woman from the Highlands, who was so different to the theatrical women of his acquaintance.

Others, too, found Beth MacKintosh the Highlander a sharp contrast to the punchy, romantic writing of Gordon Daviot. Margaret Harris of the Motleys, always attuned to dress and appearance, remembered Gordon as a 'very tweedy lady, with brogues, you know. And a hat. I seem to remember she wore a hat all the time'. Gordon was, as ever, smartly dressed for her trips to London. Margaret Harris felt that '[s]he didn't sort of throw her weight about at all, she was very quiet and we didn't really get to know her at all'.[15] In common with most of the theatre people Beth was meeting, Margaret knew her only as 'Gordon Daviot' and wasn't sure what her real name was. Gordon Daviot didn't talk about where she came from, or her background, and Margaret was left with the impression that she had once been a history teacher, and could only marvel: 'She was a strange little austere lady who had written this very romantic play'. Although Gordon was becoming friendly with John Gielgud, her hands-off approach meant that she was initially a little estranged from others involved in *Richard of Bordeaux*. It was a surreal experience: Beth was, on the one hand, a successful playwright, but, on the other hand, very much still rooted in her Inverness life with Colin and not involved with the development of the play.

The rehearsals for *Richard of Bordeaux* did not always go smoothly.[16] Daviot and Gielgud altered a fair amount of dialogue and moved some scenes around, and there were a number of strong personalities among the actors. The long cast list included a number of well-known faces, not only Gwen Ffrangcon-Davies, but also established character actors such as Francis Lister, Richard Ainley and Donald Wolfit, and theatrical father and daughter Ben and Margaret Webster. The final dress rehearsal was a shambles. John Gielgud had almost lost his voice after all the shouting he had done in his capacity as director. There had been arguments amongst the cast. The Motleys were unhappy that Gielgud had sawed the top off one of their designs for the scenery, because he'd thought the audience in the gallery couldn't see him properly.

Theatre was hugely popular all over the country in the 1930s, with cinema, of course, still in its infancy. Gordon Daviot had shown in her writing that she was a huge fan of the London West End, with the knowledgeable and entertaining descriptions in *The Man in the Queue*. She would also have had plenty of opportunity to see both professional and amateur shows in Inverness. Touring productions came regularly to the town, and the amateur circuit was well established, with several companies. In schools, as a pupil and a teacher, Beth would have seen and been involved in productions, and students' recollections of Anstey College included memories of theatre.[17] The opening night for *Richard of Bordeaux*, however, was in a different league.

Opening nights for the theatre in the 1930s were big events. Red carpets, full evening dress of long gowns for ladies and black tie for men, and crowds outside watching to see which of the aristocracy would glide up in long cars. Some people made a point of attending as many first nights as possible. A few years earlier, when Fred Astaire and his sister Adele had made their London stage debut, Fred had noted that black tie was rare, as audiences were usually in the smarter 'white tie', with women wearing accessories like diamond tiaras.[18] Gielgud and his colleagues would have considered Astaire and his contemporaries like Tallulah Bankhead and Noel Coward to be the old guard – pre-cinema and not quite so serious – but the theatre retained much of their spirit. Astaire described the Gallery First Nighters, many of whom were still attending plays like *Richard of Bordeaux*, while producers like Binkie Beaumont, at one time part of Tallulah Bankhead's entourage and soon to follow Basil Dean as Dodie Smith's producer, provided yet more links with the glamorous 1920s theatre world. The New Theatre is now called the Noel Coward Theatre, and is still in business, retaining many of its original features. The Noel Coward, or New, backs onto the other Albery family theatre, the Wyndham, and they are connected by a linking corridor-bridge that runs above the alleyway between the two theatres. The narrow streets in the area are full of shops selling theatrical memorabilia and other specialist goods like second-hand books and plays, and dance wear. This is the heart of theatreland, with a feeling that any of the cafés in the area could be peopled with actors and backstage staff taking a break from rehearsals. During the day, people queue at the box office to try and get last-minute tickets and returns for sell-out shows, and boards outside advertise the performances, with the actors', writers' and producers' names in lights. The audience arrives early, crowding into the foyer as uniformed attendants stand in front of the doors to the auditorium, and making their way upstairs to one of the theatre's bars. Champagne sits in ice buckets on tables, as well-dressed people meet friends and covertly glance in the large mirrors around the edges of the room to see who else is there. The theatre is still decorated as it was in the twentieth century, with photos of all the famous performances decorating the stairs down to the stalls. Two photos of Gwen and John, posing under the Motley's simple archway scenery, are among them.

Gordon Daviot attended her own opening night. The audience watched attentively during the performance, and, at the end, clapped enthusiastically. There were good comments flying around. Gordon went backstage and congratulated John, and then left. The actors, more used to the slow pace of backstage, waited, receiving flowers and telegrams of congratulations, and speaking to the newspapermen who wanted to know more about the play. A first night party was given by Dame May Whitty, whose husband and daughter were both in the play – Ben Webster was playing John of Gaunt, while Margaret Webster had small parts.[19] It's not clear whether the retiring Gordon Daviot was at this party. Cast members did remember the petite, unknown author making a short speech to the assembled company on the opening night, but this was probably at the theatre. May Whitty and Ben Webster's parties were more informal, almost a theatrical drop-in where people were always welcome. Gordon was to become friendly with May and Ben's daughter Margaret, but this friendship, as with Gordon's other relationships in theatrical circles, took a little while to develop.

———

After the first night, there was the tradition of sitting up to wait for the first editions of the newspapers, to read the reviews. These were universally good, but there was still a somewhat muted feel. Gwen Ffrangcon-Davies wrote a long letter to her mother after the first night, saying that booking was good and they were hoping for a reasonable run, but she was more interested in the idea that *Richard of Bordeaux* might encourage Bronson Albery to put on some Shakespeare for her and John Gielgud later, and concentrated on telling her mother about a conversation she had had with playwright John van Druten at May Whitty's party, where van Druten had said he hoped Gwen would be in one of his plays.[20]

When John Gielgud went back to the theatre the next day, he discovered that box office takings were only £77.[21] The first night had also clashed with a major ballet opening, so some of the respected critics had attended that instead. However, *Richard of Bordeaux* turned out to be a play that did not need positive critical reviews in order to succeed. The morning after it opened was the first indication that something special was about to happen. The box office had been so quiet that the manager gave permission for his assistant to head out for an extended lunch break. The manager carried on with his work, but suddenly became aware that a long queue was forming, right out from the theatre doors, across the street, and down St Martin's Lane. *The Man in the Queue* had given a picture of London theatreland from the point of view of the audience: 'No one moved away from the long line. Those who were doomed to stand for three hours more seemed indifferent to their martyrdom. [...] who would not stand, and be pleased to?'[22] These descriptions of the long queue of punters waiting to get in to see the smash hit play of the season match almost exactly Gielgud's later descriptions of people queuing to get into *Richard of Bordeaux*. Gordon Daviot's fiction had become a reality. The cast of *Richard of Bordeaux*, waiting to go on stage, had to wait an extra fifteen minutes before the curtain finally went up, to allow the unexpectedly large audience to have time to take their seats.

Richard of Bordeaux became a massive popular hit, with

audience numbers growing through word-of-mouth. The Old Vic audience played a large part in that. In her letter written after the first night, Gwen mentioned to her mother that 'all the old Vic enthusiasts were there in full force and have announced their intention of coming every Saturday during the run'.²³ The Old Vic regulars were thrilled to see their actor, John Gielgud, play a Shakespearean king – but in modern language. They loved the pairing with Gwen Ffrangcon-Davies, and the memories it brought back of their pairing as Romeo and Juliet. They were enthralled by the story of the doomed love affair, and the scenes with the interjections from 'commoners' were perfectly judged to capture their imagination. Their enthusiasm was contagious. People returned over and over again to watch the play, up to thirty or forty times. The anticipation in the audience before favourite lines was palpable. Richard II's emblem, a white hart, was sewn onto handkerchiefs, drawn on postcards, and gifted to Gielgud in every possible way. Dolls were produced of the main characters, wearing reproductions of the beautiful Motley costumes. The Motleys started to take orders from ladies anxious to have evening dresses modelled on the clothes Gwen wore in the play. John Gielgud was interviewed and photographed and painted and followed home by fans. He lived in St Martin's Lane, right by the theatre, and was totally immersed in *Richard of Bordeaux* for the whole of its run. *Richard of Bordeaux* ran for over a year before touring regionally for six further weeks and transferring to Broadway in New York. With fourteen months and 472 performances, *Richard of Bordeaux* was seen by something like 400,000 people in London alone. It made a star out of John Gielgud, and was the turning-point of his career as well as Gordon Daviot's. They were both stars – if they wanted to be.

When it became obvious that *Richard of Bordeaux* was going to be a hit, there was huge interest in the identity of the unknown author 'Gordon Daviot'. As mentioned, a few years earlier, Dodie Smith had written *Autumn Crocus*. Similarly, this was her first play, and it also went on to be hugely successful. Dodie had come from 'nowhere' (really from a failed career as an actress and from a background steeped in the theatre, but, as far as the public were concerned she was an unknown) and the papers absolutely delighted in telling her story – as Dodie delighted in finally getting the recognition she thought she deserved. Headlines screamed 'Shopgirl Writes Play'; Dodie's photograph was everywhere; and journalists fought to interview her.[24] Dodie's chosen gender-neutral pen-name of C. L. Anthony didn't last, and soon the name in lights above theatres was 'Dodie Smith'. In some ways, Dodie's career is a template for what Gordon Daviot's could have been – but Gordon chose to go a different way.

John Gielgud said, many years later, that Gordon deliberately avoided the press.[25] She certainly did not give interviews after the launch of *Richard of Bordeaux* in the way that Dodie Smith did after the launch of *Autumn Crocus*, but the biggest difference was that Gordon was not resident in London. The press and photographers could not show up at her place of work, as they did with Dodie, because Gordon was already heading back to Inverness. For the London press, this seemed very strange, and increased what they thought was a mystery.

A popular impression has persisted that Gordon Daviot was hounded by the press, and that, horrified, she backed away from all interviews, trying desperately to preserve her anonymity. The reality is perhaps a little different. There was no tabloid-style exposé – 'Former PE Teacher Writes Play'; in fact Gordon Daviot's identity was already an open secret, 'revealed' several times. Articles had already appeared after the publication of her first novels, from as early as 1931, and, after the initial two showings of *Richard of Bordeaux*, the *Glasgow Herald* printed a short article, on 24th January 1933, explaining that 'Gordon Daviot' was in fact a woman – which the *Herald* should certainly have known, since Gordon had been writing for them. *Richard of Bordeaux* opened for its full run a couple of weeks later on 2nd February, and interest in the identity of the author grew from that point on, but there was certainly none of the paparazzi-style attention we would understand as part of press harassment today. In July 1933, Gordon was even happy to write and give biographical details for one short piece in a Scottish writers' newsletter – though details she gave were brief and slightly inaccurate.[26] Even though Gordon's identity became fairly well known through press reports just after *Richard of Bordeaux* opened, newspapers were still able to run 'exclusive' reports on her identity over a year later – particularly in America, where her identity was 'revealed' once more in the *Boston Globe* of 17th January 1934.

However, the success of *Richard of Bordeaux* was much greater than she had expected or prepared for, and there's no doubt that Gordon did not go out of her way to look for publicity. She was a genuinely modest person. She may, in fact, have found the constant 'reveals' more trying than one big story would have been. She might have done herself a favour if she had granted one interview to one newspaper, as that way she could have controlled her image, and presented more of what she wanted, while also satisfying the public demand for information.

There was another factor at work. Gordon was still considering the impact of her novel *The Expensive Halo*. This novel had potentially adversely affected family relationships, particularly with her father, because of her portrayal of characters who were too close to her family, and made Gordon more wary of promoting herself and her work. The *Inverness Courier* had been following the progress of *Richard of Bordeaux* since its first trial performances in 1932, running articles about 'the daughter of a well-known Inverness businessman'. 'Inverness has reason to be proud of a new playwright', they wrote, quoting 'Eulogies by London Critics'.[27] There was no direct quote from Gordon Daviot herself, and a slight hint began to creep into the articles that Gordon Daviot wasn't playing the game. She wouldn't even give quotes to the local paper and she wasn't acting like 'our local author'.

There was one other major factor that made Beth shy of courting publicity. Gordon Daviot suffered further when London newspapers not only revealed her identity, but also published reports saying that she was being sued for plagiarism by Gillian Oliver, author of a 1930s novel about Richard II called *The Broomscod Collar*.[28] Daviot's working methods and research are clearly shown by the materials held in Inverness Museum, but, at the time, she was an unknown author, and her relative anonymity made it easy for other people to make claims that, to an outsider, seemed to have some justification. The case was arbitrated by a Professor Oman, who came to the conclusion that the two texts showed similarities because both writers had done their research in the same places, both going back to original documents in the British Museum, but Gordon found the accusations extremely upsetting, and chose to settle with the complainant rather than put up with the publicity associated with defending her work in court. Gordon did not discuss the accusations publicly, and information about the case was hard to come by.

No further accusations were levelled at any of her future work, and her long writing career in itself shows that Beth was a talented writer who did not steal ideas. A treatment of Richard II's life was not a new thing – it was a Shakespeare play, after all – and other authors had written about him. These accusations of plagiarism were unfounded, but they did not help Beth's attitude towards publicity and the press, and encouraged her to hide behind pseudonyms.

CHAPTER TEN

The Laughing Woman

In some ways, Beth had split into two people, living two entirely separate lives. In Inverness, she got up, looked after Colin, sat at her kitchen table and wrote out the ideas for two new plays. In London, Gordon Daviot was fêted by the press. '*Richard of Bordeaux* was an achievement for the stage', said the *News Chronicle*, greeted by the audience 'with a glorious full-throated roar such as the West-end seldom hears in these sophisticated days' (*Daily Telegraph*); 'Vigorous in movement; in its dialogue, modern but without anachronistic flourishes; and in its search of human nature, watchful and diligent' (*The Times*); a 'really fine piece of work' (*Sunday Times*) and the answer to people who said that cinema was killing the stage (*Sunday Observer*).[1] It was watched and praised by theatre luminaries such as Ivor Novello, politicians like Stanley Baldwin (then part of the National Government), and finally had its own royal performance, in front of King George and Queen Mary.[2] An amusing short story, found among Gordon Daviot's family papers but possibly never published, gives a flavour of Gordon's own experiences, as it describes some fortune-hunters desperate to invite the new play-wright 'Alexander' to their party, only to be horrified to discover that 'Alexander' is a pen-name for a woman.[3]

The *Inverness Courier* collected the good reviews for *Richard of Bordeaux* together, but struggled to assimilate them with Inverness life.[4] 'Inverness is rapidly cultivating a dramatic sense,' the paper said, 'for not only are there seven entries from the town alone for this week's Dramatic Festival when last year there were none, but during the last few days there have appeared in all the most influential London papers, long and admiring criticisms of a new play by an Inverness playwright'. It is a little unfair to criticize a local paper for being local, but the Inverness drama festival and London's West End are hardly comparable. The slightly antagonistic tone that the *Inverness Courier* begins to take towards Daviot, which sometimes seems to be reflected in Invernessians' attitude to her today, starts to be visible in this article, as it continues by expressing a wish that Daviot 'will now turn her attention to some of our own historical personages, and make them live before our eyes in as wonderful a manner as she has succeeded in doing for the English King': the paper comes across parochial on a Scottish scale as well as an Invernessian one. Daviot was interested in Scottish and local history, as works such as her biography of Claverhouse, and play about Duncan Forbes (in *Leith Sands*) show, but there began to be an air of resentment that she did not use her fame to promote Inverness and Scotland, something that may be linked to Daviot's refusal to back the Scottish National movement.

The arts scene in Inverness was strongly linked to both the Gaelic revival, as Mairi MacDonald's writing shows, and the rise of Scottish nationalism, as personified by Neil Gunn. Mairi MacDonald herself believed that *Richard of Bordeaux* was a turning-point in Beth's relationship with Inverness – she thought that Beth was aggrieved because she was fêted in London but ignored at home.[5] Mairi's own explanation for this was that Inverness was such a religious place that it could not support a playwright, but, while there may have been an element of truth in the idea that some northern churchgoers did not approve of the theatre, Mairi's hypothesis is not borne out: local papers regularly talked about the theatre, and Inverness had no problem supporting male or Gaelic writers. Perhaps Inverness simply did not know how to respond to Beth as a success. While a visiting London playwright would have been celebrated, a playwright who was a fruiterer's daughter whom they all knew was a confusing social situation. Mairi, an untravelled Highland writer, was pleased with her achievements in getting articles into the *Scots Magazine*. She never really understood that Beth, who was about to consider whether Laurence Olivier was good enough to be in her plays, was in a different league.

If Dodie Smith was the London exemplar of what Gordon Daviot's career could have been, Neil Gunn shows what Beth's Scottish writing life could have been.[6] By 1933 Gunn was an establishment figure in Inverness: a published, full-time writer, he had become formally involved in the Scottish National movement in 1929, when he had gone to a sparsely attended meeting at Inverness Town Hall led by speaker John MacCormick, and after the meeting, along with three other like-minded souls, had formed a local branch of the National Party of Scotland and started drumming up support. Over the next few months Gunn and his colleagues had recruited over 500 members and embarked on some serious fundraising. During the next few years, and over the course of hard campaigning for MacCormick in the General Election of 1931, they had managed to attract support in Inverness in the person of the town's former provost Sir Alexander MacEwen. MacEwen had published *The Thistle and the Rose*, his view of Scottish independence, in 1932, while Neil Gunn was pursuing his troubled friendship with C. M. Grieve (Hugh MacDiarmid) and working on his book *Sun Circle* (published 1933).

It is in this context that Highland reviews of *Richard of Bordeaux* have to be read. In London, journalists could not understand the Highlander Gordon Daviot, but in the north of Scotland Gordon Daviot did not fit the mould that was being created of what a Highland writer should be: she was not involved with the local community in the way Gunn was, not a friend of ex-provosts, not a nationalist, not writing in Gaelic (or Scots), and not writing about overtly 'Scottish' subjects. Gordon Daviot's phenomenal success did not lead to her being accepted into the local writing community. If anything, she was even more excluded. She had chosen a different route and had gained success on a British stage without engaging with the Scottish arts community. She was not in the least interested in becoming part of Gunn's world, but this separation from both the writing scene where she lived and, by distance, from the artistic scene she could have fitted into more easily in London did have the effect of making her strangely isolated: an anomaly and mystery. This separation gave her the advantage of a different perspective, adding much to the originality of her work.

The poet T. S. Eliot visited Inverness in 1933 and stayed with Neil Gunn. Eliot was, as he saw it, visiting a far-away place with its own literary scene based on its own history and culture, and he was staying with one of his own Faber authors who exemplified that culture. It is unlikely Eliot was aware that the most successful London West End play of the moment had been written just a few minutes up the road from Gunn's house.

Gordon Daviot's work continued to be in demand. *The Man in the Queue* was translated into French and published as *Le Monogramme de Perles*. *Richard of Bordeaux* continued to play to full houses, and theatre producers in London were keen to have another Daviot play ready for production. Dodie Smith, like T. S. Eliot, was also holidaying in Scotland in 1933, and, as far as theatre producers were concerned, she was the sort of playwright they wanted. Like Gordon Daviot, she had come from 'nowhere', but she settled down to consistently write one high-quality, crowd-pleasing blockbuster after another. But Dodie was steeped in London theatre and craved the applause; she always considered the mass audience. Gordon Daviot was in Inverness, thinking about her writing and her reading and her own interests, and the next play that she submitted for consideration was very unlike *Richard of Bordeaux*.

In the same way that the settings of her published short stories had moved from Scotland down to England and France, Gordon Daviot's second play *The Laughing Woman* was also set in France and London. The published version of *The Laughing Woman* makes the source of Gordon Daviot's interest in the story clear at the outset in an author's note, stating that the play was 'suggested' by the life of sculptor Henri Gaudier and his partner Sophie Brzeska. Daviot had long had an interest in art, even considering art college when she left school, and her interest in and knowledge of French art and culture had been deepened by the trips she had made to the continent after the war, especially when her sister Jean was working there. *The Laughing Woman*'s subject matter is consistent with Daviot's rejection of Highland culture, and interest in a wider stage, and two influential biographies of Gaudier had not long been published. However, Henri Gaudier and Sophie Brzeska's relationship was something of a strange fit for Daviot, who worked best when she wrote of things she understood. She had proved she had a real feel for history in *Richard of Bordeaux*, and had handled the contemporary scene adequately in *Kif*, but she doesn't seem to have fully grasped the reality of the Gaudier/Brzeska relationship.

In real life, Henri Gaudier was a sculptor, and Sophie Brzeska his Polish muse, who gave up her own dreams of becoming a writer to live with and support Henri in England. They had a rather twisted and controlling relationship, which was also the subject of a 1972 film by the English film-maker Ken Russell. Ken Russell is best known for *Women in Love* and *The Devils,* and his film-making had a flamboyant and sexualized style. He is a particularly unlikely bedfellow, as it were, for Gordon Daviot. *The Laughing Woman* is an attempt to understand why a woman would give up her own creative dreams for a man, but with the sex and mental illness of Gaudier and Brzeska's relationship taken out it is a sanitized, intellectual version of a melodramatic love affair. Daviot does make it clear in the introductory note to the play that she did not want to write an entirely truthful depiction of the relationship, but in leaving out what later interpreters of the Gaudier-Brzeska story would see as the crucial points, she is left with a story with a large plot hole. Daviot's 'Ingrid' and 'Rene' are not suffering repressed sexual tension – instead Ingrid is stifled in her creativity because, as a woman, she is forced into housekeeping to keep Rene's artistic dreams alive. *The Times* reviewer thought this was a fair point: 'the play contains a more intelligent and persuasive study of an artist than is at all common on the stage'[7] – but it certainly doesn't make its artists likeable or attractive, and it makes the play an interesting character study – but not a dramatic night out for the audience.

Having chosen the basis for her story, and decided not to stick to it too closely, Daviot then made a couple of other dubious choices for *The Laughing Woman*. The first was the structure of the play. While *Richard of Bordeaux* had its particularly effective opening and crowd scenes breaking up its structure and pacing the story, *The Laughing Woman* takes its smaller set of main characters through events in a linear fashion, with pacing that slowed to the pedestrian. Daviot's habit of writing scenes that explored character development rather than showed action could detract from the drama – it was a characteristic that reviewers began to notice. To a certain extent, *Richard of Bordeaux* did this too, but, as part of its charm was its historical sweep and the way it covered a large period of time, it worked better in that play.

However, the strangest and most challenging choice in writing *The Laughing Woman* was for Daviot to choose for her main protagonists two non-English speakers. One of *Richard of Bordeaux*'s main attractions had been the language; the way that a medieval king was rendered understandable and attractive by speaking in modern English. Daviot had clearly thought about the way she would represent 'foreign' English, taking the time to change the real-life Sophie, who was Polish, into the Swedish Ingrid. Beth MacKintosh had experience of speaking to Swedish women through her gymnastic training at Anstey. A keen observer of others, Beth was well aware of the differences in speech of a native speaker and a Swede speaking English, and perhaps felt she had a better grasp of this than of a Polish accent. Her time in France, particularly when her sister Jean was living there, would have accustomed her to French-accented and influenced English. But the fact remains that her main male character was French and her main female character was Swedish, and at no time could they speak to each other in their native tongue, while at all times they had to speak to the audience in a third language. There are a few lines in French in the play, but essentially Daviot was asking her two main actors to maintain foreign accents all the way through the play, and asking her audience to listen, not to carefully structured and attractive English, but to a representation of how foreign people speak English, an extraordinary demand for a play-going audience. Rene at times becomes a caricature – he speaks and behaves how an English person thinks a French person speaks and behaves. It is a masterclass in 'writing Foreigners': you string a bunch of fairly simple words together in a long sentence (because of course foreigners don't construct sentences correctly), then you add in some funny noises (especially if they're French) and make sure you never use contractions (are not instead of aren't) and finally make sure to phrase your questions oddly:

> RENE What has that to do with it? I'm me. I could have murdered the men who sat next to you. If you had been kind to them I should have died. But you are very cold. You smile and are pleasant and they all hope and then poof! That is all. You are not interested in men?[8]

In fact, Daviot's leading man was to struggle with the accent so much that he eventually dropped it altogether.[9]

The Laughing Woman has some affecting moments, as well as amusing scenes where artists and critics clash over the meaning of art as opposed to the business and selling of art. The play ends with the outbreak of the First World War, which shows Daviot's continuing preoccupation with this theme, while her interest in class consciousness is also clearly shown from the standpoint of the foreigners looking in at English mealtimes. And as a meditation on creativity it shows how Gordon Daviot understood that, for women, caring for men and running the day-to-day household routine could be death to productivity. It's hard not to relate this to Beth, caring in Inverness for Colin, but frustrated at not being able to take up all the opportunities that *Richard of Bordeaux* was offering her in London.

Richard of Bordeaux continued its run throughout 1933, and had made a matinee idol out of John Gielgud. He was followed by fans, photographed for the covers of magazines, and praised by critics and theatregoers. It was essentially his biggest career moment, and he always acknowledged this: 'if the fans had their way,' he said, 'I would have gone on being Richard for the rest of my life [...] it was to the brilliant inspiration and sympathy of

Gordon Daviot that I owed the biggest personal success of my career'.[10] John and Gordon kept up a friendly correspondence, though *Richard of Bordeaux* could run now without any more input from its author. The playwright has a strange disassociation from the cast of a play: responsible for their jobs, yet no longer needed. Making only occasional trips to London, it was only the very long run of *Richard of Bordeaux* that enabled Gordon to make friends among the cast.

Gordon greatly admired the acting of her leading lady Gwen Ffrangcon-Davies, and was drawn to her charming personality. In the Gwen Ffrangcon-Davies archive there are a number of letters between the two women, with the first surviving one from Christmas 1933, when Gwen had been playing in *Richard of Bordeaux* for almost a year. 'Anne, my dear, how lovely of you!' Beth writes, using her character's name, to thank Gwen for a Christmas gift.[11] She signed herself 'Gordon', and sent Gwen some hyacinths in return. One of Gordon's prized possessions was a cushion made for her out of scraps of material from every costume featured in *Richard of Bordeaux*, a lovely idea and a present from Gwen and the other cast members that shows how highly Gordon was regarded.[12] After the Christmas letter there are some fragmented letters, and then, after some face-to-face visits, the correspondence grows in length and detail, and starts to include Marda Vanne, Gwen's partner.[13]

Gwen herself, in an interview filmed near the end of her long life, remembered that Gordon had visited her backstage and spoken with her about her dream parts – the people Gwen would, as an actress, one day like to portray.[14] Gwen had said that she had always dreamt of playing Mary, Queen of Scots. Gordon said she didn't like Mary, and had always preferred Elizabeth of England. At this point in the story, Gwen rolled her eyes, and said that she'd then forgotten all about the conversation until Gordon showed up a few months later with the script of what was to become her third play, *Queen of Scots*.

Richard of Bordeaux showed no sign of ever running down, but, after over a year in the same parts, some of the actors, including John Gielgud, wanted to move on. John was sensible of just how perfect a part Richard was for him. On a rare day off he had slipped into the theatre to watch from the back and became enamoured with the part again, watching how his understudy essentially had to play Gielgud in order to reproduce the role. Now he wanted a new challenge.[15] *Richard of Bordeaux* finally finished its run at the New Theatre in April 1934. On the last day the police had to be called to keep back the crowd that surged to the stage door when John and Gwen tried to leave. The play then went on the road, touring regional theatres around Britain, with the male lead role taken by John's London understudy Glen Byam Shaw. The *Inverness Courier* reported that the rights to the play had also been sold in Europe, with productions planned in Prague, Vienna, Bucharest, Budapest and Warsaw.[16]

Almost simultaneous to *Richard of Bordeaux*'s regional tour was its production in America on Broadway, which opened on Valentine's Day 1934 at the Empire Theatre.[17] Richard was played by Dennis King who, like Gielgud, was also producer, while Gwen's part of Anne of Bohemia went to Margaret Vines.[18] Gordon Daviot was only involved in this production through her agent, who negotiated for her. It's worth comparing this again with playwright Dodie Smith, who was far more personally involved in her American negotiations. This was another opportunity for travel and networking that Gordon Daviot did not take up, because of her commitments in Inverness and her aversion to publicity.

The American run was not as successful as the London one, lasting only around a month on Broadway before touring regionally, but it still garnered exceptionally good reviews. The *Inverness Courier* of 1st June 1934 printed an extremely complimentary critique from the *Chicago Journal of Commerce*. Whether or not the *Inverness Courier* was parochial, and whether or not they resented Daviot not speaking to them directly, they were following her career assiduously and making sure all their readers knew of her success – Gordon Daviot was news. The Chicago tribute includes the lines: '*Richard of Bordeaux* is everything that *Richard II* isn't. I re-read Shakespeare's dull study of the man before I went [to see the play] [...] I liked the nerve of this Agnes MacKintosh [sic.]

who dared to follow the Bard and improve on his lesser effort.' There surely can't be greater praise for a playwright than to be compared to Shakespeare and come out on top.

Back in London, *The Laughing Woman* had directly followed *Richard of Bordeaux* at the New Theatre, starting on the 7th April 1934.[19] The producers, wanting to develop their star playwright, and appreciating that this was a very different play to *Richard of Bordeaux*, had cast it carefully. Gielgud had originally angled for the lead role, but eventually admitted it was not the part for him, allowing Stephen Haggard (great-nephew of the writer H. Rider Haggard) to take the part of Rene.[20] Most of the cast of *Richard of Bordeaux* were out on tour, and another new actor was engaged for the female lead, Veronica Turleigh.[21] Haggard and Turleigh did not have the same connection with their audience as Gielgud and Ffrangcon-Davies; both were minor actors, who never went on to dominate the stage, but they were well suited to the parts and there seems to have been a deliberate attempt to show Gordon Daviot as an intellectual playwright, not just the populist of *Richard of Bordeaux*. Haggard struggled with the French accent demanded of his part, but Veronica, in particular, appreciated the role, and she and the rest of the cast and crew remained friendly with Gordon Daviot, who was becoming more accustomed to the stage world and easier in her interactions with it.[22]

To a certain extent, the strategy of quiet difference worked, as the play was well received by the critics. Popular magazine *Theatre World* highly recommended it, although the *Glasgow Herald* noted that *The Laughing Woman* was 'essentially the author's rather than the actor's work'.[23] To audiences expecting some sort of sequel to *Richard of Bordeaux*, seeing a play by the same author and in the same theatre, *The Laughing Woman* appeared rather strange. Although, like *Richard of Bordeaux,* it was historical, it was set in the much more recent past, just before the Great War. And although, like *Richard of Bordeaux*, it had a relationship between a male and female character at its centre, the relationship between 'Rene' and 'Ingrid' is nothing like the romance between 'Richard' and 'Anne'. Gordon Daviot didn't write primarily to entertain, she wrote to understand the world. Her writing fits into a moral framework: how and why people deviate from it is her concern, throughout her plays and her Josephine Tey detective fiction. She focused on topics that interested her, and which fitted this personal quest for understanding. When considering *The Laughing Woman* in the context of all of Beth MacKintosh's work, and in the context of her life, it makes sense – but to the audience and critics in London, the fans of *Richard of Bordeaux,* it was a strange follow-up. It wasn't exactly a failure, but they weren't entirely sure how to take it.

Behind the scenes, Gordon Daviot was working closely with Gwen on developing the next play, *Queen of Scots*. Along with John Gielgud, Gwen Ffrangcon-Davies was being fêted by both audiences and the press for her role in *Richard*, profiled by magazines and followed by fans. *Richard of Bordeaux* had made her and John stars – and made them a lot of money. Both she and Gielgud earned enough to buy houses, country cottages outside London in the Essex countryside. There was a small area around the villages of Finchingfield and Stambourne which was becoming a sort of artists' colony, familiar to anyone who has read the Josephine Tey novel *To Love and Be Wise*. Playwright Dodie Smith had bought a picturesque country retreat in the area with the proceeds from her plays; Gielgud used his *Richard of Bordeaux* money to buy a house and garden, and Gwen and her partner Marda bought Tagley Cottage, a small white house in Stambourne that was to become a place of sanctuary and home comforts for all Gwen's friends, including Gordon Daviot.

On the 7th April 1934, when *The Laughing Woman* was about to open, Gordon Daviot sat for the studios of Sasha, a leading photographer of the London theatre in the 1920s and 30s. Specializing in formal portraits, Sasha was in great demand, a fiery and competitive celebrity photographer who would spend a long time posing his subjects in exactly the right light (he was particularly interested in technical aspects of lighting and invented the Sashalite, an early flash bulb), all the while shouting at his assistants, whom he ordered to press the button on the camera when he felt the time was exactly right. Gordon was thirty-seven years old when Sasha took her photo, but she looks very youthful. Her short, waved dark hair and her shirt and tie are the epitome of 1930s chic, and she seems carefully but not overly made-up. Her pearl earrings, a gift from her father Colin, and her checked shirt show up particularly well in one black and white image. Beth was always interested in fashion, and used her trips to London to buy new clothes. Mixing with the leading actresses of her generation meant that she was able to see new fashions displayed to their best advantage, and her financial position after *Richard of Bordeaux* meant that she could indulge her love of quality tailoring. In one of the photos, she is wearing a tweed jacket, a purchase made with her first big pay packet. Compared with the photos taken by Inverness photographer Andrew Paterson when *Kif* was first published, Sasha manages to invest Gordon Daviot with a certain aura. Paterson's photographs show Beth, the former schoolteacher – Sasha's photographs very definitely project the image of a Writer. Gordon posed for several photographs, which were used on the covers of some of her books, and which are the stock images still used today when she is referred to in newspapers. Unlike Sasha's glamorous images of actresses, though, Gordon is portraying a more serious face: she is a playwright, not an actress, and she looks thoughtfully and directly at the camera with only a hint of a smile. This is the mysterious Gordon Daviot, the 'Enigma' who was not understood either by her London friends or her Highland neighbours.

In an unposed snapshot, taken around the same time, we see another side of Gordon Daviot.[24] Taken on holiday, it shows Gordon with Gwen, Gwen's partner Marda Vanne, and their friend the actress Margaret (Peggy) Webster. Gordon is relaxed, smiling and happy with friends. Her dark hair is in the familiar style from the well-known Sasha portrait, and she is wearing a blouse with a pussy bow at the neck in a similar 1930s fashion. She is also wearing her glasses, which she always removed for official photos, but which she needed. She is smiling and looking directly at Gwen, while Gwen shields her eyes from the sun. Gwen is immaculately dressed, and looks as elegant as ever: every inch the leading lady. John Gielgud wrote that Gordon was devoted to

Gwen, and Gwen had welcomed Gordon into her circle of friends.

Gwen was a dedicated actress, and a committed Christian Scientist, who felt that she had a 'calling' to make the best of her talents.[25] She worked to the fullest of her abilities to further the arts and thus help others, and her consideration for other people and caring nature are frequently mentioned by contemporaries. She was also enormous fun, and existing biographical programmes about her, recorded in the 1980s, show a woman who could tell hours of entertaining stories about backstage life at the theatre. She had a youthful voice well into old age, and retained a sort of theatrical slang in her speech; a quick, clear 1930s way of speaking that seems very close to the way that Gordon Daviot wrote in her personal letters. To listen to Gwen Ffrangcon-Davies speaking is to get a real insight into how she and her contemporaries would have spoken to each other when Gordon first met them all: the speech rhythms are different, and of course different slang was used than today, but it is the speech of people who were well-educated and who worked with words every day. In many of her later interviews Gwen would astonish and impress her audience and interviewer by quoting from memory large speeches from *Romeo and Juliet*, or from other famous plays she had worked in. For Gordon, as a writer and playwright, Gwen's company was refreshing and stimulating, but simultaneously a place where she felt at home. Gwen's dedication to stagecraft must also have struck a chord with Elizabeth MacKintosh the trained gymnast, as Gwen was interested in understanding how the whole body worked on stage, particularly through the Delsarte method.[26] To watch Gwen walk across a stage or screen, even when she was in her 90s, was an education in balance and ease. Ffrangcon-Davies practised postural and movement exercises every day, took singing lessons, read widely and studied Shakespeare. She was dedicated to her craft, and it was not at drama school that she learnt how to be an actress but through her own personal wide-ranging studies and practice. This approach to personal improvement appealed to the self-taught Gordon Daviot: Daviot had not learnt to be a writer by going on a writing course, but had honed her craft by her own version of these daily exercises: reading (her work shows how literate she was) and writing (letters, poems and short stories, as well as her novels and plays). It was very enjoyable for Gordon to spend time with people like Gwen Ffrangcon-Davies – people who took their craft seriously and were willing to discuss it; who took Daviot's talent seriously (and for granted, as she had already demonstrated it through her successes); who developed their work through daily practice; who had creative jobs that did not involve going to work every day but working to deadlines and for set periods of time; who were conversant with popular culture and interested in the theatre, in writing, in ideas. It was a great contrast to the way in which Beth MacKintosh lived in Inverness.

One of the most important people in Gwen's circle of friends was her partner, the actress Marda Vanne. Later commentators on *Richard of Bordeaux* have emphasized the undercurrents of sexuality in the play; the relationship between John Gielgud as 'Richard' and his male friend 'Robert' – but any of these under-currents came directly from John himself, as lead actor and direc-tor.[27] In 1932, when Beth first met John, there was absolutely no discussion of Gielgud's homosexuality.[28] It was not something that could be discussed openly, and many of Beth's new acquaintances would not even have referred to it in private. It was completely unlike the entertainment scene of today, where actors can openly come out as gay, and Gordon Daviot had no knowledge of it at all. Similarly, she did not at first understand that Gwen Ffrangcon-Davies was anything other than close friends with Marda Vanne. Indeed, Gwen had previously had serious relationships with men, and both she and John Gielgud were very careful of their public images, with articles in theatre magazines promoting John's matinee idol status, and reinforcing Gwen's femininity. However, many of Gwen's circle of friends were either gay women, or sympathetic to lesbianism, including actress and director Peggy Webster, the artist and socialite Caroline (Lena) Ramsden, and writer and dedicated theatre fan Angela du Maurier. In their 30s, and members of the generation who had lived through the Great War, many of these women had taken a complex route in life to get to where they now were. They wanted to enjoy life to its full, not cutting themselves off from either love or a career. Gordon's letters to her friends show a careful, yet growing awareness of how things were: it was, she explained obliquely, 'something so foreign to my understanding that the chatter of Martians would be limpid sense by comparison'.[29] Gordon did not really understand it, but she had no real problem with it. The friendship of these talented, creative, driven women was far more important to her than any consideration of their sexuality. Gordon wanted to write, and wanted to work with Gwen as an actress. In the mid-1930s, it seemed that Gordon could have everything: she had found the elusive balance she wanted, could discharge her family responsibilities in Inverness, have time to write, and yet still manage to be a part of a literary and artistic world in London, communicating by letter to her friends, and making regular trips to see them. It was one of the happiest times of her life.

CHAPTER ELEVEN

Queen of Scots

When Gordon Daviot went to London, she usually stayed now in the Cowdray, a club for professional women in Cavendish Square.[1] It was not a club for writers or 'artistic' women – unlike Dodie Smith and Gwen Ffrangcon-Davies' beloved 'Three Arts Club' – and Gordon was actually a member because of her work as a VAD in hospitals – many other members were nurses. Gordon was pleased, however, to have a London address that she could use for business. *Richard of Bordeaux* had made Gordon a wealthy woman, and, unlike Gwen or John, she had no need to spend on property, since she was still living with Colin in Inverness. Gordon, like her father, was good with money and invested wisely; she wasn't a big spender, but did like to buy quality.[2] The Cowdray was a good base for her to meet people, and meant that she was in the centre of town, and able to come and go as she pleased, without relying on staying with her sister Moire, or any of her friends. Lena Ramsden remembered the pleasure she felt whenever Gordon Daviot called her up: Gordon didn't like to phone on the crackly line from Inverness, so Lena knew that whenever Gordon called she was in the Cowdray Club and ready to meet up and have some fun.[3]

Lena, like many of Gwen Ffrangcon-Davies's circle, was a passionate supporter of the arts, a regular theatregoer and friends with actresses like Martita Hunt, and writers like Angela du Maurier and Marguerite Steen. Lena's parties were legendary, both the ones that involved a lot of sitting around chatting and exchanging opinions, and the ones that got a little wilder: Lena did like a drink. The interwar years that Gordon had described in *The Expensive Halo* were full of parties: John Gielgud remembered an all-white party at the Motley's design workshop, where everyone dressed in white and the food was all white.[4] It's a little difficult to picture Beth, the daughter of Colin, fitting in entirely at these parties, but she was there. Lena remembered her as more comfortable watching from the sidelines, ready with a droll comment, rather than the centre of attention as many of the actresses were, but always a part of what was going on.[5]

Lena and Gordon began to develop a strong friendship, and Gordon made a trip with her to Manchester, Lena's home town, to see a repertory version of *The Laughing Woman*.[6] Bronson Albery, impresario and owner of the New Theatre, was very pleased with the performance: it was a financial success and he hoped that other rep versions would follow. Gordon was more interested in the idea of a touring version of the play, as had happened with *Richard of Bordeaux*, but she was now confident enough in her position as playwright to refer to 'the cautious Bronny' when describing this conversation to Gwen and Marda. Gordon was also more concerned with some of the details of the performance: both she and artist Lena had been horrified and amused by the actor's depiction of Rene's work as a sculptor: 'It sounds incredible, but apparently no one in all the Manchester Rep. had any idea how one worked in clay [...]. And then when Rene graduated to stone he appeared with a mallet the size of a tar-drum and whacked away cheerfully and continually all through two scenes. That finished us.' As usual though, Gordon was not involved in the production in any hands-on way, but used the rest of her time in Manchester to go to the races. Lena's father was Chairman of the Manchester Racecourse Company, and Lena was a huge fan of horse racing, as well as, at various times, an enthusiastic horse rider and racehorse owner. Although Gordon never placed a bet, while the rich Lena liked the thrill of winning and losing money, the two women found they enjoyed each other's company immensely, and Gordon had a standing invitation to Lena's flat in Primrose Hill in London.

In the 1930s, West End actresses could still afford to live near their theatres, and Gwen and Marda lived fairly nearby at Holly Place – an address that might sound familiar to keen Josephine Tey fans. Once Gwen and Marda had bought Tagley Cottage though, they started to persuade their London friends to make trips out to stay with them in the countryside. Lena described the long car journeys down what were still single-track roads, with Marda's yappy little dog Snuffles annoying everyone in the back of the car.[7] Gordon Daviot insisted on buying Gwen and Marda a tea set from Harrods for their new house – they had to choose it, and the saga of the purchase went on over several letters. Gordon began to write directly to Marda too, as well as Gwen.

In early summer 1934, Gordon went on holiday with Gwen, Marda, Lena, and their friend the actress Peggy Webster, to Portmeirion.[8] This planned village in Wales was a very popular holiday spot, visited by the likes of Noel Coward and Alfred Hitchcock, and is well known today for, among other things, being the set for the TV show *The Prisoner*. The run of *Queen of Scots* was about to start in June 1934, and the holiday was probably a last chance for Gwen to relax before playing her lead role, and a final opportunity to discuss the role with her playwright, Gordon. Peggy, who had had small roles in *Richard of Bordeaux*, was also in *Queen of Scots*, but had not long begun what was to be her main role: that of director. Peggy was to become one of the premier female directors, and the first woman to direct a major Shakespeare production on Broadway. In a way, Gordon Daviot had been responsible for her career too. During the run of *Richard of Bordeaux* Peggy's part had been too small to give her much creative scope, but too large for her to take on another part in a different play, so she had turned to directing as a new outlet for her interest in the stage.[9] Marda, a character actress, had a steady stream of fairly reliable jobs, while Lena was working seriously as an artist and sculptor. It was an astonishingly creative group of women, and the photo of Gordon relaxing with her friends on holiday is also a photo of some very powerful women in the arts world. In Beth's family archive, there are a number of other informal snaps of the holiday: Gwen in her printed cotton frocks, Gordon in her inevitable tweeds, Peggy in what looks like a leather jacket and gloves, Gordon in sunglasses, the three women all drinking, the sun shining in their eyes and their arms around each other.

It was a hot summer. *Queen of Scots* opened on the 8th June 1934 at the New Theatre. While *The Laughing Woman* was the play that was to show off Gordon's versatility to the critics, *Queen of Scots* from the start was meant to be a follow-up to *Richard of Bordeaux*, a star vehicle for Gwen, directed by Gielgud. It was written in the same way as *Richard of Bordeaux*, as a chronicle play moving through the story of Mary's life, with humorous inter-jections from 'common' people breaking up the royal story, and a central doomed romance between Mary and her third husband, Bothwell. The casting of Bothwell caused some problems when the original holder of the part, Ralph Richardson, left the play only a week before curtain-up, saying he felt he wasn't suited to the role.[10] He was also not finding Gielgud's direction helpful. A replacement was needed fast, and was found in the person of Laurence Olivier.

Like Gielgud when Gordon Daviot first met him, Olivier was at that time a promising young actor, but not yet a household name. Daviot was very grateful to him for taking on the role at such short notice, afterwards inscribing a copy of the published play for him:

> Dear Larry, I may forget how well you played Bothwell. I may even forget the blue doublet and how you looked in it! But I shall remember always the gallant way you took over the part, the way you worked at it in those last crowded days, and the peace and reassurance your coming brought us. Bless you! Gordon Daviot.[11]

Olivier was pleased to accept a role in such a prestigious play, which was an important stepping-stone for him in establishing himself as a leading man and gave him an early opportunity to meet and work with Gielgud. Gielgud and Olivier's styles and personalities are famously opposite, and Daviot and Olivier never developed such a close friendship or working relationship as

Daviot and Gielgud, though, as comments in *The Daughter of Time* show, Daviot continued to follow Olivier's career.

Other parts were easier to cast, with the important role of Mary's second husband Darnley going to Glen Byam Shaw, Gielgud's understudy in *Richard of Bordeaux*. Peggy Webster remembered that the rehearsals for *Queen of Scots* were particularly harmonious. She thought it was possibly the best cast of any play she ever worked on, before or since, with attention paid even to the casting of the smaller parts – Bothwell's manservant Paris was played by a young James Mason.[12] The only criticism over the final casting was that Laurence Olivier was too good-looking to play Bothwell – but this didn't hurt the play's publicity, as shots of Gwen in Olivier's arms were prominently displayed inside theatre magazines, while Gwen's image, in full make-up as Mary, was plastered over the front covers.[13]

The tragic story of Mary, Queen of Scots is well known, and Gordon Daviot's play began the action after the death of Mary's first husband, the French king, describing her arrival back in Scotland as a young woman, and then her disastrous marriage to Darnley. Gordon then chose to present Mary as falling in love with Bothwell, who was to become her third husband after Darnley was murdered, and the play ends as Mary flees Scotland into what was to be captivity in England.

Mary was Gwen's dream part. Gwen, with all her charm and grace, understood Mary's character, and could have played her perfectly; a tragic, romantic, beautiful woman whose story would have complemented Gwen's biggest success as the doomed Juliet Capulet. Unfortunately, Gordon Daviot could not fully sympathize with Mary, an emotional, Catholic woman, who lived her life trying to follow the good advice of others and failed miserably every time she took her destiny into her own hands. Gordon Daviot was the later biographer of the principled, Protestant Claverhouse, and, however unfortunate Claverhouse turned out to be, his was a very different sort of tragedy from Mary's. Mary was representative of a different sort of Scotland, and a different era of Scotland. Gordon Daviot tried to shape her play in such a way that it made the story acceptable to both herself and Gwen, and the two women researched the historical period avidly, but the audience is left with the strong impression from the beginning that Mary is unlikeable: we never really want her to succeed, and the driving force of the play is diluted.

It's hard to see whom Daviot does like in the sixteenth-century Scottish court: she could have chosen a character to sympathise with and built the play around them, but the commitment to historical truth that served her so well in *Richard of Bordeaux* or *The Daughter of Time* here leaves her unable to commit to any character completely. James Stewart, Earl of Moray, Mary's half-brother who became an extremely popular Regent after Mary abdicated, comes close to being a sympathetic character, but even he, in the stage notes, is described with reservations. The only character Gordon Daviot might have managed to build the play around successfully is Bothwell, Mary's third husband: Daviot herself was unhappy with the play, and admitted that she felt little sympathy with Mary. In later comments, she felt that it was her misunderstanding of the character of Bothwell which had caused some of the problem. If only Daviot had known more about the Protestant, principled Bothwell, he may well have become the sort of character who would have appealed and could have been written up well by her.

'If I had seen Bothwell's handwriting before I wrote *Queen of Scots*', said Daviot, 'I would have made him a very different man. The handwriting is a shock. Educated, clear-minded, constructive, controlled. The complete opposite of the man we have been led to believe in. More like Claverhouse's than anyone else I can think of. And the handwriting doesn't lie.'[14] Bothwell apologists often feel an affinity with Richard III apologists, and Beth MacKintosh gave Richard III his best chance yet at justice in *The Daughter of Time*. (Opinions of Bothwell vary wildly. Robert Gore-Brown wrote one of the best studies, whilst acknowledging the darker parts of his character, in his book *Lord Bothwell* – which was published around the time of Daviot's biography of Claverhouse, and in fact advertised on the dust jacket of *Claverhouse*.) Bothwell was played with great energy by Laurence Olivier, a style that probably didn't help Gordon Daviot reinterpret his character.

Jumping around on stage, Olivier broke his ankle and had to be replaced by his understudy.

Character was Daviot's great strength in writing, and with problems in her understanding of some of the roles, her other shortcomings, or idiosyncrasies, as a playwright began to stand out more. She preferred to emphasize dialogue, rather than action, but she made some strange choices about which events to show on stage. The murder of Mary's secretary Rizzio, for example, would appear to be a gift of a set-piece for a playwright. Mary was six months pregnant and, late at night, unable to sleep, was playing cards with Rizzio and some of her other servants in her room, lit by a blaze of candles, when a gang of armed men – all of whom were high-born noblemen and known to her and who were led by her husband Darnley – ran into the room. One of them held a pistol to Mary's pregnant belly while the others grabbed Rizzio, stabbed him more than fifty times then threw him down the stairs, leaving Darnley's knife ostentatiously sticking out of his back. Daviot shows us none of this on stage. Instead, she gives us a scene with two serving men, one French and one Scottish, who are teaching each other dance steps before becoming worried about the noise coming from the Queen's room. This is followed by a scene where Darnley tells a crowd of well-wishers outside the castle that there has been a bit of a disturbance because French and Scottish servants have had a disagreement, and yes, the Queen is all right. Daviot's scene with the serving men dancing is a subtle, humorous exploration of culture clash, but there is a feeling of missed opportunity.

John Gielgud thought that Gordon Daviot's refusal to include anything about the Casket Letters – supposed love letters from Mary to Bothwell – weakened the play, but I don't think they would have added anything, as the evidence in them is so discredited nowadays, with agreement that many of them were whole or partial forgeries.[15] However this adds to the consensus that there was something in Daviot's interpretation of Mary and her love life that was not working. Daviot just did not appreciate the charm of Mary Stuart, and saw the story as a tragedy that could have been avoided, not a doomed romance (romance either of a country or between people). The audience, waiting for a strong partnership such as Richard and Anne's in *Richard of Bordeaux,* were disappointed. Daviot herself, faced with a play that would have been a success by anyone's standards but her own, began to feel frustrated, and resented the interference with her vision by her producer and even her actors. Gordon finally recognized her lack of control in the rehearsal period of the play, and began to object to any more suggested changes.

Queen of Scots was not a failure – its cast was stellar, and it managed a respectable if unimpressive run of 106 performances, closing on 8th September 1934, three months after opening. It was reviewed well, and would probably have run for longer if it had not come up against one final hurdle in the weather. The summer that it opened was oppressively hot, and theatre audiences across the whole West End dwindled.[16] Even in the particularly cold, snowy March when I visited the New Theatre the inside got uncomfortably warm, and it is a fair excuse to say that the weather could be a factor in a play's success there.

It was a tricky moment for Gordon's new friendship with Gwen. Gwen was naturally disappointed with the failure of the play, but, as charming as ever, she did not hold it against Gordon, and moved on, as usual, to the next project. Her partner Marda Vanne, however, felt strongly that she should defend the gentle Gwen.

Marda was a complex, somewhat hard character: a determined actress, a foreigner in London and a divorcée whose attitude to relationships could be promiscuous.[17] Unlike Gwen, who had fallen into a same-sex relationship when she fell in love, and who remained loyal for the rest of her life, Marda was more open about her sexuality, and had a series of relationships with different women. Marda was born Margaretha van Hulsteyn in South Africa to titled Dutch parents, Sir Willem and Lady van Hulsteyn, and her national loyalty remained to South Africa, something which was to be important in the war years to come. She had wanted to be an actress since she was a child, and had established a solid career from an early age, but that career had been interrupted by an unsuccessful marriage, which lasted just under a year, to Johannes Gerhardus Strydom, a lawyer who later went into politics. Strydom became Prime Minister of South Africa in 1954 and was a prominent supporter of segregation, pursuing and implementing the policies that led to apartheid. Marda cut off all contact with him after their divorce, changing her name and moving to London in 1918, where she successfully restarted her life. Photographs of Marda from the 1920s show her posed in a variety of fashionable outfits, with a round, open face, and short dark hair.[18] She was always a character actress, and never achieved the level of fame that Gwen did, but she did appear on the cover of magazines, a fashionable if not trendsetting beauty, and worked continuously throughout her life.

Gordon wrote to Marda and Gwen equally as their friendship grew, and empathized with what she saw as Marda's 'difference' – but to Gordon, that difference came, not from Marda's sexuality, but from not being a Londoner, from not being from the same background as Gielgud, Olivier and her other acting colleagues. 'Do those South African words give you the same kick as Highland words used to give me?' Gordon wrote to Marda in December 1934, 'It's always an asset to be brought up in a "special" country – a country with marked peculiarities, I mean. One has the common inheritance plus something else.'[19] Marda and Gordon misunderstood each other. Gordon's letters to her are chatty and friendly. She was so pleased to be in with this group of creative women and finally able to write to equals about her writing, and, as she always did in her correspondence, she described her life, finding happiness in things like nature and the flowers in her garden. Marda and Gwen were keen gardeners, but they couldn't really understand that, for Gordon, in Inverness and far from the theatre, these simple pleasures were hugely important. Marda did not deny herself anything: she cut herself off from her South African family when she wanted, she took lovers even while in a relationship with Gwen, and she had no understanding of the sort of duty that had led Gordon away from the independent life she may have preferred, to look after Colin. Marda's attitude caused Gwen great pain, and began to be the source of trouble amongst Gordon's new group of friends.

Marda did not even understand the way that Gordon dressed. To Marda, tweeds were a secret sign of lesbianism, an embracing of a masculine way of dressing.[20] To Gordon, they represented Highland craftsmanship, old money and an artistic, yet classic Chanel-like fashion. Marda felt the 'failure' of *Queen of Scots* deeply, and continued to write about it in her voluminous diaries, some of which she began to write as a love-letter directly to Gordon. These diaries, not all of which were ever sent to Gordon, began around March 1935, and in April 1935 Marda spoke her mind about the play:

> You should have known better than to write Mary of Scotland for her out of some emotion other than your own enthusiasm. If your hatred for Mary had been robust you might have done a better job, but you merely disliked the woman, but there again your affection for Gwen marred your integrity as a playwright. You are not among those who can write to order. I wish you had left her [Gwen] her dream that a play could be written about Mary, and that she could play that tiresome, glamorous woman. Now that's gone, and her hope of playing Juliet ever again [John Gielgud had cast Peggy Ashcroft instead of Gwen in his new production], and the little creature feels like a shrivelled acorn.[21]

It's hard to imagine the talkative Gwen Ffrangcon-Davies as being 'like a shrivelled acorn', so much of this analysis must be attributed to Marda's own dramatic and extreme personality, but it gives a snapshot of the developing, intense emotions that Marda was feeling for Gwen and Gordon.

Gordon was oblivious at first to these developments, and her own letters to Marda and Gwen are full of a new project, one that these women were not involved in. She was moving from script-writing for theatre to scriptwriting for cinema. This important detour into the film world has not previously been written about in any analyses of Gordon's life.

The technology to produce talking films had been around for a few decades, but it was not until the late 1920s and early 30s that cinemas around the UK, outside the main towns as well as in London, were really equipped to handle sound. Once sound had arrived, it became a phenomenon. One of the reviews of *Richard of Bordeaux* had stated that this was the film to bring audiences back to the theatre, but the reality was that audiences were leaving theatres in droves.[22] Gordon Daviot loved theatre, but she also loved film. There were several cinemas in Inverness, and she developed a habit of going to the pictures at least a couple of times a week.[23]

The films that she saw were very diverse. One of the major discussions over the advent of sound film in the UK was how that would affect film that had previously been brought in from Europe.[24] Silent film had meant that films could be spread widely across Europe, with language no barrier, but now things were in a state of flux. Dubbed scripts were not as appealing to the general audience as the American films that were flooding in, and the British film industry – and the British government – felt that cinema was becoming too Americanized. This would, it was felt, not do. There was no certificate system, as there is now, and films were essentially either 'U' (Universal) or 'A' (Adult), and children were taken to see everything. The audience for film was overwhelmingly working class and there was a developing moral panic over what they should be allowed to see. It was felt that Britishness and a sense of Empire must be promoted – and the many British cinema jobs must be protected – and so a quota system was introduced: cinemas had to show a certain number of British films. This system had mixed success, providing opportunity for several real talents like Alfred Hitchcock, but it also led to the rise of the 'quota quickie' – fast-produced, low-budget British films. Gordon Daviot's first film wasn't exactly a quota quickie – it was higher quality than that – but it probably wouldn't have been made if it wasn't for the quota. Film-makers were actively looking for British scripts, and the theatre was the natural place to search for wordsmiths. Dodie Smith's breakthrough play, *Autumn Crocus*, was filmed and released in 1934 (with Dodie, as ever, involved in every stage, including a trip to film abroad on location), and Gordon Daviot, still a similar hot property in the West End, was an obvious follow-up.

Gordon's third novel, *The Expensive Halo*, had started life as a play script.[25] Unlike Dodie, Gordon did not get so involved in business decisions, and permission to sell film rights would probably have been dealt with by her agent, but, somehow, the script for *The Expensive Halo* ended up at Sound City. The sheer number of British films needed for the quota had meant new film studios had been built, and Sound City was one of these.[26] Set up by another Scot, Norman Louden, who had made his original fortune selling the hugely popular 'flicker books' of the early 1930s, Sound City was based at an old estate and mansion at Shepperton in Middlesex. He raised capital from people who wanted to become film-makers, and on the staff there were a few Cambridge graduates and some former naval officers. It was a bit like film-making for gentlemen amateurs, and the people working on the films stayed in the mansion house, giving it all a country house holiday atmosphere. Louden was a sharp businessman though, and moved Sound City from its early experiments with short films onto medium-length features. He never thought of himself as making 'quota quickies', but talked instead of 'modest second features', to be shown alongside other films, and which he sold to Americans so they could promote them with their own blockbusters in a complex way to circumvent the quota. Sound City also invested in good quality studios and equipment which they rented out to other companies, along with their location (the house exterior and surrounding land featured in all sorts of films).

The Expensive Halo was filmed in black and white by Sound City under the new title *Youthful Folly*. The 70-minute film was distributed by Columbia, first shown in October 1934, and on general release in December 1934. Copies no longer exist, but the cast list and brief synopsis show that many of the character names remain the same, and the bones of Gordon Daviot's novel is still there, though her original script was adapted by Heinrich Fraenkel, one of the many Germans who worked in the film industry and who had migrated to Britain in the wake of sound film, and European political changes. Norman Louden was the producer, and the director was Miles Mander, whose brother, a Liberal MP, was involved in many of the parliamentary discussions about quota rules. The cast included Irene Vanburgh, Mary Lawson and Jane Carr.

The film based on Dodie Smith's *Autumn Crocus* had been made in Britain, at Ealing Studios, with the British theatre director Basil Dean and British stars Ivor Novello and Fay Compton, but her other plays were optioned by American film studios, and the American cinema world was to be an important part of Dodie's later career.[27] The film rights for *Autumn Crocus* gave Dodie £1,500, but *Looking Forward*, based on her play *Service* and released in 1933, gave her £7,500 as it was made by American studio Metro-Goldwyn-Meyer. The part of Dodie's autobiography where she begins to discuss her success on stage and film is called *Look Back With Astonishment* – following on from *Look Back With Mixed Feelings*. In the 1930s, playwrights working for theatre had unparalleled opportunities to make money from their original theatre audiences, and to break into the new world of film, where the money was often astronomical – especially in Hollywood.

Most Hollywood studios in the 1930s, at the height of the studio system, had an in-house group of writers who would adapt or create material, but they were also keen to scout talent.[28] Many well-known writers, contemporary with Gordon Daviot, were equally keen to be involved, and some of the big names who worked for Hollywood included F. Scott Fitzgerald (who, of course, had been based in Paris in the 1920s, when Beth was visiting her sister there), and Aldous Huxley, who moved to Hollywood in the late 30s. London's West End was another obvious place to look for writing talent that would translate well to film. Hollywood wanted Gordon Daviot, and, in 1935, they got her. This aspect of her career has never been discussed in print, and she has never received the recognition for it she deserves. In 1935, Gordon Daviot was such a well-respected writer that Hollywood literally came north to Inverness to find her.

CHAPTER TWELVE

Hollywood and Josephine Tey

John Gielgud remembered Gordon Daviot as a keen cinemagoer who went to the pictures regularly, and often wrote to him discussing the acting and directing in the films she saw.[1] He thought one reason for this was that she had more opportunity, in Inverness, to see quality films than quality theatre. He didn't seem to realize, or remember, that her interest in film was the professional interest of a film scriptwriter. Gielgud himself was wary of the cinema, worried that his acting style might not transfer well onto screen.

Gwen Ffrangcon-Davies never made the transition from stage to screen. Her acting style, preserved, alongside Gielgud, in one small Pathé short advertising their version of *Romeo and Juliet*, harked back to a time when stage actors needed very dramatic gestures: the 'big' stage actions looked overdone and overwrought in a medium that could focus close-up.[2] Cinema also did not suit Gwen's short-sightedness, which over time gave her a slight cast in one eye, and she, along with many other serious Shakespearian stage actors, felt some snobbery about the popular and populist new medium.[3] Gordon Daviot wrote to Gwen and Marda about her work in film, but Gwen, like Gielgud, didn't ever mention in later interviews that Gordon had worked as a scriptwriter as well as a playwright, though she did remember the types of film Gordon used to watch and discuss: slick Hollywood movies, with Ginger Rogers a particular favourite.[4]

In January 1935 Gordon wrote to Marda: 'They have sent

me a book from America to make a scenario of'.[5] This was the beginning of her brief flirtation with Hollywood, an undeveloped aspect of her work; and one of the experiences that led to the creation of 'Josephine Tey'.

Gordon Daviot was signed by Universal Studios. *Richard of Bordeaux* and *The Laughing Woman* had attracted the studio's attention, and they were keen to secure this West End talent.[6] Universal is the second oldest US studio, and by the 1930s had firmly established itself with a wide range of films, including Oscar-winners like *All Quiet on the Western Front*, early animation from Walt Disney before he set up his own studio (*Oswald the Lucky Rabbit*) and horror movies like *Frankenstein* (with Boris Karloff) and *Dracula* (with Bela Lugosi).[7] In addition to their large studio complex in Los Angeles they had a European base in Germany – though Gordon Daviot's dealings were with Hollywood. Hollywood wanted her to write for them, and were not in the least bothered that she was based in the Scottish Highlands. As far as they were concerned, the UK was all a distance away, and, as long as she could occasionally come down to London for meetings, they were happy to receive and send work by post.

Universal's reputation did not overwhelm Gordon. She told Marda that she was not impressed with the book they wanted her to adapt: 'It is quite illiterate [...] I have a faint idea I'm not going to like making this scenario. In fact, I'm swithering. On the other hand if I say no to this one they may hand me over a Galsworthy, and Galsworthy would be God-awful!'[8] John Galsworthy, the author of *The Forsyte Saga*, had seen his book *Over the River* filmed by Universal in 1934. That film was notable for a rare sound appearance by the renowned stage actress Mrs Patrick Campbell, but Gordon Daviot was obviously not a fan. She was, however, very clear about the task she was undertaking, and the sort of film script Universal were expecting.

The book Gordon had been sent was *Next Time We Live*, by Ursula Parrott, a successful romantic novel which had first been serialized in the magazine *McCall's* from 1934–1935 under the title *Say Goodbye Again*.[9] The title was changed again for the film, to *Next Time We Love*, which was thought to be more romantic.

The plot concerned an actress who married a journalist: the couple love each other, but their careers keep getting in the way of their marriage and there are several enforced long absences, during which the husband's best friend falls in love with his friend's wife. Melodramatically, the story ends with the husband diagnosed with a terminal illness, but all is well because the couple reaffirm their love for each other. Gordon didn't think much of the plot.

> I wondered for a little why this particular style – so devoid of excitement or purple patches – should prove so successful with the mob, until I realised that it was the equivalent of the Over-the-back-fence tale between woman and woman. What 'They' did, and how many children They had, and who She was before She married, and how She managed on her income.

However, Gordon was keen to work in film, both because she was a film fan, and because she was well aware of the money and opportunities that could come from this line of work. A few years later, Dodie Smith was able to pay rent on her (very expensive) American house for months from the proceeds of two weeks' film writing.[10] In Gordon's usual observant way she took what she could from the book – and from the experience of a different type of writing – and worked up a script.

The lead female role in *Next Time We Love* was given to the well-known American actress Margaret Sullavan, and Sullavan convinced the studio that the person for her to play opposite was an untested leading man: a young actor called Jimmy Stewart. The chemistry between Sullavan and Stewart struck a chord with the audience, and they went on to star in several more films, including *The Shop Around the Corner*, while Stewart, of course, is probably best known to modern audiences for *It's a Wonderful Life*. *Next Time We Love* was a major motion picture with big names, a Universal Studios production, top Hollywood, at the height of the 1930s studio system, the Hollywood that has been mythologized in hundreds of films and books. When, a few years later, acclaimed Scottish playwright James Bridie made a trip to Hollywood just to have some meetings about the possibility of working on scripts this was considered newsworthy; it was reported in several different Scottish newspapers including the national paper the *Glasgow Herald*.[11] More recently, there has been a push to reclaim and proclaim the reputation of Aberdeenshire's Lorna Moon, who in a short but colourful career left her native Scotland, had three children, associated with Cecil B. DeMille – and worked as a screenwriter in 1920s Hollywood. Elizabeth MacKintosh managed to get Hollywood to come to her: she worked in film in its golden era, from her home in Inverness. Whether or not she enjoyed the experience, Beth recognized that what her Hollywood employers really wanted was good writing. She worked hard and got on with it, and she deserves credit for her achievements as a scriptwriter.

She was not alone, however. As a contract writer, she had to work with several other writers, and the script was soon found to be problematic.[12] Melville Baker is given the main credit on the final film, but shooting started before the script was even finalized, and, as Stewart and Sullavan's chemistry became clear, three other writers were brought in: Doris Anderson, Rose Franken and Preston Sturges. Baker, Anderson and Franken all had solid careers in scriptwriting and re-writing, but were never names to conjure with. Preston Sturges, on the other hand, was one of the first modern writer/directors to emerge in Hollywood – he was to become an Oscar-winning writer, who specialized in the witty, fast-paced screwball comedies of the 1930s and later worked with Howard Hughes.

Next Time We Love did not too badly at the box office and gained good reviews for its stars. It was adapted for American radio three times, in 1938, 1948 and 1951 – in the first adaptation, Margaret Sullavan reprised her screen role, whilst Jimmy Stewart did the same in the 1951 production.

The continued success of Preston Sturges, Jimmy Stewart, and the other people who collaborated on this film gives an intriguing glimpse of where Daviot's writing career could have taken her. Gordon's love of cinema didn't leave her after her short experience as a scriptwriter. Late in 1936 she was still pursuing her interest in film, spending a day visiting John Gielgud on the set of

Alfred Hitchcock's *Secret Agent*.[13] Gordon found the slow pace of on-set film-making and acting boring, though her love of films themselves was not diminished. After the Second World War, Gordon's friend Lena remembered that 'a large box of chocolates and a visit to the cinema embodied Gordon's idea of bliss. If the chocolates were from Barbellion and the star of the film Danny Kaye the bliss was transcended.'[14] Beth MacKintosh's family were convinced that, if she had lived, the next step in her writing career would have taken her back to writing for Hollywood.[15]

However, the collaborative part of scriptwriting was not something that Daviot enjoyed, and neither was it where her strengths lay. It was also logistically difficult, since she was still based in Inverness. If Gordon was to work again for Hollywood, or return to it later, she wanted to do so on her own terms. In later life, she had the possibility to do that with the plots of her hugely popular Josephine Tey novels, but in 1936 what the experience of *Next Time We Love* had given her was the idea for her next book, the first novel to be published in the UK under the name 'Josephine Tey'. *A Shilling for Candles* features Hollywood actresses and screenwriters, and a glimpse of the world that Beth was shown in *Next Time We Love* – and it was to take her back into the world of film when it was adapted by Alfred Hitchcock.

The mid-1930s was still the period when Gordon Daviot's career was in the ascendency. *Queen of Scots* had not been such a success as she hoped, but she was still in regular contact with her actress friends in London, regularly visiting them, and regularly receiving offers of work. A production of *Richard of Bordeaux* was now touring Australia, a new acting edition of the play was published, and she, or her agent, were receiving regular requests for permission to put on amateur productions of her plays.[16] She had written a new play, to be called *The Stars Bow Down*, and discussions concerning its casting were already underway. There were, however, some problems starting to arise. 1935 was the first year since 1929 when Gordon did not have a new play or novel out. 'I have had a grand year doing nothing', she wrote cheerfully to her old Anstey room-mate Marjorie Davidson.[17] It was not entirely true, as she was engaged in writing for Hollywood, but she felt no urgency to produce a new play. Her main aim wasn't to earn money, or to maintain her profile, or even to have another hit. Her distance from London gave her the freedom to write for herself, for the love of writing. However, another complication arose when her agent, David Higham, broke away from his employer, the large agency Curtis Brown, to set up on his own.[18] Gordon was happy to follow him and be part of his new agency, but Higham was, for now, specializing in literature. Over the next few years Gordon Daviot had to find different representation for her playwriting and her novels. This, along with the massive cast required, had an impact on the discussions surrounding her new play *The Stars Bow Down* – and helped her to return to crime fiction and the pen-name Josephine Tey.

Beth's experiences writing *Next Time We Love* had sparked *A Shilling for Candles*, a crime novel and sort-of sequel to *The Man in the Queue* – but the subject matter was very different from her 'serious' historical and literary plays and novels. She decided to have the novel published under the new pseudonym Josephine Tey, which she had probably first used or considered at the time of the publication of the US edition of *The Man in the Queue*. The name Josephine, of course, was taken from her mother, while she believed that Tey was the name of an English ancestor on her mother's side of the family. Having traced back Beth's family tree, I have not come across any ancestors called Tey – though, interestingly, there were some called 'Fry', and, in the old handwriting this was written in, it looked at first like 'Tey'. Perhaps Beth (or her storytelling mother or grandmother) had made a mistake with the name.[19] Beth herself said 'Tey' was the name of a Suffolk great-great grandmother, though, and the strong association with her mother – and with her favourite country, England – shows just how important Beth felt this strand of her writing was.

In 1936 *A Shilling for Candles* was published, a crime novel written by Josephine Tey and featuring an Inspector Alan Grant. Those with long memories might have remembered that Alan Grant had first featured in *The Man in the Queue* by Gordon Daviot, but no publicised connection was made with the previous book. Even in 1960, the Pan paperback edition of the book still had 'Inspector Grant's first case' emblazoned on its front cover. From now on 'Gordon Daviot' wrote plays, while 'Josephine Tey' wrote crime fiction novels. Much has been made of the distinction between the two names, but, rather than a conscious decision to separate her 'serious' and 'light' writing, the initial change may have had more than a little to do with the situation with her agent. The name 'Josephine Tey' had first shown up in that intriguing, undated note on her 1929 short story 'Deborah', so may have been in Beth's mind for some time, and its clear associations with her mother's family show that the name, and the work she produced under that name, was not in any way worth less to her than her more weighty literary novels or her plays. The new name also had the added advantage for Beth of concealing her identity once again. After the unpleasantness surrounding *The Expensive Halo*, with its too-close portrayal of her family, and the publicity and allegations of plagiarism surrounding *Richard of Bordeaux*, she could once again get on with what she enjoyed: writing.

A Shilling for Candles returns to the free, accessible style of *The Man in the Queue*: unlike *Queen of Scots* or *The Laughing Woman*, Josephine Tey was not held back by the weight of research or the need to stick to a real-life story. She was free to embroider a plot around facts that she had come to know well: the Hollywood actresses and scriptwriters she had met or heard so much about during her time working on *Next Time We Love*, and the theatrical life she had become a part of since *Richard of Bordeaux*. *A Shilling For Candles* includes characters such as the actress Christine Clay, and Jay Harmer, the Jewish songwriter. Like *The Man in the Queue*, the novel opens with the discovery of a body, and, again like its predecessor, the book features an innocent man accused of the crime. A new type of character is introduced, however, in Erica Burgoyne, the daughter of the police chief. An unworldly (but not naive) young woman, she is convinced of Robert Tisdall's innocence and helps him to prove that he did not kill actress Christine Clay. Gordon Daviot was to use this type of young woman in a later play to great effect, though personally I've always found Erica less appealing than some of her other characters: she is a girl written by a woman from memory of her own childhood, rather than, like Betty Kane in *The Franchise Affair*, from the perspective of a teacher who has taught a lot of adolescents.

Another character, Marta Hallard, Grant's actress friend, helps the reader navigate through London's West End and its relationship with Hollywood. This is a clear homage to Marda Vanne, who was beginning to assume more and more importance in Tey's life.

Fictional Christine Clay, the murdered actress at the centre of *A Shilling for Candles*, is married to Lord Edward Champneis ('pronounced Chins') introducing another stratum of society (and harking back to the aristocracy of *The Expensive Halo*), while Christine's poor background and religious brother introduce other class distinctions. The wonderfully drawn journalist, Jammy Hopkins, whose slangy stream-of-consciousness contrasts vividly with Grant's careful thought processes, shows Josephine Tey had the playwright and novelist's ability to create characters and voices that were genuinely different from each other. Tey is exploring motivations in her crime fiction, and her characters are not projections of her own identity but carefully observed, differently motivated individuals. She does manage to introduce some of her own views into the book, however, and, although the plot is driven by the underlying need to find Christine's killer, the story takes in tangents on widely varying topics from horoscopes to religion, in a manner that would have delighted Rhoda Anstey.

A Shilling for Candles also has a link with Gordon Daviot's own life in the strange will of Christine Clay. Apart from the 'shilling for candles' that inspires the title of the book, Clay leaves all her money to the National Trust, as Gordon Daviot was to do much later. Daviot was already making a considerable amount of money from her writing and, without the expense of a household of her own, she was already considering what to do with it. As early as 1940, Gordon Daviot made reference in letters to Gwen and Marda saying that she had signed away the profits of some of her writing to charity – and was having trouble with income tax because she had not filled in some forms correctly.[20]

Erica Burgoyne's unworldliness appealed to another reader,

and provided a new link in the chain of movies that surround this period in Beth's life. Alfred Hitchcock was drawn to the book, and adapted it for film. Despite his approaching Tey's publishers with a view to involving the author in the film, this time, perhaps remembering her experiences with rewrites for Universal and the day on set observing Gielgud and Hitchcock, she refused to work on this adaptation and a team of screenwriters were employed. Josephine Tey had nothing to do with the making of the film. Hitchcock changed the title to *Young and Innocent (*and *The Girl was Young* in America), and Erica was made central to the plot, with secondary characters such as Christine's brother disposed of entirely. Even Alan Grant doesn't make it into Hitchcock's version, and most of his policemen are inept, comedy figures. *Young and Innocent* is a man's version of an ingénue, instead of Tey's woman's version, and Erica is not such a sturdy, sensible girl. The movie moves further and further away from Josephine Tey's original plot until Erica drives her car into an old mineshaft and almost plunges to her doom, but there are some lines which are lifted in their entirety from *A Shilling for Candles*. This black and white film is good fun, and was Hitchcock's own favourite from among his British films.[21] In a way it provides another entry into Beth's world, showing the fashions of her time; the clothes people wore (the hats stand out); the cars they drove; and the things they saw and did every day that were considered normal by the standards of the time. Hitchcock changed the identity of the murderer, and his film ends up at the Grand Hotel courtesy of a last-minute clue of a box of matches, where the evil ex-husband (a drummer in blackface) reveals himself with a maniacal laugh.

'Based on the novel entitled *A Shilling for Candles* by Josephine Tey' was emblazoned across the screen at the start of *Young and Innocent*, just under the title and the names of the stars, Nova Pilbeam and Derrick de Marney. Beth, sitting in the dark of one of Inverness's cinemas, could see her success as a writer once again, quietly and without the press intrusion and madness of *Richard of Bordeaux* and London.

Beth was visiting London regularly at this time, and there seemed no reason to think that her career wouldn't continue in this fashion, but personal problems were starting to emerge. One of these problems was Marda. The fictional Marta Hallard is a wonderful character, a foil for Inspector Grant, an actress whose flaws the author sees clearly, a striking figure dressed to advantage in black and white. Despite her name, Marta is not a straight portrayal of Marda, but a mixture of many actresses and theatrical people Gordon now knew, from the talented Gwen to the well-dressed Dodie Smith. The real Marda was something different. Unlike Gwen, who wanted a committed and faithful relationship, Marda was promiscuous and challenging. She was far more open, within the confines of the time, about her sexuality than Gwen would ever be. As the daughter of wealthy, titled parents Marda had the confidence of the ruling class, and her status as an outsider was already established by her South African upbringing. After sloughing off her early marriage, and having stepped outwith her family and society's moral code, she now felt that she could create her own rules to live by. There was no reason, in Marda's world, to deny herself anything she wanted. If she liked a young girl, she would try to entice her into an affair. Angela du Maurier was one of the women she had an affair with. Gwen, resigned to Marda, sent them away together one weekend to Tagley Cottage, even preparing them a little food, since they were both hopelessly undomesticated. When Marda grew bored of the affair and moved on, Angela, still infatuated, altered her will in order to leave all her possessions to Marda. Marda, amused, remarked that Angela was not the first young lady to do that.[22]

From around the middle of 1935, when Gordon was working hard on the script for *Next Time We Love*, Marda kept a diary, which she wrote in the form of a letter to Gordon.[23] Marda began to convince herself that she was in love with Gordon, and wrote how desperately unhappy she was that Gordon was ignoring her. Gordon was oblivious to the romantic feelings she was inspiring in Marda, and the tension this was starting to cause with Gwen. The joint letters Gordon sent to Gwen and Marda around this time include cheerful mentions of her writing work, discussions of the weather and the plants in her garden, her walks around town and breezy thank-yous for the happy times they had spent together in London.[24] Marda continued her diary-letter to Gordon from April 1935 until January 1936. Some time in 1936, the year of publication of *A Shilling for Candles*, Gordon visited London, and Marda showed her some of her writings, and thus declared her feelings.

Marda chose to do this in a slightly roundabout way.[25] She told Gordon that she was writing a book, a diary based on her experiences. Appealing to Gordon's admiration for Gwen, she could show how she had lived through such interesting times that the book might appeal to the general reader. But the manuscript that Gordon received was a thinly disguised fiction, and mainly a description of how Marda felt about her.

There is no doubt that Marda did seriously consider writing her memoirs. Her papers survive in parts amongst the Gwen Ffrangcon-Davies archive, and there are several attempts at writing a memoir preserved there. It would, however, have been a difficult one to publish, as she meant to tell the real story of her lesbian love affairs. There was precedent, with the 1928 publication of *The Well of Loneliness*, and Angela du Maurier's own attempts to write a novel with similar themes, pleading for greater tolerance and understanding.

Gordon Daviot's handwritten reply to Marda after reading the diary is a masterpiece of restrained tact.[26] Written from the Cowdray Club in London after a face-to-face meeting with Marda, Gordon chooses to believe Marda's story that the diary is fictional and for publication, and treats it as a piece of literature, yet she also tries to gently explain to Marda that she is not only not interested in a relationship, but had not even contemplated the existence of such a relationship. 'Dear Marda,' she wrote,

I have written the report on the diary extract as I should if I were a publisher's reader [...]. I read it with interest and with an odd mixture of pleasure and regret. Pleasure in the good bits of writing, and regret that I should have been the unwitting cause of so much unhappiness. I have not often made people unhappy. Put it down not to hard-heartedness nor lack of imagination, but to inability to deal with something so foreign to my understanding that the chatter of Martians would be limpid sense by comparison. So foreign that I have continually to be chastening my sub-conscious which insists on believing that no one really does feel like that!

Gordon was tolerant of her friends' sexuality but, as her own romantic history with Hugh shows, she herself was attracted to men. Private letters from Gordon to various friends, at various times, mention other men she found attractive. Jokingly, Beth says that she 'left her heart behind' after encountering some soldiers on a train, while in later letters she discusses male cinema stars she liked.[27]

Alongside her letter to Marda, Gordon affixed a sheet of A4 with her handwritten 'Reader's Report on M.S.S. entitled MARCH'. 'This is the diary,' Gordon wrote, 'kept by a woman unhappily in love, in an effort to rationalise her world, but the love affair, far from being the central theme, is merely the background and the refrain.' Gordon recognized that Marda's 'love' was not entirely about Gordon; a lot of it was about Marda, and how she perceived herself. Marda was used to the women she liked falling at her feet. Gordon's 'report' continues its focus away from the 'love affair' by giving some extremely practical and commercial suggestions for improving the writing: 'Characters who are introduced by name only should be amplified into pencil sketches, even if it is only by the old trick of the constant epithet'. The report shows how experienced a writer Gordon was. She knew what a publisher was looking for, and gives practical examples of how to change things, giving tricks to get over common beginners' writing problems. As a report, it is far more interesting for what it reveals about Gordon's approach to writing than what it reveals about her feelings, and, as such, it must have been very disappointing for Marda.

What the letter also reveals is the gap between how Gordon really was, and how her London friends perceived her. Marda was a selfish woman, and Gordon recognized that. Her portrayal of the actress Marta clearly shows the flaws of anyone following that profession, including the showmanship that can take the place of real feeling – though it is never harsh, just impartial observation.

Marda had an image in her head of Gordon, and, used to young ladies who were emotional and somewhat uneducated, she underestimated her experience. Gordon might have been a newcomer to their London theatre scene, but she was a woman in her late 40s, who had experienced life, love and loss no less because she was not in the capital or living a public life.

In November 1937, a year or so after this crisis point in their friendship, Marda typed out an A4 sheet of paper which she entitled 'Progress'.[28] In this, she looked ahead to try to imagine where she and her friends might be in the following years. The answers she came up with are ironic and amusing, but very revealing of how she saw her friends. Gwen's 'progress' is in the world of highbrow theatre – 'Persuades Gordon to adapt a play from the Greek [...] Suggests to Peggy the adaptation of a play from the Spanish'. Peggy (actress and director Margaret Webster) is to travel, producing and directing plays: 'Goes to Rome to produce a play [...] Goes to Japan to produce a Noh Play.' Their rich friend Lena 'Buys the Globe [...] Buys Shaftesbury Avenue'. Marda herself is to have ever more fantastic love affairs; she sees herself only through that prism: 'Has an affair with Ethel [...] Has an affair with Greta Garbo [...] Has an affair with the Princess Elizabeth'. And Gordon? Beth MacKintosh, who was so resolutely fixed in Inverness caring for her father, had managed to project her preferred image of herself so successfully to her London friends that Marda saw her as a seasoned, carefree traveller: '1940 – Gordon goes to London. 1942 – Goes to China. 1945 – Goes to Lapland. 1950 – Leaves for final retreat to Tibet'. 'Progress' is a piece of fun; a tongue-in-cheek look at the world with little reference to reality, but it shows how little Marda and her London friends understood Gordon. For all her professed love, Marda never made any attempt to visit her in Inverness. Gordon, to her, was an exotic traveller she wanted to snare in her net – a glamorous, creative, passionate woman.[29] Beth MacKintosh had created this alter-ego of Gordon Daviot, who could live the writing life she wanted to have, and Marda, for one, was completely taken in.

When Marda read Gordon's letters she was trying to find evidence of her feelings – perhaps that's why neither Gwen nor

Marda made much of Gordon's film work. They saw her only in the context of their London theatre lives, and struggled to see anything outside that. Gordon's friendship with the two women survived Marda's declaration and in February 1937, Gwen was secure enough to invite Gordon on holiday to Switzerland; Gordon was disappointed not to be able to go, but it led to a subtle shift, and was a precursor to much greater changes that were to come about in their relationships.[30] In some of Gordon's letters to Gwen and Marda there creeps in a tentative note, a desire to explain and make clear, to try to get them to understand that she never means to cause offence, and to explain how she sees the world. Another undated handwritten letter from the Cowdray Club to Marda reads:

> I think it was Kitchener who said 'never explain' – and for years I've tried to live up to so God-like an ideal but am always frustrated by my propensity for saying and doing things that apparently mean something actively different to other people! [...] I've been worried in my pre-breakfast moments by a crack I made last night. When Lena was holding back about coming to supper I knew she was refusing because she was afraid that she was barging into a party already made up, and since the party was still in a fluid state it seemed true that if I started an entirely new one there would be no question barging into on anyone's part. Hence my 'let's [illegible] my party – then she'll have to come.' Which, to my horror, turned out to mean something quite different.[31]

Lena, also a lesbian, had relationships with several different actresses. Marda was a jealous woman and did not like to see any preference on Gordon's part for anyone other than herself. Gordon simply did not want to jeopardize these new friendships and the new circle she found so creatively and personally fulfilling – yet she was realizing that there were parts of it she could never fully enter into. It was a difficult balancing act, yet one that, for some years at least, before they were taken over by events, was maintained.

For all the women, even Marda, their careers often took

precedence. They were working in creative, challenging and fulfilling jobs. Peggy Webster, who had turned to directing rather
than acting due to that lull in work created by the success of
Richard of Bordeaux, was starting to shine. In 1936–37, she was
working on a production of *Richard II*.[32] Peggy had dual US-UK
nationality as she was born abroad, and her parents Ben Webster
and May Whitty had both acted in America, so Peggy was keen
to pursue opportunities there. When *Richard II* was produced,
Margaret Webster became the first woman to direct Shakespeare
on Broadway. The play attracted a huge amount of interest, not
just because of her directing and the quality acting, but because
of interest in the play's plot about a king abdicating. It was the
height of the scandal surrounding Wallis Simpson, and King
Edward VIII abdicated in December 1936. *The Laughing Woman*
had played on Broadway from October to November 1936 at the
John Golden Theatre with Helen Menken (ex-wife of Humphrey
Bogart) as Ingrid and Tonio Selwart as Rene, and the link was
made between the Shakespearian *Richard II* and Gordon Daviot's
earlier play *Richard of Bordeaux*.[33] In November 1936, John
Gielgud was corresponding with Douglas Fairbanks Jr about the
possibility of turning *Richard of Bordeaux* into a film.[34] Sadly, the
plans never developed.

In the meantime, negotiations for Gordon Daviot's next play,
The Stars Bow Down, had stalled. It had a large cast of thirty-
two people including two or three child actors, and casting had
proved to be a stumbling block. Daviot's change of agent had
slowed things up, and in 1936 what was to be J. M. Barrie's final
play went on – *The Boy David*. Like *The Stars Bow Down*, this
was a religious play, and it was felt that for Daviot to follow it
would not be a good move – it would have looked like copying,
or 'staggering with imitative gestures in the footsteps of genius' as
Daviot herself put it.[35]

Gordon Daviot was happy in the mid-1930s, and in some ways
it was a pinnacle of her career as far as respect and recognition
went. She was mixing with the actors and writers who were
shaping popular culture and there was ongoing interest in her
work from theatre producers and even Hollywood. And yet, at

the same time, with the exception of *A Shilling for Candles,* her work from this period did not survive. *The Stars Bow Down* was as yet unproduced and unpublished; her plays were successful but not as successful as *Richard of Bordeaux,* and have not remained in print; and her Hollywood writing never received recognition and even became almost completely forgotten. It was a turning point in the creation of the 'mystery' that was Gordon Daviot, as lack of understanding of this part of her career meant that people could not see the 'join' between Daviot and Josephine Tey. The slowness of production of her next plays had given Daviot time to write – and reconsider what she was writing. As the notes for *Richard of Bordeaux* show, she took her research seriously, and it was frustrating to put in considerable amounts of work without seeing any result. For her next project, Gordon Daviot turned away from the theatre. She wanted to write about the historical figure of Claverhouse, but decided a play was not the best format. Instead, she was going to write a book – and it was going to be totally factual, a straight non-fiction biography.

CHAPTER THIRTEEN

Claverhouse

Claverhouse was John Graham of Claverhouse, 1st Viscount Dundee (1648-1689). He is renowned in Scottish history and myth from two entirely different angles: first vilified as 'Bloody Clavers', he was responsible for policing south-west Scotland and maintaining order for the Crown during the 'Killing Time', the period of political and religious unrest led by the Presbyterian Covenanters. However, his loyalty to the established order led him to continue to support James VII after the king was overthrown in favour of William of Orange in the 1688 Revolution. Claverhouse then became, ironically, a popular anti-establishment figure, leading a Highland clan army and celebrated in song as 'Bonnie Dundee'. From Hollywood to Claverhouse is quite a leap. Many of Gordon's theatre friends were completely London-centric – a few years later Dodie Smith almost broke her heart leaving London during the Blitz, convinced that she would never again be able to relate to her audience or write a hit play because she had not experienced London during the war. It never occurred to Dodie that there could be other valid British experiences of war. The London one was the only one that mattered. Beth MacKintosh never put London life and experiences ahead of her experiences in Inverness in this way. Despite her success in England, and her love of the country, she gave equal consideration to the culture that she encountered in Inverness and elsewhere, and her biography of Claverhouse was an attempt not only to reinterpret the life of a historical figure who fascinated her, but to seriously grapple with important political and cultural events in Scotland and the Highlands. Beth had been reading about Claverhouse for some time, and discussing her interest in him with several people.[1]

Like her best-known Josephine Tey book *The Daughter of Time*, *Claverhouse* takes a serious look at how history is understood. In a forerunner of *The Daughter of Time*'s dedication and title, *Claverhouse* is dedicated 'TO THOSE WHO *may not prefer Scotland to Truth, but certainly prefer Scotland to enquiry*'. This quote is originally from Dr Johnson, and was also referenced by Walter Scott.

By 1937, when Beth was researching and writing *Claverhouse*, Neil Gunn had left his day job as an exciseman and become a full-time writer.[2] As he was no longer a civil servant, he was now free to openly state his political views. In 1934, the two main Scottish nationalist parties had combined to form what we now know as the SNP, and Gunn, along with his friend ex-Inverness provost Alexander MacEwen, had worked hard behind the scenes to make this happen, pushing more conservative, less radical ideas, such as prioritizing devolution before full independence. Leading SNP figure John MacCormick, supported by MacEwen and Gunn, had stood for election for Inverness twice, once in 1931 and again, after the new SNP was formed, in 1935. SNP policies had been well and truly discussed in Inverness, and, through Gunn and his friends, were intricately linked with the literary scene. Neil Gunn very much enjoyed his position as literary lion of the Highlands, and in 1934, between political campaigning and starting an affair with MacEwen's young daughter, had hosted the Inverness leg of the International PEN conference and tour, which had been based in Scotland that year. PEN, formed in 1921, aims to promote harmony between writers of all nations, using literature as a tool to promote freedom of expression and understanding. The Scottish branch was formed by C. M. Grieve (Hugh MacDiarmid) in 1927.[3] It was an organization that meant a lot to many people, particularly in Europe during the 1930s and onto the years of the Second World War, when it supported writers whose work was banned by the Nazis.

In 1934, the highlight of the Inverness PEN tour was an opera in Gaelic called 'Ishbel of the Shealing [sic]'.[4] Gunn and MacEwen were the hosts (Gunn's affair with MacEwen's daughter being, for the time being, a secret), along with a Gaelic expert, and Gunn was also invited to the main Scottish event in Edinburgh, where he met the guest of honour, H. G. Wells. In 1936, the Scottish branch of PEN had met again in Inverness – tying the meeting to the Mod, the annual celebration of Gaelic music. Beth MacKintosh, in 1937 probably the most successful author working in the Highlands, was not involved in any of this.[5] She was certainly aware of Gunn and his work, and knew MacEwen as well – later, Beth was to become friendly with one of MacEwen's daughters (not the one who was having the affair with Gunn) and MacEwen also worked for the solicitor's firm that Beth and her father Colin used.

Beth was never officially involved in Scottish PEN, whose membership list, as initiated by Hugh MacDiarmid, shows a distinct bias towards writers either sympathetic to the nationalist cause, or strongly linked to the Gaelic revival.[6] Beth did contribute some money as a donation towards the 1934 conference, but she was not part of the organising committee, and no further involvement after that one 1934 donation has been found.[7] Scottish PEN had acknowledged Gordon Daviot's work as early as 1933, when one of the organizers, the writer Marion Lochhead, had included a short profile of Gordon Daviot in a series she wrote on Scottish writers, but the relationship had not progressed.[8] Marion and Gordon Daviot corresponded briefly, but while many of the Scottish women Marion profiled wrote her long, detailed letters which Marion carefully filed, some of the Daviot-Lochhead correspondence seems to be missing, and Gordon's surviving letter to Marion is, if not unfriendly, uncharacteristically short, and perhaps more formal than usual. Anything that Beth might have gained from associating with local writers was lost because their meetings and discussions were generally not centred on the craft of writing, but around politics. Beth found far more fulfilment in discussing the creative process with her London friends – but she did not disengage entirely from what was happening around her, as the donation to PEN shows. *Claverhouse* shows her creative engagement in Scottish history and identity as well, in her own unique way.

Claverhouse is not one of Gordon Daviot's well-known books, and for the first two-thirds of the book the reader may wonder why she wrote it. The answer is in the final section: the powerful descriptions of the battles, which Daviot makes modern and relevant by referencing the Great War; the insights into the character of Claverhouse and his troops; and the descriptions of their terrain, the Scotland over which they fight. In this final section, Claverhouse, his men, and his country, come alive, and Gordon Daviot conveys vividly why she is interested in this man. The biography format and Daviot's tendency (already shown in her plays) to always tell a story from the beginning to the end with an assumption that the audience has a good grasp of the historical facts masks the fact that the most interesting thing about Claverhouse is the sweep of his whole life, and the way he was judged afterwards. It was a structural problem that Daviot was not able to solve in her writing until *The Daughter of Time*, with its unusual framing and much better known figure of Richard III. In *Claverhouse*, the contradiction between 'Bloody Clavers' and 'Bonnie Dundee' and how these two images can both be applied to the same man, is what makes him so interesting – but the essential problem for his biographer is that not enough people know who Claverhouse is in the first place. Gordon Daviot even admitted as much herself, saying in a letter to fellow playwright Dodie Smith that 'I can't believe his activities are of any general interest to anyone south of the Border'.[9]

In this book, Daviot was writing a character study, which she thought would be of interest to people interested in history in her own country, Scotland – but she needed to make that clearer. Her sense of history and truth would not allow her to make overt links between 1930s nationalism and Claverhouse, but an understanding of the political situation at the time she was writing sheds light on her decision to write this biography. Claverhouse is a Scottish hero she could respect whilst still being pro-British: he leads a romantic Scottish Highland Clan uprising but is essentially a conservative figure who did not want change to the established order. Daviot explained the attraction to Dodie Smith by saying, although '[t]he Covenanting period is a dreich period in Scottish history [...] Claverhouse is a man after my own heart'.[10] Protestant and honourable, Claverhouse was the sort of person Gordon Daviot could respect. In a way, Claverhouse is the figure that Bonnie Prince Charlie should have been, honourably dying in the victory charge. However, in order to respect Claverhouse as a Scottish hero, it is necessary to somehow get around his image as 'Bloody Clavers', the killer of the Covenanters, and it is this problem that Daviot's *Claverhouse* biography is trying to solve.

The choice of the Covenanting period of Scottish history was not an arbitrary one – it was one of the touchstones of the history that the SNP was referencing. Neil Gunn's friend Maurice Walsh wrote about the Covenanters in a fictional novel around the same time, while 'the National Covenant' was the SNP's chosen name for their 1940 campaign for devolution.[11] Gordon Daviot is engaging with Scottish nationalist rhetoric in this biography, by showing a Scottish figure she thinks is worth respecting, but she is doing so in her own way. It is impossible to read this book as a response to the political ideas of her day – the increasing Scottish nationalism – because it is so much on Daviot's own terms. But, conversely, it is difficult to understand why it is important without understanding that Daviot was trying to present her own view of what was important in Scottish history partly because there were many other people at that time who were picking and choosing what *they* saw as important in order to build up a new nationalist ideology, an ideology that persists until the present day. Daviot's book presents a new version of what is important in Scottish history, in the same way that her fictional books present an entirely different version of the Scotland of her time to that presented by her contemporaries. In personality, the principled, logical and Protestant Claverhouse was much closer to Elizabeth I of England than Mary, Queen of Scots, and *Claverhouse* held Daviot's interest in a way *Queen of Scots* had not. The suggestion to write a straight biography had come from a publisher, but that suggestion had grown out of Daviot's real interest in history: she had been talking about her reading to anyone who would listen.

Claverhouse was her return to writing what she was interested in: writing for herself.

Claverhouse was published by Collins, who, on the dust jacket of the book, made much of Daviot's success on the stage, while talking up the excitement of the current work. It was maybe not quite the right approach to take – fans of *Richard of Bordeaux* might not have found what they wanted in this academic discussion of Kirk policy and her emphasis on the importance of bureaucracy in the bloody dealings in Galloway. Daviot was a difficult author to market: her publishers probably understood as poorly as her theatrical friends just why she was interested in life outside of London.

The book received some good reviews, but, although it was acknowledged to be useful for students of the period, it did not get the response that Daviot hoped for. 'The Manchester Guardian,' Beth wrote, 'hovered on the verge of libel and refused me permission to answer their reviewer's really shocking accusations'.[12] Daviot acknowledged that she was not a historian, but felt she was more than capable of reading sources critically, and that she had something new and important to say, which would rehabilitate Claverhouse's reputation. She didn't want to be judged as a historian, but felt that the common-sense she applied to her reading of history books gave her a fresh and important perspective – something she was later to manage to express to its fullest potential in *The Daughter of Time*.

However, Daviot no longer had the anonymity of *Richard of Bordeaux*, but was now known as a female ex-PE teacher. The dust jacket made it clear that Daviot was a woman, and, in the text itself, Gordon Daviot makes a couple of wry observations on a previous biographer of Claverhouse, stressing that the author has drawn certain conclusions 'because she is a woman'. Gordon Daviot was no longer writing anonymously but would be judged, not only in Inverness but in the wider press, on her sex as well as her previous achievements. Daviot noted in her letter to Dodie Smith that the reviews had generally agreed that *Claverhouse* was 'not a woman's book'.[13] Reviewers also felt that her view of Claverhouse tended more towards 'Bonnie Dundee' than 'Bloody

Clavers', and her portrayal of his soldiers does seem far more courteous and bloodless than the reality could ever have been. Daviot, reading the criticism of her book, summed it up in a letter to Dodie Smith, saying 'I couldn't find bad things to report about [Claverhouse], with the inevitable result that I have been accused of using pink spectacles.'

Beth also wrote at length about the reception of the book to one interested and interesting 'fan', who had written to her with a page of intelligent criticisms – Miss M. E. M. Donaldson. Mary Ethel Muir Donaldson, or MEMD as she called herself, was another remarkable woman of the period, a writer and gifted photographer, whose views of the Highlands are still widely disseminated. Something of a kindred spirit to Beth in her search for historical truth, she had recently published *Scotland's Suppressed History: Talks on Scottish Church History for Young People, etc.* 'The first thing I did after reading your letter,' Beth wrote to MEMD, 'was to get your book from my bookseller, and I have read it with vast enjoyment [...] I hope to see Scotland's Suppressed History in a prominent position on the Literature Stall at the Empire Exhibition. (What is the betting that it isn't? Eighty to one against and no takers!)'[14] Sadly, the friendship had no chance to progress, but Gordon's letter to MEMD covers three enthusiastic, closely typed pages, and she shared one of her favourite reviews of *Claverhouse*, from an irate Reverend.

Beth never again attempted to write straight, non-fictional history: from now on, all her historical writing was fictionalized. She had found the constant referencing needed in a more 'academic' work tiresome, and in the future she focused on the story, and her own interpretations of events. In this way, she managed to achieve something greater, and showed that education, information and truth were available to anyone who chose to spend time researching. *The Daughter of Time*, her most well-known historical piece, sets out not only the historical story of Richard III but also the way in which Alan Grant and Brent Carradine research this story. Grant and Carradine's searches through the archive for contemporary materials are a good indication of how Beth herself approached research. For the amateur historian, the search itself is part of the joy; the discovery of the original sources is part of the exhilaration; the chase for the truth and the realization that this is something that can be done by anyone with a good education and access to the right libraries are particularly well conveyed in *The Daughter of Time*. In Inverness, Beth had access to the Inverness Central Library, and other subscription libraries, such as Boots, would also have been easily available. Her trips to London gave her access to the larger public libraries, and *Claverhouse* is fully referenced, with Beth's sources clearly stated. *Claverhouse* is a response to how she saw the movements in Scottish politics and culture, and an important and prescient one, but she never allowed that to come to the front, always focusing only on the real history. This makes it a much better history book, but perhaps a less enjoyable read.

Daviot found the writing of *Claverhouse* hard going at times: 'the "woik" is fair bluidy!' she wrote to Lena Ramsden in 1937, planning a holiday in the sun when it was all over.[15] Once *Claverhouse* was done, it seemed like things moved on in Inverness. Neil Gunn left the town, selling his house on Dochfour Drive and moving further north after various personal problems, including his wife's miscarriage and probable discovery of his affair with Margaret MacEwen.[16] Beth, too, was more concerned with family, as her sister Jean announced that she was getting married.

Beth's youngest sister Moire was still fixed in London, working for the Gas Board and generally enjoying life. Jean had moved around a little more in her secretarial work, occasionally coming back to Inverness between jobs.[17] She had been with a firm in London in the late 1920s, until 1931, and sometime after had moved north of London to Buckinghamshire. It was here she met her future husband, either through their shared love of horse riding, or possibly because she worked for him as his personal secretary. Jean was in her late 30s and her father Colin might have been forgiven for thinking that none of his three daughters was ever going to marry. Jean's marriage was something of a surprise, particularly as her future husband was twenty-two years older than she was with two children from a previous marriage. His elder son was actually older than Jean.[18]

Jean, no less than Beth, had been affected by the First World War, surviving in a post-war world where there were far fewer men of her age to marry, and where she had tasted the freedom that a career could give her. Her secretarial work had given her plenty of opportunity to travel, and, like Beth, she had enough money to enjoy her hobbies. She and Beth shared an interest in horses, though Beth was always more interested in watching racing, while Jean liked riding. 'Jean and her gee-gees', Moire used to say dismissively, but this love of horses was a shared hobby with her new fiancée, Vice-Admiral Humphrey Hugh Smith, DSO.[19] Humphrey was a navy man who had been aboard ship through the old-fashioned style of training, on old-fashioned sailing ships, starting when he was thirteen or fourteen.[20] He had served with distinction in the First World War but had been retired (against his will) in 1926, and had settled down with his wife and children to write his memoirs (which was why he needed a secretary). His two volumes of memoir are vastly entertaining, full of bluff, amusing anecdotes about his travels and the people he worked with, completely sincere in his devotion to the navy and his general belief in people's essential goodness.

Photographs of Humphrey show a very smartly dressed man with a wry smile and eyes surrounded by laughter lines. He had married his first wife, the aristocratic and well-connected Blanche Scott-Murray, around the same time that Colin MacKintosh had married Josephine, and they had had a happy marriage, despite Humphrey's long absences at sea, but Blanche had died in January 1937. Humphrey was not the sort of man who could manage on his own, and he and Jean were pleased to find companionship together. They were married in late spring/early summer 1937, less than six months after Blanche's death. Humphrey was a Catholic – not the easiest link for the daughter of a Free Church family to make – but however Colin, Beth and Moire felt about the marriage in the first place, there was no doubt that Humphrey was accepted into their family, visiting Inverness and Colin, and making Jean happy. Beth was happy to refer to her sister 'marrying into the navy' in letters to her friends.[21] Several photographs of Humphrey remain amongst the MacKintosh family possessions, and Josephine Tey was surely thinking of him when she wrote in *The Singing Sands* about the journey to Inverness and the dreadful sleeping-car attendant who was rarely challenged except by 'an Admiral of the Fleet or something like that [who] would venture an opinion that it was damned awful tea'.[22]

The contrast between Beth's home life and working life was stronger than ever: 1937 was the year that *A Shilling for Candles* was adapted by Hitchcock as *Young and Innocent*, with the film coming out in November, but, although Beth was not involved with the filming at all, her family were certainly too busy with their own affairs to be very involved in her writing life. Colin, Jean and Moire were proud of Beth, but did not understand her work. Colin was more concerned with his hobby of angling: the *Inverness Courier* of Tuesday 13th July 1937 reported that 'Fishing the Ness Castle Pools yesterday, Mr Colin MacKintosh, a well-known local angler, had a beautiful salmon, which scaled 24½ lbs'. As the year went on, Colin was also very concerned with his property on Castle Street: the street was not in a good state of repair. A contemporary description of the flats in the street, from the mid-1930s, described how number 67, where Colin and his family used to live, was crawling with cockroaches.[23] Number 51, where Colin was now the landlord, was described by the same person as 'a bit more up-market', with indoor toilets, a well-maintained drying green outside, and a well-kept stone staircase entrance. Colin was friendly with his tenants, and the grandchild of one of his tenants remembered that '[o]ne of the things he always did when he got new potatoes in, he would take a pail of them up to my grandmother to get her to try them out for him – she was the official taster'. But regardless of how well Colin kept his property, Castle Street as a whole was giving the council cause for concern. In 1932, there had been a landslide under the castle, which had led to the demolition of all the shops and flats on that side, including the original building where Colin's family had opened their fruit shop. The street looked entirely different – much closer to how it does today, as the buildings on the castle side were never rebuilt – and the appearance of the old town, with its narrow streets and alleyways, was starting to go. The council were keen to close up more of the alleyways, and demolish more of the buildings which were felt to be dangerous. Castle Street, with its problem tenements, did not fit in with their image of a bustling town – but, as is the way with councils, the whole project was thought to have been handled in the worst way possible, as the council would have preferred to demolish the problem rather than spend time fixing it, and the ensuing battles began to take up more and more of Colin's time and energy.

In May 1938 the council closed two rights-of-way leading from Castle Street to Castle Wynd, and Colin was moved enough by this action to write to the local paper complaining – in a beautifully expressed letter that shows at least some of Beth's writing talent was inherited from her father.[24] Colin also had the distinction of being one of the few correspondents on the matter to openly sign his name, as others chose to hide behind pen-names. In later analyses, both Colin and Beth were criticized for their lack of engagement in the social and public life of Inverness, but this incident shows clearly that Colin was involved – though not necessarily on the side of the class of people who were running the council and who made these later analyses.[25] Beth, too, was engaged with what was happening in Inverness, taking time out from her serious writing to produce a crossword for her old school newspaper, with a prize offered for its completion.[26] It was a fitting contribution for someone who was to become well known as a mystery writer, as crosswords and their clues are so often associated with crime writing. Crosswords were still a relatively new fashion at the time, invented only around 1913.

Colin's complaint about the right-of-way in Castle Street was supported in the leader column of the next week's paper, and further letters complained that shops were losing custom because customers could not get to them. The council reacted by refusing to discuss the matter at their next meeting, and, after a couple of months, the butcher who owned the shop further down the street from Colin, cheered on by the other residents of the street, took his butcher's saw to the council-erected barricades and forcibly re-opened the right of way.[27] The council gave a long-winded response about how wrong this was and how they could close the rights-of-way if they wanted to. They then backed down and agreed to try and fix the roads. The local paper went back to complaining about the council's other big problem of the moment – their planned reforms to the Public Library. Reading the *Inverness Courier* of the 1930s is essentially the same as reading it today.

While Colin's attention was fixed in Inverness, Beth looked elsewhere for discussion of her writing career and literary interests, continuing to meet up with her sisters regularly and maintaining a correspondence with playwright Dodie Smith.[28] Beth's acquaintance with Dodie deepened around this time. Where Gordon Daviot had had one brilliant success with *Richard of Bordeaux* and then not quite followed it up, after her breakthrough play *Autumn Crocus* Dodie Smith had hit after hit.[29] Both writers were concerned with observant humour, though Dodie always set her plays firmly in the middle-class house or family. In 1937 *Bonnet Over the Windmill* was running, the successor to *Call It A Day*, *Touch Wood* and *Service*, and Dodie was writing what was to be one of her most enduring plays, *Dear Octopus*.

Dodie Smith was a small woman with a big personality. Photos of her at this time show her with short, dark hair, fashionably curled at the ends; eyebrows plucked into the thin line of a 1930s Hollywood fashionista, and a small mouth with rather big teeth. She had been a full-time writer for some years, having extricated herself from her shop job at Heal's (and her affair there with her boss), and by 1938 she was well established on the theatrical scene and enjoying that life to the full. Dodie had known Gwen since they were both young women in the Three Arts Club – Gwen a rising star, and Dodie a struggling actress. Now Dodie was doing well enough for her and her partner Alec not only to have bought a Rolls-Royce, but also to have customized it to their own requirements. When they went out to the US some years later they paid to ship the car out with them. Dodie's life very much shows the different route Beth could have chosen to take, if, after *Richard of Bordeaux*, she had chosen to move to London and immerse herself in the commercial, hit-making side of playwriting. Dodie lived with (though, typically unconventionally was not married to) her partner Alec Beesley, a younger man who had worked with her at Heal's but was now her manager. Her social life revolved entirely around the theatre and she was far more immersed in the gossipy world of acting than Beth, and more openly interested in and involved in the relationships between actors. While Gordon Daviot focused on historical and religious subjects for her plays, Dodie Smith drew on her own relationship experiences, particularly her affairs before her marriage. She was later to befriend Christopher Isherwood and to be intrigued by his gay lifestyle, and often tried, through her writing, to question social mores of the day. That is one reason many of her plays have not stood the test of time as, by engaging so wholeheartedly with the ideas of the 1930s, they now seem very dated.

Although they had both come from relatively modest middle-class backgrounds (Dodie was originally from the north of England) Beth and Dodie's writing styles and approach to their careers were very different. However, the four extant letters written from Daviot to Smith show a correspondence between two women writers working as equals, with respect for each other's views and an emphasis on their shared interest in the theatre and women's work in the theatre. Gordon wrote cheerfully to Dodie about her trips to Paris and England, the plays she had seen and the people she had visited, but was compelled to refuse Dodie's invitation to spend Christmas in Essex because of her commitment to Colin in Inverness. Dodie seemed unaware of Colin, but she was often seemingly unaware of anything or anyone that wasn't in her beloved London theatre world. This mismatch between their lives is apparent in a later letter, where Gordon felt she had to write quickly to explain comments she had made earlier – it harks back to the slightly apologetic tone in some of her letters to Gwen and Marda: although Gordon wanted to live by the maxim 'never explain, never apologize', some more explaining was necessary if she was to maintain her London friendships, as it was too easy for them to misunderstand her. Gordon knew that if she lost these friendships it would be a greater loss for her than it was for Dodie, or Marda, or Gwen.

Each of the letters from Beth to Dodie is signed 'Gordon', rather than 'Beth'. Daviot had met Smith through her professional life as a playwright, and kept that persona when corresponding with her. This is not to say, however, that the letters are impersonal, and contain no details of her private life: they include an amusing sketch Beth writes about visiting her dentist, and a funny description of her troubles getting the home help to make Christmas pudding. One intriguing reference, in the last letter, talks about Daviot's 'other half', who is not encouraging when Daviot comes up with new ideas for plays. Beth MacKintosh sometimes comes up with new ideas, but the 'other half' of her personality, Gordon Daviot, rejects them. This same idea, of an inner contradictory voice, is present in the Josephine Tey novels for both Alan Grant and Brat Farrar, while Miss Pym talks about 'her other half [...] which stood watching her with critical eyes [...]. It had sent her into fights with her knees knocking, it had made her speak when she wanted to hold her tongue, it had kept her from lying down when she was too tired to stand up'.[30] That was Beth and Daviot, or Beth and Tey. However, in these letters it is the discussion and analyses of plays that is exercising Gordon Daviot and Dodie Smith's interest.

The main discussion of content is in the first letter: Gordon advises Dodie to write about something other than 'Young Love'. Dodie was sometimes obsessed with analyzing her relationships, particularly the affairs she had before marriage, but the play she was working on which was to become so successful (*Dear Octopus*) is far more focused on family relationships. Gordon's advice perhaps struck a chord with her at this time. It also reflects what Daviot herself thought important enough to write about: her books are certainly not about 'young love'. The discussion of writing in the letters is not focused solely on the content of plays but also on the things that surround the writer and playwright: more than one letter comments on critical reviews, either of *Dear Octopus* or of Daviot's biography of *Claverhouse*. This is the analysis of two successful professionals who have nothing to prove to each other, who see each other as equals with whom they can discuss the drawbacks of writing success, rather than the correspondence of writers who are yet to become established and are still fixated on the process of writing. Daviot also saw Smith as an important colleague in another respect: she makes frequent comment in the letters about 'women playwrights' or 'women's writing'.

After *Claverhouse* had been published in late 1937, 1938 became another year in which Gordon Daviot had no new publications or theatre productions, though new editions of her work continued to be published. She was busy writing, but the full production of her play *The Stars Bow Down* had been postponed indefinitely, and she began to explore other options for it. It was to be published in book form in 1939. However, adaptations of her plays continued to appear, and, after the success of *Young and Innocent* and her other experiments with film, there were other media options to explore. Gwen Ffrangcon-Davies, paired this time with actor Andrew Osborn, reprised her role as 'Anne' for an adaptation of *Richard of Bordeaux* for the new medium of television.[31] At this time, television plays were filmed live, with the actors on a regular stage, rather than pre-recorded on location. It was a new and exciting development which presaged the many TV adaptations that would later be made of Josephine Tey's mystery novels – but in 1938 there wasn't even a television signal in Inverness, let alone any television sets, so the new medium had little impact on what and how Beth wrote. The broadcast has not survived or been preserved in any way.

Beth took another holiday around this time in 1938, travelling on the continent to Denmark and Germany with her sister Moire – but they ended up cutting their holiday short as there were now growing concerns about events in Europe.[32] References start to crop up in Gordon's letters to Germany and Hitler, though public opinion in Britain continued to be against any suggestion of war. Neil Gunn, now settled further north out of Inverness, was also travelling in Europe, making two visits to Germany in 1938 and 1939 – though, unlike Beth and Moire he was not on holiday, but had been invited to speak there by some young Germans, who were interested in his vision of Scotland and his nationalist politics. 'It would be much to the purpose,' Heinz Mollwo wrote to Inverness ex-provost Alexander MacEwen, 'if we knew something about the views which Mr. Gunn is inclined to-day to hold on young Germany and its problems'.[33] Heinz had been a guest at MacEwen's house in August 1936, where he had met Gunn.[34] Gunn, somewhat naively, accepted his invitations abroad, but in later life his friends did much to protect his reputation against any accusation that he had been pro-Nazi. The idea of 'nationalism' was beginning to take on a different meaning.

CHAPTER FOURTEEN

The Second World War

During the Second World War, John Gielgud and Gwen Ffrangcon-Davies met Gordon Daviot in Edinburgh, while they were touring their production of *Macbeth*, their own contribution to entertainment of civilians and troops for the war effort.[1] Gielgud's description of Gordon Daviot at this time is of a deeply depressed woman, who spoke with extreme bitterness about war and its aftermath, and who made reference to her own lost love from the First World War. Gielgud was very much struck by how Gordon appeared to him at this time, and his description of her in 1941 is one of the enduring images of the enigma 'Josephine Tey'. He wrote about it in his introduction to her collection of posthumously published plays, and it has been quoted by almost every commentator on her life since. The Second World War is often seen as the most 'mysterious' part of Tey's life; a period of silence where, commentators mistakenly write, she produced no work and where her movements were unknown. The reality, of course, is a little different, but the Second World War radically interrupted Gordon Daviot's writing, once more forcing her to rebuild her life as it destroyed everything she had so carefully built up since her mother's death.

As with so many of the myths around Beth's life, the reality of what war meant to her, and the reason why so many of her friends struggled to understand this, was bound up in what it meant to be living in Inverness. As with the First World War,

Inverness, as a major military hub, was affected to a very great degree, with large numbers of troops stationed and training there. Once again, Invernessians' movements were restricted and citizens had to carry a pass – the whole of Scotland north and west of the Caledonian Canal was 'closed', which was a considerable inconvenience to Invernessians, since the canal cuts through part of town and people must have crossed it regularly in Beth's time. 'This Closing of Scotland north and west of the Caledonian Canal is a bit of a nuisance,' said Colin with some understatement in a letter to his youngest daughter, 'It means that no one can cross the Canal without a permit. You have to fill up reams of paper, get two photos, your registration card, how far you want to go and god knows how much more. But the powers that be seem to think it necessary so what can we do.'[2] The Longman too, then an open area where Colin enjoyed walking, was closed and made into an airfield.[3] Around this time, he sent postcards of Shieldaig to Moire, so it seems he did manage to travel to his birthplace during the war years, but wider travel had certainly become more difficult, affecting Beth's journeys to London. However, Beth was actually on her way home by train to Inverness in September 1939, just after war was declared, and she did travel to London during the time of the Blitz.[4] Of Beth's two sisters, Moire was in London itself, while Jean was just outside and, as a veteran of the Zeppelin bombings, Beth was well aware of what dangers aerial bombardment might bring. Equally, in the north of Scotland, German planes were not unknown, and Colin's regular letters to Moire at this time obliquely mention 'visitors' to the night skies. Colin's business was affected, and his letters also discuss the difficulties of running a fruit shop in a time of rationing, the problems he had getting fresh fruit delivered and the tension it caused amongst his customers when there was not enough to go round.

We were 18 days without tomatoes and when they came we only got half the ordinary allotment. My allotment is 56 12lb baskets and most of the 28 baskets were over ripe. On an average there are 75 to 100 women daily at my place asking for tomatoes, and I take it that this happens at all other shops in town.[5]

When he could, Colin sent fruit down to Moire, but even he and Beth were going short as the war progressed.[6] Jean had less need of food parcels, but her husband Humphrey decided to re-enlist in the navy and rejoin active service.[7] As Commodore, he was in command of Atlantic convoys, a dangerous position under attack from U-Boats.

Professionally, one of the first notable things that happened for Gordon Daviot the playwright when the Second World War broke out was that all the theatres in London were closed.[8] They were quickly re-opened, as theatre and culture was publicly declared as being both important to morale and one of the things to fight for, but playwrights' work was difficult to continue in its same form with so many actors away fighting in the army, while those who remained, like John Gielgud, often focused on the classics, or on pieces that their managers knew would definitely attract an audience. Gordon was not in a good position, as the performance of her last two plays at the box office would not convince a manager to take a new one on at a risky time. With the exception of revivals or the inclusion of scenes from her plays included in revues, the theatre was effectively closed to Beth for the duration of the war.

Beth's London friends reacted differently too. Some of them were, frankly, rich enough to try to buy their way out of war. Acquaintances such as writer Marguerite Steen and her painter husband sold their London home and moved out to the country.[9] The honourable exception was Lena Ramsden, who, for the duration of the war, resolved to put her art and theatre-going to one side, and signed up to do war-work in a factory making aeroplane parts. Decidedly wealthy and artistic, Lena was at first something of an outsider in the factory, but eventually won over her colleagues with her attitude to hard work, her charm, and her love of placing a bet on the horses. Several of Beth's friends made their way to America, for various reasons. Peggy Webster, who had dual nationality, was already based there, while Dodie Smith had moved out because of the pacifist convictions of her now-husband Alec Beesley. Alec, several years younger than Dodie, was worried that he would be forced to join the army, and had convinced Dodie to take advantage of offers to work in Hollywood.[10] Alec spent the war working with other conscientious objectors to promote pacifist views, while Dodie, freelancing in a well-paid job as a scriptwriter and beginning to write novels, wrote endlessly to her friends in London, horrified to be missing out on what was developing in Britain. Gwen Ffrangcon-Davies was also persuaded by her partner to leave Britain, though Marda Vanne's motives were slightly different.

On 7th January 1940, Gordon wrote a long and revealing letter to Marda, discussing the war.[11] Marda, as a South African not feeling much British patriotism, had asked for advice on whether or not she should continue to persuade Gwen to leave England and come with her to South Africa. Gordon was very much against the idea of Gwen leaving, partly because she felt it would be a professional misjudgement: 'Already letters are beginning to appear in the film trade journals asking: "What is So-and-so doing in Hollywood? Hasn't he got a country any more?"' Gordon also tried to illustrate what she felt by discussing both her own personal feelings, and those of her family, including both her sisters – a rather rare occurrence in a letter to her theatre friends, where she tended not to focus on her family and private life and only to speak about her work. Gordon explained to Marda:

When the last war ended, my life drifted away from Service matters, both naval and military. Inasmuch as I had lived till I was eighteen in a town that was a Regimental Headquarters and within bugle call of a barracks, I would always have an interest in the army; but in England I met few Service people, and my daily interests led me further and further from them [...] And no one mentioned the war. No one, it seemed, had been marked in any way by those four years, or remembered them except to mention a butter shortage. To me, who could never quite forget, that seemed odd; but as the years went on I came to believe, without ever thinking definitely about it, that it was I who was odd, and that for the great bulk of the British people the war might never have happened.

Gordon particularly noted that for her sister Moire, who was eight years younger than her, the war did not seem to have much meaning – but she had recently been surprised to hear Moire say of someone at her work, 'He's not very popular. He didn't serve', – meaning that he hadn't joined up during the war.

Marda was not convinced, and she and Gwen went to South Africa.[12] Gwen was persuaded that it was the right thing to do, because the two women were invited to try and start a national theatre. They began a high profile and successful administrative, organizational and acting mission to improve South African theatre, with the aim of bringing two races together – meaning, of course, the two white races, English and Afrikaans. Marda, with her high-profile connections in South Africa, cleared the way for the two women to get invitations to the highest rank of society, where they worked hard to raise funds and raise the profile of the arts. For Gwen, it was part of her vocation to promote the arts, though as time went on she found her relationship with Marda more and more difficult, and was persuaded back to the UK in 1941 by John Gielgud, who offered her the part of Lady Macbeth. It was on the tour for *Macbeth* that Gwen and John met Gordon in Edinburgh.

By 1941, the war had already had a very personal impact on the MacKintosh family. Jean's husband Humphrey was killed in action in September 1940 when the flagship he was commanding was torpedoed and sunk by a U-boat.[13] Fifty-eight men were killed. Humphrey's body was washed ashore in Ireland, and he was buried in that country. Jean was not as good a correspondent as Moire and Beth, and there were periods when she did not keep in touch with her father Colin and her sisters as much. Beth in particular sometimes found her difficult to get on with. By the time Jean had managed to write to Moire and her family in Inverness, Beth had already read in the papers about Humphrey going missing, as the loss of his ship had been reported. Beth kept the knowledge from Colin at first, who heard it from Moire. He wrote at once to Jean, and worried to Moire about how she would be left financially. Humphrey, of course, was survived by his children and grandchildren from his first marriage as well as his second wife. In the event, things were arranged to everybody's satisfaction, Jean remaining in Buckinghamshire, on good terms with her stepchildren.

Beth managed a trip to visit her youngest sister in London in April 1941, during the Blitz.[14] On arriving in town, just off the sleeper train from Inverness, she found the city depressing and badly damaged, but was impressed to see cheerful women walking to work with bright lipstick and smart clothes, not looking at all as if they had been up all night. She went to Moire's flat where, she wrote ironically afterwards, she realized that the reason these women could live through Blitz nights being bombed but still get up and look lively and smart was that they all had a 'sleeping sickness', which Moire had picked up as well:

I know now how Moire has lived through the winter in London and come out looking not a day older. It is for the simple reason that there is no sound known to God or man that can keep her awake. At the height of last Saturday's blitz, about two in the morning, in her top floor flat, with pandemonium all around that drew the teeth from your head, – guns, shells, bombs, falling shrapnel, and ambulance gongs – she woke up suddenly, said with great distinctness: 'I really have a horribly guilty feeling that I should be staying awake when I have a guest.'

Moire then flopped over on her other side and resumed her snoring, leaving her 'guest' to face the three hours still to come with what philosophy she could! Beth remained awake, alone, quaking all night as the bombs continued to fall.

Moire was personally affected by the Blitz, as her flat was bombed out.[15] She herself was unhurt, but, as with so many other women, the war sharpened feelings that she had for one of her colleagues, and she soon after wrote to her father with the announcement that she was getting married. 'So you have made up your mind to get married', Colin wrote back to her. 'Well, well. I hope you will be happy.'[16] He had never met her fiancé, Donald Stokes, and wanted to know all about him. He thought he had a good Highland name but, jokingly, said that he was rather sad that Moire was marrying an Englishman. Colin had seen Jean very little since her marriage, and, if Moire married an Englishman, that would mean that she would be permanently based away from him – and from Beth. With men now being conscripted into the armed services, and with Jean's widowhood still raw, Colin and Beth could see that there were other unknown dangers ahead for Moire, while for Beth it brought back memories of both Hugh McIntosh and her World War I soldier.

Beth's situation was in contrast to her sisters. Now aged forty-five, she was the last unmarried MacKintosh daughter, a spinster caring for her aging father, and, with the difficulties of travel, the closure of the theatres, and the choices of her London friends, now cut off from parts of the professional career and the friendships that meant so much to her.

However, Gordon's depression, which Gielgud wrote about so movingly, was not solely linked to her own personal situation, but also to the wider implications of the war. As a sensitive, observational writer, Beth watched the people and society around her. War meant many different things to different people, but the First and Second World Wars in particular caused a rupture with the world that had gone before them, and perhaps Beth saw this more clearly and more immediately than many people of her generation. Beth was not only unhappy at the loss of a lover or a friend in the First World War, she was unhappy at the loss of a whole way of life. She herself had rebuilt her life more than once, reinventing herself as a teacher and later as a writer, and now she could see that she would have to do it all again, and that the whole society she lived in would have to do it again. *Kif* had reflected her understanding of what war can do to a society; *Richard of Bordeaux* had shown that she understood what grief could to a person and a nation.

Beth was born in 1896, when she had an uncle who drove a horse and cart; by 1952, when she died, she was living in a world of cars and nuclear bombs. As a writer whose career was based on observation, and a single woman whose life wasn't invested in her family, but was often turned outwards through her experiences, Beth saw these changes more clearly than many of the people around her. After the war, she wrote mainly detective fiction, and her books as Josephine Tey, her masterworks, although decidedly modern, are full of longing for a world that does not exist any more: the England before the war, or between the wars. The passages in *Brat Farrar* where Brat, coming home from America, describes England, are an elegy for something that was disappearing. Beth was an Anglophile, but, by the end of her life, she knew that she could never return to England even if family commitments and money allowed her to, because the England she wanted was one that no longer existed, that two World Wars had destroyed. Beth saw early on what the Second World War meant for her and for her country. Everything was going to change again. It took her a while to figure out how to deal with this, and her written output decreased sharply when the war began.

Another, more practical obstacle in the way of publication, as well as the lack of theatres in which to put on her plays, was paper rationing, which meant the number of books printed was limited. After turning already from writing for the stage to writing novels and biography, Beth needed to find a new format if she was going to continue publishing her work. However difficult it might be for her to reinvent herself and rebuild her life again, Beth was not going to give up. Even at the end of that depressing meeting in Edinburgh which Gielgud described so vividly, he noted that only a few days in his and Gwen's company seemed to revive Gordon. She might miss her friends and her pre-war life down south, but she was a writer, and all she needed to write was right there in Inverness. In 1941, she made a return to the format of the short story, and the first of her radio plays was broadcast.

At the outbreak of war, John Gielgud had publicly stated that he would do everything he could to entertain troops and boost morale.[17] There is a famous quote, attributed to Winston Churchill in the Second World War, in which he is reported as saying that culture was one of the things worth fighting for.[18] Accordingly, the role of ENSA, the Entertainments National Service Association, was given prominence, with actors touring round the serving troops providing entertainment. Binkie Beaumont, the theatre manager, organized a tour of army camps for Gielgud in the mid-1940s.[19] The entertainment generally consisted of several short pieces, rather than one long play, as that held the audience's attention better, and meant that pieces could be kept light and short. Noel Coward's plays were included in Gielgud's 1940s run, as were extracts from Gordon Daviot's play *Queen of Scots*. Extracts from the hugely popular *Richard of Bordeaux* also went down well on Gielgud's later ENSA tour to Gibraltar. These short extracts and shorter forms were where Gordon Daviot began to find an outlet for her writing.

Magazine readership – and, in fact, reading in general – went up in the Second World War, as long blackout evenings meant people had to stay indoors and find their own entertainment.[20] Short stories were in demand, and in February 1941 *Lilliput* magazine published a new Gordon Daviot story, *Bees*. *Lilliput* was a small-format magazine aimed, if the pictures of tastefully almost-naked women are anything to go by, at men, but with a good reputation for its fiction. Other authors featured around the time include James Thurber, Antonia White and Dorothy Whipple (whose novels have recently been republished to great acclaim by Persephone Books), while in its lifetime the magazine also published Doris Lessing and Evelyn Waugh. The brief biography given by Gordon Daviot for the magazine describes her as 'best known as the author of *Richard of Bordeaux*, *The Laughing Woman*, and other plays, but before taking to the theatre was a writer of short stories, as readers of the *English Review* and *Westminster Gazette* may remember'. Daviot added, 'I retired from the theatre; punch-drunk, in 1936. Still have a liaison with my first love.'[21] The story *Bees* is about a naval man who returns to service – owing something, undoubtedly, to Jean's late husband. It's the only short story I have been able to identify in published form from this period, but there were almost certainly more, particularly as amongst Beth's papers were manuscript versions of other short stories – 'The Thing That Knows The Time' seems to be a contender for being written at this time in her life.

Gordon Daviot was also busy writing short plays. John Gielgud's brother Val, whom she knew, was in charge of the BBC drama department, and, with the wartime reorganization of the BBC's service into a national programme with little regional variation and a strong duty to encourage patriotism, he was actively looking for quality writing. Gordon Daviot's plays had already proved popular on the radio, with *The Laughing Woman* adapted and broadcast near the start of the war, John Gielgud finally getting to play the title role of 'Rene' which he had so coveted.[22] Gielgud reprised his lead role in *Richard of Bordeaux* for another radio adaptation in 1941. Gordon Daviot published a collection of short plays entitled *Leith Sands and other plays* in 1946, but no explanatory note was put into the published book and it is not generally realized that most of these plays had been performed on BBC radio during the war. However, recent archiving projects have revealed the broadcast dates for several of her one-act plays during the war: *Leith Sands*, in 1941; *The Three Mrs Madderleys* in 1944; and *Mrs Fry has a Visitor*, also in 1944. *Sara*, *The Mother of Masé* and *Rahab* were collected together as 'Three Women', in three instalments just after the war ended, in June 1945. Gordon Daviot's full-length play *Queen of Scots* was adapted for radio in 1942; *Remember Caesar*, also in the *Leith Sands* collection, was broadcast in 1946; while two plays not in the *Leith Sands* collection – *The Pen of My Aunt* and *The Balwhinnie Bomb* – also appear to have been broadcast in 1946.[23]

Leith Sands was broadcast on BBC Radio Scotland in 1942.[24] The BBC had merged its stations into one 'Home Service' at the start of the war, but there were still some regional opt-outs and, as a play based on Scottish history, *Leith Sands* must have been thought to appeal particularly to the Scottish audience – it is one of Gordon Daviot's short plays which is often remembered and mentioned by an older audience. Leith Sands is an area in Edinburgh, but the play's hero is actually a Highlander, a well-known name for those in Inverness – Duncan Forbes. Gordon Daviot never engaged with the history of Culloden, the most famous historical incident near Inverness, but in *Leith Sands* she came close. The Forbes family were known for their appeals for clemency after 1746, and, despite their support for the government troops, the Forbeses paid for the monument to the Jacobites which still stands on the battlefield. Duncan Forbes was a character guaranteed to appeal to Gordon Daviot: a British-supporting, logical man, who tried to do the right thing even if it meant going against what people thought. *Leith Sands* is a one-act play focusing on an incident during his training as a lawyer in Edinburgh, where men are mistakenly hanged for murder. The play is set in a bar, where Duncan Forbes is not afraid to stand up against the anti-English sentiment of the other drinkers, who believe the hangings were right and necessary. He is finally proved right when the supposed murder victim walks in and asks for a drink. A prostitute, Belle Hepburn, is guilty of supplying the misinformation that led to the hanging, but Forbes also blames the bystanders for being swept up in the moment and not carrying out justice properly. It is a very 'Gordon Daviot' theme: she likes to set straight historical misconceptions. It also seems a play with some bold themes to broadcast during wartime: the idea that everyone should be responsible for justice and not get carried away with punishment could equally be applied to British attitudes towards Germany – though I think Daviot's main aim in writing the play, as with most of her work, was to elucidate a historical point.

Gordon Daviot's work was often broadcast on the BBC, particularly after her death, when many adaptations were made of her Josephine Tey novels. In the 1940s, when they produced *Leith Sands*, she was pleased enough to get the plays performed anywhere, given the wartime conditions, as she later wrote to her friend Lena Ramsden: 'At the time, it was found money. I just "used them up" on the BBC before collecting them.'[25] Beth was not financially dependent on her writing since Colin was still housing her and running his shop (and she still had considerable proceeds from *Richard of Bordeaux*). However, she later became dissatisfied with the wages that the BBC had paid her, explaining to Lena Ramsden in the same letter: 'Where the Corporation is concerned, I remember that before the Authors' Society screwed them up to a minimum they got my one-acters – brand new and unacted – for the price an amateur hack gets from a provincial daily for writing an article on a fortnight in Brittany for the Saturday page. But that rankles *now*, not then.'

The BBC certainly do not seem to have done a terribly good job in promoting her plays, given that many serious critics of Gordon Daviot's work still assert that she wrote nothing during the Second World War. Josephine Tey – and Gordon Daviot's – work is still being broadcast on the radio in the present day, so the BBC perhaps should have tried harder to develop a better relationship with Beth. Certainly she later turned down offers from the BBC because she was unhappy with the way they had treated her, and was unhappy with the quality of the adaptations they made. In a lengthy letter to her friend Lena, Beth explains her thinking on the manner, which sheds some light on her professional relationships. She was not happy with the BBC's pay, but had not attempted any negotiation. She preferred the financial side of her work to be taken care of by an agent, and did not wish to enter into discussions. Her lack of financial dependence on her writing influenced her attitude, and she treated her work in a personal, rather than detachedly businesslike manner. She had drifted into the agreements with the BBC because they suited her at the time, but when she became aware that the BBC were not paying her a fair rate, she instantly took action by refusing to give them any more stories – and then continued to refuse them stories in the future. She was later able to write that 'of course where the BBC are concerned Tey is out, since they won't pay my prices. (I get more pleasure out of bucking the Corporation than I ever could have had out of their measly few pounds.)' Beth was also unimpressed with some of the Scottish opt-outs of the BBC programming.[26] She felt these did not take the Highlands into account, and had too many Central Belt accents. In the North of Scotland, she said, these sounded almost more foreign to her than an English accent.

During the war, however, the BBC work was useful to Beth, particularly as, alongside her return to short stories, the short play format was encouraging her to experiment with different ideas. Her writing began to develop in new ways. *Leith Sands* was a fairly typical 'Gordon Daviot' historical play, but *The Three Mrs Madderleys* was completely different. After the bout of depression at the start of the Second World War, *The Three Mrs Madderleys* marked a change towards a lighter tone, reminiscent of *The Expensive Halo*. In this case, the story is very slight and has no moral – unless it is never to run around after a man, or believe what he says. Mary, Margaret and Marion meet over pink gin, and gradually find out that they all know the same, rather disappointing man: one woman is his current partner, one is his ex-wife and one is his mother. In the late 1990s, *The Three Mrs Madderleys* was one of the plays chosen to be performed by the local drama group in Inverness for a 'Gordon Daviot evening' – its humour still appealed, though it seemed dated.

Of the other plays broadcast on the BBC in wartime, *Mrs Fry has a Visitor* is another historical piece, with a twist in the tale rather like an early Daviot short story – it was to have an afterlife as a BBC children's television play, reflecting its gentle nature.[27] *Remember Caesar* is as light as *The Three Mrs Madderleys*, with gentle humour and an understanding of city life as opposed to country life:

> LADY WESTON   And the kitchenmaid thinks that she will stay in London after all.
> WESTON   Stay in London?
> LADY WESTON   Yes, she was leaving because she found London so quiet after the country.
> WESTON   Ridiculous!
> LADY WESTON   In the country, she said, if there wasn't a wedding there was a wake. It was never dull. A pleasant girl. I am glad London is being livelier for her.[28]

The Pen of My Aunt is the only play to have an explicitly wartime setting, set in France where a young man evades capture. It has echoes of *Kif*, but with a strong female lead this time, an older woman who helps the young man escape. Finally, *The Balwhinnie Bomb* is probably Gordon Daviot's very best short play, a genuinely funny slice of Highland life that has stood up to numerous revivals by amateur dramatic companies, and which easily translates to a modern audience.

It is obvious from the sheer number of publications and performances that Gordon Daviot was to produce in 1946 that she spent the Second World War writing. At the age of forty-eight, she no longer felt the need to volunteer, as she had done as a VAD in the First World War, and the time she wasn't writing was spent housekeeping and caring for Colin, who was now in his eighties.

He was still going to his fruit shop every day, but, although he had assistants to help out with the day-to-day serving behind the counter, wartime rationing made this job stressful, and he wasn't as able as he had been. 'I haven't been too well lately', Colin wrote to his youngest daughter in 1943, 'so I went to see Dr Campbell, who thinks I am wonderful for my age. I usually get to Castle St [the shop] about 10:30'.²⁹ Just as Beth couldn't travel south in wartime, so Moire found it difficult to travel north, though she and Jean did their best, arranging, so that they wouldn't disturb Beth and Colin too much, to stay in one of the two hotels in town that were not in Government service. Colin complained to Moire that Jean was not good at keeping in touch in between visits, and complained, too, that continual bad weather was taking its toll. In several letters Colin said he was struck down with colds and niggling bad health – 'Beth is not too well,' either, Colin added, 'but makes no reference to it in any letter.' (Beth wrote separately to Moire.) Beth carried on stoically working through any ill-health she was enduring.

When the collection *Leith Sands* was published after the war, it contained seven plays in total. By the time of publication, six of the seven had been broadcast on the radio. Just after the war had ended, *Sara*, *The Mother of Masé* and *Rahab* had been collected together as a series, entitled *Three Women*. These three plays, broadcast on three subsequent Sundays, continue the re-telling of Biblical stories in modern-day language that Gordon Daviot had started to explore in *The Stars Bow Down*: *Rahab* is about the walls of Jericho, but is chiefly concerned with longevity, and wishing one's name to be remembered after one's death. *The Mother of Masé* is about Moses (Masé being Daviot's version of Moses), and *Sara* is a one-act play that was later developed into the full-length production *The Little Dry Thorn*, and is about Sara and Abraham. Each story is told with considerable feeling for the Biblical characters. Beth was trying to make them into real people, whose stories and choices were relevant to understanding character, not just religious emblems. The final, apparently unperformed, play included in the collection is *Clarion Call*, about a family reunion engineered by a newspaper. Gordon

Daviot had written knowledgeably and with understanding about newspapermen since her first novel, though her experiences after *Richard of Bordeaux* had not improved her opinion of journalists. Interestingly, she keeps the same fictional name for her newspaper, *The Clarion*, consistently throughout her work, much in the way that she carried place names from her very early short stories through into her Inspector Grant mysteries.

The seven plays in the *Leith Sands* collection are as variable in subject matter as the rest of Gordon Daviot's output, and reflect her wide-ranging interests. From 1941's *Leith Sands* to 1944's *The Three Mrs Madderleys*, Gordon Daviot's mood seemed to have lightened considerably. Perhaps she came to feel, in common with other writers like Georgette Heyer, that, during wartime, a writer's duty is to entertain. Certainly the depressed Gordon Daviot that John Gielgud described meeting in 1941 had somehow found some sort of peace by the end of the war. She had turned the closure of the theatres and the rationing of paper to good account, turning the artificial interruption of wartime to her advantage by using the shorter formats that were available to her to experiment with new ideas and styles, and was to continue to develop this in her post-war writing. She had obviously also continued to read widely and to explore new subjects that might interest her. *Valerius*, about the Romans, dates from the 1940s, while a short play about Richard III, *Dickon* could possibly be dated as early as the mid-1940s. It dealt with the mysteries surrounding Richard III, the subject that she was to return to so successfully in *The Daughter of Time*.[30] A few other longer plays, which were posthumously published but don't appear to have been performed in her lifetime, may also date from the 1940s – *The Pomp of Mr Pomfret* for example, or *Lady Charing is Cross*, which are close to *The Three Mrs Madderleys* in style; or *Reckoning*, which seems closest to *Kif*, but with strong cinematic influences. *Barnharrow* too returns to the themes of her pre-war *Claverhouse*.

Beth's depression in the early years of the war was replaced by 1946 with her renewed focus on her writing. Her talents had grown and developed over the wartime period until, afterwards, she was able to produce some of her best work. As the war ended in 1945, Beth MacKintosh was about to enter one of the most creative phases of her writing career. She had got through the war, and had managed, once again, to hold onto her identity and her work as a writer, and to continue to have a life that she enjoyed despite the restrictions around her. She was entering the third stage of her career, where Beth MacKintosh and Gordon Daviot were soon to be taken over by Josephine Tey.

PART THREE

Josephine Tey
1946–1952

CHAPTER FIFTEEN

The Citizens Theatre

Although it was after the Second World War that Beth wrote most of her Josephine Tey novels, 1945 started with a return to the theatre as Gordon Daviot – and another reinvention with a new project under a different third pseudonym. It was a new phase of creativity and optimism.

Post-war theatre was entering a new phase, as cinema had won away the popular audience. In London, the big project was Olivier's National Theatre. In Scotland, the Citizens Theatre Company had been formed in 1943 by James Bridie. 'James Bridie' was the pseudonym of Glaswegian Oswald Henry Mavor, a doctor who had switched careers in the 1930s to focus on his hobby, and become a full-time writer. His plays had been successful on the London stage for some time, with *Tobias and the Angel* running concurrently to Gordon Daviot's *Richard of Bordeaux* in 1933. Bridie, through his involvement with the Citizens and, later, the RSAMD (Royal Scottish Academy of Music and Drama[1]) has earned the title of the 'father of modern Scottish theatre'. Unlike Gordon Daviot, he was involved in all aspects of the theatre world, from writing plays to setting up theatre companies, to discussions with actors, to screenwriting jobs (like Daviot, he worked with Hitchcock). The library at Glasgow University Union is named after him, as is the Bridie dinner that takes place in the University each year (it was at the University of Glasgow that he first studied to be a doctor, and he kept up his links with the place for many years). In short,

Bridie was a public figure. And yet, this man, whom so many saw and still see as 'Scotland's best-known playwright', considered that 'Scotland's greatest living playwright' was Gordon Daviot.[2] He founded the Citizens Theatre Company to promote Scottish playwriting and acting, as opposed to bringing up shows from London, and when he was looking for a new play to showcase his company's talents, one of the first playwrights he turned to was Daviot.

The Citizens Theatre Company had been based at the Athenaeum Theatre in Buchanan Street in Glasgow for the first two years of their existence, but found it too cramped.[3] In 1945, with the end of the war, they began looking for a new building. They were offered a lease of The Royal Princess's Theatre in the Gorbals area of Glasgow. This was an old building, with a memorable theatrical past (including a well-known story about a riot caused when an elephant on stage panicked). It was renamed the Citizens Theatre, and still thrives today. It has a distinguished theatrical history, partly because of the radical blueprint that Bridie drew up when he opened: the Citizens Theatre, he hoped, was to be a theatre that would genuinely appeal to every citizen in Glasgow. Tickets were to be accessibly priced, programmes were to be free, and it would showcase the very best in home-grown Scottish playwriting. The venue is still a major producing theatre, staging new work by Scottish playwrights, and still has an extremely competitive pricing structure, including cheap tickets that enable Glasgow students to see the likes of new plays by Liz Lochhead and professional revivals of classical Greek drama from the cheap, uncomfortable seats near the back. The Citizens Theatre has a special atmosphere for its audience and for the actors who play there, and Gordon Daviot helped to build its foundations. However, her dislike of publicity, and her desire to hide behind a pseudonym, means that her total contribution to the Citizens, and to Scottish theatre, has not always been recognized.

The Citizens Theatre Company officially opened in their new home on 11th September 1945 with a production of *Johnson Over Jordan* by J. B. Priestley.[4] They wanted to follow this successful run with new plays by Scottish writers, to firmly establish their aim to be an innovative Scottish company. By October 1945, Mathew Forsyth of the Citizens Theatre Company was in negotiation with Dramatic Agent Mrs T. C. (Evelyn) Dagnall (in association with A. M. Heath & co), London, to put on a new play by Gordon Daviot. The play was called *The Little Dry Thorn*, and it was an expanded version of the one-act religious play *Sara* that was soon to be published in Daviot's collection *Leith Sands*, and which had just been broadcast on BBC radio in June of 1945.

The Citizens Theatre Company agreed with the agent that they would be the first to perform *The Little Dry Thorn*. It would not be performed anywhere else in Scotland before their production, and it would not be performed by anyone else in Scotland for a year after the Citizens Theatre production (though an exception was carefully made for a possible one-off production in Leeds). Essentially, the Citizens wanted to make sure that they were the first and only theatre company to have Daviot's new play. They also agreed to pay Gordon Daviot 5 per cent royalties. After the initial negotiations with the agent were completed, and Gordon Daviot had signed the contract, the Citizens Theatre Company began to write directly to the playwright herself. From this moment on, the correspondence becomes more and more chatty and familiar. Gordon Daviot liked her agent to do the initial legal negotiations over money and rights for her, but once she herself was involved, the letters become far more informal. The administrator at the Citizens Theatre also becomes more informal in his letters to her agent, as they start to build up a working relationship. Several letters were necessary to sort out all the details, and the correspondence filed by the Citizens Theatre for *The Little Dry Thorn* continues long after the contract is signed, into June 1946. Gordon Daviot spent some time on correspondence like this, not only for this play, but also for all her previously produced work. As her work was very successful, the administrative tasks associated with her writing needed time and effort as well as the new writing she was doing. For example, at this time she was also in negotiations with the BBC, who produced an adaption by Hugh Stewart of *Richard of Bordeaux* for broadcast on their 'Saturday Night Theatre' radio programme on 26th July 1946, as well as, that same year, the first broadcast of Gordon Daviot's one-act play *Remember Caesar*.[5] Gordon has been criticized for not taking part in the 'tea party' circuit in Inverness, but it's doubtful if her neighbours understood how much time she needed for her work. She was not a loner who did not want to join in, she was a busy working woman. Gordon was not a hermit; she was in constant contact by letter with her professional colleagues, and her friends. The Citizens Theatre Company – or at least representatives of it – were also among the small number of her professional colleagues who made the effort to travel to Inverness to visit her: a letter from 1946 states 'looking forward to seeing you in Inverness', and it seems Gordon Daviot received visits both before the production started in Glasgow, and later when it toured to Inverness.

The Citizens Theatre Company archive contains copies of most of the correspondence between Daviot, her agent and the Company, but, frustratingly, letters are not always signed, as only the carbon copy was kept on file. This sometimes makes it hard to know who was writing, but Gordon Daviot was mainly in touch with Mathew Forsyth, and with James Bridie himself. Mathew Forsyth, the Citizens' producer, had been the stage director for *Richard of Bordeaux* at its first performances in 1932 and Daviot specifically said that she gave her play to the 'Citz', 'because of Mathew Forsyth [...] he was very sweet and kind to me when I was new in the theatre'.[6] It was Mathew Forsyth who had first written to ask if she had a play, and she had obliged with *The Little Dry Thorn*. Gordon Daviot was well known for her ability to make friends, and keep up friendships with, the backstage staff at her productions, the cushion she had received from the backstage crew at *Richard of Bordeaux* being the best illustration of this.

These friendships have not seemed as glamorous to later admirers of Daviot as her friendships with leading actors, but they were, perhaps, ultimately more useful to her. *Richard of Bordeaux* was well known for being a production with a number of 'new' people working on it – it was the Motley's first production, Daviot's first play, and so on – and many of these backstage people, not just the actors, had gone on to have successful careers in theatre. Another key figure working backstage at the Citz was set designer Molly

MacEwen, the elder daughter of Alexander MacEwen, ex-provost of Inverness, and sister of Margaret, who had by now ended her affair with Neil Gunn. Gordon Daviot became very friendly with Molly, who was about twelve years her junior.[7] Neil Gunn, incidentally, was well aware of Daviot's shows at the Citz, and was in correspondence with James Bridie himself throughout the 1945 negotiations for the post-war season, though mainly about their nights out – meals with the literati (all male). Another connection between the two men was Bridie's cousin, the Reverend Ivan Mavor, who was based in Inverness for a time and whom Gunn had met through Alexander MacEwen.[8]

Inverness was closely linked in to the Scottish literary world – Scotland is a small place and connections are easy enough to make – but there were barriers set in Gordon's way. Bridie was very much a man's man, and, although he was happy to take Gordon Daviot's plays, he would never have socialized with her in the way that he socialized with Neil Gunn. When Gordon Daviot met Bridie, it would have been with his wife Rona, in a more family setting – though, since Rona had connections to the Black Isle and the Inverness area, this was congenial for Beth, and Rona always remembered her fondly. The rub was that when Bridie and Gunn met socially, along with other people like Hugh MacDiarmid and the painter J. D. Fergusson, their discussions about things like the formation of a Scottish Academy rather set the scene for Scottish literary culture – and thus excluded Gordon Daviot, not just from attending and influencing these meetings, but from later analysis.[9] Gordon Daviot and James Bridie got on very well, but when scholars later looked at the Scottish literary scene, Bridie's polite negotiations by letter with Gordon Daviot have not been seen as being as significant as nights where Bridie, Gunn and MacDiarmid met in the pub.[10]

But it was not just Gordon Daviot's contacts that helped her to get plays produced. She was well aware of how things worked. The quality of her writing was always the key aspect that attracted people to her work, and she wanted to make sure that this always shone through, and was never overshadowed by any publicity or associations with her name, sex or previous work. In 1945,

Gordon Daviot decided to try out a third pseudonym. This third name was never revealed during her lifetime, and, even now, over sixty years after her death, it is barely known. In 1945, at the same time as she was carrying out negotiations with the Citizens Theatre Company for Gordon Daviot's *The Little Dry Thorn*, Beth MacKintosh was also negotiating with the Citizens Theatre for *Cornelia*, by F. Craigie Howe.[11] Actively on the lookout for new scripts, when the Citizens Theatre Company received the comedy *Cornelia* by F. Craigie Howe, they were very keen to put it on. *Cornelia* was to be one of the successes of their new programme at their new theatre, and the 'mystery' of the author was news in all the Glaswegian and national Scottish papers. Although journalists at the time tried their hardest, in this instance Beth MacKintosh managed to fool everyone. The only person who knew the identity of 'F. Craigie Howe' was James Bridie, and he took the secret to the grave with him. The pen name was not revealed until after both Bridie and Daviot had died.

Beth MacKintosh had recognized a change in her writing during the Second World War. I have highlighted the lightening of her mood, which was evident in the short one-act plays which were broadcast on the BBC, and later collected in *Leith Sands*. *The Three Mrs Madderleys* was startlingly different in tone to *Sara* – and *Cornelia* was startlingly different in tone to *The Little Dry Thorn*. Beth decided that she did not want the name 'Gordon Daviot' to be identified with a light Coward-esque romantic comedy, and she chose her new pen-name for this reason.[12] Craigie Howe is a place name on the Black Isle, near Inverness. Beth was a dedicated walker, and had thoroughly explored the countryside where she lived, so it seems certain that this is where she got the name. She was always fond of names with secret meanings. To get to Craigie Howe from her home in Crown, she could walk up to the water in Merkinch, and then take the ferry over to the Black Isle. Walking round Ord Hill, she would eventually come to the steep cliffs which are known as Craigie Howe. It is a long walk, but nothing for a former Anstey student. Shallow caves at the bottom of the cliffs look out over stony beaches to the water of Munlochy Bay. At the entrance to the cave at the bottom of the hill known as

Craigie Howe there was once a natural spring, though nowadays it is just a muddy pool. It's easy to imagine Elizabeth, contented in this isolated place, exhilarated from the walk to get there, and making plans for her future. There's no indication of what the 'F' in 'F. Craigie Howe' might have stood for – 'Female'?

The Citizens Theatre Company archive is now housed at the Scottish Theatre Archive in the University of Glasgow. A member of the library staff found the file on *Cornelia* for me easily enough, but then had a whispered consultation with one of her colleagues. According to their records, the file was 'restricted' – but no one could remember why. The initial negotiations for *Cornelia* were carried out between the Citizens Theatre Company and a theatrical agent, much like the negotiations for *The Little Dry Thorn*, but then the secret of F. Craigie Howe's identity had been revealed, in the strictest of confidence, to James Bridie only. Bridie had been sworn to such strict secrecy that the file was still marked 'restricted' after all these years.

Beth MacKintosh had signed the contract for *Cornelia* in October 1945, two months before the contract for *The Little Dry Thorn* was signed. The terms were similar, with productions being reserved for the Citizens Theatre Company first, and Beth to receive 5 per cent of the profits. The contract letter was sent to 'Mr. F. Craigie Howe esq., c/o Crown Cottage, Inverness'. After the formalities were over, the Citizens Theatre Company (probably in the person of James Bridie, as the style is his confrontational, over-honest best) wrote to Beth,

Dear Gordon Daviot,
I read with great delight your play of Abraham, and now am going to have the temerity to say, as a pious writing it is delightful, but as a play Craigie Howe's Cornelia is much better. Abraham on his own is an amusing and extremely interesting study, but has absolutely no dramatic shape, and while I am looking forward to doing "Cornelia" by F. Craigie Howe, I am still hoping for a 'good play!!' from yourself.
Thank you very much for letting me read 'The Little Dry Thorn'.

———————

241

As with her experience on *Richard of Bordeaux*, Beth was happy to let her writing do the talking. She didn't rely on her 'name' or position as an established writer to get her work produced, but instead wanted it to be accepted as a quality piece of work that could stand on its own. Most people would agree with James Bridie that *Cornelia* is more enjoyable than *The Little Dry Thorn*, but with some qualifications.

Cornelia Taft from Forks of Sagataw in Labrador in Canada is one of Gordon Daviot's ingénue heroines, a little like Erica Burgoyne in *A Shilling for Candles*. This kind of heroine can be rather wearing in her relentless unconventionality and energy, but Cornelia does have her appealing moments, and the unrealistic, Cinderella-in-reverse quality of the play makes it rather good fun. *Cornelia* has more 'dramatic shape' than *The Little Dry Thorn* in that it has a clear beginning, middle and end, and the conclusion is nicely set up, with pointers leading to it rather in the way a mystery novel needs its clues to get to a satisfactory conclusion. *Cornelia* is well constructed. Cornelia herself dramatically arrives in a taxi in England, where she is met with incredulity and a little indulgence by the butler Parkin (a very Bunter-esque figure) and her new guardian Lucas:

PARKIN   I beg your pardon, sir, but I don't seem to have enough to take care of the taxi.

CORNELIA   Take care of it? Who wants to take care of it?

LUCAS   All right, Parkin. (Feeling in his pocket) How much is it?

PARKIN   Eleven pounds, seventeen shillings, and ninepence, sir.

LUCAS   What!

CORNELIA   (equably)I was afraid it might be quite a bit.

LUCAS   Cornelia, How far have you come by cab?

CORNELIA   From the docks.

LUCAS   You mean you came all the way from Southhampton by taxi-cab?

CORNELIA   No; from Liverpool.

LUCAS   But why didn't you take the train?

CORNELIA   I didn't like the look of them.[13]

She has arrived at Liverpool rather than Southampton because she took a working boat from Canada, rather than the luxury passenger ship. This sets the scene for Cornelia's unconventional attitude to class, which is easy to indulge with the amount of money her guardian lavishes on her. She gets herself a new fur coat and, her heart's desire, a pair of utterly impractical high heeled shoes and proceeds to learn how to fish, beat everyone at golf and show how good she is at shooting, while making remarks about how things are done in the little town she comes from, interspersed with the homely wisdom of 'Barney from the store' and a cutting analysis of socialist politics. So long as it's not seen as being in any way realistic, it is a bouncy, readable play that rattles along to its satisfying conclusion.

The Little Dry Thorn is quite different. It tells the Old Testament story of Sara and Abraham, Abraham's conversations with God and his journeys, and Sara's struggles with fertility and her arrangement with her handmaiden Hagar to bear Abraham's first child. It breathes life into names that have become symbols, endowing the Biblical characters with personality, charm and humour, and shows real insight into character. Sara has to deal with practicalities as well as religious concepts, as we watch her and Hagar pack away her clothes before they follow Abraham. Clothes can be 'a great comfort' says Sara. 'It is very odd having to say goodbye to one's clothes [...]. One *grieves* for them.' The genuine sadness and confusion Sara feels at leaving her home is expressed through descriptions – hers and others – of her clothes, and the occasions when she wore them. In this, and other flashes, we can see not only her characters but also Gordon Daviot's personality.

However, as James Bridie summed it up privately to Gordon Daviot, although delightful, it has very little shape. To a serious scholar of the Bible, who takes it as read that every Biblical story is of inherent interest, it is a play which can stimulate debate and provide food for thought. For the audience who is less familiar with the story, it has an inherent shapelessness: there is little dramatic tension. The play is not expressly religious, and its point is not to convince the audience of the existence of God, it is an exploration of people's lives, but by making it less overtly religious the audience are never entirely clear quite why these people's lives should be of interest. Publicly, James Bridie told the press that *The Little Dry Thorn* had 'gentle clarity', while on the accompanying programme handed out to all the audience members at the Citz, Gordon Daviot said it was 'a simple folk tale from the Middle East'.

Gordon Daviot helped the Citizens Theatre considerably with publicizing *The Little Dry Thorn*. Daviot has often been described as being wary of the press, and she certainly avoided them after *Richard of Bordeaux*, but her attitude had changed after the Second World War. The renewed optimism with which she was attacking her writing career seems to have spilled over into a willingness to speak about herself, her opinions and her writing. From this point on, if she was asked, she was quite happy to volunteer information. Several articles, over several days, in the Glasgow *Evening News*, the *Evening Citizen* and the *Daily Record* quoted Daviot directly, as she publicly said that she was an 'enthusiastic supporter' of the Citizens Theatre.[14] The *Evening Citizen* reported that she had been writing plays from her schooldays, while the *Evening News* recalled the success of *Richard of Bordeaux* and drew its readers' attention to the fact that Mathew Forsyth of the Citz had worked on that production. *The Observer* noted another link to Daviot's home town of Inverness, pointing out that the new scenic designer at the Citz was Molly MacEwen, daughter of a former provost of Inverness. Both the *Evening News* and the *Daily Record* reported Daviot's opinions on modern theatre-going, characteristically expressed in her forthright manner, including her dislike of smoking in the auditorium and, particularly, intervals in plays. Daviot thought the social aspect of play going should be satisfied before and after a performance, not during: 'How can a man who has been out to the bar, bought a packet of cigarettes, greeted five separate acquaintances, stood a friend a drink, damned the government, arranged a golf four for Saturday, and cast an eye over the local houris, be expected to care two hoots what happens to imaginary characters in Act II of any play?' The *Daily Record*, interested in the Citz' intention of focusing on Scottish plays by Scots, expressed an interest in this eminent Scottish playwright's opinion of the current vogue for writing in Scots, but Daviot said bluntly, 'there's no special virtue in the Doric'. She was never keen on any expression of Scottish nationalism, and, as a native of Inverness, would never have spoken any form of Scots, so it was particularly irrelevant to her.[15]

Meanwhile, the press campaign for *Cornelia* was managed expertly. For about two weeks from 15th April to 26th April 1946, the play, and its mysterious author, were the hot topic in all Glasgow's newspapers. Clippings saved by the Citizens Theatre Company include articles with titles like 'New Play By "Mystery" Scots Author' in the *Daily Record*. Even the producer and the cast had no idea who 'F. Craigie Howe' was, and the papers were desperate to find out. The cast of *Cornelia* were reported to have received telegrams wishing them every success from the mysterious 'F. Craigie Howe' postmarked in London, and there was much speculation over whether it was a Scot in exile. As well as these 'news' items, in the entertainment columns of the papers were gossip articles with profiles of the play's stars and details of the costumes they were to wear. One article would, I think, have particularly appealed to that lover of clothes, Beth MacKintosh: a special exposé of how a prominent Glasgow department store had lent the Citz' costume department £3,000 worth of fur coats.

The publicity did not stop at previews. Once *The Little Dry Thorn* and *Cornelia* were running the press enthusiastically reviewed the shows, and then followed their progress, and the progress of everyone connected with the Citz. A party of Church of Scotland ministers made a special trip from Edinburgh, where they had been attending the General Assembly, to see *The Little Dry Thorn*. And it seems that no fact or rumour about James Bridie's negotiations with Hollywood to work on a script was too small to be avidly reported. The Citizens Theatre Company's spring 1946 season, their first in their new theatre, was a roaring success, and it was mainly down to Beth MacKintosh. They were resting their reputation for good Scots plays on not one, but two of her productions. This showed massive confidence in her ability – and it shows one reason why James Bridie, no mean publicist, felt it was imperative to keep F. Craigie Howe's identity a true secret. Paper after paper praised the Citz for promoting Scots writing, saying that two plays of this quality, *The Little Dry Thorn* and *Cornelia*, proved that the Citz was doing the right thing supporting Scottish-born authors as clearly there was plenty of talent out there. If James Bridie had let slip that both plays were by the same author, he would have undermined the manifesto he and the Citz were trying to create. Beth's awareness of this, and her continuing friendship with Bridie, might be one reason why she never returned again to the F. Craigie Howe pseudonym. She also found another outlet for that lightness of tone in her Josephine Tey novels, while the positive reception of *The Little Dry Thorn* may also have convinced her that 'Gordon Daviot' had much yet to give. The Citizens' approach to her as Daviot confirmed for her that her name was not forgotten, and her point had been made when she got *Cornelia* accepted – her writing was always good enough to stand on its own merits.

The fact that neither reviewers, nor any of the Citz' actors, worked out who F. Craigie Howe was, is a real testament to Beth MacKintosh's writing ability. Several of the actors and actresses who played in *Cornelia* from 15th–26th April, went on to play parts in *The Little Dry Thorn* from 29th April–10th May. The actress Rona Anderson played Cornelia in the first play – her first major role – and then went on to play Hagar in *The Little Dry Thorn* – a major part. And yet, although some reviewers guessed that F. Craigie Howe was a woman, the characters in *Cornelia* and in *The Little Dry Thorn* were so well drawn that no one, not even Rona Anderson who would have carefully studied every word of Cornelia's and Hagar's speeches, recognized that the same author had created all these different parts. This strength and ability to draw characters and work on completely different subjects was both a strength and a weakness for Beth MacKintosh. Many later critics have picked up on the section in her novel *The Daughter of Time*, where Inspector Grant laments the 'sameness' of most authors' 'new' novels, and how similar they always are to their previous work. No one could ever accuse Beth MacKintosh of churning out the same recycled themes: *Cornelia* is as wildly different to *The Little Dry Thorn* as *Brat Farrar* is widely different in theme to *Miss Pym Disposes*. Equally, however, it meant that playgoers and readers never quite knew what to expect. There was no 'new Gordon Daviot' play, and, as with *The Laughing Woman*, sometimes her audience stayed away out of disappointment when they did not recognize anything they knew in her new work.

The Citizens Theatre Company's staff carefully noted the reactions of the audience at all performances of *Cornelia* and *The Little Dry Thorn*.[16] Performance reports were written up, and the notes used for the following night's performance, as well as being kept in the Citz archive files. Between calculations of timings (the play was about two hours long, with an interval, despite Gordon Daviot's dislike of breaks in the performance), prop plans and lighting cues, there are notes that *Cornelia* received '3 calls – excellent reception!' Later performances got up to four curtain calls. *The Little Dry Thorn* ran the following week. From surviving photos and posters, the lead actor and actress Edmund Bailey (Abraham) and Enid Hewitt (Sara) were dressed in Egyptian-looking costume against backdrops that aimed towards the Motleys' high standards. The play was received in the more serious manner it was written, with fewer laughs and curtain calls, but the careful notation of audience numbers and box office receipts shows that from 4th–11th May 1946 it took over £650 and played to over 3,300 people over eight performances (including matinees). Gordon Daviot considered that it was '[O]ne of my MAJOR TRIUMPHS'.[17]

Amongst the good reviews of both plays, and the speculation over the identity of 'F. Craigie Howe', one article had noted that the cast of *Cornelia* were sent 'good luck' telegrams from London. Beth MacKintosh had not attended the original performances of *Cornelia* (though she did attend *The Little Dry Thorn*) in April, because she was away on holiday. Now that the travel restrictions in place during the Second World War had lifted, Beth had accepted an invitation from her friend Lena Ramsden to attend Newmarket races in England.

Lena Ramsden was the sort of woman who could have been a model for 'Cornelia': resolutely unconventional, with the money to back up and excuse any sort of eccentric behaviour, she was a sometime sculptor and great lover of the theatre who lived in a studio in Primrose Hill. She was friends with Gwen Ffrangcon-Davies and had known Gordon Daviot since the 1930s. During the Second World War, wishing to contribute to the war effort, and despite her age and total lack of experience, she had found work as a lathe turner, interspersing this difficult factory work with hospitality from sympathetic friends, visits to various pubs, and the odd broadcast on the BBC. She was part of a creative set of women that included many of Gwen's Tagley Cottage friends, and also the writer Marguerite Steen.

Through Lena, Beth must surely have been aware of Marguerite: the opinionated Steen, mistress of the well-known portrait painter William Nicholson, must have made a vivid contrast to the sort of literary society available in Scotland.[18] Although *Cornelia* was pure fantasy, Beth MacKintosh did have some experience of the social round she described 'Cornelia' rejecting. Lena, though, had more in common with Beth than Marguerite the writer had, in their shared passion for horse racing. With Gwen and Marda still in South Africa, and with the shared experience of living in Britain during wartime, Gordon became much closer to the garrulous, enthusiastic and friendly Lena, and their friendship deepened in the 1940s.

Lena, after spending the war working very hard, was looking forward to a holiday, and was delighted to see her Scottish friend after so long. The two women travelled from London to Newmarket races by car (Lena drove).[19] Although Lena doesn't record whether or not the two women discussed the theatre, she does provide a vivid picture of the journey they made each day from the races to the house where they stayed:

At one sharp bend there was a garden in which grew an apple tree, which was unfailingly obliging with a full show of blossom. I shall always remember with pleasure Gordon's delight in that tree. In spite of the vagaries of spring weather, on the day we arrived it was always covered with tight, pink buds, which by the end of the week were so fully opened that they were almost white. Each day, as we approached the turning on our way back from racing, Gordon craned forward to see what progress had been made, and I stopped the car so that we could jointly admire the tree before driving on. I looked on the tree as a talisman; a guarantee of Gordon's continued enjoyment of that particular holiday.

Gordon returned with Lena to Newmarket several times. In January 1948 she wrote to Lena: 'your letter comes, suggesting Newmarket again. And I remembered the peace of that house, and the nice green Newmarket world, full of space, and the apple tree – No things to un-remember about it.'

Whatever feelings of depression Gordon had at the start of the Second World War were now completely gone: she was full of renewed optimism and hope for the future. Her writing career was blossoming forth, and would soon be in full bloom.

Miss Pym Disposes

1946 was a year of great change for Beth, a reawakening after the difficult years of the Second World War. Now that two of her plays had gone down well, offers for her theatrical work began to come in again, though, as the nature of theatre changed post-war, so the offers of work changed. *Leith Sands*, her collection of short plays, was published and, most importantly, Josephine Tey began to take over from Gordon Daviot, as *Miss Pym Disposes* was published, the first of six mystery novels. Beth opened up to the press and re-established her ties with not only her London friends but also contacts from her college years – and became an aunt for the first and only time. Her creative circle widened, as shown by her friendship with James Bridie, and it seems that it was around this time that she also became friends with the successful Scottish author and journalist Elisabeth Kyle (real name Agnes Dunlop).[1] Yet, paradoxically, as Beth's life expanded after the restrictions of wartime, and her circle of family and friends got larger again, it was at this very time that the perception of her as a 'loner' in Inverness grew.

Other theatre companies had noted the success of Gordon Daviot's *The Little Dry Thorn*, and the Citz began to receive communications from the Wilson Barrett repertory theatre company.[2] Wilson Barrett staged a production of *Richard of Bordeaux* in both Glasgow and Edinburgh in summer 1946, a well-timed repeat which capitalized on and took advantage of the renewed interest in Daviot's plays, and they wanted to secure the rights to *The Little Dry Thorn* as well.[3] The Citz referred them to Gordon Daviot, but, as with all her business negotiations, she passed them on to her agent and did not want to deal with them directly. It was clear, though, that Gordon did not want *The Little Dry Thorn* to become a play for what she saw as second-rate repertory. She still wanted a professional London run: '[my agent] knows', she wrote to her friend Mathew Forsyth at the Citizens, 'that I don't want the play to become "small change" before we get a West End showing, and perhaps can tactfully discourage him for the moment. The THORN will not date and is fore-ordained to be God's gift to repertory for years to come, so there is no need to cash in on it.'[4]

Instead, the Citizens Theatre Company took *The Little Dry Thorn* on a short tour to Edinburgh, but letters rumbled on between the Citizens Theatre Company and Wilson Barret. Mrs Dagnall, Gordon Daviot's agent, finally settled the matter, writing to confirm that Wilson Barrett did not have permission for any performances, as she was in negotiation for a West End contract. The Citizens Theatre Company wrote back immediately, wanting to know more about this contract, and, producing their trump card, saying that they themselves had had an invitation to perform the play in London, as part of an 'exchange' visit with the Lyric Theatre in Hammersmith – which eventually took place in 1947. They also extended their tour of *The Little Dry Thorn* around Scotland, including a visit to Inverness, where it played at the Empire Theatre on the 12th August 1946 and Beth MacKintosh met up with her friends and colleagues from the cast.[5] The play was reviewed and mentioned by the *Highland News*, *Inverness Courier* and the *Northern Chronicle*, though, in contrast to the Glasgow papers, there were no interviews and no special mention of Beth MacKintosh. Beth might have been happy now to do interviews, but she was still not the sort of person to do publicity. She would attend a literary party in London that she had been invited to, but the thought of phoning up someone at the local paper to promote her new play would never have occurred to her. Not only did she not need the publicity, she probably felt, since the family-owned *Inverness Courier* still had staff members who went to school with her, that the journalists should be doing their job and seeking her out. Professionally she didn't need the publicity, and personally she was not going to beg for recognition. The Beth who had written 'His Own Country' still felt ambiguous about Inverness, and was now the Beth who disagreed with the nationalist politics of the prevailing literary scene in Scotland. Her Josephine Tey novels always had reference to Scotland and Scottish characteristics, some more cutting than others, and this was the light in which she approached much of her dealings with the local press. She had been well reported in the Glasgow press, but the Highland press seemed to have forgotten the identity of Gordon Daviot.

The national London-based press, however, had not. As well as the previews and reviews for *The Little Dry Thorn* and *Cornelia,* the administrators at the Citizens Theatre carefully kept and pasted into their scrapbooks a cutting from *The Observer* of Sunday 28th April 1946. Alongside good reviews of the Citizens productions, the show business reporter Mamie Crichton wrote an article entitled 'Author reveals a thrilling secret'. In this, Mamie Crichton described meeting and talking with Gordon Daviot at a party. 'Because we, two Scots, both know a little Sussex village so unexploited that few except its inhabitants ever seem to have heard of it, we got chatting, the secret slipped out and Miss Daviot allows me to publish it' – i.e. Gordon Daviot and Josephine Tey were the same person. This secret 'was to have been disclosed in the autumn anyway, when my next whodunit comes out', Beth is quoted as saying. Beth went on to reveal a little more about her writing: 'As against historical plays, thriller-writing is "like a piece of knitting: it's my way of relaxing"'. In the same piece Beth stated that she had not yet decided on the title of her next novel. It was to become *Miss Pym Disposes*. Compared to the research needed for *The Little Dry Thorn*, or for *Richard of Bordeaux*, writing *Miss Pym Disposes* must certainly have required a very different approach.

This interview with *The Observer* must have taken place during Beth's spring holiday, at the same time as she had visited

Newmarket with Lena. Her renewed enthusiasm for life and confidence in her work is clear. She was now happy to attend literary parties and chat to journalists in a way that she had not really done in the days of *Richard of Bordeaux*. Ironically, however, next to Mamie Crichton's article in *The Observer* were their two reviews of the Citizens' productions: one for Gordon Daviot's *The Little Dry Thorn*, and one for F. Craigie Howe's *Cornelia*. The reviewer had no idea that Daviot and Howe were the same person. Beth was still keeping some secrets.

This piece in *The Observer* is also the first time in print that Beth referred to her mystery novels as 'knitting'. It was a phrase she was to return to, and her friends remembered and repeated it, until it became something that critics and analysts of her novels continually referred to.[6] The idea that Beth saw her writing as Gordon Daviot as serious work and her writing as Josephine Tey as unimportant 'yearly knitting' became established. However, her work under the two names was always intertwined, and she never prioritized one over the other. All of her work was important to her. When Beth first tried to describe the different feelings she had about writing mystery novels and plays, she didn't realize the interpretation later critics would put on her work. Composing a novel is a different process to composing a piece of theatre based on historical research. *Miss Pym Disposes* came from a very different place to *The Little Dry Thorn*: from her own life, from experiences she had had over twenty years, now seen from a mature standpoint, and with the added confidence of a writer who has mastered her craft and is able to construct a story. Beth MacKintosh was now fifty years old, and *Miss Pym Disposes* might have seemed to her like easy writing after the research necessary for a historical play, but there is fifty years of research in the novel; fifty years of living and observing, and twenty or more years of practice at the craft of writing.

Miss Pym Disposes is a rather strange mystery book, as the reader doesn't even know what the mystery is until chapter sixteen (of twenty-two), and even then it's not immediately clear if it is a murder mystery or not. Nevertheless, it is compulsively readable from the start. The common memory of the insistence of school bells and the nerves of those preparing for examinations give the book its initial sense of urgency, and then the reader, like Miss Pym, starts to want to know what will happen to the students. *Miss Pym Disposes* is particularly absorbing because of its strongly drawn characters, and the strange world it describes.

The novel is set in 'Leys Physical Training College', a fictional establishment, but one that is based very firmly on Beth MacKintosh's real-life college, Anstey. 'Leys' is a local Inverness place name, perhaps the name of the hospital where Beth was a VAD, one more example of her enjoyment in choosing names for her fiction. The book is so accurate in its description of the college building and grounds that a former Anstey student could pinpoint the exact room where 'Miss Pym' stays.

Miss Pym is a visiting lecturer, and old schoolmate of the headmistress Henrietta, who comes to give the students a talk on psychology, and stays because she likes the atmosphere and then becomes interested in the students themselves, before becoming involved in the mystery surrounding the student Rouse's death.

Rouse's death had its real-life counterpart in Beth's accident in the Oban High School gym in the 1920s, while the impetus behind the crime reputedly was based on how Beth felt when she was passed over for first prize in art and recommendation to art college when she was at the IRA.[7] However, it is not entirely certain that the murder is the real 'crime' in the book. In some ways, Henrietta's short-sightedness in not offering a prestigious teaching post to Mary Innes and offering it instead to Rouse is presented as equally dreadful. Innes herself also accepts blame for being unable to control her reactions. It is an intensely moral book. The mystery is not just who committed the crime, but who is to blame and why, and it shows how small decisions are more important than large ones in creating criminals – and creating people.

The world of women at Leys College is described in detail, as are Miss Pym's impressions of people and her shock when her assessments turn out to be wrong. The appearance of her characters was important to Tey, as she was describing girls in a physical environment, but they are always linked for her with description of character. Josephine Tey has a keen eye for describing the sporting: 'Except for a string of two-year-olds in training, Lucy could think of nothing more attractive to mind and eye than that set of burnished and controlled young creatures busy dragging out the booms.'[8] She was well aware of the physical training and control necessary to produce a gymnast, but did not stint on the descriptions of the injuries that training could produce. In *Miss Pym Disposes* characters are revealed not only in physical description, but also through insights about what details (such as the type of shoes a character wears) mean about a character's background (Mrs Innes is poor) and what that might then mean for the development of not only that person, but also the others they come into contact with (how would being poor have affected Mary Innes?). The minutiae of everyday life lead to revelations about the self and others. This is the way both Miss Pym and Alan Grant approach understanding their suspects – in fact, the way they understand all of those around them.

Miss Pym Disposes is a murder mystery where the mystery does not happen until the final third of the book, and we are not even sure there has been a murder until even later. Tey was playing with the conventions of mystery or crime writing, and she was getting better at it with each novel. She was also subverting other restrictions by using the crime genre: if *Miss Pym* had been marketed as a 'straight' novel it would probably have been aimed at women, whereas 'crime' novels cut across this problem, being generally read equally by men and women. Crime fiction may not have been taken seriously by all critics, but it had many benefits for the author, and many authors were taking it extremely seriously indeed.

Josephine Tey had written two successful crime novels already, and was starting to see the possibilities of the genre: the way the author can use the framework and structure to build upon and climb through, leading the reader to unexpected places, and exploring whatever topics please them safe in the knowledge that the reader will follow, so long as the author never forgets to present a solution to the book's central crime. In *The Man in the Queue* the murder happens in chapter one; in *A Shilling for Candles* we are given the familiar character of Grant to identify with. In *Miss Pym Disposes* we have an unknown central character, the unusual and untypical setting of a girls' physical education college, and no immediate mystery. There is a lot of psychology, face-reading and, finally, a murder that might not actually be the main crime in the book after all. The title hints at the moral, religious core of the book: Miss Pym is advised to 'let God dispose' – but chooses not to. We have to make up our own minds, as readers, whether or not she has made the right choice. Josephine Tey's character development and the way that she played with unorthodox structure were the strengths of her crime writing, and they were what she used to advantage in all her novels from this point onwards. This character-driven approach was also typical of crime novels of the period. Although Josephine Tey had started writing in the Golden Age of the crime novel, and is usually associated with this era and the strange halcyon summer of the interwar years, most of her mysteries are actually from the late 1940s and early 1950s, and can be seen as a bridge between the more 'classic' crime novel which centres on a puzzle, and the modern crime novel with its focus on character and realism. Her Tey books, though often very 'modern' in feel, are sometimes vague about dates, occasionally mentioning 'the war', but not going into other details.

Beth was always a great reader, and she continued to read the detective fiction that was being written. There are two that come to mind when reading *Miss Pym Disposes* – *Laurels are Poison* and Dorothy L. Sayers' *Gaudy Night*. *Laurels are Poison* had been published in 1942, one of the long series of crime novels written by Gladys Mitchell and featuring her detecting character Mrs Bradley. Grouping Mitchell, Tey and Sayers together shows how broad a church 'crime fiction' can be: although superficially *Laurels are Poison*'s setting of a women's teacher training college foreshadows *Miss Pym Disposes*, Mitchell is writing a different sort of breezy entertainment. Her books have dated faster than Tey (or Sayers) because of some of her views of morality, as well as her then-up-to-date discussion of lunacy, or her depiction of black servants. Gladys Mitchell's work is currently being reprinted, and is undergoing a minor revival, well deserved as it brings readers her bracing, puzzle-solving plots. Mitchell was a fan of Gordon Daviot and Josephine Tey, and makes reference to this in her novel when Deb plans to suggest that her students put on a production of *Richard of Bordeaux*.[9] Some critics have seen echoes of Gladys Mitchell in Tey, and it seems Tey had read Mitchell's work.[10] There's every chance Mitchell and Tey met in person, albeit briefly, as they crossed the same literary circles, though Beth preferred to observe, while Mitchell was a joiner, a member of the Society of Authors, PEN and the Detection Club.[11]

The Detection Club was set up in 1930, and was a social meeting place that counted among its members Dorothy L. Sayers, Agatha Christie and G. K. Chesterton, among many others. The club still exists, but there is no record that Josephine Tey was ever a member.[12] She may, however, have met Dorothy L. Sayers elsewhere, as they shared an agent in the early 1930s. Josephine Tey's mystery novels have more in common with Dorothy L. Sayers's than with others of the Golden Age of crime writing, but in person the two women were very dissimilar, as Dorothy was as loud and outgoing as Beth was quiet and reserved. There are rumours that they did meet, and that Sayers was unimpressed.[13] Their careers have many parallels, though, and by the 1940s Sayers had moved towards the theatre, and towards religious topics. Her radio plays, such as *The Man Born to Be King*, had been broadcast during the Second World War, and were controversial to some for the way that she chose to put modern language in the mouths of historical, Biblical characters – the same approach that Gordon Daviot had taken both in *Richard of Bordeaux* and in her own recent Biblical plays like *The Little Dry Thorn* and the shorts in *Leith Sands*. The thoughtful subject matter of the best of Sayers's Wimsey novels, and their strong sense of morality – such as Wimsey's unhappiness at condemning criminals to the death penalty – are appealing in the same way that Josephine Tey's characters are. 'Neat but not gaudy,' says Alan Grant in *The Daughter of Time*, echoing Sayers, and *Gaudy Night* is an obvious companion to *Miss Pym Disposes*.[14] The books both deal with the return of the author to her alma mater, but where Sayers meditates at length on the fitness of women for Oxford life, and the constant clash between intellectual and social life – the endless choice for women between a career and a family – Anstey students have a calm certainty about their careers and their futures.

Beth herself had managed to find the balance between work and her family obligations caring for Colin – but, unlike Dorothy L. Sayers, who had a child and was married (though not to the father of her child), Beth had not had the choice between marriage and work.[15] Circumstances had taken that choice away from her when Hugh McIntosh died. *Gaudy Night* is concerned, on one level, with whether marriage can take place between intellectual equals, and how this can be negotiated. Miss Pym mentions vaguely 'the Alan years', but, now that she is older and the choice of marriage is no longer open to her, she sees the advantages of her single life. Dorothy L. Sayers is equally clear that marriage should only be undertaken to the right man. Harriet Vane's creator wrote her someone perfect, but Josephine Tey shows that, even if there isn't someone perfect, there is still plenty to live for.

Beth always said that she never regretted her choice of Anstey, and the college was a supremely good training ground for life. It achieved for its students the elusive balance between the mental and the physical, with the potential to produce well-rounded individuals. *Miss Pym Disposes*, in its murder theme, shows how the intense training could be flawed, but in writing the book Josephine Tey showed how well the training could work. Given the subject matter of the novel – unfairness, death, murder – the reader might be expected to be left with a bitter aftertaste after reading, but instead is left feeling that the book has created a world that we want to re-enter: we want to know, as Lucy does, how Desterro's wedding will go. The characters live on after the book is finished. They have hope.

Miss Pym Disposes became a cult novel for students at Anstey, where it was received with delight.[16] Anstey produced a yearly magazine, which was sent to Old Girls, and Beth, still at her 'home' address, had never lost touch with the college. The communications with Old Girls had become more frequent towards the end of the war, which was probably one impetus behind the writing of *Miss Pym Disposes* – the reason being that the college was making arrangements to celebrate their Jubilee year, the fiftieth anniversary of the founding of the college, in 1947. Two major events were held for Old Girls, the first being a dinner at the Normandie Hotel in Knightsbridge, London. The lunch was well attended, and students and Old Girls were surprised and pleased to find the author of *Miss Pym Disposes* had made the effort to attend. Many other students who had not been in touch with the college for years also appeared. Anstey held fond memories for many of its students. Its reputation had only been enhanced in the fifty years since it was founded and its longevity and health were rightly seen as a great achievement. An 'almost pre-war lunch' of three courses, followed by coffee, was offered, and then students from several different eras gave short speeches reminiscing on their time at college and the changes that had taken place.[17] No one from Beth's time spoke, and none of the other students from her graduating year were there. The atmosphere, however, was extremely welcoming and positive, and the report in the following college magazine read in part, 'it seemed almost incredible that so many people could have benefited and gained such privileges from one person's initiative and energy and I only wished Miss Anstey could have seen the happy result of all her effort'.

Rhoda Anstey had founded an impressive college which had provided a strong foundation for several generations of women students, who had gone on to do remarkable things. The college magazine gave brief summaries of many of the former students' careers, which ranged from being organizer of PE for Wolverhampton, owner of a country inn, selector for Midland Women's Hockey Association, housewifery at home and as far away as Kenya, and appointments in the Ministry of Education. At the bottom of one page is the listing for E. MacKintosh, authoress, mentioning both *Richard of Bordeaux* and *Miss Pym Disposes*, alongside pleas for news of other graduates of 1917, and testimonials from other former students: '[I] have had a very busy time since May,' wrote one Mrs Williamson, 'with farm and poultry work, as my husband broke his leg very badly just below the knee. *How very useful I have found my training in Massage and First Aid!* The doctor is astounded at the wonderful full recovery and use of the knee.'[18]

259

Anstey students were nothing if not varied, and Beth found their company at the meal in London congenial.

A further lunch was held at Anstey itself in July 1947. The principal of the college was now Miss Squire, who had taken over in 1927 from the Mrs Bridgeman whom Beth would have remembered from her own time at Anstey.[19] The new principal, Miss Squire, had trained at Bedford before working for a time in Edinburgh and then in Bristol. Miss Squire had made an impact from the beginning of her appointment, and, increasing student enrolment, she continued to push for official recognition for the college, and the highest, university level certification, as well as keeping up with new trends in physical fitness such as the interest in mountaineering and outdoor pursuits. Just two years later, by 1949, the college was sending students to the Highlands to train, to Glenmore Lodge in Aviemore.[20] Beth felt on familiar ground with both Anstey and the new principal. A large photograph exists of all the students, Old Girls and staff who attended the second Jubilee event at Anstey itself, but it's not clear enough to distinguish whether Beth attended this second event. In the second row, a smiling woman in dark hair, seated next to some of the staff, looks familiar. Beth certainly kept up her connection with the college now that she had re-established it, and was to visit the college again at a crucial point in her life.

Josephine Tey was not trying to hide her past any more. Although she was still using a pseudonym she had exposed part of the secret to a journalist and had become much more comfortable with it, and she was returning also to her earlier life as Beth MacKintosh. 'Mary Innes' in the novel makes a resolution at an early age that will take her back to a home town that she hates: was it the right decision or not? I think Beth's personal assessment of her own life led her, after the Second World War, not only to re-think her past and to use it as a basis for fiction, but to come to accept the choices that she had made. It was this acceptance that led to the renewed creativity that gave us the Josephine Tey books. Living in Inverness and caring for Colin was not always easy, or her preferred choice, but she felt it was the right choice, and had made it work.

Beth's personal situation in Inverness, after the Second World War, had changed considerably. When she was little, she had been part of an extended family, and, although she was a private person, she had plenty of relatives around her. After the Second World War, it becomes harder to trace many of Beth's relatives. Partly this is because records are not made public until after a certain amount of time has passed, and 1946 is still relatively recent compared with researching Beth's ancestors from the late 1800s, but partly it is because Beth and her father Colin had grown so distant from her immediate family. She had become quite isolated in Inverness, partly through her own choice, but partly also because of the losses and changes of the Second World War. Inverness, even after the troops, evacuees and prisoners of war left, was no longer the same sort of town with the same old people. The class system that Colin had fought so hard against was changing, new families were moving in, and the housing shortages after the war led to a building programme that was to expand the town dramatically, with new houses, for example, being added to the post-World War I building projects in Dalneigh.

From being at the centre of those two hopeful families, the Hornes and the MacKintoshes, Beth was now on her own with only Colin. Although he maintained some links with Applecross and Shieldaig, Colin had grown apart from the other members of his family living in Inverness, though he still had close friends who lived nearby. At over eighty, Colin was now in failing health, and neighbours remember Beth having to support him when he walked.[21] Although Colin still owned and ran his fruiterer's shop, he relied more and more on his two shop assistants, Annie Macpherson and Barbara Cameron. Perhaps worried about his health, Colin wrote a will in 1946 which shows that he valued his shop assistants' help highly, making financial provision for each of them.[22] He did not, however, leave any provision for any of his other relatives except his daughters. His nephews and nieces were not mentioned by name, and it becomes difficult to trace what happened to Colin and Josephine MacKintosh's brothers and sisters and their children. Certainly at least one of Beth's cousins, Peter Horne (son of Josephine's younger brother Robert) had died in the First World War, and other cousins had died young, but there seems now to be no one left in Inverness who claims kinship with Beth MacKintosh.[23]

The cousins who had grown up and married had either moved away, or had gradually lost contact with Colin and Elizabeth. For example, there is no further trace of Colin's older sister Mary, or her illegitimate son Donald.[24] Robert Horne had remarried after the death of his first wife, but he too had died in 1943, and his 'second' family don't seem to have kept in close contact with Colin and Beth. Colin had simply outlived many of his siblings and in-laws, and those of his family who were still in town simply had little in common with him, and so had lost touch. Robert Horne, for example, was a school janitor, and although his family tree, and the repeated use of certain names, clearly shows the interest he took in his family history, it was the Ellis and Horne connections that he favoured – there was no interest in his brother-in-law Colin, or literary works by one Elizabeth MacKintosh.[25]

After Humphrey's death in the Second World War, Beth's sister Jean had remained in England.[26] This refusal to move back and share the care for Colin, even after she was widowed, may partly explain why Beth is said to have not got on with her middle sister, though both Jean and Moire did visit Inverness several times in the late 1940s. Moire, now married to Londoner Donald Stokes, also stayed down south – but in 1946, Moire had news. She was pregnant. The whole family were delighted. 'Dear Ett,' Colin wrote to her (he always used her baby name), 'this is great news. I look forward to this event. It gives me the greatest pleasure that life can give me now.'[27] He went on tell her to be careful. Jean wrote to Moire too, a long letter that detailed a church service she had attended for Humphrey, where a pennant was unfurled in his memory. Jean's letter shows that it was not just Beth who had a ready pen and a sharp tongue – the sarcastic sense of humour that Beth sometimes surprised people with, and which delights Josephine Tey's readers, is evident when Jean writes:

> I'm glad to hear your egg is incubating satisfactorily. Have you been sick yet! Or are you past the stage when one begins that

horror! I spent the last 3 nights with Olivia – her two are adorable, but it took me a long time to get over having known the younger one for the less pleasant stage of her existence! Now she's '2 & a bit', I feel better about her! But '4 in August' is <u>exquisite</u>.[28]

Jean arranged to come and see Moire, bringing some fruit, as rationing was still in place. Colin, too, was busy posting Moire some eggs, and making up new parcels of fruit to send down.

Moire's child was born in October 1946, a son. She called him Colin, after her father.[29] Colin senior was delighted with his new grandson, and immediately amended his will to make him a bequest of £300 (more than the £200 he wished to leave to Moire).[30] The later 'Josephine Tey' novels are full of warm references to young children, such as Laura's baby in *The Singing Sands* or the opening scenes of *Brat Farrar*, showing the keen interest Beth took in her new nephew, as far as she could from the distance of Inverness.

CHAPTER SEVENTEEN

Amateur Dramatics, Valerius *and*
The Franchise Affair

A year after Beth's nephew, Colin Stokes, was born, the Citizens Theatre Company finally took *The Little Dry Thorn* to London. Before that, 1947 saw some very different performances of Gordon Daviot's plays.

The theatre scene had changed dramatically after the war. Angela du Maurier, an inveterate theatregoer, described in her autobiography the shock and disappointment she felt when attending a post-war first night: instead of the white ties and tiaras of a 1920s or 30s first night, the audience was casually dressed.[1] The sense of theatre in the audience itself was gone. The community of first nighters had changed forever. The audience for 'popular' plays, like *Richard of Bordeaux*, had departed to the cinema. Changing entertainment taxes had also taken their toll, and the lavish productions with sumptuous scenery that Dodie Smith had excelled at were no longer as viable or appealing to theatre managers, as they would not guarantee a return on their investment. Dodie Smith herself was still in America, but she felt totally out of touch with the theatre scene in London, and saw clearly, and with a deep regret, that she was never going to come back in the same way.[2] Critics didn't like her sort of theatre anymore; they appreciated a new type of play, with a grimmer, less middle-class aesthetic. Straight plays were going out of fashion too, since the cinema could tell realistic stories with real backdrops. Theatre writers started to explore something different, like painters faced with photography and turning to impressionism to express themselves. Gordon Daviot's set of actor and producer friends were no longer in the ascendant and the professional contacts she had made, and which she had never maintained as strongly as, for example, Dodie Smith had, were no longer as useful to her. Whereas before the Second World War, the impresario Binkie Beaumont, who was still renting Dodie's house in Essex while Dodie and Alec were in the US, had seemed like a colourful, larger-than-life figure of power, ready to create magic on stage and with huge influence over both actors' and audiences' lives – now he seemed like an old man.[3] The all-night meetings about castings no longer seemed like power sessions that could make or break careers, but instead like sordid, alcohol-fuelled attempts to recapture dreams.

Gordon Daviot had written about the Bright Young Things of the 1920s in *The Expensive Halo*; now in the 1940s she was over fifty years old, and her theatre friends were no longer the new guard. In 1948, she had to write a consoling letter to Peggy Webster, still in America, on the death of her mother May Whitty. In it, Gordon remembered 'a furious letter' May had written to her about the New York production of *The Laughing Woman*, 'where the very pen strokes were protest and repudiation so that even if you looked at it upside down you would get the gist of it'.[4] It was a letter that Peggy treasured, as Gordon had captured some of the essence of her mother's character, but it was a letter about old times: actors and plays that were firmly now in the past.

Unlike Dodie Smith, Gordon Daviot did not try to go back to this world, and did not waste her time hankering after it. She still wanted London performances of her plays, but in a changing theatrical world, she did not turn down other ways to get her writing out in public. Gordon Daviot's plays, starting with *Richard of Bordeaux*, had always been very popular with amateur theatre groups. With their large casts, they were perfect for groups who wanted to include as many actors as possible, and their popularity with the public meant they would be guaranteed to sell tickets. Amateur dramatics was still very popular across the country, and there were active groups in Inverness. Beth had never previously been involved with these, but in 1947 she was persuaded to allow an Inverness amateur dramatic society to perform three of her one-act plays, *Rahab* and *Leith Sands*, from the *Leith Sands* collection, and a comedy, *The Balwhinnie Bomb*.[5] It was an outward sign of a new development in her career. She had been writing these short plays since the Second World War, originally for radio, but she was now finding that they were very popular with editors of collections. Acting groups and schools often wanted collections of short plays which they could study and put on, and Gordon Daviot's work appeared in many of these, often ending up, as a result, in very strange places. The short play *The Pen of My Aunt*, for example, was first broadcast on BBC radio just after the Second World War. It was anthologized, and repeated on radio in 1950. By 1963, as a result of its dissemination in various collections, the play was picked up by Finnish television, and made into a TV movie, translated as *Tätini kynä*.[6] This sort of willingness to try new formats and allow her work to be published in different places – both when she was alive and, afterwards, because of the way her work was managed – is partly what has made Beth's work survive and do well.

Gordon Daviot's association with community theatre in Inverness was not conducted solely through her agent. Beth was persuaded to take part by a member of the society, Barbara Bruce-Watt, who simply walked up to her in the street and asked her if she had any plays the local acting group could put on. This was considered rather bold of Barbara, as Beth was seen as unapproachable, but she was actually delighted to be asked. As far as Beth was concerned, she felt that Inverness had never honoured her, nor asked her to be involved in the community. As soon as she was asked – in her capacity as a writer – she responded immediately, much as she had before the war, when asked to contribute to the IRA school magazine.

The amateur dramatic society in Inverness was the Florians. Set up originally to entertain the troops stationed in the town during the Second World War, the group is still going today. The first play of Gordon Daviot's that they performed was *Rahab*, in 1947, the Biblical short published in *Leith Sands*. *Leith Sands* itself followed in 1948, and *The Balwhinnie Bomb* in the 1949 season. Other amateur dramatic groups were also using Gordon Daviot's plays, and, at a Scottish Community Drama Association event on the 15th February 1947 at the Empire Theatre in Inverness, Beth was in the audience to see productions of both *Rahab* and *Leith Sands*. The SCDA events took the form of a competition, where the best group was awarded a prize. Beth stayed to watch all the plays, but, characteristically, didn't watch the judging. The end goal for Beth was always to see her work performed as well as it could be, not to please the critics. She was back again the following year to watch the Inverness group perform *Leith Sands*.

Gordon Daviot's short plays remained extremely popular with amateur groups, and newspaper searches bring up many references to groups performing her work to great success. *Rahab* comes up in newspaper articles about a performance in Aberdeen in 1947; *Leith Sands* is mentioned in the *Dundee Courier* in 1948, and won a competition for a Stirling amateur group in 1948.[7] The excellent play *The Balwhinnie Bomb* was one of Gordon Daviot's most enduring short pieces, which holds up particularly well today, with a superb beginning (though it slows down a little by the end). Telling the story of a suspect package delivered to a rural post office, it is peopled with Daviot's usual cast of well-drawn characters, and it is rather modern in its take on the Highlands. Roddy Ross the postman, Annabella Morrison the postmistress, Finlay Macphail and Peter the Polis could quite easily slot straight from their 1940s debut into a modern BBC Scotland drama. The play is full of lines that draw a laugh of recognition from anyone in the Highlands:

> 'It's a scandal, that's what it is. How is anyone to catch a train only an hour late? One of these days it will be on time, and then there will be nobody there to pick up at all.'
> 'Man, it's an awful thing ambition. Believe it or not, there's people will climb *mountains* just to sit on the top and look at places they knew were there all the time.'[8]

The humour in the play makes it seem, out of all Daviot's one-act plays, the most ripe for revival.

Another major theatrical event in 1947 did not include Gordon Daviot at all.[9] The Edinburgh International Festival, now one of the biggest arts events in Europe, started that year, but none of Gordon Daviot's plays was performed there and she was not invited to take part. The 1947 Festival was deliberately planned to provide cultural respite and boost cultural tourism after the Second World War. It was supported by the British Council and Edinburgh civic leaders and with the aim of bringing the world's very best performers to the city. Shakespearean plays and dancers from Sadler's Wells were among the first to be included in the programme. Gordon Daviot did not have a presence at the Festival until 1951, when *Richard of Bordeaux* was performed there as part of the Scottish Community Drama Association's programme.[10]

Gordon Daviot had not lost sight of full-length plays, however, and now returned to *Valerius*, the story of a Roman legion in Scotland defending Hadrian's Wall against the Picts. There is an 1821 novel of the same name by J. G. Lockhart, Walter Scott's son-in-law, which at least one critic saw as direct inspiration, though the plots are not the same, and the style is very different. Gordon Daviot had actually written *Valerius* 'just after the blitz and put [it] in a drawer'.[11] She had been in London in September 1939 when war was declared, and during the first days of evacuation and uncertainty the streets had been empty and the atmosphere tense. Beth described it as being like the end of civilization, and imaginatively likened it to the past London of Roman times, before the barbarian hordes descended.[12]

Although *Valerius* is a well-imagined idea of how the Romans felt defending an indefensible last stand, the added context of the parallel with the Second World War was not brought out in the production, and neither is it obvious to the reader. Anyone brought up in the tradition of broad classical education, of the type that Beth received at the IRA, would see no reason why the Romans should not receive attention, even in the Highlands, where there is less obvious Roman influence on the landscape – but the reader is left searching for Daviot's inspiration. The play is well written, well paced and interesting, but has elements of an intellectual exercise without that extra context. *Valerius* is a frustrating play as it is almost a return to Daviot's best form as a playwright, and she was certainly very happy with the production, but it did not go on to a longer run. Of all Daviot's full-length plays, if there was some way to bring out that parallel with the Second World War, *Valerius* could well be the best one to revive. The claustrophobic atmosphere increases the tension, and the descriptions of the wall are extremely evocative, even reminiscent to the modern reader of George R. R. Martin's fantasy Wall which stands against the forces of darkness in his Song of Ice and Fire series – something fantastical that looms over everything – while the tragic end of the play is very affecting. We get a sense that civilization is being threatened, and that Valerius and his fellow soldiers on the wall are the last stand against chaos, but this isn't over-emphasized. As in her Biblical plays, Gordon Daviot's aim is to bring history to life by showing normality, but that normality eases the dramatic tension – and, incidentally, shows how much *Richard of Bordeaux* benefitted from Gielgud's direction and the sharper parallels that were drawn between that historical play and its context of 1930s appeasement.

Daviot returned to *Valerius* because she had been contacted by The Repertory Players, whose leading actor was Andrew Osborn. They put on a one-off London show at the Saville Theatre on 3rd October 1948. Osborn played the title character 'Valerius', and, although his name at first meant little to Gordon, she soon realized that he had a long Daviot pedigree, including playing 'Richard' in the 1938 TV version of *Richard of Bordeaux*, opposite Gwen Ffrangcon-Davies. Osborn knew and liked Daviot's work, and was pleased to be involved, and she in turn was happy with the performance 'with the Valerius out of all others that I would have chosen [...] my star was [...] perfect for the part!'[13]

Daviot was very involved with the rehearsals for *Valerius*, more so than with many of her plays. She went to rehearsals from 10 am to 6 pm every day of the short preparatory process, and then attended the final performance. One reason the play had not been performed when it was written was that, obviously, during wartime there had been a lack of male actors, and it was a wholly male cast. Daviot had felt uneasy about submitting a play with an all-male cast in the early 40s as she hadn't wanted conscientious objectors to take good parts, but now the war was over, she found it strange to think that men who had, only a few years before, been fighting in the front line, were now play-acting on stage. Some of the people Daviot knew had not come back from the war, and in the late 40s Daviot's consciousness of war – which she was always very sensitive to – was still strong. She also felt there was a gender split in the audience, with men and women responding differently to her tale of soldiers. She felt that female audiences did not like it as much, and that this would prevent *Valerius* from ever being a West End success. The Saville was in the West End, and had seating for just under 1,500 people, comparable in size to *Richard of Bordeaux*'s home in the New Theatre, but, unlike *Richard*, *Valerius'* one-off performance did not lead to it being picked up for a longer run.

Daviot's approach to her theatre writing, her even-handedness in showing off the good and bad points in all the characters, is far more suited to a novel. What became drawn-out and overlong on stage was more acceptable in a book, where the reader is happy to take a little more time. The detective novel framework, in particular, allowed Daviot to talk about the many different things that interested her, yet still leave the reader always wanting to read on, because in a detective novel there was always the underlying goal, which Daviot never forgot when she was writing. The reader might be interested in the characters and the digressions, but they also want to solve the crime and know what happens. *The Franchise Affair*, published the same year that *Valerius* was performed, was the next Josephine Tey novel, and it has been one of her most popular.

The Franchise Affair is not a crime novel where there is a murder and a detective to solve it, but a novel where there is a mystery and the reader wants to know the truth. Solicitor Robert Blair's quiet, pedestrian life is disrupted when Marion Sharpe calls asking for his help. Marion and her mother have been accused of abducting a young girl, Betty Kane. Betty's story is plausible and detailed, and the thought that it is entirely without foundation

seems fantastic – but Robert Blair is convinced of Marion's innocence. Like *Miss Pym Disposes, The Franchise Affair* plays with
conventions, but, unlike *Miss Pym,* Josephine Tey was becoming
comfortable enough with her status as a 'mystery writer' to refer
to her own work by reintroducing Alan Grant, though he only
makes a very brief appearance when another character remarks
that he is not happy with the case. The mystery solving is left to
Robert Blair.

Coming immediately after *Miss Pym Disposes,* which was so
firmly rooted in Beth's life experiences at Anstey, and after Beth's
period of reflection on her own experiences during the Second
World War, it is interesting to see what *The Franchise Affair* can
tell us about Beth's own life. Its central story concerns a mother
and daughter who, like Colin and Beth, are in a community but
not of that community. Marion Sharpe and her mother have just
enough money and status to set them apart from the rest of their
village, to the extent that the village is able to believe they are
capable of horrible crimes against young Betty Kane. Marion and
her mother are proved completely innocent, and the questioning
of their way of life is shown to be petty and based on stupidity.
In the final chapter of the book, which is a sort of coda, Robert
Blair follows the Sharpes out to their new home in Canada. He
has proposed marriage to Marion, who has rejected him because
she has to care for her aged parent – he then rejects this rejection.

It's hard not to read a little of Beth MacKintosh's life here.
Despite her willingness to be involved with community theatre
in Inverness she was still generally seen as unapproachable, and
any man who married Beth would have had to take Colin on as
well. To make her book's hero capable of this is a rather wry
in-joke for her. However, Beth's own possible romance with
Hugh Patrick Fraser had a lot more in its way than just Colin:
there was also the inescapable fact of Hugh's illness – and there
is an amusing portrait of a young man with literary aspirations in
Robert Blair's nephew Nevil. One of the reasons that Beth's relationship with Hugh seems so real is that any reference to poet or
'young love' or Scotsmen who do not fit the Alan Grant-Murdoch
Beaton-Colin MacKintosh dark-haired 'type' are always realistic

and well-drawn: Beth's relationship with Hugh was more than a crush, it was a real relationship where she saw the good and bad – but it was also a long-ago relationship.

Beth did draw to a certain extent on her own life to write her fiction, but not to the extent that some commentators believe. Many critics have been tempted, in the absence of an authoritative biography, to see Beth's life through her fiction. After *The Expensive Halo*, she certainly never put Colin or her family so clearly into her work, and, although she did draw on her own personal experiences, the intersection between fact and fiction is more complex than straight borrowings from real life. For example, the Irish lawyer in *The Franchise Affair*, Kevin Macdermott, lives in a small flat in St Paul's Churchyard, London. Kevin is not a real person, but his flat was real enough: Beth's sister Moire had a friend from college, Celia Kelly, who lived at 76 St Paul's Churchyard.

The Franchise Affair has other roots, very far from Beth's life. It has been widely reported that it is based on a true story – not Beth MacKintosh's, but the eighteenth-century trial of supposed kidnap victim Elizabeth Canning – the similarity between this name and Betty Kane is obvious. The 1753 Canning trial had been the subject of contemporary books, such as *Elizabeth is Missing* by Lillian de la Torre in 1945. The story interested Beth, and she fictionalized it, simplifying and changing several elements, but with no doubt that in her own book Betty Kane was guilty and the Sharpes innocent. The teenage Betty Kane, unlike the genuinely innocent 'Erica' or 'Cornelia', is the sort of adolescent girl a teacher could easily describe, and she comes across as a complex, believable and plausible character, while the whole fantastical story of *The Franchise Affair* is endlessly readable. Any summary of a Josephine Tey novel, however, never comes close to what they are really about. The reason they are so re-readable is that the characters are so fresh and real: every time, they strike the reader as being alive – and not just the main characters, but each incidental person met along the way, from Ben Carley, the other lawyer in Robert Blair's town, to the illiterate Gladys, whose evidence in the witness box is given in such a strong country accent that the court struggles to understand her.

The Franchise Affair was critically well received as a superior detective tale.[14] It went on to be adapted several times, and remains one of Josephine Tey's most popular stories, with modern writers like Sarah Waters citing it as an inspiration.[15] *The Franchise Affair* was published in the US, like all Josephine Tey's novels, almost immediately after its UK publication, and was adapted into a major UK film in 1951.

The US publication had been quickly followed by the book's release in paperback in the UK, and the negotiations over the rights are a clear indication of just how happy Beth was with her new incarnation as crime writer Josephine Tey.[16] Tey's publishers, her trusted friends Peter and Nico Davies, carried out most of the negotiations for the paperback rights, which were given to Penguin. Even by the early 1950s, Penguin were still keen to mention the more recognizable name of Gordon Daviot somewhere on the cover of the book, but Nico Davies explained to Penguin that both the Peter Davies firm, and Beth herself, wished the Tey name to be built up separately. They compromised on allowing Penguin to include a biography, which Beth wrote herself. The biography is a clear summation of her career as she herself saw it at this point in her life. 'Josephine Tey', she began in the biography, 'is the reverse side of Gordon Daviot'. Beth was also clear that 'Josephine Tey' was a crime writer. Her recent books, such as *Miss Pym Disposes, Brat Farrar,* and *The Franchise Affair,* were such unusual crime novels that Penguin still felt it necessary to check whether it was okay to issue *The Franchise Affair* under their green 'mystery' covers. In her biographical note, Tey explains that she had found the structure of the novel, such as *Kif,* a less exciting medium than poems, short stories or plays, but crime novels, she stated, were 'a medium as disciplined as any sonnet'. Beth had found her niche, and recognized that her strengths as a writer – her original thinking and her characterization – were shown to their best advantage within the formalized structure of crime fiction. Beth's comment comparing writing detective fiction to creating a sonnet is the clearest statement of how she saw her writing. This, rather than any remark about 'knitting', is how her crime fiction should be viewed.

Beth was happy as Josephine Tey, though did not mind the linking of this name to Gordon Daviot. What she did object to, though, was her real identity being revealed. Most of the negotiations for the paperback were done between Penguin (in the person of Eunice Frost, former secretary and now the most powerful woman at Penguin) and Peter or Nico Davies. Tey only wrote directly to Penguin when one of their proofreaders made a plot query that struck her fancy. Was Tey sure, when describing Robert Blair's repetitive daily life, that she'd given him the right biscuit on the right day? She signed that reply 'Josephine Tey'. Meanwhile, the only time Tey's agent got involved was when he conveyed his client's violent opposition to having her photograph on the back of the book. Josephine Tey wanted to write in peace and focus on writing only; she did not want to do any self-promotion. In her biographical note, Beth was keen to stress that, apart from *Miss Pym Disposes* she did not use her own personal experiences in her novels – not strictly true, but a point that she reiterated, saying also that her first novel *Kif* had been 'notably unautobiographical'. She admitted to being from the Highlands, but rather cagily ended her potted biography by saying that 'now she is reduced to domesticity [Tey] divides her time between the Highlands and London'. This was how Beth wanted to be seen.

The Franchise Affair did well for Penguin, and they continued to ask for paperback rights to Tey's work. *The Franchise Affair*, meanwhile, was adapted for television in 1958, again in 1962, and once more in 1988, while Penguin reissued it several times in the 1960s, and on into the 70s.

CHAPTER EIGHTEEN

The Malvern Festival and Brat Farrar

Following the success of *Miss Pym Disposes* and *The Franchise Affair*, Josephine Tey continued to write mystery novels, working on what was to become *Brat Farrar*. Beth found the writing creatively satisfying, and her books as Josephine Tey became more and more popular. With publication of her novel both in the UK and the US, Josephine Tey built up a loyal audience in both countries. Gordon Daviot's plays, however, were also still in demand, and 1949 finally brought to a conclusion the unsatisfying story of *The Stars Bow Down*.

The Stars Bow Down was written as early as 1936, but, as discussed in Chapter 12, problems with casting meant it had never been produced.[1] The script had been published, but not until 1939, when theatreland was not in a position to look for new material. After the war, however, it was not forgotten. Gordon Daviot's plays had been finding new outlets, with her short plays, such as *Remember Caesar*, in 1949, anthologized, and others broadcast on the radio.[2] *The Stars Bow Down* was finally produced as a radio play in 1948 for the BBC's Saturday Night Theatre programme.[3] This in turn influenced the programmers of the culturally important Malvern Festival, who decided to pick *The Stars Bow Down* as one of their 1949 festival plays.

The Malvern Festival was founded by Barry Jackson and Roy Limbert in 1929 to celebrate the playwright George Bernard Shaw.[4] In Gordon Daviot's time Shaw was considered by many to be the greatest playwright after Shakespeare, with actors clamouring to appear in his plays and audiences flocking to see his work.[5] Popular demand had established the Malvern Festival as an annual, critically acclaimed fixture in the arts calendar. The Malvern Festival was not just dedicated to Shaw in name only; the playwright was a regular attendee, writing plays specifically for the festival, but equally happy to share the stage with other dramatists. Both classic plays and new works by living playwrights had been performed at previous Malvern Festivals, with previously produced playwrights and plays including Ben Jonson, Christopher Marlowe's *Dr Faustus*, *Lady Precious Stream* (a popular Chinese play by S. I. Hsuing), James Bridie, a version of *Jane Eyre* by Helen Jerome, as well as Shaw's *Pygmalion*, *Saint Joan*, *Caesar and Cleopatra*, and many more.

In 1949 the event was in its twelfth year (it had not been running during the war) and included six plays which were performed several times each over the course of the whole month of August and into September.[6] Three of the plays were by Shaw, and the other contributors were Lewis Wood, Denis Cannan, and Gordon Daviot. Mathew Forsyth, who had worked with Daviot at the Citizens Theatre and on *Richard of Bordeaux*, was the overall producer. Other linked events were tea-time talks on a variety of subjects, including the theatre and Isaac Newton; a literary luncheon featuring Compton Mackenzie; a Shakespeare festival; and church and choral singing.

Malvern and the Malvern Hills are near Birmingham in the West Midlands. The area was familiar to Gordon Daviot from her days studying at Anstey Physical Training College – she wrote fondly of remembering Christmas in the Malvern Hills in a letter to Dodie Smith, and she was delighted to see *The Stars Bow Down* finally get a full on-stage production with a good cast at such a prestigious festival.[7] She arranged her holidays to fit in with the dates of Malvern, and invited her good friend Lena Ramsden to join her there.[8] Colin MacKintosh, now elderly and frail, was left in the capable hands of a housekeeper, whom Beth hired in order to get a couple of weeks' holiday and respite each spring and autumn.[9] Beth was still free to travel, but she had to now spend more time organizing each trip, making sure that Colin was not left alone. Money to hire a housekeeper was not a problem.

In her autobiography, Lena Ramsden described their activities during the week they spent at Malvern, saying that they climbed the hills above the town and visited nearby towns such as Cheltenham and Tewkesbury – but she doesn't mention the two women watching or commentating on the other plays in the festival.[10] Lena was an avid theatregoer, but it seems significant that her description of the week focuses on the many other activities they did: Gordon Daviot enjoyed writing plays, and enjoyed watching them – but she did not enjoy talking shop, and would not have considered her holiday well spent if she had sat in the theatres all day, speaking only to theatre staff, management or actors. She wanted to see the countryside and spend time with her friend, and was happy to wait until the Friday to make a special trip to see her own play performed.

John Gielgud, way back when *Richard of Bordeaux* was produced, had said that Gordon Daviot was the best of playwrights for an actor or producer because she left everyone to get on with it, and her attitude had not changed in the meantime. Dodie Smith had far more control over her plays – and ultimately far more success – but Gordon Daviot had far less stress. She had faith that what she had written would easily be interpreted by the actors. Dodie Smith had been an actress, and was intimately interested in the nuances of performance and the technical work needed to bring a drama to life on stage. Gordon Daviot was a writer. She wrote, and that was the end of her job. A question often asked of dramatists is whether they find it strange to see their work performed, as actors must surely change what they have written and interpret it differently to how it was intended, but sometimes the reverse can be true: sometimes it seems impossible for the actors to interpret it differently, and it can seem as though the writer's mind is just being laid bare onstage. Gordon Daviot saw actors in a very different way to Dodie Smith. Dodie, as an actress herself, felt that parts were open to interpretation, while Gordon simply saw her writing as something the actress must read and perform. Dodie Smith's autobiography is full of descriptions of actors and their personalities and the difficulties of casting. Gordon wrote no autobiography, but her letters rarely talk about actors, only about books and plays as entities in themselves.

On the day of the performance of *The Stars Bow Down*, a day when a writer like Dodie Smith might have been taking a last look at changes or at the theatre or the stage sets, Gordon prepared by having a rest.[11] She took her meals in her room and remained in bed all day. Lena looked in on her a couple of times – by invitation, she is careful to add – and asked Gordon what she was thinking about. 'Nothing,' Gordon replied, 'absolutely *nothing* – I've had a wonderful time'. Given the stress of her private life in Inverness at that moment, it is easy to see, with hindsight, why she needed a rest. The theatre was not her whole life – her father Colin, now very elderly and frail, was taking up a lot of her time and energy, as were problems with his business, not to mention the beginnings of a concern about her own health. The Malvern Festival, for Gordon Daviot, was not a career opportunity, a chance to mingle with producers and get her name out there again – it was an end in itself. She was enjoying the moment of having her play produced, without seeing it as any sort of stepping stone to the future. Malvern was her holiday and her rest time; it was not part of a carefully devised career plan. Dodie Smith spent a long time after the war trying to re-establish herself as a dramatist, speaking with managers like Binkie Beaumont, trying to cast new plays, writing works that were rejected. Dodie was always worried about the next project; Gordon simply enjoyed what she had. Of course, another key difference was that Dodie was the main wage earner for herself and her husband Alec, whereas Gordon still used her earnings for extras. Colin's business was still nominally the MacKintosh's main income.

Gordon Daviot did not have to do any extra self-promotion to gain status at Malvern, as she already had top billing in the festival programme.[12] Her introductory essay comes first and takes up more space than is given to the other two featured dramatists. Her photograph is included, but no mention is made of her real name and there is no biography given other than what she herself chooses to mention in her essay. It's the same for the other two playwrights, and the general impression is that the reader of the festival programme is expected to be cognisant of the dramatists' work and to accept at face value the festival's programming as being of high quality. Daviot is in illustrious company, and her play is being given serious critical attention merely by being included in the programme. Critics have seen some similarities to Shaw in Daviot's work, citing her assured dialogue and seeing his influence on *Queen of Scots* and *Cornelia*.[13] This sort of critical attention is in contrast to the cheerful comments about Josephine Tey's crime writing, which, although praised, was not always received with such serious consideration. Crime reviewing has become more serious over the years, but it is worth reiterating that in 1949, Elizabeth MacKintosh would have seen a clear distinction between Gordon Daviot's work being invited to join the Malvern Festival, and Josephine Tey's crime novels being published in popular paperback editions. They were seen as very different types of writing, and this coloured how Beth spoke about her own work, even if it didn't affect how she approached the writing itself.

Gordon Daviot's introductory essay in the festival programme provides interesting comment on how she saw the popularity of her own plays.[14] She discusses *Richard of Bordeaux*, and how she felt it was somewhat misrepresented by critics as being a work of pacifism, rather than an exploration of Richard's revenge on those who had tried to thwart him. She then says that, despite this, she did not return to novel writing, but carried on writing plays, because that was 'the thing I liked doing best in the world'. Remembering that the programme had no potted biography, this assumes that the Malvern audience had some knowledge of Daviot's novels under her own name, as well as her Tey work. Daviot explains, however, that she has now chosen to write plays on Biblical themes, and, while admitting that this may not appeal to the regular playgoer, she defends her choice, and hopes that the play she is presenting at the Malvern Festival, *The Stars Bow Down*, a rewriting of the story of Joseph and his brothers, will appeal. This essay gives some insight into how she viewed her critics, and her own writing. She writes purely for enjoyment, rather than for the audience – or for the money. Her Biblical scholarship is serious, and she wishes to see Biblical characters not only in their religious but also in their historical context. This chimes with the interest in history found in many of her other works. She also gives some indication of how she approaches playwriting and plotting, explaining that she is interested in moments of conflict, whether this is personal and individual or wider political or religious conflict.

The plays at the Malvern Festival were performed mainly by the Malvern Company, with the addition of extra actors as needed. The Malvern Company was a group of actors and actresses who were based at the Malvern Festival Theatre, but who also travelled across Britain doing shows elsewhere as a repertory company. Daviot's play has a cast list of thirty-two people including two or three child actors, a considerable cost and logistical challenge for the Malvern Festival. Although many of the actors doubled up to play parts in the other plays, Daviot's cast requirements are significantly higher than the other playwrights' (twelve listed cast members for Shaw's *Buoyant Billions*, for example, plus nine people for *The Tressinghams* and eight for *Max*, the other two plays). None of the actors are really household names today, but they were all hard-working professionals who appeared in numerous well-known plays, television series and films.

Gordon Daviot's own photograph is prominently featured in the Malvern Festival programme, and it shows a very different woman to the young, diffident playwright in Sasha's pre-war studio portraits.[15] At fifty-three, she now looks confident and mature, rather than having an air of being dressed up for the camera. She is wearing the same pearl earrings as in the Sasha portraits, which were a gift from Colin. She is much more relaxed and almost smiling, with her head resting on her hand. Her dark hair is swept up and back from her forehead, and, although the photo is just as posed as the Sasha ones were, this time it seems as if Gordon is in control, rather than the photographer. A full-length photograph showing Gordon in the same outfit, and so presumably taken at the same sitting, was kept by the MacKintosh family. This print is signed by the photographer: Angus McBean. McBean was a well-known figure in the theatrical world, a friend of the Motleys, for example, and of similar stature to Sasha. He is seen in the world of photography as a forerunner to David Bailey because of his post-war work with celebrities, and he photographed many well-known people, including, in 1963, the Beatles, for the cover of their first album. The fact that he photographed Gordon Daviot shows that she continued to have stature in the theatre world.

The attractive cast photos provided in the festival programme, along with the adverts and a certain datedness in the copy, bring home the difference between 1949 and now. Actors are photographed smoking cigarettes, few of the men are without a tie or smart jacket, and the women's hair and make-up has an attractively retro appearance. The Malvern Festival of 1949 was a very different beast from the self-promoting book festivals that authors have to attend today. Given what we know about Gordon Daviot's personality, it seems eminently her sort of place. A snapshot of Gordon at Malvern also survives: taken in the street, it shows her and Lena sightseeing – two extremely well-dressed women enjoying a cultural holiday.[16]

The Malvern Festivals continue today, with an ongoing commitment to cultural, high-quality entertainment. Drama now takes more of a back seat, with writers, film-makers and other artists now featured as well, but the Malvern Theatres still have a full year-round programme. The significance of Gordon Daviot's attendance at the festival is worth noting: she was still being assessed as a major British dramatist post-war.

Beth was very pleased with the reception of *The Stars Bow Down*, and said proudly in a letter to the mother of her Anstey room-mate, 'it got a first night reception that made history at Malvern', and describing her (largely positive) reviews.[17] Whereas the Gordon Daviot of the first performances of *Richard of Bordeaux* was overwhelmed by her reception, now Beth was pleased and comfortable with it. Gwen Ffrangcon-Davies returned to Britain permanently from South Africa in 1948.[18] Beth wrote to her shortly after the Malvern Festival, again describing the good audience reaction to her play: 'According to a cutting, the MALVERN Gazette announces that what it calls "the locals' favourite" was THE STARS BOW DOWN. Which pleases me far more than it has any right to do!'[19] She also describes some of the socializing that went on, and her meetings with festival founder Roy Limbert and sponsors the Beauchamps – all of whom would have been well known to Gwen. Gwen had appeared at the Malvern Festival herself, and knew founder Barry Jackson well through her work with Birmingham Rep at the start of her career. Beth's letter to Gwen is much like their letters of the 1930s, full of references to people they knew and books that Beth was reading, but it is the only surviving post-war letter between the two women.

After the Second World War, Gwen's position in theatre was slightly different, as, just as Beth had feared, there was a general feeling that she was 'one of those who had left' while the war was on. The old problems between Gwen and Marda were still not resolved, and Marda did not come back to Britain at the same time as Gwen.[20] Marda stayed in South Africa for a while longer, partly to continue the work she and Gwen had done on establishing theatre there, but partly also because she was not homesick for Britain in the way that Gwen was. It was also because Gwen wanted a break from their intense relationship. There was a suggestion that Marda was drinking too much. Beth's group of friends had all been affected by the war, and they were all, not just Beth, forced to rethink their lives and work. Dodie Smith, like Beth, had also turned to novel writing, and at the time that Beth was at Malvern, she was overseeing the US and UK publications of her hugely successful and beloved novel *I Capture the Castle*. This book perfectly captured a 1930s Britain with an atmosphere that worked in print but would no longer work on stage.

Beth, too, was focusing on her novels. 1949 was the year of publication of Josephine Tey's next mystery novel, *Brat Farrar*. Lena Ramsden, one of the few of Beth's London friends who had not only remained in Britain but who had made an effort to engage with the war effort, was particularly friendly with Beth in the post-war years, and *Brat Farrar* has as its subject something that was dear to both Lena and Beth: horses and horse racing. Beth wrote to Lena during the planning and preparation of *Brat Farrar*, and her letters and discussions shed some startling light on Beth's method of writing.

Captain Murdoch Beaton, the inspiration for the fictional
Murray Heaton

Elizabeth MacKintosh's first 'author photo' – never used

The New Theatre, London (now the Noel Coward)

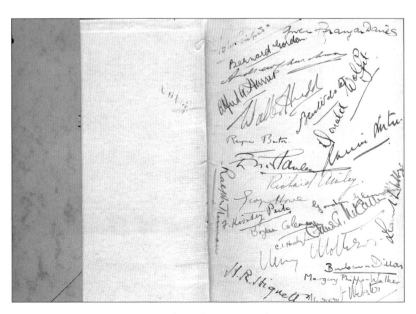

Gordon Daviot's own copy of "Richard of Bordeaux", signed by the cast

Magazines featuring Gordon Daviot's first three plays

Peggy, Marda, Gwen and Gordon. Portmeirion, 1934

Gwen, Gordon and Peggy. Portmeirion, 1934

Tagley cottage today

Humphrey, with Jean in
the background

Jean's husband, Humphrey Hugh Smith

Moire

TELEGRAMS: "MACKINTOSH, FRUITERER"
TELEPHONE 299

COLIN MACKINTOSH
:: Fruit Importer ::
and
Vegetable Merchant

47, 49 & 53 Castle Street,

Inverness, 6th May 1936

Dear Ltt—

This is great news,

I look forward to this event—
to give me the greatest pleasure
that life can give me now.

Be careful— no stretching to lift
something above you, quite right
about coal Holiday.

Posted you some eggs today

Love to both

Dad

Hope to post you a different—
Parcel next week Dad

Colin wrote to congratulate his youngest daughter on her pregnancy

Josephine Tey

Beth, 1949

Lena (centre) and Beth (right), Malvern 1949

Gordon Daviot. Malvern Festival, 1949

Colin and Beth, 1949

Colin and Josephine MacKintosh's simple grave marker

9.35 John Gielgud 27.9.52.
in **'RICHARD
OF BORDEAUX'**
by Gordon Daviot

Richard II....................John Gielgud
Anne of Bohemia, his Queen
....Joy Parker
The King's uncles:
John of Gaunt, Duke of Lancaster
.........................Leon Quartermaine
Thomas of Woodstock, Duke of
Gloucester......D. A. Clarke-Smith
Edmund of Langley, Duke of York
.............................Bryan Powley
Richard, Earl of Arundel
.................................Arthur Young
Michael de la Pole, Chancellor of
England........................Ivan Samson
Sir Simon Burley, the King's tutor
.................................George Howe
Robert de Vere, Earl of Oxford
.................................Robert Eddison
Henry, Earl of Derby, Bolingbroke,
son of Lancaster........Ivan Brandt
Thomas Mowbray, Earl of Notting-
ham........................Godfrey Kenton
Mary, Countess of Derby
.................................Margaret Ward
Agnes Launcekron, the Queen's wait-
ing woman................Patricia Hilliard
John Maudelyn, a page, afterwards
the King's secretary...Robin Lloyd
Edward, Earl of Rutland, Aumerle,
son of York................Richard Bebb
Sir John Montague...Roderick Lovell
Thomas Arundel, Archbishop of
Canterbury................Walter Hudd
A page.......................David Spenser
Narrator.......................Hamilton Dyce

Music by Herbert Menges
conducted by the composer
Adaptation and production
by John Richmond
(BBC recording)
Stephen Williams writes on page 7

27.9.52.
7

...WILLIAMS

...NES

*John
Gielgud
as
'Richard
of
Bordeaux'*

Scotland. She sent *Richard of Bordeaux* to John
Gielgud. He saw possibilities in it, but he was
cautious at first and tried it out at two Sunday
night performances at the Arts Theatre at a
total cost of £300. The play passed the test
triumphantly and when it was produced at the
New Theatre it became one of the outstanding
successes of 1932-3. Many still consider that as
Richard the Second, with his charm and
graciousness in youth, his petulance in contro-
versy and his dignity in adversity, Gielgud gave
the finest and subtlest performance of his career.
He plays the part again in *Saturday-Night
Theatre.*

* * *

IT was John Gielgud who revived in London in
1944 *The Cradle Song,* that gentle idyll of the
convent by Gregorio and Maria Sierra, and incidentally gave me one of the most enchanting evenings I have ever spent in the theatre. A woman of
the town leaves her baby on the convent steps. The
good sisters bring up the child and when she has
flowered into womanhood relinquish her—gladly
and sadly—to the man of her destiny. The charm
of the play is in the gradual and beautiful kindling
of the mother instinct in these devoted souls who
can never become mothers themselves. The authors
do not unduly sentimentalise the situation. No
doubt it takes all sorts to make a sisterhood, and
besides those for whom stone makes not a prison
make, there are, we surmise, others for whom iron
bars make a cage against which they beat their
wings in vain. (*Home Service, Sunday afternoon*)

* * *

IT is astonishing how drastically the English
'costume' play has altered during the last thirty
or forty years. In my boyhood a play dressed in
the fashion of a remote century was, *ipso facto,*
unreal: a cloak-and-sword romance, the dialogue
bristling with Gadzookses and gramercies, in
which the malapert caitiff was eventually out-
witted and a sawdust-stuffed doublet-and-hose
swept off to the altar an animated doll calcu-
lated to bore him to death in two weeks. Nowadays we have instead an honest endeavour to
analyse the minds of people of a past age and
relate their motives and passions to our own.

Such a play is *Richard of Bordeaux,* with its
shrewd historical perspective, its sense of character, and its essay naturalistic dialogue. Gordon
Daviot's real name was Elizabeth Mackintosh,
and before she achieved fame as a playwright
she was a games mistress at a girls' school in

"Richard of Bordeaux" was reprised as a BBC radio drama shortly after
Beth died – Moire's collection of cuttings

Beth's novels and plays were reprinted many times

Beth wrote to Lena frequently in the late 1940s, often about horse racing.[21] She described, on one of her still-regular visits to the cinema, seeing a particularly good horse race in the newsreel before the main feature started, the St Leger, won in 1949 by Michael Beary on his horse Ridge Wood. To Lena, whose father was chairman of the Manchester Racecourse Company, the jockeys like Michael were people she was on first-name terms with, whom she met at parties and socialized with. Josephine Tey, in Inverness, was still at arm's-length to this society, as she had been to London theatreland before the war, but, unlike the people around her watching the newsreel in the cinema, she could write about Michael as someone she was aware of, and had perhaps met. Tey had knowledge of horse racing as a connoisseur, but also the personal connection that her friends knew the jockeys. This is another illustration of her slightly strange position in society, in that, if she had been living in London, she would have been associating with very different people. In Inverness, Beth was still the daughter of a shopkeeper who – rather strangely, it was thought by her neighbours – went to the cinema on her own. In England (and to Lena) Gordon Daviot was an established playwright who would be invited to parties along with leading sports stars, actresses and Lena's other well-to-do artistic friends.

Lena said herself that 'Gordon was a grand person to have as a friend [...] her visits to London were infrequent, but we communicated regularly, and our letters were like conversations, broken off and resumed from time to time'.[22] Gordon had been particularly keen to draw on Lena's knowledge of horses and jockeys in the previous year, when she had been planning and writing *Brat Farrar*. Lena reveals in her autobiography the rather startling fact that, although Brat Farrar and Simon Ashby's lives were completely fictional, Brat had a physical counterpart: the way he looked was based on a real person. Apparently Brat looked, sounded and moved like a racing personality of the day, Frank Moore O'Ferral. O'Ferral was a wealthy Irishman who co-founded the Anglo-Irish Bloodstock Agency, exporting Irish horses and promoting Irish racing and horse breeding to wealthy clients, particularly Americans.[23] He was an extroverted, noticeable character in the horse-racing world of the time, though one that Beth would only have come across through her association with Lena and others behind-the-scenes, not someone Beth could ever have met as simply a horse lover from Inverness.

Beth went to the length of getting Lena to find out everything she could about O'Ferral, asking her to obtain a photograph of him and also make a sketch. Lena was not acquainted with him, but she sent what information she could up to Inverness. Gordon wrote back saying,

> I hope you will go on dishing the dirt. If you don't happen to be familiar yourself with this kind of interest, it is difficult to explain it to you. It isn't a question of wanting to meet him – which I should actively dislike. It is a quite detached curiosity about him and his. What he thinks, reads (I suppose he can?), says, eats; whether he likes his bacon frizzly or flaccid; how many children he has, their sex and ages; how many back teeth he has had filled and how often he has broken his collar bone. It always happens with someone I see casually, like that; and once my curiosity is satisfied my interest finishes. But until the picture is complete the curiosity is devouring. I think it is one tenth sex, four tenths writer's instinct, and five tenths urge to detection.[24]

The basis for a Josephine Tey character is seen here: the people in her books are always described precisely, with their facial characteristics often a key to their characters, such as Richard III in *The Daughter of Time*, or 'The Dago' in *The Man in the Queue*. Little details, physical or personality traits reveal characters' motivations. Beth was a very observational writer, who was supremely interested in psychology and character motivation and this glimpse into her planning for *Brat Farrar* is a key insight into the way she approached novel writing and the creation of her plots. It backs up the idea that other fictional characters were based, in looks at least, on people she had known, such as Murdoch Beaton/Murray Heaton in *Kif*.

Eventually, as Beth wrote to Lena, the fictional character she created in her mind would take over from the real person: 'It was lovely of you to send the drawing of Himself [O'Ferral], but you have made him *far* too good-looking [...]', Beth continued,

> When I was in town this last time I thought that, apart from a well-fitting new suit, there was nothing in the world that I wanted. And then I thought that yes, there was. I wanted a camera that looked like a handbag, or a compact, or something. So that one could photograph a person standing two feet away and be looking in another direction altogether while one was doing it. This has nothing to do with Himself; it is a permanent need with me. I am always seeing faces that I want to 'keep'.

This extract from Beth's letter to Lena is interesting not only because of its connection to *Brat Farrar*, but also because of what it reveals about Beth herself: this is the woman that people knew in Inverness; one who did not want to engage, but who held herself apart – one who did not even shop for clothes locally, but always went to London ('to town'). Beth seems to see this part of her personality in a positive way, as being something that is essential to her as a writer, rather than something that held her back socially. It is interesting too to note that Beth, who once considered art school, and who wrote about artists in *The Laughing Woman*, is still very interested in portraiture, yet dismissive of her own talents. The word pictures that Beth could create in her novels were far more satisfactory to her than her drawing talents.

Brat Farrar is one of Josephine Tey's most popular novels. Before its US publication in 1950 it was first serialized, in a slightly shortened form and under the title *Crooked Penny*, in the US magazine *Ladies Home Journal*, and over the following years it went on to be adapted for TV several times, made into a movie (with some creative licence) and adapted for radio.[25] Moire remembered that Beth would sometimes ask her for ideas for plots, and Josephine Tey's characters are so strong that she is often described as a writer who prioritizes character over plot, or even a writer whose plots are weak.[26] But when considering *Brat Farrar*, especially coming after *The Franchise Affair* or *Miss Pym Disposes*, it's clear that once Josephine Tey did find a good idea, she was capable of evolving some impressive storytelling. *Brat Farrar*'s plot is clever, turning on a case of mistaken identity and twins, which is eventually revealed as a murder mystery. The title character, orphan Brat Farrar, is approached in the street by Alec Loding, a stranger who mistakes him for Simon Ashby. Building on this unlikely coincidence of appearance, Loding convinces Brat to insinuate himself into the Ashby family, posing as the long-lost Patrick, Simon's elder twin and heir to the family home and business.[27]

Twins are a fairly standard literary device, but they did run in Beth's family. Her grandmother, Jane Horne, had a brother and sister who were twins, James and Anne Ellis. Jane Horne had probably mentioned the twins and the large family they came from. The Ashbys, in *Brat Farrar*, are a very convincing large family, with two sets of twins, Simon and Patrick, and Ruth and Jane. The opening scenes of the book, with the family around the dinner table talking and squabbling, may come as a surprise to someone re-reading the novel, because they do not relate to the plot as it is remembered or described, but they do show how at home Josephine Tey was writing large families. She had her childhood memories of her two sisters to draw on, as well as her new baby nephew – and even her other sister Jean's stepchildren and step-grandchildren. Jean, like Beth, was a horse lover, and the Ashby home is reminiscent of the English home of Jean and her husband Humphrey, the house at Wilfred's, Radnage where Jean now stayed alone. Jean's real name was 'Jane', and, in another of Josephine Tey's in-jokes with names, the horsey daughter is Jane. Moire's middle name, Henrietta, had been used in earlier work. Other names include Ledingham, a name common in Inverness, while the unseen twin, who dies young through no fault of his own and with whom our hero (Brat) feels an affinity, is given the symbolic name Patrick – Hugh McIntosh's middle name recurring again.

Tey continues to build her fictional world, with Kevin Macdermott QC reappearing, and the paper *The Clarion* showing up, as it did in her play *Clarion Call*. Local paper the *Westover Times* seems very similar to the *Inverness Courier*. The intersection between truth and fiction crops up in strange places, as do Beth's own views. 'What I can't get into [people's] blind blinkered minds', she had said to Marjorie, her Anstey room-mate, 'is that luxury isn't owning Rolls Royces, or having the royal suite on the Olympic, but not having to do something you don't much want to do'.[28] This sentiment appears in *Brat Farrar*, but it is the villain, Alec Loding, who echoes it: 'Riches, my boy, don't consist in having things, but in not having to do something you don't want to do. And don't you forget it. Riches is being able to thumb your nose.'[29] Alec, the old actor, is an ambiguous villain.

Beth spent much of her time living in her mind; her reality might be in Inverness but *Brat Farrar* has an element of wish fulfilment, a way of writing out her longing for her former home before her mother's death and the Second World War. Brat is the most unlikely hero, yet the reader cannot help but like him, despite what he does, and Bee Ashby comes to think of him as family. Brat, the outsider, loves and appreciates England, and, despite everything that stands in his way, through his detection and his ultimate desire to do the right thing, he gets to be part of the Ashby family. 'The close, fine turf slipped by under them [...] England, England, England, said the shoes as they struck. A soft drum on the English turf. I don't care [...] I don't care. I'm a criminal, and a heel, but I've got what I wanted, and it's worth it. By God, it's worth it. If I died tomorrow, it's worth it.'[30]

These are Brat Farrar's words as he rides in England, a passage so full of emotion it can even make someone who is not English feel for the country. Brat wants to be part of an old English family who pay pensions to their old servants, who live in a pre-war landscape, surrounded by animals. The image is tarnished by Simon, but it is still something Brat aspires to.

It seems unlikely Beth would have remembered and romanticized England as she does in *Brat Farrar* if she hadn't been living in the Highlands for over twenty years. During her holidays, and throughout the time she was preparing *Brat Farrar*, Beth was mentally focused on England and her life there – Malvern, and her sisters, nephew and friends – but in reality she was dealing with questions of money, her father Colin's illness, and worries about her own health. Post-war, Beth was managing to pick up the threads of her old life successfully, reconnecting with friends like Lena Ramsden, still receiving commissions for her playwriting, and moving her creative output in a new direction towards novel writing, but Inverness life kept disrupting the pattern she wanted to establish.

The photos of Gordon Daviot the successful playwright in Malvern are offset by some family snapshots from the same year. In these, Colin and Beth stand side by side outside. Colin, dressed in a heavy coat and hat, is an old man. He stares challengingly at the camera, looking every inch the strict father he undoubtedly was. Beth, as in so many photographs, doesn't meet the eye; she looks away from the camera and down at the ground. She is just as smartly dressed as she was at Malvern, in a tweed jacket and skirt, with her dark hair neatly up, and the beautiful bone structure of her face highlighted by shadows, but it would be clear to anyone looking at this photograph that she is the daughter of Colin. There is almost a graceful, adult version of childish awkwardness in the photo. As Colin's daughter, she must do what she has to for him, putting him before herself.

Brat Farrar alternates its point of view between Brat himself, and Bee Ashby. Brat gets England by any means, but Bee, faced with a family tragedy and dependents who needed her, has given up her single life in London with regret, but not a moment's hesitation. And, no matter what Eleanor has planned for the future, it is Bee, in the end, who gets to live with Brat, that substitute for Patrick.

CHAPTER NINETEEN

To Love and Be Wise

Beth's father Colin was now in his late eighties and, although still going down to his shop each day, was becoming more and more frail.[1] Beth herself was not keeping well. Lena Ramsden talked about her at the Malvern Festival, saying that her idea of a good day was to lie down doing nothing, and this probably reflects both her need for a rest from looking after Colin, and her own niggling health worries.[2] Lena also recalled in her autobiography that both she and others, like Gwen, were worried about Beth's health in about 1950 – perhaps even a year earlier, in 1949.[3] Certainly Beth had been experiencing some health problems for a few years, which had gradually got serious enough to become obvious to her friends. Another friend, the Scottish writer Elisabeth Kyle, was concerned that she only had help in the house one day a week, and that even on that day Beth herself had to work hard at the housekeeping.[4]

Given the choice, Beth often did just ditch the housework and go out: she much preferred taking the train to Aviemore and doing a day's hillwalking around Rothiemurchus to spending her limited energy tidying. However, she wrote to Lena saying, 'If you have seen Gwen you probably know that I have been reprieved, and am not likely to turn invalid. A nice simple treatment by tablet should bring me back to normal in about a year.'[5] They had been planning a trip to Newmarket races again, and Beth did indeed manage Newmarket, for all three days of the races, but Lena said later, 'There could be no doubt that she had enjoyed herself, but, all the same, to her friends the cloud was still there – small, but persistent.'[6] Beth always presented a cheerful front, ignoring any illness as much as possible and continuing her quiet life in Inverness, interspersed with trips south.

As the correspondence with Lena shows, Gordon Daviot was back in regular contact with her theatre friends, including Gwen Ffrangcon-Davies. In 1950, Josephine Tey published another mystery novel, *To Love and Be Wise*, which owes rather a lot, not only to her knowledge of theatre and her actress friendships, but also to the Essex villages where people like Gwen, Dodie Smith, Binkie Beaumont and John Gielgud had made their homes. It was country that Josephine Tey had got to know well, and she drew a sly, rather mocking, but ultimately affectionate portrait of this rural retreat from London in *To Love and Be Wise*, showing an artistic community causing waves in the country.

The name of the village where Gwen Ffrangcon-Davies was based at Tagley Cottage – currently alone, as Marda was still in South Africa – was Stambourne.[7] Dodie Smith's house was in nearby Finchingfield (theatre manager Binkie Beaumont was still living there as Dodie and her husband Alec continued their extended exile in America), and John Gielgud and other theatrical personages lived close by. Gwen and John owed their homes to their financial success in Gordon Daviot's *Richard of Bordeaux*, and the whole area had come to symbolize for them a retreat from London, where they went when they were 'resting' between jobs, but still wished to be in contact with the theatre community. Carfuls of their friends had been going out there since the 1930s.

This southern English county of Essex is very different from the Highlands. The flat, fertile fields, bounded by high hedges, far away from the sea, create a type of landscape that is not found in Scotland. Old thatched village cottages, with thick roofs and white walls and small windows, are still preserved – although they are often now owned by the richer Londoner, because of their position within commuting distance of the city. A village or small town in the Highlands would be nothing like this vision of England. A Highland small community would have houses built to withstand the weather, oriented towards the sea. Farming and fields would be on a far smaller scale, and with less productivity there is more of a feeling of wrestling a living from the land. For a Highlander, the feeling of difference and contrast is huge. Thatched cottages and rurality would not have been so alien to Beth, but the physical contrast of a larger, flatter inland landscape, would still have been there. The policeman Rodgers says as much in *To Love and Be Wise*, contrasting the inland village with his own upbringing by the sea.

Beth was at once drawn to the way of life Gwen and her friends lived, and slightly sceptical of it. As a native of the Highlands, and coming from a fairly small town herself, she was used to small town life, and able to see the village both as the villagers did, and as her theatre friends could. Small communities often attract people who have removed themselves from the city to 'find themselves' in the country, incomers who appropriate local customs but are never quite totally accepted as they never quite want to become truly local. There are a few scathing remarks in *To Love and Be Wise*: 'A once beautiful English village', Liz says, 'that is now occupied territory'.[8] The matter-of-fact, country born Sergeant Williams sums it all up, saying countryside always looks more appealing to those who weren't brought up there, and who don't have to do any actual work in it. Beth enjoyed and understood the country, but was clear that towns were really what appealed to her. She wrote to Gwen, 'I know in my heart that three-minutes-from-a-station-and-two-minutes-from-a-cinema is my idea of comfort and convenience, and that I would rather spend my days in the country and come back to the comfort and lights of town at night'.[9]

Josephine Tey's portrait of 'Salcott St Mary' – and its inhabitants – is thus not entirely flattering. *To Love and Be Wise* sees the proper return of Alan Grant, who had only had a walk-on part in *The Franchise Affair*, and it also sees the return of Alan's friend, the actress Marta Hallard. Marta is given some unflattering personality traits. She's certainly not described in an idealized way, and the other 'theatre' personalities mentioned are equally flawed. In the case of Marta, however negatively she is described, Grant obviously still thinks a lot of her. However, her slight phoniness and tendency to take her acting into her everyday life is alluded to in the same scene, and Grant sums her up by thinking,

> In general knowledge Marta was as deficient as a not very bright child of eleven; her attention automatically slid off anything that was alien to her own immediate interests, and the result was an almost infantine ignorance. He had seen the same thing in hospital nurses and overworked GPs. But put a script in her hands, and from a secret and native store of knowledge she drew the where-withal to build her characterisation of the author's creation.[10]

It's a pretty damning assessment of an actress – but, on the other hand, it's recognizable and has a definite air of truth. Perhaps, given the even-handedness and Grant's appreciation of Marta's talent, and obvious affection for her, Beth's actress friends would have been rather flattered by the portrayal after all. They were certainly a group of friends who encouraged bracing criticism in the pursuit of high art.

Marta's name is, of course, recognizably similar to Marda Vanne's, and there is the usual number of in-jokes with real names and real places throughout *To Love and Be Wise*. My favourite is the book publishers Ross and Cromarty (the name of an area north of Inverness), and there is also Lee Searle's address in London (9 Holly Pavement, Hampstead) which almost matches one of Gwen and Marda's real London addresses (8 Holly Place, Hampstead).[11] Marta Hallard dresses dramatically in black and white, in the manner of Dodie Smith, and various comments about upgrading country houses to suit artistes seem rather similar to comments Dodie made in her autobiographies about the real Essex and its artistic inhabitants.[12] There are also rather more mentions of Scotland than a non-Scot would be likely to put into a book about the south of England. Lee Searle paints Scottish scenes, including Suilven, as her alibi, while Grant acknowledges a Scottish grand-father from Strathspey. With a background knowledge of Beth's life – the real village, the friendships with actresses, the interest in art – something is added to the book, but equally it can be enjoyed without any of this knowledge.

To Love and Be Wise begins by introducing us to an artistic community of writers and theatre people, before bringing in a newcomer to this world, photographer Leslie Searle. Alan Grant encounters Searle by chance through his friendship with actress Marta Hallard. He feels there is something odd about him from their first meeting, but is shocked to be called in to investigate his mysterious disappearance. *To Love and Be Wise* is a crime novel where you get to focus entirely on the process and go through all the emotions associated with disappearance, murder and discovery, without the horror of violently killing off characters. It is extremely interested in character and place and, as the conclusion of the book shows, how to be grown-up about love and passion. But at the same time as exploring character and motivation in this way, it is a good read: the pacing is perfect and the reader wants to know what happens next. In *The Man in the Queue* Tey showed from her first chapter cliff-hanger ending that she knew how to keep her readers wanting more. There is a similar chapter one cliff-hanger here, but this is a more sophisticated book than *The Man in the Queue*. In terms of technical writing, any of the awkwardness of phrasing that was evident in Beth's early short stories is completely gone; she is now playing with words confidently. *To Love and Be Wise* does make reference to earlier Inspector Grant adventures like *The Man in the Queue*, when Grant's superior talks about Jerry Lamont, but there are none of the authorial asides that we had in Grant's first book. Tey is happy here to let her characters talk for her: she is now a confident enough writer to let the story flow through them.

The plot in *To Love and Be Wise* hinges on what Grant calls 'transvestism'. In this way, Tey is able to discuss something which was integral to the theatre world she knew. *To Love and Be Wise* would have been a very different book if, in 1950, Beth had written openly about gay people. Around this time, Dodie Smith showed her American publisher a draft of a novel featuring openly gay characters and was told it had to be revised for publication because it would be considered obscene, while authors such as Dodie's friend Christopher Isherwood who wrote about gay characters were writing a different kind of literature.[13] It would have been almost impossible for a 'mystery' novel to include an openly gay character and still be marketed as popular Josephine Tey novels were. Since Marda's declaration of 'love' Beth had been painfully aware of the homosexuality amongst her London friends, and *To Love and Be Wise* deals with her feelings about this in a measured way. Other hints of knowledge appear in earlier books – Brat and Alec Loding's first meeting and talk about 'propositioning', for example – but there was no way that Beth could write about it openly in 1950.

Dodie Smith, in her novels, tried to deal with issues surrounding homosexuality, but her then-liberal attitude now comes across as dated. Josephine Tey does something that seems far more modern, in showing that homosexuality is incidental to the characters' morality; it is not the crime. Grant knows something is 'off' about Leslie, and feels uncomfortable around him from the first time he meets him at the publishers' party, but Grant's moral judgement is reserved for Leslie's later crimes, and is tempered with a feeling that Leslie has been rather clever. The character of Serge Ratoff, the fading Russian dancer who is obsessed with playwright Toby Tullis, approaches the idea of a same-sex relationship, but here, too, Josephine Tey has other, overriding concerns: Serge is the only one of the incomers who is fully accepted by the village, partly because he enjoys being part of village life, chatting in the post office and drinking in the bar, but also because he is seen by the villagers as having a 'childish quality [... they treated him with] the same tolerance that they used to their own "innocents"'.[14] Another reason why Serge is able to move between the two groups, the artists and the villagers, is that, as a foreigner, Serge is out of the class system which is accepted throughout the book. Leslie Searle, the other outsider, outrages the playwright Toby Tullis by leaving him in the pub to talk to his 'friend' Bill Maddox, the garage owner. Toby is upset because Searle is not acknowledging his fame and status, and is instead spending time with a villager. Class is far more important in Josephine Tey's depiction of English country life than sexuality and that, ultimately, is how she saw it. It wasn't their sexuality which set her London friends apart from her life in Inverness, and not even their theatrical backgrounds, it was their class and upbringing. When Beth was with Gwen and Lena, she was a playwright. But in Inverness, Beth was still a fruiterer's daughter.

Beth's Inverness life, and her relationship history, is referenced in *To Love and Be Wise* in one other way: the book contains a clue to Beth's relationship with Hugh McIntosh, when Grant quotes some lines of poetry which he attributes to 'an army friend of mine'. 'That's good that is,' says his colleague. 'Your army friend knew what he was talking about.'[15] The lines are carefully attributed in an acknowledgement at the start of the book. If it wasn't for these ten small lines of poetry quoted by Josephine Tey, Hugh McIntosh's work and short life would be completely forgotten.

In Inverness, Colin MacKintosh was now so frail he needed someone to lean on when he walked.[16] He still visited his late wife Josephine's grave every Sunday afternoon, but he now had to go by taxi. Over the years, Beth had come to dislike these ritual visits, and retained a hatred of putting fresh flowers on graves. There were many meaningful graves in Tomnahurich for her, but she was always the type of person to look forward, rather than dwell on the dead. Sometimes, she waited for Colin in the taxi outside the cemetery, reading the Sunday papers, though, if Colin was ever unable to go, she would take the flowers to Josephine's grave for him. Colin's fruiterer shop and landlord business were still a going concern, but he had to rely more and more not only on his daughter to help him, but also on his long-serving shop assistant, Annie Macpherson.[17] Although Colin was still comfortably well off, with constant money from rents and investments and no real need to worry about finances, his fruiterer business had never quite regained the standing it had before the war.[18] In common with most Scottish women of her class, it is likely that Beth not only knew her father's exact financial situation, but also that she managed the household accounts, if not all the business accounts as well. Colin, however, probably didn't know the extent of Beth's fortune. Father and daughter liked to spend their money on practical things – furniture, clothes, or expensive jewellery – but neither was ostentatious.[19] Beth always preferred, for example, a plain, smartly cut suit of expensive material to following the latest fashion. They bought good furnishings for their house, but Beth's greatest expenditure was probably her holidays and trips to London and to see friends. Beth never wrote solely for money – her aim was not to provide a living for herself and Colin, but to write literature she enjoyed and which helped her to cope with the restrictions of her life in Inverness.

While the fruiterer business could be left, to a certain extent, to shop assistant Annie, Colin's landlord interests really needed more attention, and neither of the MacKintoshes seemed to be putting in the time here. The value of the shop buildings, stores and flats on Castle Street had gone up over time, but only because of a general rise in prices. In reality, they were very run down.[20] Colin had always maintained his flats to a higher standard than many others in the street, but the problem was the basic structure of the old buildings: they were falling down. By 1949, five of the rooms that Colin rented out were condemned and could no longer be used – he had only four tenants left, as opposed to the nine he had in 1918.[21] No new tenants and rents could be found until a serious amount of work was done. The tenants in the remaining flats had remained fairly stable, with the Diack family still occupying the flat they had been in since about 1918. Colin was lenient with demands for rent now that Mrs Diack was a widow, and she was a few months behind.[22] In 1950, local cinema owner and film-maker Jimmy Nairn made a short feature called *Homes for a Highland Town*, where he illustrated the changes in housing in Inverness by contrasting the new family sized, three-bedroom council houses with gardens being built in wide, planned streets in Dalneigh, with the crumbling old tenements of Castle Street.[23] In the short silent movie, which was shown alongside newsreels before the main feature in cinemas across Scotland, it's not possible to identify Colin's flats or shop, but small children stare out of narrow alleyways in the old town in Inverness as the camera pans slowly up the crumbling brickwork and faded, peeling window frames. This illustration of how Invernessians were encouraged to view the old flats of landlords like Colin, may explain once more why Beth felt antagonistic towards Inverness. As a keen cinema-goer, she would not have found it pleasant, however uninterested she was in the landlord business, to have seen her father's flats, which he had worked so hard to buy, held up as an example of the opposite of progress and modernity.

Castle Street was no longer a prospering area. Shops nearby had not changed much in the last few years, with a cycle shop and a confectioner next to Colin's fruit business, but several shopkeepers were living in the little flats above their shops now, rather than being able to afford big houses in Crown.[24] There is a description of a sad little street in *Brat Farrar* that sounds suspiciously like Castle Street: 'the row of cheap shops on the opposite side of the road; some of them not much better than shacks. Dingy cafés, a cobblers, a bicycle "depot", a seller of wreaths and crosses, a rival seller of flowers, a greengrocer's, and anonymous businesses with windows painted half-way up and odd bills tacked in the window'.[25] As Colin became more ill, the worries over the shop and the tenants became Beth's. She was plainly not interested, and preferred to spend her time with her writing and on holidays, but Colin's illness now deteriorated to the point where she had to take action. She typed a letter to Moire in early September 1950, saying that she had had to call in the doctor.[26] Colin was taken in for treatment at a private nursing home at Rossal, 31 Island Bank Road; a large half-timbered house a little way up from the River Ness. Beth's letter is quite positive – Colin, she writes 'asks you to excuse him from writing because "he doesn't feel like it" – the sober truth being that he is so deep in a work by Ian Hay that he can hardly put it down to eat'. Ian Hay wrote popular novels and Colin, like Beth, was still an avid reader. Beth ends her letter by saying that she 'is having an unbroken night's sleep for the first time for eight months. Smasheen.' Despite the cheerful tone and the last word (an in-joke for anyone familiar with the Invernessian accent), it's clear that Beth has been finding the task of looking after Colin difficult.[27]

Beth wrote again to Moire shortly after, to say that Colin had undergone a successful operation which had left him much more comfortable, though she was still concerned about him – 'Up to yesterday his normal dictator complex was in full swing, which was a good sign if very hard to bear. Today however he is lethargic and sweet, which is a much less healthy sign.'[28] Colin had definitely rallied, but the ups and downs continued. It was a difficult time for Beth, alone in Inverness with sole responsibility for her father.

Colin died in the nursing home, at quarter to seven in the evening on the 25th September 1950, less than a month after he had first been admitted.[29] He was eighty-seven years old. On his death certificate, the cause of death was recorded as hypertrophy of prostate and pulmonary hypostasis. As on every official document, his occupation of 'Fruiterer' is carefully noted, but so also is the fact that he was the 'Widower of Josephine Horne'. Colin had come a long way from the isolated croft at Shieldaig, and through his own hard work had established himself creditably in business and established his family in a substantial house. He had paid for his daughters' education, and seen two of them happily married, while his eldest daughter had dedicated much of her adult life to caring for him. Colin has sometimes been portrayed as an autocratic, domineering father who forced Beth to stay at home. While he was undoubtedly strict, his upbringing shows why this was: he cared very deeply for his family and wanted the best for them. He was always a fair man, a hard worker who did his best, and who did not always get a just reward for that work. He had missed his wife very much in the decades since her death, and he was finally buried next to her in Tomnahurich cemetery.[30] 'If one had prayed for his life to end in one special way,' Beth wrote to her school friend and Anstey room-mate Marjorie, 'one would have prayed for it exactly as it happened'. Despite Beth's flurry of letters to Moire, it had actually only been three weeks since Colin took a turn for the worse, and he had not suffered too much pain. 'Moire', Beth continued, describing Colin at the end, 'said how extraordinarily good-looking he had become and that was true'.[31]

Beth did not go to the registrar's office to record her father's death. This duty was carried out by her father's close friend, Alexander Finlayson. In his will, Colin had named three men as his executors or Trustees: Alexander Finlayson, Alexander Martin and David Brass. Finlayson lived at 15 Lovat Road and was a cashier who had worked at the MacKintosh's solicitors, Stewart, Rule and Co, the firm which employed ex-provost and friend of Neil Gunn, Alexander MacEwen. Alexander Martin was a chartered accountant, living in Lombard Street, and Brass a commercial traveller living in Broadstone Park. From the addresses, all the men were living close to the MacKintosh's house in Crown, so it's possible that all three were Colin's close friends, though, from their job titles, it is also possible that Martin was a business acquaintance Colin may have thought would be useful in administering the financial side of his will.[32] Many people choose relatives to act as executors, but perhaps Colin felt men of his own generation would be better able to deal with his business, or perhaps he wished to spare his daughters any further stress and upset.

Colin's will was not overly complex, but his financial affairs took time to settle, and he made personal requests which cast some light on his family affairs.[33] The will had first been drawn up four years earlier, in 1946, but Colin had made some changes to it, the most recent in 1949. Colin's assets amounted to £3,826 11s 4d before taxes. As well as his business and house, he had savings in more than one bank, and stocks and shares. Colin had bought a substantial amount of British Government war stocks, which would have been sold to help the war effort, and he also had money in various other assets, such as Associated Newspapers shares and the Eagle Star Insurance Company, chosen probably for their returns rather than any particular association. His business was valued at £156, and his household furniture and personal effects at £131. His rents for the shop and flats were not completely balanced, and his tenant Mrs Diack's account in particular needed attention, as Colin had allowed the widow to fall behind on her rent when she had trouble paying. Colin's total assets were a reasonable amount, given inflation. An average wage in Scotland in 1950 would be around £350, and the Highland economy was always poorer than the rest of the country. In today's money, Colin left just over £87,000.[34]

In the written statement of the will, Colin was careful first to make provision for all his sickbed charges, funeral expenses, debts, and expenses incurred by his Trustees to be paid. He added that, for the trouble of administering his will, each of the three Trustees was to get a sum of £25. Having settled his debts, Colin then wished to give his daughters 'Mrs Jane Ellis MacKintosh or Humphrey Smith and Mary Henrietta MacKintosh or Stokes the sum of Two hundred pounds each'. Elizabeth, 'who has kept house with me since her mother's death', was to get a larger sum of £1,500. Any left-over money from his capital, once the debts and bequests had been paid, was to be divided equally between his daughters. Jean and Moire, as they were married, were, in Colin's eyes, more financially secure. He wanted to make special provision for Beth as she was single, and because she had helped him for so many years. The money was not his main legacy to Beth, however. She was also to have the house in Crown, and a half share in his shop.

Colin was very proud of his business. In the absence of a son to whom he could have left the business outright, he wanted to leave half the shop to Beth and half to his loyal shop assistant, Annie Macpherson. Annie was also to get a sum of £200. He further added that 'it is my earnest wish that [...] the said Annie Macpherson, should, after my death, continue to manage and direct my said business for the joint behoof of my said daughter Beth MacKintosh and herself'. Colin's fruiterer business was at this point established at numbers 47, 49 and 53 Castle Street, and Beth and Annie were to get 'all stock-in-trade, furnishings, implements, utensils, fittings and all others of my business as Fruiterer'. Colin also made provision in his will for any shop debts and problems with 'legacy and Government duties' (presumably death duties) to be dealt with by his executors/trustees before the business was handed over to Beth and Annie, so they could have a clean start.

Colin had added a special amendment to the original will on 17th December 1946, saying that his new grandson, Colin Stokes (son of his youngest daughter Mary Henrietta) was to get £300. He had also altered a previous legacy, where he had wished £150 to go to his shop assistant Barbara Cameron, because she had left his employment.

In his will, Colin's closeness to his eldest daughter Beth, and his gratitude for her help, is clear. Of his family, he mentions only his immediate descendants, no nephews or nieces or cousins, and he also mentions his good friend Alexander Finlayson and his loyal shop assistants, which probably gives a fair picture of his social circle at the time of his death. His family had become scattered and less close over the years, while his wife, brothers and sisters had predeceased him. Colin had spent much of his adult life providing for his family financially, looking after his sister and his parents when he was a young man, and then his children as he grew older, but over the years they had all become independent, surely thanks in part to Colin's support. Colin's national pride is clear in his large holdings of British Government war stocks, while his new pride in his grandson is shown by the amendment he made after little Colin's birth. Finally, Colin's pride in the business he built up from scratch is clear in his wish that it should be carried on.

As one of Inverness's oldest shopkeepers, Colin's death was noted in obituaries in the local papers. The day after his death, 26th September, the *Inverness Courier* ran his death notice in their classified section, and a short obituary in their main news section.[35] The *Courier* reminded its readers that Colin was 'one of the oldest businessmen in Inverness. He was in his 88th year, and he had been in business as a fruiterer in the town for over sixty years'. The obituary is not signed, but is clearly written by the paper's staff, rather than by a family member. It says of Colin that 'He was possessed of a keen sense of humour, and he was the most generous of men, doing many kindly and helpful actions quietly and unobtrusively' and that he 'took a lively interest in the affairs of the town and in its welfare'. It also mentions his birth 'on the west coast of Ross-shire', and his hobby of angling – 'he was acknowledged to be a first-class fisherman'. Colin's daughters are also mentioned, both 'the well-known authoress' Gordon Daviot (no mention of 'Josephine Tey') and his other two daughters, now married and living in England.

There is one slightly sour note in the obituary. After noting Colin's interest in Inverness affairs, the writer feels compelled to point out that Colin 'did not associate himself actively with any public boards'. This was almost the same criticism that was to be later thrown at Beth on her death: the idea that the MacKintosh family didn't give quite enough to Inverness, didn't contribute to the public life of the city, and held themselves aloof. Colin was concerned with his immediate family, but did not feel under any obligation to the city where he had struggled and worked for his own success. The MacKintoshes did not move in the same social circles as the family who owned the *Inverness Courier*, so the *Courier* did not feel that the MacKintoshes were completely involved in the fabric of Inverness society.

The contrast between Colin's life and that, for example, of ex-provost Alexander MacEwen, shows how little the writer of the *Courier*'s obituary understood of the different upbringing that Colin had experienced. To read about MacEwen's life is like reading about a different world. He was a colonial child, born to well-off parents, educated privately then trained as a lawyer, automatically given a place in an Inverness firm, encouraged to stand for local government, and later knighted for services to local government and public health in Scotland. MacEwen's gentle upbringing meant his energy was saved for battles when he was an adult. Colin had already fought his way through life when he was fourteen and had to start bringing in a wage for the family. MacEwen saw public life as a duty that successful businessmen should engage in; Colin saw his successful business as the end result. MacEwen moved in the same circles as the Barron family who ran the *Inverness Courier* (though they did fall out over politics), and Colin did not.[36] More consolingly, one of the sympathy letters Beth and her sisters received came from the manse in Colin's home village of Shieldaig, where Colin was remembered as 'a kind friend to us on many an occasion and in particular I shall not forget his goodness when my mother was ill and died in Inverness'.[37]

Another local paper, the *Highland News*, also ran an obituary for the 'Late Mr C. MacKintosh', and it did not feel any need to criticize Colin.[38] The *Highland News* is the more tabloid of the two papers, publishing weekly in a smaller format, and it has more west coast and Gaelic connections. They ran an obituary on Saturday 30th September, beginning 'Inverness has lost its oldest and one of its most respected members of the business community'. It describes Colin's progress in the business world in more detail, writing that 'He came to Inverness as a youth and gradually built up an influential business, his clientele including prominent families in the three Counties'. Colin's interest in Inverness and the wider Highlands is mentioned, with no qualifications, and a personal insight into his hobbies says that he was interested in fishing and reading: 'he lòved to converse about the great literature and political figures who dominated the Victorian stage'. It ends, 'His geniality and hospitality were striking characteristics'. This is the Colin who had common interests with Beth; who gave his wife and daughters presents of beautiful and expensive jewellery; whom Beth honoured and respected, even if she found looking after him a chore; who had worked hard and made something of himself.

Sadly, the *Courier*'s portrait of a man who wasn't interested in public affairs is sometimes the one that seems to have prevailed. Recent articles on the history of Castle Street have omitted any mention of Colin's business's sixty-year presence on the street, and his shop seems, unlike many others of a similar vintage, to have faded from public memory. Perhaps the fact that he sold to big houses and on contracts, rather than always directly to the public, has influenced this, but there is also a selective memory at work. Many researchers of Tey's life have used the same written archive – the *Inverness Courier*'s – and repeated the same facts without an understanding of the background. I have found no photographs of Colin's shop – it would have been difficult to take a good one of the shop from the narrow darkness of Castle street – and it has seemed at times as if he was never there. He could be proud of what he had achieved for his daughters and grandson, but his pride in his business was Colin's (and perhaps his wife Josephine's) alone.

Beth did not want to carry on the fruit shop in the way that Colin wished. His final illness and death had been very stressful – it was around this time that she said to Lena Ramsden at the Malvern Festival that her idea of a good idea was to lie in bed and do nothing – and it took her a while to recover. She was also suffering from illness herself. It took time to sort out Colin's affairs after his death, and things did not work out exactly the way Colin – or Beth – had wanted.

CHAPTER TWENTY

You Will Know the Truth

After Colin's death, Beth wrote to Marjorie, her friend from school and Anstey, that 'I have not yet decided on plans for the future. The present is too full of horrible practicalities like lawyers, and values, and inventories, and what not. And it is so long since I had a life of my own that it is difficult to accustom myself to the idea that I am free.'[1]

Beth did not want to keep on running the shop with Annie Macpherson, and did not need the income. Plans to sell the shop and flats, however, took time to carry out, particularly because there were sitting tenants whose rents still had to be collected, not to mention the fact that the building was not in a good saleable condition because several of the flats were condemned. It wasn't until later in 1951 that the shop and attached flats passed into the possession of Estate Agents John Macmahon of Huntly Street in Inverness.[2] Beth was still writing to Moire about the finer financial details in October 1951.[3]

What Beth did want to do was keep writing, and what she wanted to keep writing were mystery novels. However much she might talk about 'knitting', her Josephine Tey novels were very important to her.

Colin had missed the publication of *To Love and Be Wise* by a matter of days. In October 1950, the month after his death, Beth made a trip to London. She no longer had to wait on Colin's convenience to take holidays, and she also wanted to see her sisters after their father's death, as well as sort out some of her writing business, meeting Nico Davies for lunch. Both Nico and Peter had become good friends. Later, from her club in Cavendish Square, Beth wrote to Nico discussing a letter she had received from a fan after the publication of *To Love and Be Wise*.[4] The fan seems to have questioned a couple of points in the novel, and Beth defended her book robustly. Her letter to her publisher also sheds more light on her writing methods, as she mentioned that when she wasn't sure about police matters she would ask the local Chief Constable. This suggests not only that Beth did some of the technical research so beloved of contemporary crime writers, but also that her social circle in Inverness was wider than is popularly believed. The Chief Constable in Inverness in 1950 was William Paterson, a local man who had worked his way up the ranks. This letter to Nico is not publicly available; it was advertised, along with detailed photos and a partial transcription, for private sale on the internet, and has a particularly interesting footnote. Written in Beth's usual execrable handwriting, she tells her publisher, 'It's a very strange thing but I got more kick out of seeing Tey in the middle of the 'Times' window than I ever did out of seeing my name in front of the New [Theatre]'.

Walking around London, Beth had seen a prominent display of her new novel, *To Love and Be Wise*, in a bookshop window featuring novels from the Times Book Club. She was also keen to finish her next novel, which involved checking some research at the British Museum. Throughout the time Colin was ill, she had been thinking and writing about another man who was trapped, ill, in a hospital bed, creating what was to become her best-known novel, *The Daughter of Time*. Like *To Love and Be Wise*, this once again featured Inspector Grant as the main character, but it was a very different story to anything Josephine Tey had written before – in fact, it was a very different sort of mystery to anything anyone had done before. *The Daughter of Time* and her subsequent novel, *The Privateer*, may have been attempts to fuse her 'Gordon Daviot' and 'Josephine Tey' writing, by mixing serious historical facts with entertaining novelization and story. *The Daughter of Time* succeeded spectacularly in this aim, and it remains many people's favourite Tey novel. *The Daughter of Time* is also an 'Elizabeth MacKintosh' novel – not because she reveals anything more of herself, or sets the story in her Inverness world – but because it is exactly the book to read to find out about Beth herself, the things she thought about, and how and why they mattered to her.

The title is a quotation from Francis Bacon, 'Truth is the Daughter of Time', and the plot concerns the hospitalized and bedridden Alan Grant, who becomes interested in the historical mystery of Richard III, and whether he was responsible for the deaths of his nephews, the Princes in the Tower.[5] The action doesn't leave the one hospital room, and mainly involves Grant reading books about Richard and his time, discussing him with his friends, and drawing his own conclusions, and yet the book is unputdownable. Josephine Tey manages to make us care about Richard III and challenge received opinion about him. As with her biography of Claverhouse, she has picked a historical figure she thinks has been maligned, and tells us why. The difference is, unlike that biography, the literary device of using Alan Grant, a character who her readers already cared about, and showing why truth is so important to him as a serving police officer, demonstrates why the interpretation of history matters.

Grant is in hospital because he has broken his leg badly while chasing after criminal Benny Skoll. Bored and restless, Grant rants about how much he hates the books his friends have brought into the hospital for him to read during his convalescence. They are all the same and nothing new, he argues, dismissing the new novel by 'Silas Weekly' as 'earthy and spade-conscious [...] mother lying-in with her eleventh upstairs, father laid-out after his ninth downstairs, eldest son lying to the Government in the cow-shed, eldest daughter lying with her lover in the hay-loft, everyone else lying low in the barn'.[6] Josephine Tey is a confident writer who can use five different versions of the word 'lie' in one pithy sentence, but, however much Grant likes books normally, Tey here gently satirizes contemporary fiction, including her own, and recognizes that there is a point when even the most avid reader no longer wants to read. Josephine Tey understood that the lies of fiction are not always satisfying, but she ultimately reaffirms Grant's faith in books by presenting him with a different subject to read about. Marta Hallard, with her actress's intuition about character, provides Grant with the perfect way to pass the time. She brings a brief and welcome blast of her aura of theatre and glamour into the hospital ward, leaving Grant a selection of historical pictures to study, each with a mystery attached. Grant the policeman believes he can spot a criminal on sight, and is struck by a portrait of Richard III: he cannot believe that this man, with his sensitive face and hands, is the hunchbacked child killer he remembers from school history lessons and Shakespeare's play. His interest is sparked, and he embarks on a course of reading and research, ultimately convincing his 'associate', a young American academic called Brent Carradine, to write a book of their findings.

The Daughter of Time is not the first thing Beth wrote about Richard III. That was a play called *Dickon*. This play remained unpublished until after her death, but was probably written in the 1940s.[7] *Dickon* dramatizes a period in the life of Richard, from just before the death of his brother, through his ascension to the throne and up until the night before the battle in which he lost his life. Like *Richard of Bordeaux*, it is a straight historical play. *Dickon* and *The Daughter of Time* both treat the same subject, and a comparison of them shows why one was a success and the other was not. It shows what was different in Beth's novel writing to her playwriting, and why her novels have lasting popularity while her plays do not. It also shows some of the decisions Beth made as a writer, the way that she separated her 'Gordon Daviot' and 'Josephine Tey' identities, and how she brought them together towards the end of her life.

In some ways, Beth's plays are more polished than her mystery novels. The plays are like the final resolution, whereas the novels show their workings. The trouble is that the workings are sometimes more interesting. *Dickon* doesn't argue against the portrayal of Richard III as an evil man, it just presents a picture of him as a good man. *The Daughter of Time*, in contrast, shows how Richard III was seen as the villain, before showing why this is not true. The real interest lies in how Tey reveals that what was previously believed is not true. Daviot's play loses this altogether by choosing only to present the truth. Writing about history is always suffused with the attitudes of the period you are writing in: *Richard of Bordeaux* is not just a play about medieval times, it is a 1930s play about medieval times. *The Daughter of Time* is not only a book about the 1400s, but also a 1950s book about the 1400s. It is the prejudices of our time that create the mystery of Richard III, because it was after his death that opinions of him were revised. A play set in the 1400s loses this, but a novel set in the 1950s shows that it is not just the man himself that matters, but our interpretation of him.

None of the flaws in *Dickon* make the play a bad piece of writing, but it is not outstanding, as *The Daughter of Time* is. In *The Daughter of Time* Alan Grant is the moral centre, and having established this it is easier for Tey to then create other characters around him, such as the boyish Brent Carradine. By using her established characters of Alan Grant and Marta Hallard, and by using the familiar framework of detective fiction, Tey was able to concentrate on Richard III. The reader does not need pages of explanation about who Alan Grant is and what he does – they know that a detective looks for the truth. Beth MacKintosh often gives the impression that she wasn't writing primarily to entertain, she was writing to understand the world. Her work, both crime fiction and other works, such as *Kif*, fits into a moral framework: how and why people deviate from it is her concern. In *The Daughter of Time* this morality is matched perfectly with mystery and entertainment, creating a readable and thus more effective book.

The Daughter of Time succeeds over *Dickon* because it has a point: *Dickon* doesn't tell us *why* we should care about Richard: *The Daughter of Time* tells us something interesting (about Richard III) and also tells us, passionately and eloquently, why it matters. The real story of *Dickon* is given in the footnotes after the play while the play itself relies on the audience either knowing the story already (or reading the footnotes afterwards). *The Daughter of Time*, on the other hand, starts with a child's history book and a child's knowledge of history, then talks the reader through it, convincing them completely as it goes. Even the reader who has little or no interest in or knowledge of history can be swept along by Grant and Carradine's conviction, skipping the parts about the Wars of the Roses if they get too confusing. Everything in the book – all of Tey's knowledge of theatre and people and hospitals – is directed towards the one aim: to convince us of Richard III's innocence – but we also care about her other characters, feeling Grant's frailty, Marta's kindness and sympathizing with Carradine when he comes dejected into Grant's room.

In 2013, the dramatic discovery of Richard III's remains under a Leicester car park was widely reported, with a documentary following the entire process broadcast on Channel 4.[8] The documentary had to set the scene by doing what Tey achieved in *The Daughter of Time*: show the average viewer just why a group of people (the Richard III Society) cared so much about a dead king's reputation that they were willing to put enormous time, effort and money into the seemingly impossible task of finding his body. The Richard III Society exists to promote the revisionist ideas about Richard which Tey puts across so forcefully. They more generally aim to promote balanced historical research, rather than allowing history to be written by the victors, an admirable aim which even the least Ricardian can understand.

The Richard III Society has been around since the 1920s. Josephine Tey was never a member, though, as *The Daughter of Time* shows, she was of course aware that other historians shared her view of Richard. Tey's 1951 novel brought the views of the Society to a more general audience and increased their popularity so much that the Richard III Society website still dedicates a special section to Tey's life and work for all enthusiasts who come to their society by that route. After Josephine Tey's death she left the copyright to all her novels to the National Trust, who then had to field many queries about *The Daughter of Time* and its authenticity. Coincidentally, the person who took those queries, volunteer Isolde Wigram, was also the secretary and a prime mover in the revival of the Richard III Society, and so was well able to answer any question on the topic, and took great joy and pride in doing so.[9] Since the 2013 discovery of Richard III's body, Josephine Tey's novel has attracted attention again. The novel has never been out of print, and is a constant fixture on bookshop shelves and in lists of the best-ever crime novels, and, in 1990, was voted the number one crime novel of all time by the UK Crime Writers' Association.

By the time of writing *The Daughter of Time* Tey was a confident enough writer to put in a few in-jokes: Grant knows all about Richard II because he saw Gordon Daviot's play *Richard of Bordeaux* (four times). Marta is upset that a playwright is not writing plays for her because she is concentrating on her detective fiction. Mary, Queen of Scots (subject of a Daviot play) and the Covenanters (subject of a Daviot biography) are discussed at length – but in each of the discussions Grant expresses the kind of memorable opinions that are missing from Daviot's treatment of each of those subjects. For example, here is Grant on the Covenanters: 'The Covenanters were the exact equivalent of the I.R.A. in Ireland. A small irreconcilable minority, and as bloodthirsty a crowd as ever disgraced a Christian nation.'[10] This is seventeenth-century Scottish history seen through the eyes of a man in the 1950s with Alan Grant's moral code. We can read it and see it in context and enjoy hearing what Grant has to say, and how it relates to his argument about Richard III. Daviot's *Claverhouse* is just as opinionated, but at rather convoluted length:

This was that Solemn League and Covenant which has been the banner of the Presbyterian church ever since. Even more than the other covenants it was a worldly and bargaining document. Its six clauses (four civil and two ecclesiastical) added up to this: that the Scots would provide an army to help their brothers in God, the English non-conformists, against their King, on condition that Presbyterianism was imposed on Episcopal England.[11]

The opinionated Josephine Tey who skims over myriad subjects as she continues on to her main argument is more fun and a better read than the sensible Gordon Daviot who explained thoroughly, but the key is that behind both Tey and Daviot is a woman who has thoroughly explored the topics she writes about, and who excels at her craft.

In *The Daughter of Time* Beth MacKintosh achieved something brilliant, as she managed to make a genre that in the 1950s was sometimes dismissed as pulp fiction, a mystery novel, into something worthy of serious critical attention. By adhering to her own morality, and writing what she wanted, she achieved the respect she wanted and deserved. The structure of *The Daughter of Time*, with Alan Grant looking into a historical mystery, is superbly conceived, difficult to categorize, and made people sit up and take notice. Beth MacKintosh had found a way to synthesize her serious interests as Gordon Daviot and her popular form as Josephine Tey. It is tragic that this book was written just before her untimely death. Between this and the luminous *The Singing Sands* she was a writer coming into the full breadth of her powers.

The Daughter of Time was first published in June 1951, and was reprinted the following month, and again in October.[12] It was published first by Peter Davies, and they were very pleased with the sales. When the rights for a paperback edition were offered to Penguin's Eunice Frost, and she wondered if the title might be too obscure for the book to sell well, Peter Davies took pride in relaying how many copies they had sold (15,000 at 9s 6d) and pointed out that they were onto their fourth reprint.[13] Josephine Tey was a bestseller, and, although Penguin still wanted to put Gordon Daviot's name somewhere on the book, her work was in demand. From the time Penguin published the book, through all the following decades, the book's appeal to the general reader was made abundantly clear to them. In the Penguin archive, the file for *The Daughter of Time* is full of letter after letter from fans of the book who wrote to the publisher for more information about Richard III, and about Tey.[14] Meanwhile, Daviot's *Richard of Bordeaux* made its Edinburgh Festival debut in August 1951 as part of the Scottish Community Drama Association's programme; *To Love and Be Wise* joined all Beth's other novels by being published in the US; *Next Time We Love* was once more adapted for American radio; and the film industry came calling again as *The Franchise Affair* was made into a movie.

The Franchise Affair was a British production, directed by Lawrence Huntington and starring real-life husband and wife Michael Denison and Dulcie Gray as Robert Blair and Marion Sharpe. Betty Kane was played by Ann Stephens. Unlike other adaptations of her work, this film was faithful to the source material. With a solid cast, the film was well received when it was released towards the end of the year.

Opportunities were crowding in, but Beth was still feeling unwell, unable to take advantage of the freedom she now had. She visited her doctor in Inverness, and was told that the pain she was suffering was not life-threatening, and prescribed pills and rest.[15] Given the fact of Colin's recent death, and the stressful period Beth spent caring for him in the months before his death, it seemed a reasonable diagnosis. Beth followed her doctor's orders, making no radical changes to her life (such as selling her house or moving away from the Highlands) and continuing with her work researching and writing – though she began to struggle with more physical aspects of housework. She stuck to the routine she had established before Colin's death, taking a holiday in the springtime in Wadhurst in East Sussex, the part of England she liked best. This destination is close to Tunbridge Wells, where Beth's last teaching post had been, before her life had been interrupted by the need to care for her parents. Her enjoyment of the holiday, however, was spoilt by constant nagging pain. What Beth's doctor in Inverness had failed to diagnose was that Beth was suffering from liver cancer.

Beth was already in a race against time – one that she seemed to be aware of, as her writing output increased, almost as if she knew she had to fit in as much as possible in the time available to her. January 1951 had brought more sad news, as the playwright James Bridie died. He was sixty-three years old. Beth had got on well with both him and his wife, and it was another unwelcome reminder of mortality. As Beth's own health problems refused to clear up she coped by focusing on writing.

The Privateer, like *The Daughter of Time*, was a fusion of the historical and the entertaining, but whereas *The Daughter of*

Time was a Josephine Tey mystery novel, Beth chose to write *The Privateer* under the name of Gordon Daviot. It was three years since a Daviot play had appeared, and it was the first novel to appear under the Daviot name since *The Expensive Halo*, back in 1931. The publicity for the book mentioned *Richard of Bordeaux*, but didn't really make the connection with Josephine Tey. The book was targeted at a different audience to Beth's mystery novels, and was seen as serious historical fiction. Unlike *The Daughter of Time*, it has not remained in print. Frankly, it is almost a disappointment considering it comes between two of her best Josephine Tey novels. It certainly has a very different tone, and it was probably right to market it as being by Daviot. Many critics disagree with this assessment however, with some even seeing it as a highlight of Beth's writing career. The book has been praised for its drama and suspense, and the characters' well-drawn friendships, and was well received at the time, with a positive review in the *New York Times*.[16]

The Privateer details the life of Welsh buccaneer Henry Morgan, a historical figure who may not be a household name today, but whose life story was well known at the time Beth was writing, as various books and films had been dedicated to him, including 1942's *The Black Swan*. Gordon Daviot casts him as another of her 'good men': honourable and upright British heroes. Daviot had more time to dedicate to research now that she didn't have to care daily for Colin, and there has obviously been considerable research and thought put into the book – but it doesn't have the impetus and freedom of her mysteries and she seems tied down by the historical facts, unable to let her own opinions alter the story too much. Despite the vividness of the scenes abroad, and the lush green of Morgan's homecoming to Britain, Daviot's depiction of Morgan's love affairs, in particular, just doesn't ring true. She is up against the problem of trying to impose the morality of her own times on him, and it doesn't completely work.

Beth worked on *The Privateer* throughout 1951, but she also had other writing going on, including the manuscript that was to be posthumously published as *The Singing Sands*. She was working at a furious rate, and, no matter what her doctor's official diagnosis was, I think Beth must have sensed the need to finish what she could. She had actually written her will – and a remarkably individual will it was – in March, probably before taking her spring holiday to Wadhurst.[17] In addition to this return to the scene of her last job and the end of her teaching career, she made one other trip to the 'past'. The reassessment of her life which she had begun during the Second World War, and which had resulted in such a burst of creativity, was now superseded by a reassessment with a more personal urgency. After Colin's death, a period of reflection would have been natural, but Beth must have been aware, at some level, of the potential seriousness of her illness.

At an Anstey College reunion in 2012, I spoke to one former Anstey pupil who had a strong memory of Beth re-visiting the college in 1951.[18] Pupils were told some time in advance that Josephine Tey, the author of *Miss Pym Disposes*, would be coming to Anstey, and were very excited to have the chance to meet her – there was an idea that she might be giving a talk. The novel's depiction of college life was judged to be fair, and they were happy to feature in a bestselling mystery series. By 1951, the Scotswoman Miss Squire was principal of Anstey. She was to be the last principal, before the college linked up with other institutions and ceased to be independent. Miss Squire had many links to Scotland, and had met Beth at the Anstey Jubilee luncheon in 1949. Anstey was much bigger now than when Beth attended, with around 100 students, but it was still recognizably the same institution. It still meant a lot to Beth – she wanted to see it again. However, Beth didn't meet any of the current pupils, and did not give a talk. Her health by this point was failing noticeably.

At the start of October 1951, Beth wrote to Moire.[19] It is a cheerful letter, but she expresses the wish that someone would help her just a bit more; organize things for her:

I have always subconsciously HATED having to decide for myself, and all my life I have had to do it, in big things and small. As I became middle-aged the thing became a conscious longing to be

able to sit back and have things decided for me; to be 'cherished',
in fact. To have someone else book the tickets and look after the
luggage and reckon the tips and deal with the bad manners [...].

It's an aside, but it paints a clear picture of someone who has
always had to deal with the difficult things in life, and would
like a rest. Although Beth mentions her doctor, it is only to
say that he called her to say that he had seen a full-page article
about *The Daughter of Time* in *The Field*, and offered to bring
it round. Dr Iain Macleod may well have been choosing a subtle
way of checking up on a patient, but Beth just thought it was a
kind thing for a busy doctor to do – describing to Moire how
much Dr Macleod had changed since they were pupils at the
Academy together. There's no real discussion of illness or how
ill Beth is feeling. When Beth visited Moire towards the end of
October, it was the first time they had met in person for some
time, and Moire was shocked at the physical changes she saw
in her sister. Moire insisted that Beth should go to her own GP,
a Scotswoman called Janet McAllister McGill, for a second
opinion on her illness. Dr McGill referred Beth immediately
to the South London Hospital for Women. This well-respected
institution on Clapham Common had been absorbed into the
new NHS but it retained an all-female workforce.[20] It had been
one of the first hospitals to train women to be specialists, and all
staff, from porters upwards, were women. Although NHS rules
meant it now had to admit men, it still specialized in women's
treatment and care. Beth underwent an exploratory operation at
the hospital, but it was too late. All that the nurses and doctors
could do was to gently tell her that she was suffering from inop-
erable cancer, which had spread from her liver to her abdomen.
She had only a matter of months left to live.

Beth was too ill after the operation to return to Inverness, and
there was no question of her living alone. After all these years
of Beth caring for her family, it was Moire's turn to care for her
sister. She stayed in Moire's family home in Streatham, along
with Moire's husband and their little son Colin, who was only
five. Beth could do no more writing. Moire tried to make her

comfortable, but Beth was not well enough even to travel into London or Essex to see her friends. Moire did not know any of her sister's friends, such as Lena or Gwen, personally, and the Stokes' family life was a world apart from the racing, party-going lifestyle of Beth's theatrical friends. If Beth had asked, Moire could surely have arranged for Lena or Gwen to visit – and they would have been happy to do so – but Beth just wanted peace.

Beth grew closer to Moire again in the few months that remained of her life. The two sisters had spent most of their adult lives apart, living in very different ways, in different countries, and, however much they had kept in touch by letter, Moire had not ever really been involved in Beth's private writing life. Colin and Beth had much more in common, in some ways, with Colin's interest in literature and shared love of the outdoors, but Moire had for many years been occupied with her single life in London, her work, then her husband and son. She was there, however, when Beth needed her. Beth made a couple of special amendments to her will to reflect this, leaving Moire £1,000 extra than she originally planned.[21] Beth also asked Moire to sort out her affairs in Inverness, something that was obviously preying on her mind, as she had not left the house in Crown expecting never to return. Beth felt she had unfinished business, particularly as regards her playwriting, and her idiosyncratic will reflected that.

There was nothing more Moire could do except make Beth as comfortable as possible. Beth's nephew Colin Stokes retained only a hazy impression of Beth's last weeks: a sick room that he could not enter, and a house that had to be kept quiet. Beth lasted through Christmas but died on 13th February 1952.[22]

Moire sent a notice to *The Times* newspaper, perhaps hoping belatedly to inform all of Beth's friends. The notice was filed under 'Daviot', rather than 'MacKintosh', and it was printed on 14th February, the day after Beth's death: 'DAVIOT: On Feb. 13, 1952, in London, GORDON DAVIOT, Playwright and Novelist. Cremation at the South London Crematorium, Rowan Road, Streatham Vale, S.W.16, on Monday Feb 18, at 11am.' As at the funerals of their father and mother, Moire requested mourners not to bring flowers. Beth had a strong personal dislike of flowers on graves – perhaps because of all those weekly visits to Tomnahurich.

The death notice in *The Times* was widely picked up. King George VI died on 6th February, and huge crowds had assembled in London for his funeral. Newspapers were reporting the event, and everyone in London was avidly reading about it. Moire's short notice was seen by several of Beth's friends, and her mention of 'Gordon Daviot playwright and novelist' was also picked up by journalists the length of the country, showing that the name Gordon Daviot was well known enough to be afforded space even when most column inches were being dedicated to royalty. A long obituary was printed in *The Times* the day after the original notice, on 15th February, while the *Inverness Courier* printed an obituary in its Friday edition, also on the 15th. The *Highland News* ran an obituary on the Saturday. Moire had effectively got the information out in time for Beth's friends to attend the funeral, but many of them were very upset to learn about the death of their friend in this way. Beth was still relatively young – fifty-five – and, in the postwar years, her friends had become unaccustomed to reading obituaries of their contemporaries.

John Gielgud was the first to spot the death notice.[23] He was playing in *Much Ado About Nothing* at the Phoenix Theatre, and read his evening paper between acts. He was shocked to learn of Beth's death. He knew she had been ill the year before, but Beth's optimistic attitude had led him to believe she had been cured. He had to wait for his fellow cast members to come offstage before he could share the news, and then had to go back onstage himself for the final scenes of the play. His colleagues were busy telephoning Lena Ramsden to try to find out more. Lena, too, hadn't realized the extent of Beth's illness, and hadn't yet read her evening paper. She received the phone call with great shock.

Lena, and the rest of Beth's London friends, had got used to Beth appearing in their lives at regular intervals, and between those visits communicating only sporadically by letter. Gwen used to say that it was hard enough to get London people to leave their comfort zone and come out to Tagley Cottage in Essex; Beth had never even tried to persuade her friends to visit her in Inverness.

She had met John and Gwen when they had toured in Scotland, but it was always Beth who did the travelling to see her friends.

Beth's friends' shock at hearing of her death was perhaps mingled with some guilt that they had not kept in touch more regularly. There was a general feeling that Beth should have told them about her illness, that they should have been more involved. When her friends were later interviewed about her death this realization that Beth had been alone in her last few months came through as being in some way her own fault. Her friends were all genuinely upset and saddened by her death, but the way that her silence about her illness has been reported is a little unfair to Beth. 'Her sudden death [...] was a great surprise and shock to all her friends in London,' wrote John Gielgud in the foreword to Gordon Daviot's collected plays. 'I learned afterwards that she had known herself to be mortally ill for nearly a year, and had resolutely avoided seeing anyone she knew. This gallant behaviour was typical of her and curiously touching, if a little inhuman too.'[24] This quote has been repeated over and over again, and become central to analyses of Beth's personality and work, but it is not the whole truth. Beth, and her friends, had known she was unwell for some time, but Beth herself had not known the full extent of her illness until the operation in London. After that, she barely had the energy to contact any of her friends, and her sister Moire would not have known how to contact them on her behalf – even if she had the time, when looking after both a small child and an invalid. If Beth's friends had wanted more regular contact, they could have established that themselves, many years before. The only one of her theatre friends who had ever visited Inverness, it seems, was James Bridie, when he had toured there with the Citizens Theatre production of *The Little Dry Thorn*.

James Bridie's widow Rona made the trip down from Glasgow to London to attend the funeral, noting that 'Gordon had always got on so well with her husband, that she [Rona] felt she wanted to come, to represent them both'.[25] Lena drove a small party of Beth's theatre friends out to the crematorium in South London, where they were joined by others who had heard the news. Among the attendees at Beth's funeral were John Gielgud, the actor

George Howe (currently performing in the same Shakespeare play as Gielgud), Veronica Turleigh (who had played the lead role all those years ago in *The Laughing Woman*), actresses Edith Evans and Betty Makeham, and writer Elisabeth Kyle.[26] Gwen Ffrangcon-Davies was in South Africa, and Peggy Webster was in America. Beth's family was represented by Moire and Jean, who met Beth's theatre friends for the first time at the funeral. Lena Ramsden talked to Beth's sisters, but was left with the impression that Beth had only arrived in London two weeks before, and had stayed at her club in Cavendish Square before heading to Moire's. Beth had of course been at her sister's since October 1951. Perhaps she had been able to make one last trip in to her Club before her death, but, if so, she must have been very weak and would have struggled to make contact with her friends.

It's a pity that there was this misunderstanding about the length of time Beth had been ill. Perhaps Moire, like Beth, was in denial about the cancer, or perhaps she was acting in accordance with Beth's wishes, but, either way, it didn't spare Beth's friends any distress. Lena was very upset to know that Beth had been so ill and so close and yet she had not seen or helped her, and talked of the incident with some emotion in her autobiography, written thirty-two years later. By this stage, Lena's memory of the events were not perfect: she confused the years, and thought that Gielgud had been starring in *The Winter's Tale*, rather than *Much Ado About Nothing*. John Gielgud also repeated the story, and it became one of the most persistent myths about Beth. Sadly, after her death, Beth's desire for privacy didn't translate into a silence or lack of knowledge about her, it translated over the years into a false picture that bore little relation to the reality of her life.

Beth's Will, and Plays

The main bequest in Beth's will is well known, and has been mentioned on the cover of almost all the reprints of her books since her death. 'I, Elizabeth MacKintosh,' she wrote in Inverness in March 1951, 'desire that everything of which I die possessed, whether money, goods, property, personal possessions, investments, play book and film rights and royalties, or any other belongings whatsoever, shall, except as hereinafter provided, be devoted to furthering the work of the National Trust for England'.[1] This is the first line of a personal, somewhat idiosyncratic will. To read it is to hear once again Beth's voice; the strong opinions and outspokenness familiar to readers of Josephine Tey novels. After a lifetime spent largely looking after her family, Beth decided that, in death, she was going to do what she wanted.

The idea of leaving money to the National Trust had been in her mind for some time. The heroine of her second Josephine Tey novel, Christine Clay, does the same thing in her will, and Beth had made donations to charity out of her writing income as early as the mid-1930s.[2] However, there were a number of codicils to the will, and it is a fairly lengthy document. The picture is not quite as clear-cut as that first sweeping statement makes out, and not quite as stark as the little note in Beth's published work suggests. Beth did remember friends and family, and she did also remember Scotland and her home town of Inverness.

The second thing that Beth requested in her will was that she wanted her unpublished Gordon Daviot plays to be printed – and if her agent couldn't find an interested publisher, this was to be done at her own expense, money for the purpose being taken out of her estate before the remainder was handed over to the National Trust. Her writing was the most important priority.

Beth then specified a number of personal items that were to be given to her youngest sister Moire. These included jewellery and other items that had belonged to their parents: a pearl and wreath diamond brooch, an amethyst brooch of their mother's, and their father's gold watch and seal. Beth also wanted her own personal jewellery to go to Moire or her descendants: the pearl earrings Colin had given her, which she had worn in her official author photographs; a diamond crescent and a diamond brooch. Some household items of value from Crown Cottage were also to go to Moire, including valuable silver spoons and Moire's own choice of some of the furniture from the Inverness house. As can be seen from this growing list, Beth's assets were of considerable value. Assessing the value, and disposing of her estate was something that would take some time, particularly given Beth's strict conditions and the fact that Moire was based at the other end of the country.

Beth had been careful to stress that 'If at the time of my death I still own Crown Cottage, no sale of the contents shall be permitted until the said contents have been removed from the house to a sale room: nor shall any inspection of the house by prospective purchasers be allowed until all the contents have been so removed'. In an addition to her will made in November 1951, she added that on her death, her sister should get the keys to Crown Cottage, and no one was to enter the house until Moire had time to gather and sort Beth's personal belongings and papers. This condition is witnessed by two nurses, and was made around the time that Beth had her operation in London. Beth had left Inverness in autumn 1951 in the expectation that she would return, and had left her house accordingly. The reference to 'papers' shows that Beth was particularly concerned about her written work, and it's likely, given the posthumous publication of material, that Beth gave Moire specific instructions about what she should look for.

As with the instruction in the main body of the will about her unpublished Daviot work, Beth was trying to ensure that her final writings were published. For her help, Moire was allowed to take anything from the house that she found useful, and, in addition, at the end of January 1952, just over a week before her death, Beth asked her GP, Dr McGill, to witness a statement saying that Moire should get an additional £1,000.

There was another possible reason why Beth was so keen not to let anyone into her house after her death. She knew that, given the chance, some local people would have loved the chance to snoop around. Quite apart from her worry over her literary work, left lying and unorganized, Beth did not have a perfect relationship with her neighbours. Niggles like noise complaints from her and complaints of unfriendliness from them meant Beth did not look too kindly on them and did not like the idea of them looking through her personal belongings.[3] She may also have known that there was interest in the property itself. After her death, her house was bought by neighbours, and they showed a particular interest in Beth's work and life that could be construed as nosiness.

Beth added a similar caveat when she stated that none of her clothes were to be disposed of locally. Inverness was still a small enough town that people could have recognized the original owner of clothes distributed through charitable organizations, particularly if they were of exceptionally good quality, as Beth's were. She did have a preferred recipient for her clothes: Celia Kelly, of Wren's View, St Paul's Churchyard, London was to get those, including her furs, currently in storage in the London branch of Debenhams. Celia Kelly was Moire's friend from college, and her flat had been used by Josephine Tey for her fictional character Kevin Macdermott. As an adult, Moire's son was particularly pleased with the idea that Beth had remembered Celia.

Finally, contrary to popular opinion, Beth did not forget her home town in her will. Although she left the bulk of her fortune to the National Trust, she had made a special provision in her original will that Inverness Museum should receive not only personal possessions, but also items pertaining to Beth's career, and items of particular interest to the town. The Museum and

Library (then housed in the same building) were to get a valuable Victorian ring which Beth habitually wore, and the original script of *Richard of Bordeaux*. Beth also stated that she had already lent the museum a collection of tartans and a silver spoon, which they could now keep. Even in her final days, Beth was thinking of Inverness, as she made an undated addition to the will while she was in England, adding another gold ring to her donation to the Public Library, and reiterating that the script of *Richard* should be placed there. The tartans and spoons had been part of a contemporary display organized by well-known local librarian and curator Miss Margaret MacDougall, who was a specialist in both tartan studies and old Inverness silver. These have now been subsumed into the general museum collections.[4]

The script for *Richard of Bordeaux* now forms part of a special collection, available on request, and the two rings are kept with the script, though recently the Victorian emerald and diamond ring was on public display.[5] The two rings have been the subject of some speculation as to their origins, but it's clear from a letter in the family archives that the Victorian ring was a twenty-fifth birthday present from Josephine MacKintosh to her daughter Beth. The double gold ring is a wedding ring, made by James Ferguson of Inverness some time around the mid-1800s, and matches the description of a ring in Josephine MacKintosh's will – which probably means it belonged to Beth's grandmother, the long-lived Jane Ellis, who had told the young Beth so many stories. Beth wore both these rings throughout her life. In this way, Beth made sure that both Josephine and Jane had a presence in Inverness history.

Beth's will was not actually registered until August 1952, six months after her death.[6] Her request that Moire should hold the keys to her house and be the first to enter held things up considerably, as Moire did not feel she could make the long journey north until the better weather, particularly with her small son and husband to look after and consider. Moire was not the executor. Beth perhaps had some idea of how difficult Moire would find it to travel north, and, given what she wanted done, she did not ask her sister, who had had very little interest or input into her literary career or life, to administrate the will. The executor's duties were split between the family solicitors Messrs Stewart, Rule & Co, in Inverness; Beth's bank in London, the Westminster; and her literary agents, Pearn, Pollinger and Higham Ltd. There were further delays when Beth's agents, in the person of David Higham, declined to take on the duties of executors. Her agents were involved in the assessment of the worth of Beth's copyrights, and the posthumous publication of plays and novels, but they had no desire to do anything other than their already established job with regards to Daviot and Tey work. Beth seems to have written much of her will without reference to the people named within it. Although her family solicitors, the main executors, were well aware of what they would have to do, she may not have discussed it with her agent, and it may only have been towards the very end of her life that she discussed it with her sister Moire. After years of looking after other people, Beth was definitely pleasing herself when she wrote her will.

Beth's assets were finally collected together and itemized. Including stocks and shares in companies like Woolworths; war bonds; cash and savings accounts; antique furniture; jewellery; and one half of her share in Colin's business. It all added up to an astonishing £24,323 18s 8d – the equivalent today of half a million pounds. Clearly, given the total of her father's assets, this had come almost entirely from her writing, and from clever money management and investments. The copyright of her books and plays was valued by her agent at £3,075.

Elizabeth MacKintosh's will, as well as being written in her own strong-minded style, shows personal bequests to her favourite sister, who helped her during her final illness; some sense of loyalty to Inverness, despite a wish to preserve her privacy there; and a strong love of her adopted home, England, where she had been unable to live due to family circumstances. It also shows how successful a writer she actually was, and how she had been able to enjoy the money she had earned. The most important clauses, however, are the provision for the publication of her uncollected 'Gordon Daviot' works, and her concern over her papers. People have often focused on her main legacy to the

National Trust, but however she felt about it, her life in Inverness is what created Gordon Daviot and Josephine Tey as we know them, and Beth knew that and gave it due recognition. Her will shows that even if it was her love of England that had sustained her and which she wanted to thank through her generous legacy to the National Trust, her other legacies to her family, friends and the town were important to her. She specifically wanted all her plays to be published first, before any money went to the National Trust. She did not forget her family; she did not forget her friends; and, in the end, her love of writing came before her love of England.

In a personal request to Moire, Beth also showed her love of the Highlands, when she asked for her ashes to be scattered at Daviot, the area just outside Inverness where the sisters had spent their childhood holidays, and which had given Beth her preferred pen-name.[7] Moire, with a husband and child to care for, found it hard to take time to make the journey north to Inverness. When she finally made it in the spring, not only did she have to deal with Beth's unorthodox will, but she also found that the house at Crown Cottage was partially flooded. The pipes had frozen over the winter and had burst when the warmer weather came. Beth had not left any spare key with neighbours, so no one had done anything to mitigate the damage, and the water was simply pouring down the street as Moire walked up to her old house. Crown Cottage was in a mess. Fortunately, Beth's papers and writings were not water damaged, and Moire was able to follow her sister's instructions. She found the manuscripts of the plays Beth had specified should be printed, and also the complete manuscript of one more Josephine Tey novel: Beth's final Inspector Grant mystery, *The Singing Sands*. There were to be four posthumously published books.

Josephine Tey's books, and Gordon Daviot's plays, had been immensely popular, and her death was seen as a loss not only by her friends and family, but also by her many readers. Almost all her books were reissued in the years after her death, with the 'Gordon Daviot' novels *The Man in the Queue*, *Kif* and

The Expensive Halo all republished under the name 'Josephine Tey'. New publications of her books received universally good reviews. BBC radio produced several adaptations of her work, with *Miss Pym Disposes* appearing on the Saturday Night Theatre programme only three months after Beth died. *The Daughter of Time* had its first US publication in 1952, while John Gielgud returned to the part that had made his name in a BBC adaptation of *Richard of Bordeaux* – recordings of which still exist.[8] Gielgud also contributed a short introduction and biographical sketch to the first collected edition of her plays, the plays Beth had in her will specifically asked to be published.

Beth had specified three plays in her will which had not been published, and which she wanted to see in print so badly that she was prepared to pay for publication herself: *Valerius*, *Dickon* and *The Little Dry Thorn*. The first and last of these had of course been performed: *Valerius* in London in 1948, and *The Little Dry Thorn* by the Citizens Theatre Company in Glasgow in 1946. *Dickon* had never received a performance, but the importance of the subject matter – Richard III – was clear, since Beth had already made it the focus of her Josephine Tey novel *The Daughter of Time*. In the event, her executors made sure that every unpublished play they found amongst her papers was printed. Three volumes of *Plays* by Gordon Daviot were published by Peter Davies, the first in 1953 and the second and third in 1954. Where they let Beth down, however, was that the plays were presented almost wholly without context. The brief foreword from Gielgud was commissioned for the first volume, but it is usually cited for its personal memories of Beth and it doesn't give a summary of Beth's writing career or life. Beth's desire to see her plays published and her willingness to fund this herself, did not give her publisher much incentive to publicize her final published works. Beth had never done any self-promotion, and her publishers were used to her Josephine Tey novels (and previous Gordon Daviot works) selling with little effort on their part. Her publishers didn't stand to lose any money on the publication of the plays, so they merely fulfilled their obligation by putting them out there, to stand alone. It may even be that, because of her fondness for privacy and pen-names,

Beth's publisher, and even her family, could not have written a comprehensive overview of her career, but it certainly did the plays a disservice to be presented without context. By the time of the publication of the third volume, there was even a newspaper article questioning why so many unperformed plays needed to be published, with the journalist apparently unaware that many of the plays included had been performed.[9]

Many of the plays in the three volumes also went on to be produced again in one form or another, *Cornelia*, for example, appearing on BBC radio in 1955; *Dickon* finding a stage home the same year; and *Sweet Coz* adapted for television also in 1955.[10] Amateur groups embraced the plays, and *Valerius* was reprinted as a stand-alone play by 1955, while *Leith Sands* continued to perform well. This last play had won a place in the Scottish Community Drama Association finals just at the time of Beth's death.

Beth would probably have been happy with this, as she always let each of her own works stand on its own merit without any publicity, and she had had enormous success this way. She put a lot of herself into her Josephine Tey novels, particularly *The Singing Sands*, and these are of a quality that has stood the test of time far better than the Gordon Daviot plays. In other ways, though, the publication of her final *Plays* was a rather shoddy finish to a successful publishing career, a career that had made Beth's publishers and agents a fair amount of money. Lacking any sort of context or assessment of Beth's life and work – including any well-publicized association with the Josephine Tey name – the publication of her final Gordon Daviot plays contributed some-what to the myths around her life – the image of her as unhappy, the unfair assessment of her father's character – and she also did not receive fair recognition for the work she had done.

The lack of context for the plays even extends to their covers. The first volume was published the year after Beth's death, and has a plain cover, as was usual for play text. The end dust wrappers have a brief blurb, stating that Elizabeth MacKintosh, Gordon Daviot and Josephine Tey are one and the same person, and giving a short summary of the three plays included, the three that Beth had specifically requested, *The Little Dry Thorn*, *Valerius* and *Dickon*. The dates of the two performed plays are listed, as are the names of the principal players. The link with *The Daughter of Time* is also flagged up. However, this information only features on the dust wrapper, so many library editions, for example, have lost this information after the dust jacket has been removed. No full list of Gordon Daviot's work is included in the volume of plays, though there are adverts for other Tey and Daviot works in print.

The foreword by John Gielgud, focusing on his personal memories of Gordon Daviot, has been used as a source by every subsequent biographer of Daviot, and it is where many of the received ideas about her come from.[11] It provides, as you would expect, a clear idea of how he worked with Daviot on the production of *Richard of Bordeaux*, and then goes on to give his personal assessment of her writing, along with a brief attempt to put it in context of other plays and playwrights. It is, however, a very personal piece, and should be read as such, rather than as a factual assessment of Beth's life and work. The foreword ends with a touching tribute: 'The theatre is the poorer for an unique talent, and I for a dearly valued friend'. Gielgud's summary, that 'Gordon Daviot was a strange character, proud without being arrogant, and obstinate, though not conceited' is a fair assessment of this complex woman.

The three plays in the first volume have all been examined in this biography in relation to the times in which they were written – or, in the case of *Dickon*, in conjunction with *The Daughter of Time*. *Dickon* finally received its first performance in 1955, while *Valerius* was resurrected for radio twice in the 1960s. The plays in the next two volumes of collected plays are harder to date, and present a very varied selection of Daviot's interests and writing styles. Like the plays in the first volume, which were from the 1940s, they are probably not Beth's final written works, but were almost certainly written in tandem with her more successful published writings. These plays are not the conclusion to her writing career, they are collected writings.

Plays 2, the second volume, has three longer plays, and three one-act plays.[12] Unlike *Plays 1*, there is no foreword, and the library copies I have seen were missing their dust jackets, so the reader was provided with minimal information about the author or the context of the plays. The three long plays are *The Pomp of Mr Pomfret*, *Cornelia* and *Patria*. The biggest omission seems to be any sort of context for *Cornelia*. There is not even a statement saying that this play had in fact been performed, let alone any sort of history of the 'F. Craigie Howe' pseudonym that Beth had used when she gave it to the Citizens Theatre Company. The mystery of its authorship was only really remarked on seventeen years after *Cornelia* was first produced, when the play was revived at the Pitlochry Festival Theatre by the Theatre's in-house company in 1963. The programme notes for this production give a succinct explanation of the play's history. This short run, however, did not touch public consciousness to any great degree, and the story of 'F. Craigie Howe' was forgotten again. It barely even shows up on the internet, which is pretty impressive given how the internet likes a mystery.

The Pomp of Mr Pomfret and *Patria* don't seem to have ever been performed in Daviot's lifetime, though *Mr Pomfret* apparently finally got an airing on the radio in 1954.[13] It is likely *The Pomp of Mr Pomfret* dates from the same period as *Cornelia* because, like that play, it has a modern English setting and is a comedy – unlike Daviot's better-known historical or romantic plays. Mr Pomfret is a politician, and the play begins with him turning some people out of their seats in a restaurant; a protracted revenge is then taken on him by brother and sister Rosa and Valenti, supported by Canadian businessman John Judd, involving poltergeists and liberating Miss Hermione Pomfret from caring for her brother. Many of Gordon Daviot's recognized interests are here: a London and English country setting; a woman forced to do housekeeping against her will; a journalist (working for Daviot's standard fictional newspaper, *The Clarion*); and throwaway comments about the 'Scotch' character.

The other full-length play, *Patria*, is more interesting in terms of Gordon Daviot's interests and character, but probably less successful as a play in its own right. It is an extended political allegory dealing with two countries, 'Creeland' and 'Tainia'. As with other Daviot plays, *Patria* suffers from having unseen drama offstage and several long speeches – with one speech, in particular, ranting non-stop over two pages in untypically uncontrolled fashion. There are odd little scenes with children, reminiscent of the scenes of 'ordinary people' in *Richard of Bordeaux*, which have charm and humour, but the general tone is polemical. And yet, despite this, it is a play that might still work in production, as its concerns are wholly modern, and the topics she expresses such strong opinions on are still current today. *Patria* is essentially a statement of how Gordon Daviot saw the nationalist movement and Scottish independence; a companion piece to her final Josephine Tey novel, the more measured *The Singing Sands*.

Given the nation-changing concerns of *Patria*, it is rather a change of pace to read the one-act plays in *Plays 2*. *The Balwhinnie Bomb* is the one-act comedy set on the west coast of Scotland that was performed by the local Inverness drama group in the late 1940s, and popular with amateur groups in the north of Scotland. *The Pen of My Aunt* had been broadcast on the radio in 1950, was later anthologized, and then had the impressive after-life of adaption into Finnish as a 1963 TV movie *Tätini kynä*. Finally in *Plays 2*, there is the strange little one-acter, *The Princess who liked Cherry Pie*. This surely must be a children's play, perhaps written for radio, or even with a memory of Beth's teaching days – or from her ongoing friendships with other teachers, such as 'Miss Mac' in Inverness, the well-known Daviot primary schoolmistress.[14] It is a simple moral fairytale with a lot of silliness.[15]

Plays 1 and *Plays 2* both have a selection of plays that had already been performed. *Plays 3* seems to be a collection of entirely unperformed pieces, though several of them were picked up after publication.[16] *Lady Charing is Cross* is one of Daviot's historical pieces, set in the middle of Edward the Seventh's reign (1901-1910). Set in high society, with the descriptions of clothes that Daviot excelled at in her historical pieces, it deals with politicians and politics, not quite in the same vein as *Patria*, but clearly from the same sort of small-c conservative standpoint. Neil is a Scottish socialist politician, who gradually drifts further and further to the right wing as he associates with Lady Charing. Daviot points out that politicians are very clever in the way they use words to rouse people, but also that there is often little meaning behind the words, an idea that also recurs in *Barnharrow*, another of the plays in this last collection. Daviot particularly pokes fun at people who say they are working class but clearly aren't, and, as in *Cornelia*, has few pertinent things to say about socialist ideas. The humour is a little like *Cornelia*, and, given that the politics are not as polemical as in *Patria*, it may well date from the mid-to late-40s.

Sweet Coz is on a different subject from almost any other Daviot play. Set in modern times, it features as its main character a woman doctor, Dinah Partridge. Dinah is a professional career woman, of the type Beth must have been familiar with from her days as a VAD and from Anstey. Other medical professionals feature as characters, surely drawn from Beth's own experiences. Despite Dinah's professionalism, however, the plot hinges on her getting drunk and being rather silly. It is in fact a farce in which she wakes up with a strange man (not in the same bed, but in the same house). This is a much more 'modern' topic than Beth's other writing, and it is rather surprising to find her writing about people being drunk and silly – though certainly Beth had her share of partying when she hung out with her theatrical friends and Lena Ramsden in London. The other main character is Hector, Dinah's brother, who is a poet, and Beth is scathing about his writing life and the man in general. Given the poet in *Patria*, and 'Wee Archie' in *The Singing Sands*, Beth doesn't seem to have had a very high opinion of male poets – something at odds with her use of Hugh Patrick Fraser's poems in her work, and her own start to her writing career. There was a particular 'type' that she didn't hold in high regard, however, and Hector is typical of this, a rather pompous man, who relies on a fading 'boyish charm'.

Reckoning also shows another side to Daviot's interests. A modern play, it seems to be set in a 1930s London similar to the backdrop of *Kif*, and covers Camden Town's underworld and its gangsters. Its plot is filmic, and suggests something of the sort of movies Daviot enjoyed – but it is tonally a rather strange play.

The first half of Scene 1 starts with a gentle portrayal of someone working in a shop, with no hint of the gangster plotline to follow. Perhaps the switch in tone was deliberate, but it is a dramatic shift for someone used to reading the rest of Daviot's work – even bearing in mind that she wrote crime novels. The romance between 'Nell' and her criminal also isn't terribly believable. It's an interesting look at retail work though, something that Colin's daughter didn't use much in her fiction.[17]

Barnharrow is a Covenanting play, Claverhouse-period. It works well as an exploration of religious fanaticism, though, as in Daviot's biography of Claverhouse, her soldiers are rather too polite, well mannered and well spoken to be wholly believable. Her portrayal of the daughter, 'Ishbel', is effective. She heads to the conventicles not out of religious conviction, but to see the boys – one of Daviot's young women in the Betty Kane mode, rather than like Erica Burgoyne.

Finally, *The Staff-Room* is a realistic look at an all-female teaching staff, and must surely give a hint of what Beth's teaching days were like. The end is something of an anti-climax, but it is an extremely believable portrayal of a staff room.

The Staff-Room was adapted for television, and broadcast as a live double-bill with *Barnharrow* on Tuesday 1st May 1956. *Sweet Coz* also made it onto television the year before, broadcast on Tuesday 4th January 1955, and it was later produced on stage as well.

The number of productions of Daviot's plays shows their enduring appeal. Even without a proper context, the quality of the plays was clear to readers and producers, and Daviot's name was enough to generate interest. The three volumes of plays achieved what Daviot would have hoped for them: all her work was collected and published, and audiences liked it. Adaptations of her work on radio and on stage (particularly with amateur groups) continued for decades after her death, but it was her Josephine Tey works that proved the most enduring. In addition to her collected plays, the last and final work published was *The Singing Sands*.

333

The Singing Sands

The Singing Sands was published after Josephine Tey's death, and was written while she knew she was seriously, if not terminally, ill. It has a plot that starts in Scotland but ranges far and wide, before tying up all the ends in a satisfying conclusion in London. The character development goes deeper into Alan Grant's psyche as he suffers from stress and claustrophobia, and finally overcomes this through his application to learning and hard work. As the culmination of Elizabeth MacKintosh's life's work, it has roots in her childhood; touches on her doomed romance with Hugh; is a personal response to the Scottish Literary Renaissance and Neil Gunn; and reflects the achievements of her adulthood in the way it is based in Scotland, but ranges much further.

Grant has been signed off work, something he finds difficult to deal with as his illness is mental rather than physical. He has been working too hard, and decides to go and stay with his cousin Laura, in Scotland, to recover. Grant's struggles with claustrophobia in the sleeper train north set the scene in detail, and the journey ends with the discovery of a dead man in one of the compartments. Grant absent-mindedly takes the dead man's newspaper, and, waiting for his cousin in the hotel next to the station, is surprised to find a short and intriguing poem about 'The Singing Sands' written on the edges of that newspaper. When he later reads the report of the death in the following day's newspapers, he cannot square the description of the man with the poem, the handwriting, or the face that he glimpsed in the compartment. The mystery of the location of the Singing Sands takes hold of him, and, as he battles his own personal demons and contemplates his future, he starts to follow the dead man's trail. The twisting plot takes in a flight to the Western Isles, Grant's romantic life, an encounter with a Scottish nationalist activist, and academic and personal jealousy amongst archaeologists and explorers.

Back in 1949, when Josephine Tey had published, in quick succession, *Miss Pym Disposes*, *The Franchise Affair* and *Brat Farrar*, Maurice Lindsay, a Scottish poet, editor and broadcaster, wrote to Neil Gunn, discussing some of the writers they knew in common, such as James Bridie and Hugh MacDiarmid (and, of course, their political views). Lindsay also touched on his own work, saying, 'The novel is nearly finished. I found out that I couldn't write a detective story. I'm just not interested in crime that flippant way. So it's now a very human story in which a murder just happens to occur.'[1] That was very much the attitude to crime fiction within the Scottish Literary Renaissance. The mystery novels that Josephine Tey was producing were not thought worthy of serious consideration. However, Gunn could not help but be aware of Tey's work, since it was garnering such good reviews.

Neil Gunn had published his best-known book, *The Silver Darlings*, during the war in 1941, but by 1949, although his adulation by the Scottish Literary establishment was well underway, and he sat on committees and received awards and honorary degrees, his most recent novels, *The Drinking Well* and *The Shadow*, had not received the reception he had hoped for. Gunn decided to try his hand at a sort of detective fiction. The result, 1949's *The Lost Chart*, is generally received by Gunn aficionados with bemusement.[2] With a Cold War spy theme, a missing chart and a detective with a shady Second World War past, the novel starts strongly, though soon becomes bogged down in ruminations on a lost Gaelic idyll. To Josephine Tey, it must have seemed as if Gunn was encroaching on her territory. The book even starts with her own preferred hobby of fishing, but, however high her hopes were for it, it's hard to imagine she would have admired the way Gunn tried to impose his vision of Scottish nationalism onto the story.

Colin's lifelong interest in fishing gets considerable time devoted to it in *The Singing Sands*, where Grant sees fishing not as a hobby, but as 'Something between a sport and a religion'.[3] *The Singing Sands* is a clear riposte, not only to *The Lost Chart* in particular, but to Gunn's political vision of Scotland, and, by extension, to the way that the Scottish Literary establishment had treated Josephine Tey over the years. It is also about fishing, and much, much more. Grant, *The Singing Sands* tells us, was 'the best sonnet-writer in the sixth form'.[4] This novel, where the plot hinges on the dead man's unfinished poem, clearly shows us crime writing as Beth herself saw it: 'a medium as disciplined as any sonnet', where a framework can be used to create something original.[5]

In *The Lost Chart*, Gunn's hero is 'Grear', a name noticeably similar to Tey's detective Grant. Grear becomes obsessed with the island of Cladday, a Gaelic paradise in the Western Isles, though he never actually goes there. Tey takes her hero Grant on a bumpy flight west to the island of Cladda in *The Singing Sands*, and shows it very clearly for what it is: not an idyll where people speak Gaelic and have discovered the meaning of life, but a collection of disparate souls living in a small place. As for Ellen, the Gaelic singer and Grear's romantic interest: what a contrast between Tey's description of Gaelic singers at a ceilidh, and Gunn's view. His lead character is barely able to hear Ellen sing a line in Gaelic without fainting from emotion. Grear regularly calls Ellen up on the phone and asks her to sing to him – something that Neil Gunn, in real life, sometimes asked his girlfriends to do – as he finds her voice so soothing and inspiring and evocative.[6] The audience in Tey's novel, faced with interminable, mediocre Gaelic singing, slip out the back of the hall and go home to watch the ballet on TV.

The Lost Chart is full of ideas about how Gaelic is the ancestral language of Scotland, and how Scots going back to the pure emotion of Gaelic, with people saluting the sun and moon and remaining unsophisticated, would be idyllic and an antidote to the Cold War. Josephine Tey, who had seen the snobbish way her father had been treated in Inverness, could not endorse that world view. By turning his back on Gaelic, Colin had given his daughters the education they needed to get on in the world. When Tey saw Gaelic speakers, she saw her uncles, people who had fought Colin in the back of his shop to try and get money out of him; she saw the poor roads and stifling religion of the Applecross peninsula and Colin's original home, as described in *The Man in the Queue*. When she thought of Gaelic women, she didn't think of dark-haired, long suffering silent types like Christina in *The Lost Chart*, she thought of Colin's mother, bringing up her family as best she could through hard work. Transferring a female character from a Neil Gunn novel into a Josephine Tey novel – or into Josephine Tey's life – would be impossible, and cuts to the root of their differences. Gunn saw the Highlands through a romantic, historical mist, with idealized female, Gaelic speakers. In *The Singing Sands* Josephine Tey presented an entirely different vision of Scotland: the Scotland that she knew and lived in.

The SNP was campaigning hard in the last years of Josephine Tey's life. In 1950, Lena Ramsden and Gwen Ffrangcon-Davies had spent Christmas together at Tagley Cottage in Essex, and Lena remembered the two of them laughing at reports on the radio that the Stone of Destiny had been stolen by Scottish students, keen to make a nationalist point.[7] Lena thought it was a tremendous joke; her friend Josephine Tey was not so sure. Tey had seen the beginning, in Inverness, of the Scottish National Party, with Gunn and his political friends, ex-provost Alexander MacEwen and lawyer John MacCormick campaigning for election. In the Scottish literary world, the idea of stealing the Stone of Destiny was not new – Hugh MacDiarmid had been corresponding (in secret) about it since the 1930s.[8] Beth had been aware of these nationalist ideas for years.

Lawyer John MacCormick, in 1950 Rector of the University of Glasgow, was heavily involved in the aftermath of the Stone of Destiny theft (which had been taken by Glasgow students), and, by 1951, was also taking the Covenant Committee up to Inverness.[9] The Covenant Committee aimed to raise the profile of the idea of Scottish Home Rule, and their meeting in Inverness was very well attended, with an audience of 2,000 congregating outside the Town House. What Lena saw, from Essex, as a fringe movement, had been at the heart of Josephine Tey's local politics in Inverness for some time, and Tey was remarkably prescient in seeing just how important Scottish nationalism would become. For Tey personally, the idea of an independent Scotland was anathema. She had not received full recognition for her achievements in Scotland. Both she and her sisters had left Scotland in order to find work. Scotland, for Tey, was where her father was eternally stigmatized for being a shopkeeper. London, and Britain, were the stage where Tey was successful. Her reasons for not supporting Scottish independence are set out clearly throughout her work, but nowhere more clearly than in *The Singing Sands*.

The Singing Sands is not a polemic against Scottish nationalism. Many of the ideas in the novel had already been explored in *Patria*, the unperformed play written around the same time.[10] As with *Dickon* and *The Daughter of Time*, *Patria* is less successful as a piece of work, while *The Singing Sands* is the finished item – more polished, and much deeper. In *Patria* Tey's attitude is clear from the name of the first (nationalist) character mentioned: he is just called WASTREL. There is some attempt, from the author of *Kif*, to discuss the role of economics and unemployment in nationalist movements, but in *Patria* the whole reason for the nationalist movement is that these people don't want to work: they want glory; they're drunk on words. The nationalist movement is even led by a poet (BERGEN), an American who has written a dramatic and lengthy poem entitled 'Flame among the Lilies'. Bergen leads his cronies in impassioned speeches at political meetings – but is brought up short by 'Margot', who appears to be his ex-girlfriend: 'dark and pale, earnest but not fanatical, obviously nervous and unhappy in her position, but driven by a conviction stronger than her fears'.[11] Margot, so similar in looks to Beth MacKintosh, certainly expresses much of what Beth says about nationalism throughout *Patria* and *The Singing Sands*. Over a long speech which spills onto two pages of the published play, Margot spells out Beth's eloquent thoughts about her country and its place in Britain, and her distrust of nationalists:

338

What you are doing is a sin, a crime. A crime against humanity and civilisation. You are rousing hatreds that were sleeping, that would have died in their sleep. [...] you rake up old injustices [...] you invent new ones [...]. You distort history as you please [...]. I love my country as much as any of you. But I'm not blinded by flag-waving or doped by cheap sentiment. I don't cheer when some fool tells me that we are the salt of the earth.

Poetry, in particular that of Hugh MacDiarmid, was at the forefront of the literary scene in Scotland, and fuelled the debate on writing in Scots or Lallans.[12] Beth, with her Gaelic heritage, makes 'Margot' (still in that same lengthy speech) say this about writing, the subject dearest to her heart:

You talk of our glorious traditions; you would revive the language and literature of the Creelanders. There isn't any literature, and you know it. All the literature the Creelanders ever produced were folk-tales, handed down by word of mouth because they couldn't write. As for the language, there isn't a single person in this hall tonight who knows a word of it. It is so dead that it has no words for anything that came into being later than two hundred years ago. It has no connection with modern life. And yet you demand that it should be learned and talked again. And when you speak a tag of it your poor dupes cheer like maniacs.

The Gaelic revival in Scotland has seen the number of speakers rise and the language maintain an important part in Highland life. In Beth's time, her former schoolmate Mairi MacDonald was typical of the Gaelic revival in that she devoted time and energy to the Mod, the showcase of Gaelic song and culture, but did not want to associate with poor Gaels such as Beth's grandparents, or even Beth's father. Gaelic speakers such as Beth's grandparents experienced real prejudice against their language, an attitude that persisted for many years, but the Gaelic revival did not simply reverse this prejudice and allow descendants of Gaelic speakers, like Beth, to accept their heritage: instead it set up new norms and new societal groupings. The Scottish Literary Renaissance honoured Gaelic writers such as Sorley MacLean, but Beth's distance from the men of Scottish literature such as Gunn and MacDiarmid meant these new Gaelic writers never came into her circle.

Gordon Daviot's play *Patria* simplifies the argument about Scottish nationalism, but also tries to include too much. It is not a successful play, because it has too much going on and too much ranting – but it is a successful exposition of complicated views about Scotland and its place in Britain, and as clear an expression as anywhere in her work (with perhaps the exception of *The Singing Sands*, which is more subtle) of Beth's complicated attitude to Scotland. She didn't hate her country and love England, as is sometimes presented. Beth liked her home and liked England as well: she was British. What annoyed Beth was that 'Scotland' was being presented as a particular entity in the nationalist debate, a romantic, pseudo-historical national entity that had room for the songs of Colin's rejected Gaelic heritage, but had no room for Colin the self-made man, or Beth the successful writer.

Beth put so much of herself into her final novel *The Singing Sands* that it is easy to trace echoes of her childhood, her young womanhood and her adult life. The novel begins with one of her descriptions of the train journey north, a journey she had done so many times before. In the annotated draft manuscript of the novel, held now in the National Library of Scotland, some of the very few alterations made to the typed text make sure that details of the train and railway are correct – while the list of passengers that have previously met 'Old Yoghurt' include an Admiral (Beth's brother-in-law Humphrey Hugh Smith) and an officer of the Cameron Highlanders (either Hugh McIntosh or her lost First World War soldier) – while 'Yoghurt's' real name of Murdo is the name of Beth's uncle, on her father's side, who had worked (as a cab driver) at the station. The book is nominally set in Perthshire, which of course Beth had links to through her maternal grandmother, Jane Ellis, but it may as well be set in Inverness. The length of the train journey, the airport, and a few other details all point to Grant travelling from London to Inverness and then out into the country to his cousin's. From the moment Grant gets off the train and walks into the Station Hotel, every part of the scenery seems familiar to an Invernessian.

The journey to Clune is a journey from Inverness to Daviot, the scene of Beth's childhood holidays (there is even a Clune near to Daviot). Laura's house is a return to childhood for both Grant and Tey. And, as Grant remembers an adolescent romance with Laura, Josephine Tey remembers her own romance with Hugh McIntosh, through Laura's son, Pat. Patrick of course was Hugh's middle name, and Pat had first appeared in one of Beth's early published short stories, written just after his death. 'Haivers', where the character of Pat first appears in Beth's fiction, was published in the *Glasgow Herald* newspaper on 18th February 1928, and essentially the story is the same as an incident in *The Singing Sands*: Pat has to present a bouquet of flowers, and doesn't want to. Details are changed – the VIP in *The Singing Sands* becomes Zoe, and has an integral part to play in the story; Cresta is forgotten; and the sympathetic uncle becomes Grant. The first person narrative of the short story is gone, and *The Singing Sands* is far more assured: it loses the pawkiness, sentimentality and quick humour of the short story in favour of the more deliberate pacing and character exploration of the novel. Although there are some similarities between the two, the novel shows clearly how Tey had developed as a writer. Pat was always a strong character but now, as Tey herself was older, she also had sympathy with Grant and Laura, and so can present a more rounded picture not only of Pat himself, but how he fits into his family. There is no question that *The Singing Sands* is the work of a mature writer who is reworking an old idea – looking again at incidents in her real life and in her writing life that have all contributed to who she is and what she can create now. Although knowledge of Tey's life shows that she was remembering her earlier romance with Hugh, Grant, as a cipher for Josephine Tey (herself a cipher), makes his views about marriage clear: he rejects marriage, almost by accident, because of his absorption in his work. He is a clear celebration of single, independent life, maintaining his links with friends and family, not isolated, but living his life as he chooses. This is a very clear statement from Beth that she had ultimately found contentment in her life choices.

Hugh Patrick Fraser McIntosh's family's attachment to Scotland was so great that he, his father and two of his sisters all insisted on being buried in Inverness, despite living and dying elsewhere.[13] When Hugh and Beth had started writing together they had submitted their work to British or English journals, but Hugh's poems had also been republished in a popular anthology of Scottish writing. As a man, Hugh would have found it easier to fit into the world of Neil Gunn and James Bridie. Beth had seen, through Hugh, the attraction of Scotland, but her life had taken a different turn. Her ambiguous presentation of poet characters in her fiction shows that she had continued to engage with Hugh's work and ideas. She didn't dismiss the idea of Scottish independence out of hand, but had explored it thoroughly, and saw more possibilities in other things. Grant begins his search for 'singing sands' in Scotland, but soon discovers that they are actually much, much further away, in Arabia. There is so much more to the world than Scotland that the Scottish Nationalist Wee Archie and his concerns become merely a subplot in *The Singing Sands*.

This is where Josephine Tey's skill as a writer, and her own original thought, raises *The Singing Sands* from polemic like *Patria*, and turns it into an extraordinarily complex novel. Given the basic framework – a body and a mystery discovered in the first chapter, and a solution found logically by the end chapter – Tey was able to work in a fantastic plot, which takes wild tangents that are always reined in by the needs of the mystery novels – but which allow her to explore not only nationalism, but also develop several characters, put in an extended storyline about pilots, explore Grant's mental state of exhaustion, visit the Western Isles and Arabia, and put in numerous other quirky details (such as the fact that Grant's housekeeper used to be a theatrical dresser, and we hear her opinion of Marta Hallard's acting in a 'modern' play) that make the book a joy to re-read. We know that Grant will solve the mystery, so, as readers, we follow him no matter where he and his author take us. The book certainly does not rely on a traditional building of tension, where the hero overcomes a series of hurdles to reach his goal, but operates in a far more subtle way, balancing several plotlines at once. The trip to the Western Isles, for example, doesn't help the main plot of discovering the murderer in any way, but it does help to resolve Grant's nervous exhaustion – whilst also giving Josephine Tey a chance to make several pertinent comments on Scottish nationalism and set up the resolution of the subplot involving Archie's criminality.

The west coast settings owe something to Tey's family knowledge of the area and her Gaelic heritage. The American characters, too, could come from family knowledge – it would be an unusual Scottish family that did not have some American relatives, and Tey was no exception, since one of her cousins had emigrated to America.[14] Tey also had more and more dealings with America through her work, both publications and adaptations. Tey uses some of her own pet names throughout (like the newspaper name *The Clarion*) locating it all in Daviot/Tey country, but in reality the island of Cladda is more difficult to locate. There are 'singing sands' on Eigg and Islay, both of which are accessible from Oban, where Grant sails from, but Grant flies back, and the plane takes off from the sands, which sounds more like Barra. The description of the aeroplane is very realistic – as is the interest in flying shown throughout the novel – and suggests Beth had experience of flying. She had the money to fly, and flights from Inverness to the Western Isles (including Islay and Barra – but not Eigg, which had to be reached by boat) had been available through Captain Ted Fresson's Highland Airways since the 1930s. Highland Airways was nationalized after the Second World War, but existed in one form or another until fairly recently, and the small planes it employed flew the mail, newspapers and passengers out to the islands in an experience not dissimilar from Grant's summation of it.[15]

Grant is pleased to be able to fly back from Cladda, as it is another sign that he is recovering from his claustrophobia and work-induced stress and breakdown. The description of his illness is an extremely sympathetic portrait of what it is like to suffer from mental illness, and Grant is in no way diminished by admitting that he is having problems. He appears here as more vulnerable than the usual Golden Age detective, and this, too, makes the book seem modern. Grant first appeared in 1929, during the Golden Age of crime fiction, but Tey continued to develop his character, making Grant, and Tey's books, a bridge between the classic crime of Agatha Christie, with its emphasis on plot, and the darker, more character-driven crime novels of later writers.[16] Tey had personal experience of illness through her nursing of Colin in his final years, but it is heartbreaking to remember that Tey herself, suffering from terminal cancer, was originally told, like Grant, that rest was the cure she was seeking.

The Singing Sands was published to excellent reviews, and Josephine Tey's work was reassessed as a whole, as her other Grant novels were also republished after her death.[17] It is her most significant work, and is a reminder that she could have achieved even more if she had lived.

Beth's legacy to the National Trust in England attracted some attention in the press after her death, particularly in Scotland, where people unfamiliar with her life story could not understand why she had not left the money to a local or Scottish charity. The initial legacy that Beth left the National Trust was spent on buying, in 1954, 142 acres of gardens in Sussex and a fifteenth-century gatehouse at Oxburgh Hall in Norfolk.[18] Oxburgh is a grand manor house, with a moat around it, which was built by the Catholic Bedingfield family in the fifteenth century. It now houses tapestries worked by Mary, Queen of Scots, a connection that would perhaps have interested Gordon Daviot. It's in the east of England, a little further north than the area Beth really liked; neither of the National Trust sites are places she had any particular connection to, but she would have appreciated that her money was spent how she wished. However, the Daviot Fund continued and continues to bring in money, more than sixty years after Beth MacKintosh died. As it has turned out, it has been a gift that has caused them some administrative difficulty, as it needs continuous management. It is now run through the publishing department of the Trust, rather than the Legacies department.[19] All monies generated are now put into the Trust's General Fund, which is used for priority projects in England, Wales and Northern Ireland.

What the National Trust does not do, however, is manage Beth's literary reputation in any way. For them, the copyright to the books is an unusual, though welcome, way of generating income. Requests to use or adapt the books are generally agreed to.

Beth had been wary of allowing the BBC the right to adapt her work in the years before her death, feeling that they did not offer a high enough fee or respect her wishes as regards changes.[20] But after her death, her novels and plays became almost a staple for the Saturday Night Theatre programme, a guarantee of good audiences. The number and type of adaptations of Beth's work increased significantly in the years after her death, and some of the adaptations took great liberties with her original plots. For example, the maker of Hammer Horror films bought the film rights to *Brat Farrar* in the year of Elizabeth's death, finally adapting the book in 1963, though their 'version' was so far removed from the original *Brat Farrar* that Josephine Tey is not named in the credits. *Paranoiac* retains enough of the original to make its source material clear though, including many of the names: Simon Ashby, a wealthy psychotic who enjoys playing the church organ, tries to drive his sister Eleanor insane to get the family money, but is thwarted by a man who pretends to be his long-lost brother. There's also a mummy, and it ends with a dramatic fire.[21]

However, the constant stream of adaptations, including some more high-quality television adaptations by the BBC, did much to keep Josephine Tey's books selling: when people saw the films and heard the radio plays, they wanted to buy the books. Beth's stories appealed to readers, and more and more people kept coming back to read them. Even *Paranoiac* had a surprisingly high quality cast for a shocker – Oliver Reed was Simon – and was dubbed and released in several countries. It was reissued on DVD in 2010. Beth was well aware of the liberties taken with adaptations – Alfred Hitchcock's version of *A Shilling for Candles* had hardly been faithful – and perhaps the benefits of the adaptations outweigh any drawbacks.

Although Beth's agents declined to be involved in the execution of her will, they have continued to manage her Josephine Tey books to a certain extent, as did her publisher Peter Davies. Peter and Nico Davies, who had been personal friends of Tey's, were very much involved in arranging the Penguin editions of Tey's books, as they had been during Beth's lifetime, but generally Tey's books were managed through the David Higham agency. David Higham is still one of the biggest London agencies, but there is now no one at the firm who remembers Tey, and, as with the National Trust, there is a hands-off feel to the management. Even Nico Davies, just a few years after Elizabeth's death, admitted that they had kept no first editions of her Daviot or Tey novels.[22] The Daviot plays, with the exception of *Richard of Bordeaux*, are all now out of print – although still readily available second-hand.

Beth's family had never been involved in her writing career and had never been in touch with her publisher or agent. As Beth had willed the management of her literary estate to third parties, her family have not had any say in what has happened to the books. Neither her family, The National Trust, her agent or her publishers have made any concerted attempt to market or promote Josephine Tey's books. Opportunities for reprints have been taken, but really they stay in print purely because every successive generation of readers since Beth's death has wanted to read them. The constant stream of adaptations has kept interest in Beth's works high, but Josephine Tey's crime novels have also been established in the crime or mystery novel canon. This extremely popular genre has increased its profile over the last few decades, and has moved from being seen as pulp, throwaway novels to serious literary fiction. Novelists such as Ian Rankin are bestsellers, and their work is given serious review space. Ian Rankin is among the contemporary authors who cite Josephine Tey as an influence, and Tey is often cited as 'Fifth' after the 'Big Four' crime writers of Agatha Christie, Dorothy L. Sayers, Margery Allingham and Ngaio Marsh – the essential exponents of crime fiction which all aficionados of the genre have at least a passing acquaintance with. Readers and critics talk about her books and recommend them to others. Like Beth's biggest hit *Richard of Bordeaux*, her continued success is built on that elusive marker of quality, word of mouth.

There has also been continued interest in Beth's personal life.

She had been seen as something of a mystery even in her own life-time, and that myth has only increased over time. John Gielgud's introduction to Gordon Daviot's collected plays was the first glimpse many of her readers had into her private life. Another small biographical sketch was written by a fellow pupil from the IRA, Mairi MacDonald, who had her essay, 'The Enigma of Gordon Daviot', published in the *Scots Magazine*, before it was anthologized in her collected writings.[23] Mairi's collected writings give a good picture of the Inverness that Beth lived in, but her essay on Gordon Daviot is based far more on research than personal recollection. Her assessment of Gordon Daviot's career is fair and comprehensive, and as an Invernessian, Mairi understood the difficulties of making the transition to London life, and explains this through her own experiences – but her air of authority and people's readiness to accept that all Invernessians know each other has led to Mairi's interpretations of Beth's character being too often quoted as 'fact'. Mairi was a snob, who could never bring herself to believe that a shopkeeper like Colin, who left school at fourteen, could ever be intelligent – and neither could a shopkeeper's children ever be given her full respect. Mixed up in this class snobbery was Mairi's own attitude to Gaelic. A pro-moter of the Gaelic language herself, she nevertheless wanted the language sanitized, denying any association with the stereotype of west coast 'laziness' that Colin fought so hard against. Mairi's own personal conflicts greatly affected her ability to write any biography of Elizabeth MacKintosh.

Mairi was also hampered by the refusal of Beth's London friends to be involved in any attempt to write a biography.[24] Mairi had proposed the idea of a full-length biography to Beth's publisher Peter Davies, apparently unaware that Peter and Nico were personal friends of Beth. She received in reply a polite but distant refusal. Writing to John Gielgud, Mairi again received a polite refusal: John wrote that neither he nor Gwen would be involved in a biography that was an 'apologia'. Mairi wanted to present Beth as someone who had disliked her home town and home country, and neither John, Gwen nor the Davies recognized the Gordon Daviot that they knew in Mairi's portrayal.

Faced with a lack of information, Mairi considered turning Beth's life, as she saw it, into a novel. The resultant notes for what she wanted to call *Small-Town Genius* are dismaying, with dreadful dialogue in an overblown romantic style. Beth, who prioritized scrupulous research and was dedicated to telling the truth, would not have been impressed with a novel that played with not only Beth's life, but that of her family. Beginning with an extremely lengthy justification of the sort of snobbery and class system prevalent in the Inverness of Beth and Mairi's youth, the proposed novel went on to mix fact and fiction in a thoroughly libellous way; painting Colin as a social-climbing simpleton and his wife Josephine MacKintosh as an English schoolteacher who married beneath her. The draft novel was abandoned after only a chapter or so. One can only hope that on re-reading what she had written Mairi caught a glimpse of how unacceptable it would have been.

Caroline Ramsden made an explicit attempt to redress what had been said about her friend in her own autobiography *Life on Primrose Hill*, presenting, unlike Gielgud, a picture of a woman who may have been shy, but who did attend parties, and who, above all, was 'a grand friend to have'.[25] But Lena's autobiography, entertaining though it was, reached only a small audience. Josephine Tey remained a mystery.

As Tey's work continued to be read and republished year after year, other attempts were made to find out about her life. A few researchers took the simple step of showing up in Inverness and asking around, knocking on the door of her old house and asking in Colin's old shop and in the local library and so on. Because Beth had been such a private person – and because most of her close friends and family had lived elsewhere, and were now resistant to the idea of a biography – these research trips tended to produce more gossip than real fact, which was then endlessly recycled into every new essay on Beth's life. For example, after her death her home, Crown Cottage, was bought by her neighbour, Hamish Macpherson. Mr Macpherson had not known much about Beth's writing career before her death, but when he moved into her house he was intrigued by the letters – and researchers – which continued to arrive for her. He was more than happy to talk to researchers and reporters who knocked on his door, and began to see himself as something of an expert on Josephine Tey. He was extensively quoted in a BBC documentary about Elizabeth MacKintosh broadcast in the 1980s, and also in articles in the *Inverness Courier* right up until the 1990s.[26] Much like Mairi MacDonald, his word was given particular credence because he had actually known Beth when she was alive. Unfortunately, he and Beth had not actually got on terribly well, and Mr Macpherson was neither particularly interested in reading or the theatre, nor a fan of Beth's work. Unlike Mairi MacDonald, he did not do such thorough research, and relied on his own memories, not all of which were complimentary. He had always felt that his former neighbour was unapproachable, and his dislike of her extended to describing her as 'strutting' down the street when she walked, something hard to believe of a former Anstey student. Mr Macpherson was also personally displeased by the idea that Beth had left her money to the National Trust in England, as he felt that she should have done more for her home town of Inverness, and her home country of Scotland.

As critics and university courses began to take crime fiction more seriously, a number of essays, encyclopedia entries and articles were published, which attempted to set Elizabeth MacKintosh's work in context. Each of these suffered because of their artificial division between her 'Josephine Tey' and 'Gordon Daviot' writing, and in particular a lack of understanding of the context of Beth's life and the full extent of her work. Writing on Gordon Daviot's theatre work is usually included tangentially in summaries of 1930s theatre, or biographies of Gielgud, Ffrangcon-Davies, Olivier, or the other great actors and actresses she worked with, with a tendency to focus on Daviot's words rather than her life. Biographical sketches remained short, and were largely based on what John Gielgud and Mairi MacDonald had said. Most contained some version of the idea that Josephine Tey the mystery writer was a mystery herself, and that writing a biography about her would be virtually impossible.

American scholar Sandra Roy produced a full-length assessment of Josephine Tey's literary output in 1980, but this book contains only a summary of Beth's life before turning to her writing.[27] It examines all Beth's work, including her writing under the Daviot pseudonym and her theatrical pieces, but it treats only her Tey mystery novels in depth. It puts her writing in the context of its time – though never in the context of the Scottish Literary Renaissance – and collects together many contemporary reviews of Beth's work, but it is essentially a work of opinion. Some of the facts are wrong (including Beth's date of birth), and it repeats some gossipy details as truth (including the idea that Beth rarely left Inverness). The book also suffers, as do many other works on Tey, from an American bias, locating Inverness as 'near Loch Ness' – which is strictly speaking true, and which would mean something to an American unfamiliar with Scottish geography, but is not how an Invernessian would ever describe their city. Someone living by Loch Ness would be considered by an Invernessian to be living out in the country – and this would be particularly true in the 1920s, when transport was more limited, and in the 1930s and 40s, when travel outwith Inverness was limited because of military activity in the area. Academic assessments like Roy's have ended up drawing conclusions which are redundant, or even plain wrong, because they are not strongly enough rooted in the reality of Beth's life.

The serious critics' love and knowledge of the novels they are writing about is what makes their essays readable, rather than what the essays reveal about how detective fiction fits into literary or sociological theory. The same could be said of the other style of essay that has been written about Josephine Tey, the love-letter to her works composed by avid fans, who are usually fans of detective fiction in general, and who have a very thorough knowledge of the genre that they love. Many blogs on the internet feature short articles of this type, and some have been collected and published. The best of these combine the author's love of Tey with another love or piece of knowledge that they have (for example, knowledge of another contemporary writer, knowledge of 1930s theatre, or something more esoteric like knowledge of transport), and so shed new light on Tey's work by looking at it from new angles. However, they too suffer from a lack of knowledge of the facts of Tey's life.

Studies of modern Scottish Literature, which might have been expected to embrace Beth's success, have generally ignored her work. There are several reasons for this omission, perhaps including Beth's reticence and fondness for pen-names, her gender, and a bias against genre fiction. Perhaps also there has been a focus on work that not only comes from Scottish writers living in Scotland and writing about Scotland, as Beth did, but Scottish writers who were explicitly focused on the Scottish nationalist cause. I have never seen any article, essay or comment that explicitly links Neil Gunn and Josephine Tey, despite the fact that they lived in the same town at the same time, knew each other's work, and responded to each other's work.

In Inverness, Tey's name is widely known, and she has many loyal readers – but she has not received the serious attention she deserves. Unlike Neil Gunn, whose admirers worked hard after his death to set up a society to his memory and publish his biography and his collected letters, Tey had no one working for her in this way. However, her books are always available in local bookshops, old copies never last long in second-hand bookshops, and at the centenary of her birth the local drama group the Florians, in collaboration with the Saltire Society, revived four of her short plays in 'An Evening with Gordon Daviot'.[28] The *Inverness Courier* reckoned "The four plays [...] offered well-defined contrasts and demonstrated Gordon Daviot's gift for mystery, suspense and intrigue', praising her 'dry Cowardesque humour' and particularly enjoying the short play *The Balwhinnie Bomb*. The organizers of the event decided that the substantial proceeds from the event should go towards a lasting legacy, and used the money to create 'The Highland Culture Award'. Recipients of this award have included writer Katharine Stewart, composer Blair Douglas and singer Mary Ann Kennedy – all people whom the Highland branch of the Saltire Society considered to have furthered the Society's aim: preserving the best of Scottish Highland tradition and encouraging any new development that could strengthen and enrich the cultural life of the region – a fitting legacy for the very original Josephine Tey.

However Beth's legacy has been managed or mismanaged, the fact remains that her books are still in print and still selling and still giving huge enjoyment to readers. They are constantly referenced by new generations of readers and writers, and the recent interest in *The Daughter of Time* shows that Beth achieved what she set out to do: to make people think about what they are reading and enjoy it. Her stories are as powerful now as they ever were.

Conclusion

Elizabeth MacKintosh had her own story to tell, but never had the time to tell it. Comparing the pictures of Beth, the diffident young woman who looks so serious as celebrated playwright Gordon Daviot in 1934, with the confident author photograph taken at Malvern in 1949, it is hard to believe that Beth was ever nostalgic for the past. Beth MacKintosh reinvented herself several times over – she always looked to the future, and felt the best was yet to come. When she died, she was at the peak of her writing powers. Her family believed that if she had lived, she could have taken up some of the very interesting offers that were beginning to come her way from America for adaptations of her Tey novels. No longer tied to Inverness, she could have travelled and perhaps rekindled her love of cinema and her film-writing career as she took advantage of adaptations of her Josephine Tey work. There were many aspects of her varied life that she had not yet explored in fiction – teaching PE to factory workers, or working in a mixed school in Oban or more about her life in Inverness. *The Singing Sands'* focus on nationalism shows an engagement with contemporary life that she could have developed further in her writing.

Beth had not always had it easy. She was never able to do all she wanted, but her writing output in the last few years of her life could not have been higher. She succeeded in completing the novels she was working on before her death, and everything she wanted to publish or have performed did eventually appear in print or on the stage. She had succeeded in creating a life for herself, and her writing gave not only her readers, but Beth herself, enormous pleasure. Elizabeth MacKintosh was Gordon Daviot the playwright and Josephine Tey the novelist, but she was also Beth the homemaker, a daughter, a cousin, a sister, a good friend, an Invernessian. She made many lives for herself, both physically when she was able to move around, but also mentally when she was confined to Inverness and living through her writing.

Beth's nephew, Colin Stokes, is the only close family member still living. Jean died in the late 1950s; Moire died in London in 1994. The gravestones in Tomnahurich cemetery tell us what happened to a few other members of Beth's family: her mother's brother John Horne died in 1955; a cousin died in 1977. None of the other cousins or aunts or uncles had stayed close to Beth, even though they continued to live in the same area.

John Gielgud, Dodie Smith and Gwen Ffrangcon-Davies all lived to extreme old age in their cottages in Essex; Gielgud as a celebrated actor, Dodie as the famous and wealthy author of *I Capture the Castle* and *The 101 Dalmatians*, and the indomitable Gwen, working in radio until near the end, forever with the youthful voice of Juliet Capulet. Gwen and John always acknowledged Gordon's influence on their careers, and cherished the memory of her friendship. Dodie never stopped regretting her life in theatre and always wished she had not gone to America when the Second World War broke out, but she forged a successful second career as a novelist, and put into fiction many of her own and her friends' experiences in 1930s theatreland. When Dodie's husband Alec died she was lost, estranged from many of her friends because of her spiky temper, relying on her housekeeper – yet always managing, despite what she said, to keep up her literary links. Her literary estate was left to the author Julian Barnes, who went to considerable trouble to deal with Disney for film rights, while her personal papers ended up in Boston University – a sharp contrast to the way in which Beth's estate was dealt with.

Gwen Ffrangcon-Davies worked for as long as she could, maintaining her cheerful countenance and enjoying being a centenarian mightily. She was made a Dame Commander of the

British Empire in 1991 at the age of 100, the oldest ever person to be made a Dame.[1] She died in 1992, and is buried in the village church in Stambourne. At her funeral, the church was filled with beautiful roses from Tagley cottage, the roses that she and Marda had planted and cared for. Marda had died in 1970, in London, reconciled in some measure with Gwen, though never totally happy. Marda left all her possessions to Gwen, and her papers are part of the Gwen Ffrangcon-Davies archive, previously held in the University of Winchester and recently donated to the Victoria and Albert Museum.

Beth's friend Lena Ramsden lived a long and happy life, which she wrote about in her aubiography *A View from Primrose Hill*. Peggy Webster forged a successful career as a director in the US and UK. At one point, Hollywood came calling, but, after a few weeks shadowing Cecil B. DeMille, Peggy decided that the sexism she would have to battle against was too much, and returned to the theatre, where she worked with many actors who are still household names today. She was quick to pick up on the talent of a young Judi Dench, and Dame Judi also worked with Gwen – remembering the incessant jangling of the many bracelets Gwen wore on her arms.[2] The theatre world Gordon Daviot knew is intricately linked to today's.

Hugh McIntosh, that dim memory of romance and what-might-have-been, is quite forgotten, with no living descendants. Almost all his family asked to be returned to Inverness after death, and are buried in Tomnahurich.

Beth is not remembered by any gravestone or marker in her home town. But her books are in every bookshop, and on many shelves in many homes.

Elizabeth MacKintosh was always an Invernessian. She did not feel that she owed the town anything, and certainly did not go out of her way to promote it or to talk up her links to Scotland, but neither was she a Scotophobe as she has sometimes been portrayed. Beth saw herself both as a Highlander and as British, and moved to England because that is where she saw the best career prospects, but it took her a while to get used to the south of the country. It wasn't until she was well established in her job in

---

Tunbridge Wells that she found an area of England that she loved and which meant a lot to her, and part of the reason for her strong attachment to the area was that she felt she had to leave before she was ready to do so.

Elizabeth's mother's death changed her life; no matter how much her career meant to her, Beth put her family first. She was Colin's daughter: he had spent years supporting his family, and had brought his daughters up with the same values, and Beth did not let him down. Although she did not always find it easy, Beth did the best she could to make her life with her father in Inverness enjoyable and meaningful.

Gordon Daviot achieved her ambition to be a playwright in spectacular style with her first play, *Richard of Bordeaux*. This play changed not only her life, but also the lives of many of the actors and backstage staff involved. It touched audiences deeply, and the story resonated for years with the people who saw it.

Josephine Tey grew her audience through word of mouth. Readers loved her books and recommended them, and have continued to do so: her books have been in print since they first appeared in the 1920s. The novels have been properly ranked as among the best crime fiction of the Golden Age, but they have not received the proper attention due to them as Scottish fiction, partly because of their genre, and partly because they have been overlooked as Beth did not support Scottish nationalism and was not closely linked to the Scottish literary scene. Similarly, Gordon Daviot has been overlooked as a 'Scottish' playwright. Beth MacKintosh's work shows us another aspect of Scottishness, and any analysis of Gunn's work, or of the Scottish Literary Renaissance, which leaves her out is an incomplete analysis. Elizabeth MacKintosh was an Anstey student, a teacher, a British playwright, and a Scottish Highlander. There should be acknowledgement of different Highland women's experiences: not just the illiterate Gael and their wealth of folklore and song, but also the extremely literate and well-educated lover of England, Elizabeth MacKintosh.

Beth used her writing to search for meaning, and, although she always tried to entertain her audience, she did not shy away from difficult topics, tackling religious themes through her plays and an extraordinarily wide range of topics through her novels, from economic troubles after the First World War to historical puzzles. History always held a strong fascination, but her main interest was always in people: she was always an observational writer, whose strength was to draw people, whether from the fourteenth century or the twentieth, that readers and playgoers could believe in.

As befits someone who understood people so well, Beth was a good and loyal friend. She stayed in touch with people from her college days and, particularly, from her time working as a playwright in the West End – but she needed to have a deep connection to people before she formed those strong friendships. She had little time for people she saw as small-minded, and did not always get on with her neighbours and fellow townsfolk in Inverness. Beth did not want to be public property, and was not interested in maintaining a media profile – she wanted to keep her life the way she wanted it: centred around family and writing.

Beth was disappointed in love, partly as a result of the First World War, which changed the hopes of so many women of her age, but she ultimately created a fulfilling life for herself as a single woman, and her writing shows how much she enjoyed and celebrated that life. As an Anstey student, she had been exposed to suffragettes and feminist thinking, but she drew mainly on her own life experiences and the strong female role models that were available to her as a child: her mother and grandmother.

Sometimes it is hard to realize that these lively young women and men are all dead and gone: Beth who wrote such funny letters; Colin, the young boy who walked alone from Shieldaig to Lochcarron; Hugh Patrick Fraser McIntosh filling in his crosswords in his bedsit in Inverness; Dodie Smith, with her entertaining autobiography; charming actress Gwen... But anyone can walk into a shop or library and pick up a Josephine Tey novel – and Beth is there, as lively and opinionated as she ever was. Elizabeth MacKintosh was Gordon Daviot, Josephine Tey, F. Craigie Howe, Beth, Mac, Bessie – she was a student Anstey could be proud of; a daughter Colin and Josephine could be proud of; a daughter

Inverness should be proud of; a writer Scotland should be proud of – she was private, spiky, friendly, contradictory, intelligent, funny, inspiring, difficult – and, above all, she is a writer that many readers simply love, without knowing anything about her at all.

Notes to the Text

1. Birth certificate. Elizabeth's date of birth is often incorrectly given online and in academic archives.

   I have checked all birth, death and marriage dates and details with the original certificates, either available through the Scottish registrar's archival services at the *Scotland's People* website; through the Highland Archive Centre (HAC); or from certificates held privately by the MacKintosh family. Census records (also available at www.scotlandspeople.gov.uk and HAC) provided extra detail on addresses, size and location of houses, and occupations. For family, records showing baptism dates were also useful. Parish records for Inverness are accessible at HAC, while records for Colin MacKintosh's family were partly accessible through the Applecross Family History Centre. The latter location also provided access to private local family history research.

   Dates were also checked against family gravestones, most of which are located in Tomnahurich cemetery in Inverness, and these often provided surprising extra details. A further check was made on dates by examining the announcements section of the local papers, particularly the *Inverness Courier*.

2. Josephine Tey, *The Expensive Halo* (London: Peter Davies, 1978), pp. 18–19. Editions referred to are from Jennifer Morag

Henderson's own collection. The text of Tey's novels was never substantially changed, except in the abridged American editions (discussed later in the text).

3. Letter from Colin to his youngest daughter, held by the MacKintosh family descendants; undated, probably from mid-1940s.

4. Incident described in a letter from Colin to his middle daughter, held by the MacKintosh family descendants; dated 21st July 1927.

5. Mary's story is traceable through the census and birth records, and Colin's support of his sister is clear in the Valuation Rolls (HAC), which show who was paying the rent on the family's houses. No reference to Mary survives in any letters, and Elizabeth MacKintosh's descendants had no knowledge of her, or her son.

6. Colin's mother's ownership of the shop is clear from the Valuation Rolls (HAC), which list 'E. MacKintosh' as a tenant, while an advert in the local press lists her as proprietor, and gives the length of time the shop had been open. Roderick's involvement is mentioned by Colin in a letter to his youngest daughter (held by the MacKintosh family descendants; undated, probably from mid-1940s.) Colin's original apprenticeship to a grocer is detailed in the census records.

7. John's story was revealed through searches at HAC, and will be discussed in greater detail in Chapter 3.

8. Details of Colin's shop were obtained partly from the Valuation Rolls of Inverness (HAC), which every year listed the owner and tenant of a building, its use, and its rental value. In 1892–3 numbers 55 and 57 Castle Street were rented by Colin from Duncan and Margaret Sutherland of Broadstone Lodge, Kingsmills Road. The Sutherlands also owned the MacKintosh family flat at number 67.

9. A useful discussion of the pupil-teacher system as it was experienced in Highland schools appears in Robert A. Reid (ed.) *Oban High School – The First 100 Years* (Oban: Oban High School, 1993), p. 51. Josephine probably worked at Farraline Park School – now Inverness Central Library – as she had family connections there, but I haven't been able to confirm this.

---

10. See 'Danny the Dago', with his Spanish dark looks, in *Kif*.
11. Mairi A. MacDonald, *The Banks of the Ness* (Edinburgh: Paul Harris Publishing, 1982), pp. 10–11.

CHAPTER TWO: *Bessie*

1. Details of Josephine and Mary's children are from census records, announcements in the *Inverness Courier*, and family gravestones in Tomnahurich cemetery.
2. Elizabeth's name is a source of confusion as she changed how she was known by family members, and she also chose to write under pen-names. On the census records of 1901 she is recorded as 'Bessie', and friends from school also remember her by this name. The second MacKintosh daughter was more consistent in her name; she was never called 'Jane', and her nephew had only ever known her as 'Jean'.
3. MacDonald, (1982), p. 114.
4. Murdo's details are in the birth, death, marriage and census records. Information and photographs of the firm Macrae and Dick, the biggest firm in Inverness employing cabmen, are detailed on the Highland Council's history and culture website, Am Baile (http://www.ambaile.org.uk/).
5. Gaelic and English language preferences were recorded in census details.
6. Information on Mary Jeans's children comes from death certificates, the announcements page of the *Inverness Courier*, and family gravestones.
7. From the private MacKintosh family collection.
8. Information on Colin's ownership and tenancy of properties, as well as the ownership of surrounding shops, is shown on the Inverness Valuation Rolls (HAC).
9. MacDonald, (1982), p. 117.
10. Details of addresses, tenants and occupations are from census records.
11. Family memory from Mary Henrietta's son.
12. MacDonald, (1982), pp. 7–8.
13. Sir Alexander Malcolm MacEwen, *The Thistle and the Rose: Scotland's Problem Today* (Edinburgh: Oliver and Boyd, 1932), p. 223.

14. As shown by the witnesses to Josephine's will.
15. From the private MacKintosh family collection.
16. Occupations shown on the census records.

CHAPTER THREE: *Secondary Schooldays, up until 1914*

1. From the private MacKintosh family collection.
2. Information on the IRA comes from two main published sources: Charles Bannerman, *Further up Stephen's Brae: the Midmills Era at Inverness Royal Academy* (St Michael Publishing, 2010), and Robert Preece, *Song School, Town School, Comprehensive: A History of the Inverness Royal Academy* (Inverness: IRA, 2011).
3. The Inverness Valuation Rolls (HAC) show Colin's rental arrangements for the shop and flat.
4. Information from family headstones in Tomnahurich cemetery.
5. Information from death certificates and census records.
6. See Bannerman and Preece, above. Additional information from MacDonald, (1982).
7. Specific information about IRA marks, prizes and subjects comes direct from the school log books for each session. These are held in the IRA school archive (unpublished; not open to the general public). See also Inverness Royal Academy Prospectuses, HAC C1/5/8/7/8 and C1/5/8/7/9.
8. Scottish Universities had their own political representatives from pre-Union times, and the Combined Scottish Universities MP was a historical relic from this old Scottish practice, which dated back to James VI and reflected the importance of Universities in early modern Scotland. The UK Parliament continued the tradition, with various modifications, until it was finally abolished in 1950.
9. Typed biography, Penguin archive DM1107/841, 00.0841 1: *The Franchise Affair*; for publication in editions of the Tey mystery novels.
10. MacDonald, (1982), p. 114 and p. 117.
11. Photographs of the new gym and art blocks are available to view on the Highland Council's history and culture website, Am Baile, and in the Paterson Collection http://www.patersoncollection.co.uk/.
12. In a letter to Gwen Ffrangcon-Davies, dated approx. 1934, she

mentions how the pipes and drums of the Camerons moved her on a 1930 trip to London, from the Gwen Ffrangcon-Davies collection, ref. AM48.

13. Specific information about Inverness and the 4th Camerons during the War was found in Patrick Watt, *Steel and Tartan* (Gloucestershire: The History Press, 2012). More general information is widely known and discussed in many general histories of Inverness, especially Norman Newton, *Inverness: Highland Town to Millennium City* (Breedon Books, 2003). Local newspapers also give a clear picture. The Am Baile website also holds various photos, with detailed captions.

14. The Inverness Valuation Rolls (HAC) show Colin's rental and home-owning prices.

15. John MacKintosh's death certificate shows place and cause of death. Craig Dunain has extensive archives, though not all are freely available to the public – events that happened more recently are still restricted or confidential. John MacKintosh's admittance to Craig Dunain and his case notes are available to view (with restrictions) at HAC.

16. In 2010 Inverness Museum and Art Gallery hosted an exhibition entitled *Homecoming* which included details of the McAskill family who underwent a similar experience. More happily, they eventually made the money they needed to buy the tenancy of a farm in Scotland.

CHAPTER FOUR: *War, and first year at Anstey*

1. See article by Jennifer Morag Henderson in the *Inverness Courier*, Friday 13th March 2015.

2. Details of IRA pupils from Bannerman, (2010), pp. 19–31.

3. Details on Beaton from Watt, (2012); Miles Mack http://miles-mack.wordpress.com/2011/11/12/murdoch-beaton-secretary-to-the-%e2%80%9cdewar-report%e2%80%9d-1912/; letter from Murdoch Beaton to his wife dated 29th May 1915 (private Beaton family collection).

4. See Watt, (2012); and issues of the *Inverness Courier*.

5. Details on Peter and Peter John from census, birth, death and marriage records; military records; family headstones in Tomnahurich; and Watt, (2012).

6. Farraline Park School Log Book 1908-1923, 18th September entry, (HAC) C1/5/3/160/1/3.
7. Bannerman, (2010), p. 29; Carol Coles, http://womenshistory-network.org/blog/?tag=anna-muncaster.
8. Details of dates and exams from IRA school archive, and Inverness Royal Academy School Prospectus 1915–16, (HAC), C1/5/8/7/8. Details of art prize from a MacKintosh family friend, who heard it from Moire (Etta).
9. Typed biography, Penguin archive DM1107/841, 00.0841 1: *The Franchise Affair*; for publication in editions of the Tey mystery novels.
10. Colin Crunden, *A History of Anstey College of Physical Education 1897–1972* (Warwickshire: Anstey College of Physical Education, 1974); Anstey College magazines; private correspondence with Dr Ida Webb, former Anstey principal; and the Anstey Old Girls (Scotland).
11. Josephine Tey, *Miss Pym Disposes* (London: Arrow Books, 2011), p. 42.
12. I thought it was pretty impressive to go to Anstey from the Highlands in 1915, but an Anstey Old Girl I spoke to told me the story of how, in 1915, her aunt went, by boat, to a PT college in Denmark.
13. 'M. Davidson' is listed in the Anstey College magazine class lists for Elizabeth's year. Marjorie Davidson is listed in the class lists for the IRA, in the IRA school archive. Copies of letters from Beth to Marjorie are preserved in Acc 7708, no. 33, National Library of Scotland – Mairi MacDonald's papers.
14. Acc 7708, no. 33, National Library of Scotland – Mairi MacDonald's papers. Letter 6, 20/9/1939, Mac to Dave.
15. Accounts of this raid are easily obtained online, e.g. http://www.expressandstar.com/millennium/1900/1900-1924/1916.html
16. Elizabeth's work as a VAD is mentioned in Catherine Aird, 'Josephine Tey, the Person' in Geraldine Perriam (ed.) *Josephine Tey: A Celebration* (Glasgow: Black Rock Press, 2011), p. 65. Aird, who knew Elizabeth's youngest sister personally, confirmed to me that Elizabeth worked as a VAD in Birmingham. The Red Cross (private correspondence) confirmed the details of the convalescent homes in Inverness, but hold no records for Elizabeth.

17. Beth's sister Etta shared many details with a friend. This friend, a writer, originally hoped to write a biography of Josephine Tey, but ultimately decided that her respect for Beth (and for the officer) would not allow her to publish private details of a love affair. She has never revealed the name of Beth's officer, but has talked to me in generalizations about Beth's wartime romance. While I respect Beth's desire for privacy, this romance was a crucial turning-point in both her personal development and in her development as a writer, so I believe it must be understood.

18. John Gielgud, 'Foreword' to Gordon Daviot *Plays* (London: Peter Davies, 1953), p. x.

19. Beth's nephew thought this man's name was Hugh Fraser, but I haven't been able to verify this when comparing it with the IRA school registers. There certainly were Hugh Frasers at her school, including one young man a few years ahead of her who specialized in music. However, this name may have been mis-remembered as it is very close to that of Hugh Patrick Fraser McIntosh (see Chapter 6).

20. Jessica Mann, *Deadlier than the Male: An Investigation into Feminine Crime Writing* (London: David and Charles, 1981).

21. There is an autograph book on display in the permanent collection in Inverness Museum.

22. Aird, (2011), p. 65.

23. Aird, (2011), p. 65.

24. Watt, (2012). Thanks to Patrick Watt for assistance with queries. More information about Alfred found online; www.edwardalleynclub.com, www.crystal-palace-mag.co.uk/remembrance.

25. Gordon Barber, *My Diary in France: experiences and impressions of active service during a period of the war with the central empires* (Liverpool: privately printed by Henry Young & sons ltd, 1917), available for reference in the military collection of the Mitchell Library, Glasgow. More information from the Commonwealth War Graves Commission website http://www.cwgc.org/, invasionzone.com forums.

CHAPTER FIVE: *Anstey's second year, and teaching*

1. Beth confused things by saying herself later that she spent three years at Anstey. The Anstey course was later extended to three

years – a change which raised its prestige as it equated to a university degree – but at the time Beth attended it was two years only, see Crunden (1974). Beth may well have attended summer courses though, making it two-and-a-half years.

2. Crunden (1974); Anstey college Jubilee magazine 1897–1947 (private collection of Dr. Ida Webb); www.connectinghistories.org

3. Mann, (1981); Acc 7708, no. 33, National Library of Scotland – Mairi MacDonald's papers, Letter 6, 20/9/1939, Mac to Dave.

4. Crunden, (1974), p. 25.

5. M. Symington's name and Inverness address is in the Anstey College graduation and Old Girl lists (*Anstey College Magazine* no. 29, Autumn 1927, private collection of Dr. Ida Webb). A search through the IRA school records revealed she was in Mary Henrietta's class.

6. IRA school records show Jean in attendance up until 1917. Jean's reference letter from her college confirms the dates. (Reference letter from James Munford, 6th November 1918, private MacKintosh family collection).

7. Leys Castle hospital opened in August 1917. Farraline Park School Log Book, entry 31st August 1917, (HAC), C1/5/3/160/1/3.

8. Letter from Josephine MacKintosh to Beth, Sun 17th Ju[l]? 1921, private MacKintosh family collection.

9. Crunden, (1974), p. 25.

10. Acc 7708, no. 33, National Library of Scotland – Mairi MacDonald's papers, Letter 2, 23/1/1919, Mac to Dave.

11. Jean's reference letters from her college and her employers are preserved by the MacKintosh family; they provide details of almost her entire career.

12. Colin's ownership of the shops and flats is clear from the Valuation Rolls of Inverness (HAC).

13. The Oban High School Log book, held in the local archives, gives dates and details of Elizabeth's employment at Oban, and her accident. Argyll & Bute Council Archives, CA/5/249/5. Details about the school in Reid (1993).

14. MS 26190, fol. 124, letter from Elizabeth MacKintosh to Marion Lochhead, 6th July 1933, National Library of Scotland; for publication in PEN newsletter.

15. Letter AM4, Gordon Daviot to Marda Vanne, Gwen Ffrangcon-Davies archive.

16. Gordon Daviot, *The Staff-Room* in Gordon Daviot *Plays* [3] (London: Peter Davies, 1954), p. 219.
17. Letter AM16, Gordon Daviot to Marda Vanne, 7 Jan 1940, Gwen Ffrangcon-Davies archive.
18. Letter AM3, Gordon Daviot to Marda Vanne, 16 Dec 1934, Gwen Ffrangcon-Davies archive.
19. Salary details from Reid (1993).
20. Letter from Mac to Dave, quoted in BBC radio programme *Gordon the Escapist* (1986), transcript available in the Scottish Theatre Archive, University of Glasgow; further information from private correspondence with Bruce Young (producer) and Tinch Minter (writer).

CHAPTER SIX: *Josephine, and Hugh Patrick Fraser*

1. Aird, (2011), p. 65.
2. Medical details, and date of death, are from Josephine MacKintosh's death certificate.
3. Details from Josephine MacKintosh's will.
4. Details on Jean's job from her reference papers, held in private family archive. Details on Etta's career from conversations with her son; date of Etta leaving school confirmed from IRA school archive.
5. Letter from Gordon Daviot to Dodie Smith, 4thDecember 1937 (Dodie Smith Collection, Howard Gottlieb Archive, Boston) mentions her 'abigail', who is helping prepare the Christmas pudding, and the laundry.
6. Some secondary sources give a different date for Beth leaving teaching. This seems to be traceable to an article in the *Inverness Courier*, published in 1933. The *Inverness Courier* is not a reliable source when it comes to facts about Beth's life.
7. http://www.nicolaupson.com/fact_and_fiction/index.html
8. MacDonald, (1982), p. 120.
9. See Aird, (2011), p. 65.
10. See Aird, (2011), p. 65.
11. Much of the information about Hugh comes from the foreword to his published collection of poems. Other information is from census records, and his death certificate, and from *The*

79th News, Regimental magazines, Jan 1920–Oct 1924, The Highlanders Museum, Fort George.

12. Hugh's birth is recorded in parish records. Because he was an older father, his birth certificate is not available (as his birth falls outwith the range covered by the official government records). Hugh's career is traceable through the MA records of Aberdeen University (http://www.ebooksread.com/authors-eng/university-of-aberdeen/roll-of-the-graduates-of-the-university-of-aberdeen-1860-1900-hci/page-19-roll-of-the-graduates-of-the-university-of-aberdeen-1860-1900-hci.shtml), and the FASTI of the Free Church of Scotland (John A. Lamb (ed.) *The FASTI of the United Free Church of Scotland: 1900–1929*). Online bell-ringers' records show some of his career (http://www.whitingsociety.org.uk/articles/scot-bells/gorbals-foundry-transcription-4.pdf), as his name is inscribed on the bell of one of his churches. I made a research trip to his church in Brockley, London.

13. Linda Taylor, *A Brief History of the First Hundred Years of St Andrew's 1882–1982* (1982), pamphlet.

14. *Sunderland Daily Echo*, Tuesday 29th March 1898; *Surrey Mirror and County Post*, Friday 16th Nov 1906.

15. National Archives, 1/380/350 CS76985.

16. *Hastings and St Leonards Observer*, Sat 3rd December, 1904, p. 4.

17. Edinburgh University Roll of Honour https://archive.org/stream/rollofhonour191400univuoft#page/464/mode/2up

18. *The 79th News*, Regimental magazines, Jan 1920–Oct 1924, The Highlanders Museum, Fort George.

19. The *Weekly Westminster* is available on microfiche at the British Library Newspaper Archives. The *Westminster Gazette* is available in bound leather volumes in the NLS.

20. See *The Saturday Review, 24 July 1926, 8 Oct 1927 and 26 Nov 1927*.

21. Josephine Tey, *To Love and Be Wise* (London: Pan, 1973), p. 140.

22. Josephine Tey collection, National Library of Scotland, Acc 4771/5. I believe the poems in this collection must have been published, as each one is dated and in some cases the name of a magazine is jotted next to them, but searches have not yet found the place of publication.

23. IRA records. Thanks to my own music teacher, Julia Gordon, for her analysis, understanding and playing of the music manuscripts from the NLS.
24. See Poems 1, 2, 3, 4 and 5 in Gwen Ffrangcon-Davies archive.
25. Josephine Tey, *To Love and Be Wise* (London: Pan, 1973), p. 139.
26. Information on Hugh's illness is from his death certificate.
27. Ernest Rhys, 'Foreword' in Hugh P. F. McIntosh, *A Soldier Looks at Beauty* (London: Simpkin Marshall, 1928).
28. Gordon Daviot, *Claverhouse* (London: Collins, 1937), p. 18.

CHAPTER SEVEN: *Short Stories and First Two Novels*

1. See Select Bibliography, The Works of Elizabeth MacKintosh.
2. *Saturday Review*, 16th April 1927, p599.
3. *Saturday Review*, 22nd Sept, 1928, p359.
4. Information from death certificate, and family gravestone in Tomnahurich.
5. MS 26190, fol. 124, letter from Elizabeth MacKintosh to Marion Lochhead, 6th July 1933, National Library of Scotland, for publication in the PEN newsletter.
6. In the MacKintosh family papers. The manuscript is typed, with the name typed at the very end in the same ink and with no sign of being a later addition. At the time this story was published in March 1929, Daviot was considering the publication of both *Kif* and *The Man in the Queue* – she had been asked for an author photograph by her new publishers, and had just revealed to them that she was, in fact, a woman. For the American edition of the book the publisher were keen to include both a photo and a biography, and so she began to consider a female pseudonym. See discussion later in this chapter, and Acc 7708, no. 33, National Library of Scotland – Mairi MacDonald's papers, Letter 3, no date, Mac to Dave.
7. Letter AM5, Gordon Daviot to Marda Vanne, Gwen Ffrangcon-Davies archive.
8. This book came up for sale at a local second-hand bookshop in Inverness, where I examined it, and has subsequently been advertised and discussed online, see, for example, www.abebooks.co.uk.

9. A short version of Beaton's life story can be found in Watt (2012); further information from Dr Miles Mack http:// milesmack.wordpress.com/2011/11/12/murdoch-beaton-sec-retary-to-the-%e2%80%9cdewar-report%e2%80%9d-1912/; thanks also to Colin Waller at HAC; and thanks to Murdoch Beaton's descendant Iain Beaton, who shared memories of his grandfather.

10. Acc 7708, no. 33, National Library of Scotland – Mairi MacDonald's papers, Letter 3, no date, Mac to Dave.

11. Paterson was well known in photographic and literary circles. He became friends with Neil Gunn and photographed Gunn, Hugh MacDiarmid and many other well-known people. His negatives are currently being archived and put online, and a book is being written about his life and work. See http://www.patersoncollection.co.uk/

12. BBC radio programme *Gordon the Escapist* (1986), transcript available in the Scottish Theatre Archive, University of Glasgow; further information from private correspondence with Bruce Young (producer) and Tinch Minter (writer).

13. See *Orlando: Women's Writing in the British Isles from the Beginnings to the Present* – biographical and literary resource; Acc 7708, no 33, National Library of Scotland – Mairi MacDonald's papers, Letter 3, no date, Mac to Dave; and manuscript of 'Deborah', MacKintosh family papers.

14. The cover art for Josephine Tey's work has ranged from the stylish Art Deco drawings of the French hardback of *The Man in the Queue*, to the photograph of Debbie Harry as a beaten-up Betty Kane on the 1971 US paperback edition of *The Franchise Affair*.

15. Since then, Josephine Tey's work has been translated into many different languages, including Spanish, German, Polish and Chinese.

16. Acc 7708, no. 33, National Library of Scotland – Mairi MacDonald's papers, Letter 3, no date, Mac to Dave.

17. Mann (1981), p212.

18. Josephine Tey, *The Man in the Queue* (London: Arrow, 2011), p. 8.

19. Acc 7708, no. 33, National Library of Scotland – Mairi MacDonald's papers, Letter 3, no date, Mac to Dave.

20. Colin sent postcards to his daughter Moire from Shieldaig in the 1940s, and often discussed the village and its inhabitants in his letters to her as well: MacKintosh family archive. In an entry to a *Saturday Review* competition published on the 31st July 1926, Gordon Daviot describes "a reedy tarn [that] lies under Shilldaig's lee". The spelling is inconsistent, and the description doesn't entirely match the real place, but it suggests that she was familiar with Colin's home.
21. Josephine Tey, *The Man in the Queue* (London: Arrow, 2011), p. 139.
22. The *Inverness Courier*, Friday 7th June 1930.
23. J. B. Pick (ed.) *Neil M. Gunn: Selected Letters* (Edinburgh: Polygon, 1987), p. 7; letter dated 18th May 1929, Neil Gunn to Hodder and Stoughton. Neil Gunn Society, inc. webpage http://www.harenet.co.uk/nmg/about/chronology.html
24. The novel was *The Lost Glen*. See Dep 209, National Library of Scotland – Neil Gunn Archive, Box 12, item 5 – rejection letter from Ernest Benn to Neil Gunn, dated 27th June 1929 (mentioning that it took a month to reply, so Gunn's original letter to Benn would have been sent in May).
25. Pick, (1987), p. 9; Neil Gunn Society. *The Lost Glen* was eventually published in 1932.
26. Jean's career is traceable through her reference papers, now in the private MacKintosh family archive. Moire's career was described to me by her son.

CHAPTER EIGHT: The Expensive Halo, *'Ellis' and Invergordon*

1. The *English Review*, 50, February 1930, p. 230
2. *Dundee Evening Telegraph*, daily from Tuesday 12th August to Wednesday 24th September 1930.
3. Josephine Tey, *The Expensive Halo* (London: Peter Davies, 1978), p. 19.
4. Article by Frank Swinnerton, 29th August 29th 1931 in *Chicago Tribune*. Swinnerton worked for the publisher Dent, as well as writing newspaper articles.
5. Josephine Tey, *The Expensive Halo* (London: Peter Davies, 1978), p. 154.
6. Mann, (1981).

7. Josephine Tey, *The Expensive Halo* (London: Peter Davies, 1978), p. 200.

8. Josephine Tey, *The Expensive Halo* (London: Peter Davies, 1978), p. 193.

9. Mann, (1981), p213; *Inverness Courier* Tuesday 24th August 1928, Friday 3rd August 1928, Tuesday 28th May 1929, 23rd and 30th July 1929, Tuesday 13th Aug 1929, Tuesday 25 Feb 1930, Friday 3rd Apr 1931, Tuesday 2 June 1931; MacDonald, (1982), pp. 12–13.

10. *The Inverness Courier*, Friday 3rd August 1928.

11. Beth's nephew recalled his mother mentioning this, but had very few details. Searches through the history of the IRA have produced no results.

12. AM38, Letter from Gordon Daviot to Gwen Ffrangcon-Davies and Marda Vanne, Gwen Ffrangcon-Davies archive.

13. AM38, Letter from Gordon Daviot to Gwen Ffrangcon-Davies and Marda Vanne, Gwen Ffrangcon-Davies archive.

14. General information on John Gielgud from John Gielgud, *Early Stages* (San Franciso, U.S.A.: Mercury House, 1989); Sheridan Morley, *John Gielgud: The Authorized Biography* (New York: Applause Theatre and Cinema Books, 2002); Richard Mangan (ed.) *Gielgud's Letters* (London: Phoenix, 2004).

15. Will of Elizabeth MacKintosh. Information on storage of the script during her lifetime from will. Information on Josephine Tey collection from Inverness Museum.

16. Information from private email with one of Moire's friends. Information on Mutiny from Am Baile website.

CHAPTER NINE: Richard of Bordeaux

1. AM38, Letter from Gordon Daviot to Gwen Ffrangcon-Davies and Marda Vanne, Gwen Ffrangcon-Davies archive.

2. Typewritten summary script, *Richard of Bordeaux*, INVMG.1952.005, Josephine Tey collection, Inverness Museum.

3. Clippings from *Daily Express*, 11th March, 1931, article by H. V. Morton; typewritten summary script, *Richard of Bordeaux*, INVMG.1952.005, Josephine Tey collection, Inverness Museum.

4. See, for example, Gielgud, *Early Stages*, p. 118, p. 134; Morley, (2002), p. 115.

---

5. Morley, (2002), p. 107; Gielgud, *Early Stages*, pp. 118–125.
6. Gielgud, *Early Stages*, p. 135.
7. For example, conversations with Helen Grime, former custodian of the Gwen Ffrangcon-Davies archive and author of Gwen's biography (Helen Grime, *Gwen Ffrangcon-Davies: Twentieth-Century Actress* (London: Pickering and Chatto, 2013)) and emails from Tinch Minter, who interviewed Gwen for the BBC in the 1980s: 'I knew her to be a nonagenarian [but when] I rang her doorbell [...] she bounded to the door in a sweet floral cotton frock and was simply delightful from beginning to end – full of lively chat.'
8. Dodie Smith, *Look Back with Astonishment: Volume Three* (London: W. H. Allen, 1979); Valerie Grove, *Dear Dodie: The Life of Dodie Smith* (London: Chatto & Windus, 1996), p. 76.
9. Paul Ibell, *Theatreland* (London: Continuum, 2009). The original Wyndham was Charles, a stage-struck doctor, who did some acting with Ellen Terry before going to America to work as a medic on the Union side of the Civil War, where he looked after the injured at Gettysburg and was mentioned by Abraham Lincoln in the Gettysburg address. Returning to London, he gave up medicine to go back to the stage, then moved to become a producer and finally theatre owner. Aged eighty, after the death of his first wife, he married his theatre's leading lady, his astute business partner the actress Mary Moore, who was the widow of playwright James Albery. Bronson Albery was Mary's son, and Bronson inherited his mother and stepfather's two theatres, the Wyndham and the New. Bronson's son Donald became a producer, as did his son Ian – who has managed Sadler's Wells theatre in London.
10. Recordings of Margaret Harris of the Motleys, 1992, interviewed by Alison Chitty, British Library NSA General Shelfmark C465/06/01-22; F3033-F3050 + F4730-F4733 C1 PLAYBACK – tape 4.
11. Martial Rose, *Forever Juliet: The Life and Letters of Gwen Ffrangcon-Davies* (Dereham: Larks Press, 2003), p. 76.
12. Gordon Daviot's nephew confirmed that his mother had always said that Gordon had found Gielgud frustrating to work with. This was one of his main memories of family talk around the play. Gielgud's biographer states that Donald Wolfit found

Gielgud particularly difficult during the rehearsals for *Richard*: Morley, (2002), pp. 116–117.

13. Morley, (2002), p. 116.
14. Gielgud, *Early Stages*, p. 135, p. 138.
15. Recordings of Margaret Harris of the Motleys, 1992, interviewed by Alison Chitty, British Library NSA General Shelfmark C465/06/01-22; F3033-F3050 + F4730-F4733 C1 PLAYBACK – tape 4.
16. Morley, (2002),pp. 116–117.
17. It would have been hard to find a school of the time that did not do some sort of show or theatrical production, and local newspapers such as the *Inverness Courier* are full of descriptions of amateur shows. Anstey theatre productions are mentioned in Crunden (1974), and were part of the reminiscences I heard at an Anstey College Old Girls reunion in Glasgow in 2012.
18. Fred Astaire, *Steps in Time: an Autobiography* (New York: itbooks, 2008), pp. 107–108.
19. Letter from Gwen Ffrangcon-Davies to her mother, F2, Gwen Ffrangcon-Davies archive. Details on the Websters from Margaret Webster, *Don't Put Your Daughter on the Stage* (New York: Alfred A. Knopf, 1972) and Margaret Webster, *The Same Only Different: Five Generations of a Great Theatre Family* (London: Victor Gollancz, 1969).
20. Letter from Gwen Ffrangcon-Davies to her mother, F2, Gwen Ffrangcon-Davies archive.
21. Morley, (2002), p. 119.
22. Josephine Tey, *The Man in the Queue* (London: Arrow Books, 2011), p. 1.
23. Letter from Gwen Ffrangcon-Davies to her mother, F2, Gwen Ffrangcon-Davies archive.
24. Smith, *Look Back with Astonishment* ; Grove, (1996), p. 77.
25. John Gielgud, 'Foreword' to Gordon Daviot, *Plays* (London: Peter Davies, 1953), p. x.
26. MS 26190, fol. 124, letter from Elizabeth MacKintosh to Marion Lochhead, 6th July 1933, National Library of Scotland. Marion compiled a series of short profiles of women writers for the Scottish PEN newsletter. See Chapter 13 for further discussion of Beth MacKintosh's relationship with Scottish PEN.
27. *Inverness Courier*, Tuesday 5th July 1933, p. 5.

28. John Gielgud, 'Foreword' to Gordon Daviot, *Plays* (London: Peter Davies, 1953), p. ix; Niloufer Harben, *Twentieth-Century English History Plays: From Shaw to Bond* (London: Macmillan, 1988), pp. 93-94.

CHAPTER TEN: The Laughing Woman

1. *Inverness Courier*, Tuesday 5th July, 1933, p. 5: 'An Inverness Playwright: Eulogies by London Critics'.
2. Rose, (2003), p. 78 (Queen Mary saw the play twice); Gwen Ffrangcon-Davies archive, letter F3.
3. Gordon Daviot, 'Alexander', unpublished; from family papers.
4. *Inverness Courier*, Tuesday 5th July, 1933, p. 5: 'An Inverness Playwright: Eulogies by London Critics'.
5. Acc 7708, no. 33, National Library of Scotland – Mairi MacDonald's papers.
6. Information from Neil Gunn Society; Pick (1987); F. R. Hart & J. B. Pick, *Neil M. Gunn: A Highland Life* (London: John Murray, 1981); Dep 209, National Library of Scotland – Neil Gunn Archive.
7. As quoted in the *Inverness Courier*, Tuesday 10th April, 1934.
8. Gordon Daviot, *The Laughing Woman* in *Famous Plays of 1933–34* (London: Gollancz), p. 383.
9. Acc 7708, no. 33, National Library of Scotland – Mairi MacDonald's papers, Letter 7 (Mac to Dave).
10. Morley, (2002), p. 121.
11. Letter IC7, 26th Dec 1933, Gordon Daviot to 'Anne' (Gwen Ffrangcon-Davies), Gwen Ffrangcon-Davies archive.
12. MacDonald, (1982), p. 120. *Richard* ran for so long that the costumes needed replaced: the cushion was made from scraps of the original costumes.
13. Gwen Ffrangcon-Davies archive, e.g. letter K5.
14. 'A Life in the Theatre', BBC television interview with Gwen Ffrangcon-Davies, 1983.
15. Gielgud, *Early Stages*, p. 141.
16. *Inverness Courier*, 17.10.1933, reprinted in 'From Our Files' article, *Inverness Courier* 17th October 2008.
17. *Richard of Bordeaux* original playbill, February 1934, see http://www.playbillvault.com/Show/Detail/3980/Richard-of-Bordeaux

18. The word 'producer' when applied to theatre in the 1930s can mean something more like what we would understand as a 'director' today. See Mangan (2004), p. 2.

19. *Theatre World*, Vol. XXI, No. 112, May 1934, 222. Dates for *The Laughing Woman* are often given incorrectly, perhaps because John Gielgud often misquoted them: he was maybe thinking of the later radio broadcast, which he was involved in.

20. Acc 7708, no. 33, National Library of Scotland. Mairi MacDonald's papers – Letter 7 (Mac to Dave). Stephen Haggard had acted with Gielgud in *The Maitlands*, the follow-up play to Ronald Mackenzie's *Musical Chairs*, produced just after Mackenzie's death. This had actually been the first play Gielgud performed in the West End after *Richard of Bordeaux*, but it was not a success, partly because the audience were surprised by the great difference between Gielgud's character in *The Maitlands* and his performance as 'Richard'. Critics had written of Haggard as a successor to Gielgud.

21. In private letters to Gielgud, Gordon had considered him for the role, with names mentioned for his leading lady including Flora Robson, Lehmen or Bergner. At this time, Gordon had the pick of the best actresses in London.

22. Veronica Turleigh was to continue her association with crime writer playwrights when she starred as 'Harriet Vane' in Dorothy L. Sayers's stage version of the Lord Peter Wimsey story 'Busman's Honeymoon' in 1936. She also played Mrs Sharpe in a 1962 BBC television adaptation of *The Franchise Affair*.

23. As quoted in the *Inverness Courier*, Tuesday 10th April, 1934.

24. Snapshot from family archive; also published in Caroline Ramsden, *A View from Primrose Hill* (London: Hutchinson Benham, 1984).

25. There are two biographies of Gwen: Rose (2003) and Grime (2013). See also BBC Desert Island Discs interviews 1962 & 1988 (available online via http://www.bbc.co.uk/radio4/features/desert-island-discs/find-a-castaway#/a-z/all)

26. As described in Rose, (2003), p. 14. The Delsarte method was founded on a Greek idea of balance – the body must be in motion or ready to move, yet balanced, at all times. A series of exercises trained the actress to be graceful, rhythmic, and aware of the positioning of her body.

27. See for example, p. 61 in Chapter 3, 'Sexuality and Discretion' of Grime, (2013); Morley, (2002), p. 115. *Richard of Bordeaux* is sometimes found in online discussions of sexuality and the theatre.

28. It might seem overly-naive nowadays that Gordon had no inkling of John's sexuality, but they were very different times. The outspoken Dodie Smith describes very clearly in her autobiographies, both of the 1930s, and later when she was friends with Christopher Isherwood, just how hidden the gay scene was. Keen to understand the taboos of her day and to live in an open-minded way, Dodie ran into trouble with censors in both her plays (in the 1930s) and her novels (much later, in the 1950s). Curiously, her work, so open-minded for its time, now seems more dated than other contemporary writing, perhaps because attitudes have changed so much that what was shocking for her audience is commonplace now.

29. Gwen Ffrangcon-Davies archive, letter AM10. This letter, which has some ambiguous phrasing, is discussed again in Chapter 12.

CHAPTER ELEVEN: Queen of Scots

1. Gordon listed her club membership in 'Daviot, Gordon', 'Who Was Who': *Who's Who* (A & C Black, 1920–2008: http://www.ukwhoswho.com/view/article/oupww/whowaswho/U236424, accessed 17 Nov 2011). The Cowdray was a club for professional women, especially nurses, and Gordon was a member by virtue of her VAD work during the First World War, and through her Anstey connections. The club's headed notepaper is used for letters to Gwen and Marda from the 1930s.

2. As both Colin's and Gordon's wills show, they both invested in stocks and shares.

3. Ramsden, (1984), p. 54.

4. Morley, (2002), p. 125.

5. Ramsden, (1984), p. 55.

6. Letter AM 38, letter from Gordon Daviot to Marda Vanne and Gwen Ffrangcon-Davies, Gwen Ffrangcon-Davies archive.

7. Ramsden, (1984), p. 67.

8. Lena includes a photo from the holiday in her autobiography: Ramsden (1984). Gordon's family had several more photos of

the same holiday. The run of *Queen of Scots*, the date of the official Sasha photo, and a perusal of the photos (especially the clothes they're wearing) date the holiday to spring/ early summer 1934.

9. Webster, *The Same Only Different*, pp. 366–367.

10. Philip Ziegler, *Olivier* (London: MacLehose Press, 2013), p. 54.

11. Quaritch catalogue item 50 (bookseller's catalogue), http://mail. quaritch.com/pdf/qpdf_29_3074865036.pdf

12. Webster, *The Same Only Different*, p. 367.

13. *Theatre World*, August 1934, Vol XXII, No 115; *Theatre World* Souvenir supplement.

14. MacDonald, (1982), p. 118. If handwriting doesn't lie then, applying the same logic to Gordon's own writing, I would say she was definitely a woman who liked to be a little difficult to understand.

15. MacDonald, (1982), p. 117. Mairi doesn't give a source for her assertion that Gielgud thought the play disappointed because it avoided the Casket Letters. Mairi herself thought the contrast between the opulent scenery and costumes of *Richard of Bordeaux* and the more muted *Queen of Scots* was a deciding factor, but a marked contrast isn't immediately obvious from still photographs of the two productions.

16. 'Horace Richards asks... "Shall Theatres Bow to the Heat Wave?"', in *Theatre World*, August 1934, Vol XXII, No 115, p. 62.

17. Information about Marda's background comes from Grime, (2013), and Rose, (2003); Marda's archive is also part of the Gwen Ffrangcon-Davies archive.

18. See, for example, *Theatre World*, Vol. VII, No. 44, Sept 1928, accessed via https://www.flickr.com/photos/42399206@N03/ 5381291350/; National Portrait Gallery http://www.npgprints. com/image.php?imgref=67031.

19. AM4, 22nd Dec 1934, letter from Gordon Daviot to Marda Vanne, Gwen Ffrangcon-Davies archive.

20. Grime, (2013), p. 55.

21. Rose, (2003), p. 80.

22. Ivor Brown, *Sunday Observer*, quoted in the *Inverness Courier and Advertiser*, Tuesday 7th February 1933, p. 5.

23. Contemporary copies of the *Inverness Courier* have listings.

24. Background to film history in the UK in the 1930s from Rachael Low, *Film Making in 1930s Britain* (London: George Allen & Unwin, 1985).
25. Mann, (1981).
26. Information on Sound City and *The Expensive Halo* production from Low, p. 179–180 and p. 413; the British Film Archive http://explore.bfi.org.uk/4ce2b6bb7781d; the Internet Movie Database www.imdb.com.
27. Smith, *Look Back With Astonishment*; Low, (1985), p. 292.
28. Thanks to Lawrence Sutcliffe of the Highlands of Scotland Film Commission for discussion about the studio system in the 1930s.

CHAPTER TWELVE: *Hollywood and Josephine Tey*

1. John Gielgud, 'Foreword' in Gordon Daviot, *Plays* (London: Peter Davies, 1953), p. x.
2. Pathe website or Pathe Youtube: http://www.britishpathe.com/, https://www.youtube.com/user/britishpathe
3. Rose, (2003), p. 159. Gwen had always been short-sighted, but problems with her eyesight got worse as she got older.
4. BBC radio programme *Gordon the Escapist* (1986), transcript available in the Scottish Theatre Archive, University of Glasgow; further information from private correspondence with Bruce Young (producer) and Tinch Minter (writer). Ginger Rogers started her series of collaborations with Fred Astaire in 1933. I always imagine that Gordon Daviot would have been a big fan of Ginger's more dramatic work as well as her dancing, for example *Stage Door* (1937), the story of aspiring actresses.
5. AM5, letter from Gordon Daviot to Marda Vanne, 17th January 1935, Gwen Ffrangcon-Davies archive.
6. Article by Anne Pettigrew in the *Evening Times*, 27th December 1954; AM8, letter from Gordon Daviot to Gwen Ffrangcon-Davies and Marda Vanne, 22nd January 1935, Gwen Ffrangcon-Davies archive.
7. Internet Movie Database www.imdb.com.
8. AM5, letter from Gordon Daviot to Marda Vanne, 17th January 1935, Gwen Ffrangcon-Davies archive.
9. Internet Movie Database.
10. Dodie Smith, *Look Back With Gratitude* (London: Muller,

Blond & White Ltd, 1985). Dodie made $2,000 a week, and up to $20,000 for one job scriptwriting and script-doctoring. Rent on one of their American houses was $600 a month, which was considered expensive. Katharine Hepburn took over the house when they left.

11. As reported at the time of *Cordelia* (1946); newspaper clippings from the Citizens Theatre scrapbooks in the Scottish Theatre Archive at the University of Glasgow.

12. The American Film Institute Catalog of Feature Films http://www. afi.com/members/catalog/DetailView.aspx?s=1&Movie=7638 credits Gordon Daviot as a Feature Writer on *Next Time We Love*, citing contemporary sources such as entertainment magazine *Variety*.

13. Letter 4, 21st November 1935, Mac to Dave in Acc 7708, no. 33, National Library of Scotland – Mairi MacDonald's papers. Gielgud played the lead role, Peter Lowe (later in *Casablanca*) and Robert Young were the other male leads.

14. Ramsden, (1984), p. 58.

15. Conversations with Elizabeth's nephew; remembering what his mother had told him.

16. Harben, (1988).

17. Letter 4, Mac to Dave, 21st November 1935, Acc 7708, no. 33, National Library of Scotland – Mairi MacDonald's papers.

18. http://www.davidhigham.co.uk/history.htm, http://www.curtis-brown.co.uk/.

19. After tracing the family back several generations, I have still not come across anyone called Tey. Beth got her stories about her mother's family from her grandma Jane, and perhaps the name had been corrupted – or was from further back than surviving records. Alternatively, Beth might have done some amateur family history research and been confused by the handwriting of an entry in a parish record: at HAC, Family Historian Anne Fraser was at first excited to discover an ancestor called 'Tey' – before realizing that she was misreading the name 'Fry'.

20. AM16, letter from Gordon Daviot to Marda Vanne, 7th Jan 1940, Gwen Ffrangcon-Davies archive.

21. *Orlando: Women's Writing in the British Isles from the Beginnings to the Present.*

22. Jane Dunn, *Daphne du Maurier and her Sisters: The Hidden*

Lives of Piffy, Bird and Bing (London: HarperPress, 2013), p. 197.

23. Rose, (2003), p. 80. See also Grime, (2013). Marda Vanne's papers are preserved in the Gwen Ffrangcon-Davies archive.
24. Gwen Ffrangcon-Davies archive. The letters are not always dated, but it's possible to work out a rough chronology.
25. See AM5, AM10 and AM11, letters from Gordon Daviot to Marda Vanne, Gwen Ffrangcon-Davies archive.
26. AM10 and AM11, letter and 'Reader's Report' from Gordon Daviot to Marda Vanne, Gwen Ffrangcon-Davies archive.
27. For example, letter 2, 23rd January 1919, Mac to Dave in Acc 7708, no. 33, National Library of Scotland – Mairi MacDonald's papers; Ramsden, (1984), p. 58. If she had been a lesbian, Beth may have wished to conceal her sexuality from Marjorie – but she would have had no need to talk around it with Lena Ramsden.
28. 'Progress', November 1937, Gwen Ffrangcon-Davies archive.
29. I wonder if Marda was the only one to see her that way: one of Georgette Heyer's mystery novels features a tweed-clad adventuring lady; a member of the Cowdray Club. (Lady Harte, in *They Found Him Dead*, published 1937).
30. Letter 5, Mac to Dave, Acc 7708, no. 33, National Library of Scotland – Mairi MacDonald's papers.
31. AM13, letter from Gordon Daviot to Marda Vanne, Gwen Ffrangcon-Davies archive.
32. Webster, *The Same Only Different*, pp. 377–388.
33. The Internet Broadway Database www.ibdb.com.
34. Mangan (2004), pp. 32–33.
35. Gordon Daviot, *The Stars Bow Down* (London: Duckworth, 1939).

CHAPTER THIRTEEN: Claverhouse

1. Beth said that she discussed her interest in Claverhouse with a publisher, who suggested she write about it: *The Franchise Affair* papers, biographical note, Penguin Archive, Bristol University. Beth also mentioned her interest in Claverhouse to Marjorie, her friend from college, saying that he was seen in the wrong way and 'someone ought to do something about it' – there's no date on the letter, but it is sent from Inverness, and she also mentions

reading Edwin Muir's *John Knox: Portrait of a Calvinist*, published in 1929, so Beth may have been reading and discussing Claverhouse for a while (she didn't think much of Muir's book).

2. Hart & J. B. Pick, (1981); J. B. Pick (1987); John MacCormick, *The Flag in the Wind* (Edinburgh: Birlinn, 2008).

3. Hart & J. B. Pick, (1981).

4. Inventory no. 9364, International PEN Scottish centre files, National Library of Scotland.

5. Inventory no. 8560 and Inventory no. 9364, International PEN Scottish centre files, National Library of Scotland – lists of members and 1936/7 programme. I checked all the available member lists and Beth MacKintosh is not listed (under any name).

6. MacDiarmid was first approached to start the club by the Professor of English at the University of Edinburgh, H. J. C. Grierson. Unbelievably, Grierson said he could not think of any writers living in Scotland except MacDiarmid and Neil Munro, and asked for any writers MacDiarmid could recommend from the Central Belt – as they would be most easily able to attend meetings. With this sort of attitude, it's easy to see why female, Highland authors were excluded, and how a club of this sort – however inclusive its name or aim – had strong elements of a boys' network. See John Manson (ed.) *Dear Grieve: Letters to Hugh MacDiarmid (C. M. Grieve)* (Glasgow: Kennedy & Boyd, 2011), p. 18, for original letters.

7. The *Scotsman* newspaper of Saturday 9th June 1934 lists additional subscriptions raised for Scottish PEN's funds for organising the international congress. 'Miss Gordon Daviot, Crown Cottage, Inverness' gives £2 2s.

8. MS 26190, f124, letter from Elizabeth MacKintosh to Marion Lochhead, 6th July 1933, National Library of Scotland.

9. Letter from Gordon Daviot to Dodie Smith, 4th December 1937, from the Dodie Smith Collection, Howard Gottlieb Archival Research Centre at Boston University.

10. Letter from Gordon Daviot to Dodie Smith, 4th December 1937, from the Dodie Smith Collection, Howard Gottlieb Archival Research Centre at Boston University.

11. Neil Gunn sometimes supplied Walsh with plots. On the 23rd February 1937, Gunn wrote to Walsh about the book Walsh

was writing, which would become *And No Quarter*, expressing
his disparagement for the Covenanters – see J. B. Pick (1987).

12. MS 9752 Letter from Elizabeth MacKintosh to Miss M. E. M.
Donaldson 16th March 1938, National Library of Scotland.

13. Letter from Gordon Daviot to Dodie Smith, 4th December 1937,
from the Dodie Smith Collection, Howard Gottlieb Archival
Research Centre at Boston University.

14. MS 9752 Letter from Elizabeth MacKintosh to Miss M.E.M.
Donaldson 16th March 1938, National Library of Scotland.

15. Ramsden, (1984), p. 59.

16. Hart & J. B. Pick (1981). The discussion of his reasons for
leaving are sometimes vague: he went on a sea voyage, which he
wrote about, but there are also hints of a serious fight with his
wife Daisy. Gunn had an accident to his eye at this time, which
was never fully explained. His affair with Margaret MacEwen
ended and she went to London to volunteer for the paper the
Daily Worker, though stayed in touch with him. Gunn's circle of
friends changed a little when he left Inverness and no longer held
'open house' at Larachan. At the very end of his life Neil seemed
to feel huge remorse about this period in his life, particularly
Daisy's miscarriage.

17. Jean MacKintosh's reference letters – private MacKintosh family
collection.

18. Actually his second son, as his eldest son died before he was a
year old.

19. According to conversations with Moire's son.

20. Information on Humphrey's life comes from his two autobiographies (Vice-Admiral Humphrey Hugh Smith, D.S.O., *A Yellow
Admiral Remembers* (London: Edward Arnold & Co, 1932);
Vice-Admiral Humphrey Hugh Smith, D.S.O., *An Admiral Never
Forgets* (London: Seeley, Service & Co, 1936)); online records
of military service personnel http://www.uboat.net/allies/mer-
chants/crews/person/37069.html; http://www.cwgc.org/find-
war-dead/casualty/2701383/SMITH,%20HUMPHREY%20
HUGH; http://www.dnw.co.uk/medals/auctionarchive/viewspe-
cialcollections/itemdetail.lasso?itemid=60253; records of his
first wife's family heritage http://www.thepeerage.com/p7543.
htm; his first wife's obituary as reported in the newspapers
(Times Archive: *The Times* Sat Jan 9th 1937), and his own

obituaries several years later (Times Archive: *The Times* Mon Nov 4th 1940).

21. AM16, letter from Gordon Daviot to Marda Vanne, 7th Jan 1940, Gwen Ffrangcon-Davies Archive.

22. Josephine Tey, *The Singing Sands* (London: Pan, 1965), p. 6. The list of people on the train is a nod to all sorts of characters in Beth's real life: 'a lance-corporal of the Queen's Own Cameron Highlanders' gets the better of Murdo the sleeping-car attendant – surely a reference to her First World War love, and perhaps another indication that they met on the train.

23. Sheila Mackay, *Inverness, Our Story* (U.K.: Inverness Local History Forum, 2007) p. 76–77.

24. See the *Inverness Courier* Friday 13th May 1938 – correspondence page – letter from Colin MacKintosh, p. 5; leader Tuesday 17th May 1938; 7th June 1938; leader Tuesday 14th June 1938; correspondence 21st June 1938; leader 5th July 1938.

25. Criticism of Colin and Beth's engagement in public life came from the *Inverness Courier*, rather unchivalrously, in their obituaries. Obituary of Colin MacKintosh, Inverness Courier 26th September 1950; obituary of Elizabeth MacKintosh, *Inverness Courier* Friday 15th February 1952. These obituaries, especially Beth's, have been quoted in many articles.

26. IRA school magazine, 1939.

27. *Inverness Courier*, leader Tuesday 14th June. The barriers at Craggie's Close and Maclean's Close were broken in broad daylight, first by 'an enterprising and public-spirited citizen', Mr Roderick Reid, butcher, 33 Castle Street 'with a saw obtained from a nearby shop'. The barricades were then broken again later in the day, and once again by two young men late at night.

28. Dodie Smith Collection, Howard Gottlieb Archival Research Centre at Boston University.

29. See Dodie's biography by Grove (1996); and Dodie's own volumes of autobiography.

30. Josephine Tey, *Miss Pym Disposes* (London: Arrow Books, 2011), p. 228.

31. www.imdb.com; Grime, (2013), p. 117.

32. According to conversations with Moire's son.

33. Letter from Heinz Mollwo to Alexander MacEwen, 18th June 1937, Dep 209, National Library of Scotland – Neil Gunn

Archive; Hart & J. B. Pick, (1981), see p. 163: 'Both she [Margaret MacEwen] and [her brother] Malcolm MacEwen suspect that Neil's invitations to Germany were connected with a Nazi attempt to use Scottish Nationalism for their own ends'.

34. 16th August 1936, Alexander MacEwen visitor books 1926-1940, D375/5/3, Alexander MacEwen archive, HAC.

CHAPTER FOURTEEN: *The Second World War*

1. John Gielgud, 'Foreword' in Gordon Daviot, *Plays* (London: Peter Davies, 1953), p. x; Rose, (2003), p. 114. Rose says that Daviot spent two weeks in Edinburgh, and that she and Gwen visited sites of interest to Mary, Queen of Scots.

2. Letter from Colin MacKintosh to his youngest daughter, Etta; dated only 'Sunday afternoon'; private family collection.

3. Letter from Colin MacKintosh to his youngest daughter, Etta; dated only '20th'; private family collection. The Longman is now an industrial estate.

4. Letters from Mac to Dave, Acc 7708, no. 33, National Library of Scotland – Mairi MacDonald's papers.

5. Letter from Colin MacKintosh to his youngest daughter, Etta; dated only 'Sunday afternoon'; private family collection.

6. Letters from Colin MacKintosh to his youngest daughter, Etta; various; undated.

7. Online records of military service personnel http://www. uboat.net/allies/merchants/crews/person/37069.html; http://www.cwgc.org/find-war-dead/casualty/2701383/ SMITH,%20HUMPHREY%20HUGH; http://www.dnw. co.uk/medals/auctionarchive/viewspecialcollections/itemdetail. lasso?itemid=60253; Obituary for Humphrey Hugh Smith in Times Archive: *The Times* Mon Nov 4th 1940.

8. For a good description of the closing of the theatres and the effect on people and business, see Chapter 17 of Richard Huggett, *Binkie Beaumont: Eminence Grise of the West End Theatre 1933–1973* (London: Hodder & Stoughton, 1989).

9. Marguerite Steen, *Looking Glass: an Autobiography* (London: Longmans, 1966); Ramsden, (1984), Chapter 10.

10. Smith, *Look Back With Astonishment* ; Smith, *Look Back With Gratitude* ; Grove, (1996).

11. Letter AM16, Gordon Daviot to Marda Vanne, 7th January 1940, Gwen Ffrangcon-Davies Archive; see also Rose, (2003), p. 105.
12. See Grime, (2013); and Rose, (2003).
13. online records of military service personnel http://www.uboat.net/allies/merchants/crews/person/37069.html; http://www.cwgc.org/find-war-dead/casualty/2701383/SMITH,%20HUMPHREY%20HUGH; http://www.dnw.co.uk/medals/auctionarchive/viewspecialcollections/itemdetail.lasso?itemid=60253; Obituary for Humphrey Hugh Smith in Times Archive: *The Times* Mon Nov 4th 1940; Letter from Colin MacKintosh to Etta, dated only 'Sunday night', private family archive; letter from Jean to Moire, dated 'Thursday 16th May', private family archive.
14. Letter 8, 23rd April 1941, Mac to Dave, Acc 7708, no. 33, National Library of Scotland – Mairi MacDonald's papers.
15. Letter from Colin MacKintosh to Etta, dated only 'Sunday night', private family archive.
16. Letter from Colin MacKintosh to Etta, date obscured, private family archive.
17. Huggett, (1989), p. 246.
18. The story goes that Winston Churchill's finance minister said Britain should cut arts funding to support the war effort. Churchill supposedly said 'Then what are we fighting for?' Whether or not he said it, it was certainly felt – as shown by the reopening of the theatres and the exemptions from fighting granted to actors like Gielgud – that the arts were important.
19. Huggett, (1989), pp. 285–288; Morley (2002).
20. This is a general statement which is repeated in many places; I've tried to check if it's true and it seems to be backed up by some academic studies. Anecdotally, I have heard people say they read more, particularly because of the blackout and the restrictions this put on going out for evening entertainment.
21. *Lilliput: the Pocket Magazine for everyone*, February 1941, vol. 8, no. 2, 93.
22. Letter 7, Mac to Dave, 19th December 1940, Acc 7708, no. 33, National Library of Scotland – Mairi MacDonald's papers.
23. Saturday Night Theatre – a Tribute to BBC Radio Drama http://www.saturday-night-theatre.co.uk/; see also the Scottish Theatre

Archive at the University of Glasgow; and Lesley Henderson, *Twentieth-Century Crime and Mystery Writers* (3rd Edition; London: St James Press, 1991). See also the BBC Genome project, the collected listings of the Radio Times from 1923 to 2009 http://genome.ch.bbc.co.uk/

24. 23rd July 1942, script in the Scottish Theatre Archive, University of Glasgow.
25. Ramsden, (1984), p. 57.
26. Letter 11, Mac to Dave, 25th January 1946, Acc 7708, no. 33, National Library of Scotland – Mairi MacDonald's papers.
27. BBC Genome project, http://genome.ch.bbc.co.uk/. *Mrs Fry Has a Visitor* was broadcast as a children's television play in 1950 and again in 1955.
28. Gordon Daviot, *Leith Sands* (London: Duckworth, 1946), p. 117.
29. Letter from Colin MacKintosh to Etta, 9th May 1943, private family archive.
30. Pamela J. Butler, *The Mystery of Josephine Tey* on http:///www.r3.org/fiction/mysteries/tey_butler.html; Elizabeth Haddon, 'Introduction', in Gordon Daviot, *Dickon* (London: Heinemann Educational Books, 1974).

CHAPTER FIFTEEN: *The Citizens Theatre*

1. Now the Royal Conservatoire of Scotland.
2. Aird, (2011), p. 66. For information on James Bridie see Ronald Mavor, *Dr Mavor and Mr Bridie: Memories of James Bridie* (Edinburgh: Canongate/National Library of Scotland, 1988).
3. Citizens Theatre Website www.citz.co.uk.
4. See Citizens Theatre Company archives, housed in the Scottish Theatre Archive, University of Glasgow.
5. Saturday Night Theatre – a Tribute to BBC Radio Drama http://www.saturday-night-theatre.co.uk/
6. Letter 12, Mac to Dave, Acc 7708, no. 33, National Library of Scotland – Mairi MacDonald's papers.
7. Christina R. Martin, 'A Mystery About This: justified sin and very private memoirs in the detective novels of Josephine Tey', PhD thesis, (University of Strathclyde, 2001), p. 128. Martin perhaps over-emphasizes the friendship between the two women. Not realizing their age difference, she assumes Molly

worked also on *Richard of Bordeaux*. She didn't. Martin also doesn't seem to realize the connections between the MacEwens and Neil Gunn.

8. D375/5/3, Visitor books; HCA/D436/7/3, Correspondence between Frank Thompson and Margaret MacEwen, Alexander MacEwen archive, HAC.

9. On the 25th November 1944, Gunn wrote to Bridie, discussing a meal out they had enjoyed together in Glasgow. At the meal, Gunn had quarrelled with C. M. Grieve (Hugh MacDiarmid). J. D. Fergusson was also in attendance. J. B. Pick (1987).

10. Bridie and MacDiarmid did not get on. MacDiarmid took umbrage (in person, at a club) at an article Bridie wrote which MacDiarmid perceived as critical. Bridie responded by letter, challenging MacDiarmid to write a play for the Citz – if he could. MacDiarmid replied only obliquely, through editorial and articles he commissioned and published in a literary magazine – sample title: 'The Citizens' Theatre: A Nuisance and a Menace'. Incensed, Bridie wrote MacDiarmid a lengthy defence of the Citz, interspersed with some pithy insults. Bridie then wrote a poem, 'The Blighted Flyting of James Bridie and Hugh MacDiarmid'. See Manson, (2011), p. 343, p. 344 & p. 360. This exchange of insults and one-upmanship was fairly typical of the Scottish literary scene, and not really a world Gordon Daviot was interested in, or concerned that she was excluded from, as she got on with producing her bestselling Tey novels.

11. Citizens Theatre Company Archive, Scottish Theatre Archive, University of Glasgow.

12. Citizens Theatre Company Archive, Scottish Theatre Archive, University of Glasgow.

13. Gordon Daviot, *Plays* [2] (London: Peter Davies, 1954), p. 75.

14. Citizens Theatre Company Archive, Scottish Theatre Archive, University of Glasgow.

15. The debate about whether or not the Citz should produce plays in Scots rumbled on: later that year, Bridie spoke publicly about it, and Mathew Forsyth was drawn into an argument with Hugh MacDiarmid, that staunch supporter of Scots, which played out on the letters pages of the *Glasgow Herald*. Alan Bold (ed.) *The Letters of Hugh MacDiarmid* (London: Hamish Hamilton, 1985).

16. Citizens Theatre Company Archive, Scottish Theatre Archive, University of Glasgow.
17. Letter 12, Mac to Dave, 24th May 1946, Acc 7708, no. 33, National Library of Scotland – Mairi MacDonald's papers.
18. Marguerite Steen talked of her recollections of Gordon Daviot on 7th December 1953, on BBC Radio's Woman's Hour. Unfortunately I have found no recording or details of the piece other than the Radio Times listing.
19. Ramsden, (1984), p. 60.

CHAPTER SIXTEEN: Miss Pym Disposes

1. Beth's friendship with Elisabeth Kyle is discussed in letters between Kyle and Mairi MacDonald, Acc 7708, no. 33, National Library of Scotland – Mairi MacDonald's papers. Kyle does not describe how they met, but, from her knowledge of Beth's life, it seems likely that they became friends later in life.
2. Citizens Theatre Company Archive, Scottish Theatre Archive, University of Glasgow.
3. They toured *Richard of Bordeaux* to Edinburgh, where one member of the audience was the future librarian of the SCDA. His memory of this performance led him to make sure that the SCDA library had a stock of Gordon Daviot plays – which I used many years later.
4. Citizens Theatre Company Archive, Scottish Theatre Archive, University of Glasgow.
5. Tour dates and arrangements from Citizen's Theatre Company Archive, Scottish Theatre Archive, University of Glasgow; press clippings and reviews also.
6. John Gielgud, 'Foreword', in Gordon Daviot, *Plays* (London: Peter Davies, 1953), p. x.
7. See Chapter 4; see also Aird, (2011), p. 65.
8. Josephine Tey, *Miss Pym Disposes* (London: Arrow Books, 2011), p. 199.
9. She says she thinks Gordon Daviot is rather good. Gladys Mitchell, *Laurels are Poison* (London: Vintage, 2014), p. 191.
10. See, for example, Martin, (2001). Martin says that Tey quoted from Mitchell, but I haven't been able to find this.

11. Mitchell was also a member, by virtue of her background in PE teaching and interest in sport, of the British Olympic Association.
12. The list of members is readily available online, e.g. http://en.wikipedia.org/wiki/Detection_Club
13. I read this once in passing, but unfortunately haven't been able to find the reference again. It seems worth mentioning as it's so likely. However, searches of Dorothy L. Sayers' published letters have brought up no references to Tey.
14. Josephine Tey, *The Daughter of Time* (London: Penguin, 1976), p. 34.
15. For a good short biography of Sayers, see Martha Hailey Dubose, *Women of Mystery: The Lives and Works of Notable Women Crime Novelists* (New York: St. Martin's Press, 2000), pp. 161–224.
16. According to Old Girls at an Anstey reunion meal I attended.
17. Anstey College *Jubilee magazine* (1897-1947), p. 10.
18. Anstey College *Jubilee magazine* (1897-1947), p. 10.
19. Crunden (1974).
20. The trips to Glenmore Lodge were remembered very fondly by the Anstey Old Girls who I met at their reunion dinner. More than one Anstey girl married an instructor from the lodge.
21. Colin wrote regularly to his youngest daughter, letters which remain in the family, and, although he never complains too much, it's clear that he is feeling his age.
22. Will of Colin MacKintosh, National Archives of Scotland.
23. See Chapter 4 for information about the Hornes.
24. Beth's nephew had never heard of these family members; if Moire and Beth had known, they had not passed on the information. As both their names are very common, and frequently spelt in several different ways, searches amongst death and marriage certificates have been futile. Census records after 1911 are not available. There is no mention of them in any surviving family letters which I have seen. No military records can be found for Donald to indicate whether he signed up in the Second World War.
25. See death certificates, and gravestones in Tomnahurich cemetery for information on this branch of the Horne family.
26. She writes to Moire from the address of the family home she shared with Humphrey (letters in private family archive).

Neighbours do remember that Colin was frequently visited by
one of his daughters other than Beth, but it's not clear if this was
Jean or Moire. Both sisters certainly visited Inverness in the late
40s and 50s, but neither moved back permanently.

27. Letter from Colin MacKintosh to Etta, dated 6th May 1946,
private family collection.
28. Letter from Jean to Moire, dated 'Thursday 16 May', private
family collection. 'Olivia' is unidentified.
29. See birth records. Colin Stokes stated that he was named after
his granddad, Colin MacKintosh.
30. Will of Colin MacKintosh, National Archives of Scotland.

CHAPTER SEVENTEEN: *Amateur Dramatics,* Valerius *and*
The Franchise Affair

1. Angela du Maurier, *It's Only the Sister* (Cornwall: Truran
Books, 2003), p. 254.
2. Grove (1996); Smith, *Look Back With Gratitude.*
3. Huggett (1989); Smith, *Look Back With Gratitude.*
4. Webster, *Don't Put Your Daughter on the Stage*, p. 146.
5. Barbara Bruce-Watt persuaded Daviot. Bruce-Watt is quoted
in BBC radio programme *Gordon the Escapist* (1986), transcript available in the Scottish Theatre Archive, University of
Glasgow; further information from private correspondence with
Bruce Young (producer) and Tinch Minter (writer); the Florians
website http://www.florians.org.uk/stuff/previous.html.
6. Internet Movie Database.
7. *Aberdeen Journal*, 11th April 1947; *Dundee Courier*, 16th
February 1948; *Glasgow Herald*, 15th March 1948.
8. Gordon Daviot, *Plays* [2] (London: Peter Davies, 1954), p. 194.
9. Edinburgh International Festival http://www.eif.co.uk/. *The
Scotsman*, 7th June 1947, p. 6, lamented the lack of Scottish
plays at the Festival, and gave Gordon Daviot as an example of
a playwright who could have been included.
10. Obituary for Elizabeth MacKintosh, *Inverness Courier*, Friday,
15th February 1952.
11. Letter 14, Mac to Aunt Tibbie (mother of Marjorie Davidson),
12th October 1948, Acc 7708, no. 33, National Library of
Scotland – Mairi MacDonald's papers.

12. Letter 6, Mac to Dave, 20th Sept 1939, Acc 7708, no. 33, National Library of Scotland – Mairi MacDonald's papers.
13. A full discussion of *Valerius* is in Letter 14, Mac to Aunt Tibbie (mother of Marjorie Davidson), 12th October 1948, Acc 7708, no. 33, National Library of Scotland – Mairi MacDonald's papers. The date of the production was included when the play was finally published: see Gordon Daviot, *Plays* (London: Peter Davies, 1953).
14. See collected reviews, including quotes from the *Chicago Sun* and the *New York Herald Tribune*, in Sandra Roy, *Josephine Tey* (Boston: Twayne Publishers, 1980), p. 119.
15. Sarah Waters, 'The lost girl', article in *The Guardian*, 30th May 2009.
16. Letters, biography and notes on *The Franchise Affair* in the Penguin Archive, Bristol University. See bibliography for publication details about individual Tey mystery novels.

CHAPTER EIGHTEEN: *The Malvern Festival, and* Brat Farrar

1. See Chapter 12. The dedication in the published version of *The Stars Bow Down* makes the dating of the writing of this play clear.
2. Max H. Fuller, *One-Act Plays for the Amateur Theatre* (London: Harrap & Co Ltd, 1949).
3. http://www.saturday-night-theatre.co.uk/; Obituary of Elizabeth MacKintosh in the IRA school magazine, 1952, HAC ref HCA/C1/5/8/11/9.
4. The Malvern Festival programme, 1949; http://www.malvern-festival.co.uk/.
5. See Margaret Webster's autobiographies, and Gwen Ffrangcon-Davies's biographies for examples of just how highly regarded he was. Other books of the time also make his status clear, while his portrait was painted by artists such as Laura Knight.
6. The Malvern Festival programme, 1949.
7. Letter from Gordon Daviot to Dodie Smith, undated, from the Dodie Smith Collection, Howard Gottlieb Archival Research Centre at Boston University.
8. Ramsden, (1984), p. 59.
9. Aird, (2011), p. 65 – Catherine Aird knew Beth's sister Moire, and is a reliable source of information about the family.

However, although Aird mentions the idea of two-week holiday and a housekeeper in more than one article, and suggests this was something that had been going on for some time, this does not fit the pattern of Beth's earlier holidays/trips to London. A housekeeper was probably only really necessary towards the end of Colin's life, when he was frailer and Moire and Jean were unavailable.

10. Ramsden, (1984), p. 59.
11. Ramsden, (1984), p. 59.
12. The Malvern Festival programme, 1949.
13. Roy, (1980), p. 27.
14. The Malvern Festival programme, 1949, p. 16.
15. The Malvern Festival programme, 1949, p. 16.
16. Private MacKintosh family collection.
17. Letter 13, Beth to Aunt Tibbie, Acc 7708, no. 33, National Library of Scotland – Mairi MacDonald's papers.
18. Rose, (2003), p. 127.
19. B14, Letter from Gordon Daviot to Gwen Ffrangcon-Davies, no date, Gwen Ffrangcon-Davies archive.
20. See Rose (2003) and Grime (2013).
21. Lena quotes from many of Beth's letters in her autobiography: Ramsden (1984).
22. Ramsden, (1984), p. 54.
23. Lena got his name slightly wrong – he was more usually known as Frankie More O'Ferrall. See More O'Ferrall Park website http://www.kildangan.kildare.gaa.ie/TimesPast/more-o-ferrall-park
24. Ramsden, (1984), p. 56.
25. *Orlando: Women's Writing in the British Isles from the Beginnings to the Present.*
26. Colin Stokes remembered his mother saying that Beth would sometimes phone when she was 'stuck' with her writing, saying 'give me a plot!' Gielgud also mentioned this 'weakness' with plots – see John Gielgud, 'Foreword', in Gordon Daviot, *Plays* (London: Peter Davies, 1953).
27. Like *The Franchise Affair*, some later critics have seen *Brat Farrar* as based on a historical mystery – the Tichborne case of the 1860s/70s. Beth was a keen student of history so it is possible, though I have found no particular evidence of this.

28. Letter 4, Mac to Dave, 21st November 1935, Acc 7708, no. 33, National Library of Scotland – Mairi MacDonald's papers.
29. Josephine Tey, *Brat Farrar* (USA: Dell, 1964), p. 168.
30. Josephine Tey, *Brat Farrar* (London: Arrow Books, 2002), p. 122.

CHAPTER NINETEEN: To Love and Be Wise

1. See Colin's letters to his youngest daughter, e.g. 9th May 1943, private family collection.
2. Ramsden, (1984), p. 59.
3. Ramsden, (1984), p. 138.
4. Letter from Elisabeth Kyle to Mairi MacDonald, April 30th 1953, Acc 7708, no. 33, National Library of Scotland – Mairi MacDonald's papers; see also letter 13, Gordon Daviot to Aunt Tibbie, no date, Acc 7708, no. 33, National Library of Scotland – Mairi MacDonald's papers.
5. Ramsden, (1984), p. 138.
6. Ramsden, (1984), p. 139.
7. Gwen and Marda stayed friends, but their relationship had changed – they were no longer so close. Grime (2013); Rose (2003).
8. Josephine Tey, *To Love and Be Wise* (London: Pan, 1973), p. 65.
9. Letter from Gordon Daviot to Marda Vanne, 17th January 1935, Gwen Ffrangcon-Davies archive.
10. Josephine Tey, *To Love and Be Wise* (London: Pan, 1973), p. 116.
11. Gwen and Marda's address is given in Ramsden (1984).
12. In Smith, *Look Back With Astonishment*, p. 169, Dodie describes Basil Dean's house in Essex, which he had ruthlessly modernized. Basil Dean produced Dodie's first plays, before she started to work with Binkie Beaumont. Dodie rented her own cottage to Binkie during the Second World War and after, while she and Alec were in America.
13. Dodie discusses this – still obliquely – in Smith, *Look Back With Gratitude*. See also Grove (1996).
14. Josephine Tey, *To Love and Be Wise* (London: Pan, 1973), p. 33.

15. Josephine Tey, *To Love and Be Wise* (London: Pan, 1973), p. 139.
16. See reminiscences of MacKintosh's neighbour Hamish Macpherson, described in the article, 'Fruit followed mystery writer's angry exchange' in the *Inverness Courier*, Tuesday 5th October 1993; and letter from Elisabeth Kyle to Mairi MacDonald April 30 1953, Acc 7708, no. 33, National Library of Scotland – Mairi MacDonald's papers.
17. Will of Colin MacKintosh, National Archives of Scotland.
18. See Aird (2011) – though the condition of the shop is obvious from the condition of Castle Street at that time.
19. See will of Colin MacKintosh and will of Elizabeth MacKintosh, National Archives of Scotland.
20. See Valuation Rolls of Inverness (HAC); Mackay (2007), pp. 76–77; *Homes for a Highland Town*, short film, c.1950, National Library of Scotland, Scottish Screen Archive, SSA ref. 4145; Newton (2003).
21. Valuation Rolls of Inverness, HAC.
22. See will of Colin MacKintosh, list of assets, National Archives of Scotland.
23. *Homes for a Highland Town*, short film, c.1950, National Library of Scotland, Scottish Screen Archive, SSA ref. 4145. Shown at a special screening in Inverness by the Inverness Local History Forum.
24. Valuation Rolls of Inverness, HAC.
25. Josephine Tey, *Brat Farrar* (USA: Dell, 1964), p. 155.
26. Letter from Beth to Moire, Sunday 10th September 1950, private family collection.
27. 'Smashing', written as spoken in the distinctive Inverness accent. It's still said. It's actually a word from the Gaelic originally.
28. Letter from Beth to Moire, dated only 'Saturday', private family collection.
29. Death certificate of Colin MacKintosh.
30. Gravestone in Tomnahurich.
31. Letter 15, Mac to Dave, 9th October 1950, Acc 7708, no. 33, National Library of Scotland – Mairi MacDonald's papers.
32. Death certificate of Colin MacKintosh. Finlayson signed himself 'intimate friend'. It was only by chance that I discovered

Finlayson's signature as witness on another document, and thus found his place of work at Stewart, Rule and Co. The addresses of Finlayson and Colin's other friends are on Colin's will.

33. Will of Colin MacKintosh, National Archive of Scotland.
34. National Archive currency converter, http://www.national-archives.gov.uk/currency/.
35. *Inverness Courier* 26th September 1950.
36. The MacEwen archives are in HAC, including notes for a proposed biography by Frank Thompson which was never completed.
37. Letter from Carmichael to Moire, 30th September 1950, private family collection. Colin was also a Mason, and the Masonic lodge in Inverness sent a condolence letter as well.
38. *Highland News*, Saturday 30th September: There were several local papers, but the *Inverness Courier* and the *Highland News* are the only two survivors. It's rather a shame that researchers from outwith the Highlanders gravitate to the *Inverness Courier* first because of its name (and because of its own promotion of its history) – it certainly means that the negative obituaries of Colin and Beth have been given undue precedence. In fact, the *Highland News* is often a better source.

CHAPTER TWENTY: *You will know the Truth*

1. Quoted in BBC radio programme *Gordon the Escapist* (1986), transcript available in the Scottish Theatre Archive, University of Glasgow; further information from private correspondence with Bruce Young (producer) and Tinch Minter (writer); see also Letter 15, Mac to Dave, 9th Oct 1950, Acc 7708, no. 33, National Library of Scotland – Mairi MacDonald's papers.
2. Valuation Rolls for Inverness, HAC.
3. Letter from Beth to Moire, 5th October 1951, private MacKintosh family collection.
4. This letter was advertised for sale online via the website www.abebooks.co.uk. I have examined detailed scans and photographs of the letter.
5. The title of *To Love and Be Wise* also comes from a Francis Bacon quote.
6. Josephine Tey, *The Daughter of Time* (London: Penguin, 1976), p. 11.

7. Pamela J. Butler, *The Mystery of Josephine Tey* on http:///www. r3.org/fiction/mysteries/tey_butler.html

8. *Richard III – The King in the Car Park*, first broadcast on Channel 4, 9pm, Wednesday 27th February 2013.

9. Isolde Wigram, interviewed by Colin White, National Trust Sound Archive, Shelfmark C1168/571/01-02, British Library.

10. Josephine Tey, *The Daughter of Time* (London: Penguin, 1976), p. 130.

11. Gordon Daviot, *Claverhouse* (London: Collins, 1937), p. 33.

12. *Orlando: Women's Writing in the British Isles from the Beginnings to the Present.*

13. Letter from John Williams to Eunice Frost, 22nd September 1952: *The Daughter of Time* files, Penguin Archive, University of Bristol.

14. *The Daughter of Time* files, Penguin Archive, University of Bristol.

15. Ramsden, (1984), p. 138; Aird, (2011), p. 67.

16. Reviews collected in Roy (1980). Roy chose *The Privateer* as her favourite of Tey's non-mystery novels (p. 43).

17. Will of Elizabeth MacKintosh, National Archives of Scotland.

18. Anstey College Scottish Old Girls Reunion, Wednesday 20th June 2012, Glasgow. See also Crunden (1974).

19. Letter from Beth to Moire, 5th October 1951, private MacKintosh family collection.

20. Aird, (2011), p. 67.
    The South London Hospital for Women, with an all-female staff until the end, remained open until 1984, when it was closed by the Tory government in the face of general opposition. The site was occupied for almost a year by some radical staff and their supporters in an attempt to keep it open, but eventually they lost their fight. The hospital was then partially demolished ten years later to make way for a Tesco, but a general outcry meant that the supermarket had to keep the building's impressive facade intact. (This story was widely reported and details are readily available online. A good starting point is http://en.wikipedia. org/wiki/South_London_Hospital_for_Women_and_Children)

21. Will of Elizabeth MacKintosh, National Archives of Scotland; original documents also held by family.

22. Death certificate.

23. Ramsden, (1984), p. 139. Lena does get some details wrong; confirmed dates and details from Morley (2002), and Mangan (2004).

24. John Gielgud, 'Foreword', to Gordon Daviot, *Plays* (London: Peter Davies, 1953), p. x.

25. Letter from Elisabeth Kyle to Mairi MacDonald, April 23, 1953, Acc 7708, no. 33, National Library of Scotland – Mairi MacDonald's papers.

26. Letter from Elisabeth Kyle to Mairi MacDonald, April 23, 1953, Acc 7708, no. 33, National Library of Scotland – Mairi MacDonald's papers; Ramsden, (1984), p. 140. Dodie Smith didn't do funerals.

CHAPTER TWENTY ONE: *Will, and* Plays

1. Will of Elizabeth MacKintosh, National Archive of Scotland. Although Beth's Will specifically refers to 'The National Trust for England', the correct name of the organisation is the 'National Trust', as it also covers Wales and Northern Ireland.

2. See Chapter 12.

3. See, for example, article 'Fruit followed mystery writer's angry exchange', in the *Inverness Courier*, Tuesday 5th October 1993.

4. See Highland history and culture website www.ambaile.co.uk for photos of Miss Margaret MacDougall organizing this display; there is also a MacDougall archive in HAC.

5. Josephine Tey collection, Inverness Museum and Art Gallery. INVMG.1952.005; INVMG.1952.003; INVMG.1952.004; INVMG.1947.001.

6. Date on will of Elizabeth MacKintosh, National Archives of Scotland. Aird, (2011), p. 67.

7. Aird, (2011), p. 65 and p. 67.

8. *John Gielgud at the BBC*, BBC radio collection audio cassette, released 2000.

9. *The Bulletin*, January 27th 1954.

10. See Lesley Henderson, *Twentieth-Century Crime and Mystery Writers* (3rd Edition; London: St James Press, 1991), p. 1006 for an incomplete bibliography. This biography contains the most complete bibliography of all Elizabeth MacKintosh's published/performed works.

11. John Gielgud, 'Foreword', to Gordon Daviot, *Plays* (London: Peter Davies, 1953).
12. Gordon Daviot, *Plays* [2] (London: Peter Davies, 1954).
13. Full details of the production of *The Pomp of Mr Pomfret* have not been found, though it is listed in some online bibliographies of Tey's work, eg http://ic.galegroup.com/ic/bic1/ ReferenceDetailsPage/ReferenceDetailsWindow?displayGroup Name=Reference&zid=223c47bd26dbfb3aa7e27d4a28a83147 &action=2&catId=&documentId=GALE%7CK2406000507& userGroupName=nysl_se_ramapo&jsid=207f8250e68e83018d 212259af30e7d4
14. Jean Mackintosh, 'Miss Mac' (1880-1971) taught at Daviot Primary School until 1950. Daviot School Log Book 1932-1961, HAC, C1/5/3/1929. Thanks to Highland Archive Centre genealogist Anne Fraser, who remembered her mum (a former Daviot pupil) talking about Miss Mac's friendship with Gordon Daviot. Despite the name, Miss Mac and Gordon Daviot were not related.
15. Gordon Daviot's play *Mrs Fry Has a Visitor* had been classified and advertised as a children's play when it was given its second airing by the BBC in 1950; this is the only other example of Daviot writing for children.
16. Gordon Daviot, *Plays* [3] (London: Peter Davies, 1954).
17. *Reckoning* is one of only four Daviot plays that seem to have never had a professional production. The others are *Clarion Call*, *Patria* and *The Princess Who Liked Cherry Pie*.

CHAPTER TWENTY TWO: The Singing Sands

1. Letter from Maurice Lindsay to Neil Gunn, 21st February 1949, Dep 209, National Library of Scotland – Neil Gunn Archive.
2. Neil M. Gunn, *The Lost Chart* (London: Faber and Faber, 1949).
3. Josephine Tey, *The Singing Sands* (London: Pan, 1965), p. 7. Like Arthur Ransome: on returning to Britain from journalistic work in Revolutionary Russia, anxious diplomats asked Ransome what his politics were. 'Fishing,' he replied.
4. Josephine Tey, *The Singing Sands* (London: Pan, 1965), p. 11.
5. Short typed biography in *The Franchise Affair* notes, Penguin Archive, the University of Bristol.

6. See Hart & J. B. Pick (1981).

7. Ramsden, (1984), p. 138.

8. See Manson (2011).

9. MacCormick (2008).

10. In Gordon Daviot, *Plays* [2] (London: Peter Davies, 1954).

11. Gordon Daviot, *Plays* [2] (London: Peter Davies, 1954), p. 152.

12. When Mairi MacDonald was writing her biographical essay on Gordon Daviot for the *Scots Magazine*, she spoke to Daviot's friend, the writer Elisabeth Kyle. Kyle wrote to Mairi that Daviot had once given a rather pithy description of a well-known Scottish nationalist as an 'elderly Sissy in a kilt'. Kyle discreetly does not mention habitual kilt-wearer Hugh MacDiarmid.

13. His sister Marianne died in Devon, but is commemorated in Tomnahurich. His father died in Wick, but is commemorated in Tomnahurich. His half-sister Jeannie (born in Aberdeenshire) and her English husband both moved to Inverness, where they lived and died. His other sister Dorothy died in Edinburgh; her resting place is unknown.

14. George Edward Jeans, the son of Mary Horne and Robert Jeans, emigrated to the USA and eventually settled in Ohio, where he became a tool and die maker. Mary, of course, was Beth's aunt – Josephine's sister (see Chapter 2).

15. Inverness Museum has a small permanent display about Highland Airways. Thanks also to former Highland Airways pilot Steven Thomson for information.

16. See discussion of Tey in Val McDermid, 'The brilliant unconventional novels of Josephine Tey', *Daily Telegraph*, 15 November 2015.

17. See introduction and blurb in reprint of Josephine Tey, *The Singing Sands* (New York: Simon & Schuster, 1996), which quotes positive reviews from the *San Francisco Chronicle* and the *New York Times*.

18. BBC radio programme *Gordon the Escapist* (1986), transcript available in the Scottish Theatre Archive, University of Glasgow; further information from private correspondence with Bruce Young (producer) and Tinch Minter (writer); Acc 7708, no. 33, National Library of Scotland – Mairi MacDonald's papers.

19. Correspondence between Jennifer Morag Henderson and the National Trust.

20. Ramsden, (1984), p. 57.
21. *Paranoiac* (1963) – www.imdb.com; *Tipping My Fedora* mystery and crime blog http://bloodymurder.wordpress.com/2012/01/10/paranoiac-1963-tuesdays-forgotten-film/.
22. In a letter from Nico Davies, advertised for sale online via the website www.abebooks.co.uk. I have examined detailed scans and photographs of the letter.
23. MacDonald, (1982).
24. See correspondence with John Gielgud, Gwen Ffrangcon-Davies and publishers Peter Davies in Acc 7708, no. 33, National Library of Scotland – Mairi MacDonald's papers.
25. Ramsden (1984).
26. BBC radio programme *Gordon the Escapist* (1986), transcript available in the Scottish Theatre Archive, University of Glasgow; further information from private correspondence with Bruce Young (producer) and Tinch Minter (writer); 'Fruit followed mystery writer's angry exchange', in the *Inverness Courier*, Tuesday 5th October 1993.
27. Roy (1980).
28. The Florians, *An Evening with Gordon Daviot*, programme; private letters from Alison Wilkie to the Saltire Society; *Inverness Courier* clippings: 'Daviot revival earns Florians a famous fan', from private collection of Alison Wilkie.

CONCLUSION

1. Although most reporting of this event focuses on the radiant photos of Dame Gwen Ffrangcon-Davies with her new honour, and discussion of her illustrious career, there have been questions over why this honour, for such a distinguished actress, came so late in life. There has been some suggestion that it was delayed because of Gwen's sexuality. See Grime (2013), pp. 196–199.
2. Private correspondence with Jennifer Morag Henderson.

Select Bibliography

The Works of Elizabeth MacKintosh
(Publication is London unless otherwise noted.)

1925 Gordon Daviot, 'A Triolet', *Westminster Gazette*, 29th August

1926 — competition entries, *Saturday Review* [various dates 24th July – 27th October 1928]

1927 — 'Pat', *Glasgow Herald*, 2nd April

1928 — 'Haivers', *Glasgow Herald*, 18th February

1928 — 'The Find', *Glasgow Herald*, 9th June

1928 — 'His Own Country', *English Review*, July, 102–08

1928 — 'A Three-Ha'Penny Stamp', *Glasgow Herald*, 3rd November

1929 — 'The Exquis', *Glasgow Herald*, 19th January

1929 — *Kif: an Unvarnished History* (Ernest Benn; New York: D. Appleton & Co.)

1929 — 'Deborah', *English Review*, March, 340–47

1929 — *The Man in the Queue* (Methuen; New York: E. P. Dutton & Co; trans. Anne d'Aurier, Plon: Paris, 1932)

1930 — 'Madame Ville d'Aubier', *English Review*, February, 230–34

1931 — *The Expensive Halo: a Fable without Moral* (Ernest Benn; New York: D. Appleton & Co.)

1932 — *Richard of Bordeaux*, The Arts Club, June 1932, directed by John Gielgud, produced by Howard Wyndham and Bronson Albery, performed by John Gielgud, Gwen Ffrangcon-Davies

1933 — *Richard of Bordeaux*, New Theatre, 2nd February-April 1934 [production and cast as June 1932]; regional tour 1934, performed by Glen Byam Shaw, inc. King's Theatre, Edinburgh, 2nd April

1933 — *Richard of Bordeaux: a play in two acts* (Victor Gollancz; Samuel French [acting edition]; Boston: Little Brown)

1934 — *Richard of Bordeaux*, Empire Theatre, Broadway, 14th February-19th March, performed by Dennis King, Margaret Vines

1934 —*The Laughing Woman*, New Theatre, 7th April, produced and directed by John Gielgud, performed by Stephen Haggard, Veronica Turleigh

1934 — *The Laughing Woman* (Victor Gollancz)

1934 — *Queen of Scots*, New Theatre, 8th June-8th September, directed by John Gielgud, performed by Gwen Ffrangcon-Davies, Laurence Olivier, Glen Byam Shaw

1934 — *Queen of Scots: a Play in Three Acts* (Victor Gollancz)

1934 —*Youthful Folly*, Sound City (UK), October, general release December, directed by Miles Mander, produced by Norman Louden, written by Heinrich Fraenkel, Gordon Daviot [adapted from *The Expensive Halo*], performed by Irene Vanburgh, Mary Lawson, Jane Carr

1936 — *Next Time We Love*, Universal Pictures, 30th January (US), directed by Edward H. Griffith, screenplay by Melville Baker (story by Ursula Parrott), ['Gordon Daviot' contract writer], performed by Margaret Sullavan, James Stewart

1936 Josephine Tey, *A Shilling for Candles: The Story of a Crime* (Methuen & Co.)

1936 Gordon Daviot, *The Laughing Woman*, John Golden Theatre, Broadway, 13th October-November, performed by Helen Menken, Tonio Selwart

1937 — *Claverhouse* (Collins)

1937 Josephine Tey, *Young and Innocent* ('based on the novel entitled *A Shilling for Candles* by Josephine Tey'), Gaumont British Picture Corporation, November; 10th February 1938 (New York), directed by Alfred Hitchcock, screenplay adapted by Charles Bennett, Edwin Greenwood, Anthony Armstrong, performed by Nova Pilbeam, Derrick de Marney

1938 Gordon Daviot, *Richard of Bordeaux*, BBC TV Drama, Alexandra Palace, 17th & 27th December; performed by Andrew Osborn, Gwen Ffrangcon-Davies

1939 — *The Stars Bow Down: a Play in Three Acts* (Duckworth)

1939 — *Mixed Grill*, crossword, Inverness Royal Academy magazine

1940 — *The Laughing Woman*, BBC Radio, 1st December [shortened version], performed by John Gielgud, Edith Evans

1941 — 'Bees', *Lilliput*, February, vol. 8, no. 2, 93

1941 — *Richard of Bordeaux*, BBC Radio, 1st June, adapted for radio and produced by Hugh Stewart, performed by John Gielgud

1941 — *Leith Sands*, BBC Radio, 13th November, 'New Play by Gordon Daviot'

1942 — *Queen of Scots*, BBC Radio, 6th December, 'adapted for broadcasting by the author', performed by Fay Compton

1944 — *The Three Mrs Madderleys*, 'a play specially written for broadcasting by Gordon Daviot', BBC Radio, 14th June, produced by Val Gielgud

1944 — *Mrs Fry has a Visitor*, BBC Radio, 6th December

1945 — 'Three Women' [series of three religious plays] *The Mother of Masé*; *Rahab*; *Sara*, BBC, 10th, 17th & 24th June

1946 — *Remember Caesar*, BBC Radio, 4th January

1946 — *Leith Sands and Other Short Plays* [*Leith Sands*, *Rahab*, *The Mother of Masé*, *Sara*, *Mrs Fry has a Visitor*, *The Three Mrs Madderleys*, *Clarion Call*, *Remember Caesar*] (Duckworth)

1946 F. Craigie Howe, *Cornelia*, Citizens Theatre Company, Glasgow, 15th April – 26th April, original production by Mathew Forsyth, performed by Rona Anderson

1946 Gordon Daviot, *The Little Dry Thorn*, Citizens Theatre Company, Glasgow, 29th April – 10th May; Empire Theatre, Inverness, 12th August, original production by Mathew Forsyth, performed by Edmund Bailey, Enid Hewitt, Rona Anderson

1946 Josephine Tey, *Miss Pym Disposes* (Peter Davies; New York: Macmillan, 1948)

1946 Gordon Daviot, *The Balwhinnie Bomb*, BBC radio

1946 — *The Pen of my Aunt*, BBC radio

1947 — *Rahab*; *Leith Sands*, SCDA, Empire Theatre, Inverness, 15th February

1947 — *Richard of Bordeaux*, BBC TV Film, 6th April, performed by Andrew Osborn, Joyce Heron

1948 Josephine Tey, *The Franchise Affair* (Peter Davies; New York: Macmillan, 1949)

1948 Gordon Daviot, *Valerius*, Repertory Players, Savile Theatre, 3rd October

1948 — *The Stars Bow Down*, BBC Radio, 13th November, 'adapted for radio by the author'

1948 — *Leith Sands*, The Florians, Inverness

1949 Josephine Tey, *Crooked Penny* ['condensed version' of *Brat Farrar*] in the *Ladies Home Journal* (August)

1949 — *Brat Farrar* (Peter Davies; New York: Macmillan, 1950)

1949 Gordon Daviot, *The Balwhinnie Bomb*, The Florians, Inverness

1949 — *The Stars Bow Down*, Festival Theatre, Malvern, 10th August, produced by Mathew Forsyth, performed by the Malvern Company

1950 Josephine Tey, *Come and Kill Me* [*Brat Farrar*] (New York: Pocket Books)

1950 Gordon Daviot, *Mrs Fry has a Visitor*, BBC TV Film, 9th May

1950 — *The Pen of My Aunt*, BBC Radio, 15th February

1950 Josephine Tey, *To Love and Be Wise* (Peter Davies; New York: Macmillan, 1951)

1950 — *Brat Farrar*, Philco-Television Playhouse (NBC TV, US), 14th May 1950 & 27th July 1952

1951 — *The Daughter of Time* (Peter Davies; New York: Macmillan, 1952)

1951 — *The Franchise Affair*, Associated British Pictures, 20th February (UK release), 28th April 1952 (US release).

1951 Gordon Daviot, *Sara*, The Florians, Inverness

1952 — *The Privateer* (Peter Davies; New York: Macmillan)

1952 Josephine Tey, *The Singing Sands* (Peter Davies; New York: Macmillan, 1953)

1952 Gordon Daviot *Richard of Bordeaux*, BBC Radio, 27th September, performed by John Gielgud

1953 Josephine Tey, *The Man in the Queue* (Hale; Peter Davies; New York: Macmillan) [republished under Tey name]

1953 — *Killer in the Crowd* [Mercury Mystery Series] (Joseph W. Ferman, New York) ['Abridged Edition' of *The Man in the Queue*]

1953 Gordon Daviot, *Plays 1* [*The Little Dry Thorn, Valerius, Dickon*; Foreword by John Gielgud] (Peter Davies)

1954 —*Plays 2* [*The Pomp of Mr Pomfret; Cornelia; Patria; The Balwhinnie Bomb; The Pen of My Aunt; The Princess Who Liked Cherry Pie*](Peter Davies)

1954 — *Plays 3* [*Lady Charing is Cross, Sweet Coz, Reckoning; Barnharrow; The Staff-Room*](Peter Davies)

1955 — *Sweet Coz*, BBC television, 4th January

1955 — *Lady Charing is Cross*, BBC television, 8th February

1955 — *Dickon*, Playhouse, Salisbury, 9th May

1956 — *Barnharrow; The Staff-Room* (double-bill), BBC television, 1st May

Unpublished works

Individual poems: National Library of Scotland, Josephine Tey collection, Acc 4771/5

Individual poems: Gwen Ffrangcon-Davies collection

'Alexander': MacKintosh family papers (Private collection)

'The Thing that Knows the Time': MacKintosh family papers (Private collection)

'Giuseppe', dated May 1951: MacKintosh family papers (Private collection)

Primary Sources
Manuscripts and Archive Material
Aberdeen University Archive: MA records (Hugh McIntosh)

Alison Wilkie material (Private collection)

Applecross Family History Centre: Parish Records

Argyll & Bute Council Archives, Oban High School Log book CA/5/249/5

Beaton correspondence (Private collection)

British Library and British Library Newspaper Archive

Edinburgh University Archives (Roll of Honour, 1914)

Highland Archive Centre:
  Inverness Valuation Rolls
  Inverness Royal Academy Prospectuses C1/5/8/7/8; C1/5/8/7/9
  Alexander MacEwen archive: visitor books 1926–1940, D375/5/3; Frank Thompson and Margaret MacEwen letters, HCA/D436/7/3
  Farraline Park School Log Book 1908–1923, C1/5/3/160/1/3

Howard Gottlieb Archival Research Centre, Boston University:
  Dodie Smith Collection, Gordon Daviot/Dodie Smith letters

Gwen Ffrangcon-Davies collection (formerly held at the University of Winchester):
  Gordon Daviot/Gwen Ffrangcon-Davies letters
  Gordon Daviot/Marda Vanne letters
  Marda Vanne papers, inc. poems by Gordon Daviot

Inverness Royal Academy School Archive

Inverness Museum and Art Gallery: Josephine Tey collection

MacKintosh collection of family papers (Private collection)

National Archives of Scotland:
  Colin MacKintosh's Will, SC29/44/112 pp1899-1904
  Elizabeth MacKintosh's Will, SC29/44/116 pp1370-1382

National Library of Scotland:
  Elizabeth MacKintosh/Marjorie Davidson letters, Mairi MacDonald's papers, Acc. 7708, no. 33
  Josephine Tey collection, Acc. 4771/5
  Elizabeth MacKintosh/Marion Lochhead letter, MS 26190, fol. 124
  Elizabeth MacKintosh to Miss M. E. M. Donaldson, MS 9752
  International PEN Scottish centre files, Inventory no. 8560; Inventory no. 9364
  Neil Gunn Archive, Deposit 209

Scottish Screen Archive: *Homes for a Highland Town* (c.1950), Ref. 4145

Select Bibliography

Penguin archive, Bristol University:
  The Franchise Affair files
  The Daughter of Time files
Scottish Theatre Archive, University of Glasgow:
  Citizens Theatre Company archive
  BBC Scotland archive: *Gordon the Escapist*, 1986 radio script,
    247 STA Jx 71/14

Newspapers and Magazines
Anstey College Jubilee Magazine (1897–1947)
Anstey College Magazine
Highland News
Inverness Courier (formerly known as *Inverness Courier and Advertiser*)
Inverness Royal Academy magazine
Lilliput: the Pocket Magazine for everyone
The 79th News (Regimental Magazine)
The English Review
The Times
Theatre World
Weekly Westminster

Secondary Sources
Books, Pamphlets and Articles
Catherine Aird, 'Josephine Tey, the Person', in Geraldine Perriam
  (ed.) *Josephine Tey: A Celebration* (Glasgow: Black Rock Press,
  2011)
Bannerman, Charles, *Further up Stephen's Brae: the Midmills Era
  at Inverness Royal Academy* (St Michael Publishing, 2010)
Barber, Gordon, *My Diary in France: experiences and impressions of
  active service during a period of the war with the central empires*
  (Liverpool: privately printed by Henry Young & Sons, 1917)
Pamela Butler, 'The Mystery of Josephine Tey' published online
  at www.r3.org/fiction/mysteries/tey_butler.html
Crunden, Colin, *A History of Anstey College of Physical
  Education 1897–1972* (Warwickshire: Anstey College of
  Physical Education, 1974)

Dubose, Martha Hailey, *Women of Mystery: The Lives and Works of Notable Women Crime Novelists* (New York: St. Martin's Press, 2000)

Dunn, Jane, *Daphne du Maurier and her Sisters: the Hidden Lives of Piffy, Bird and Bing* (HarperPress, 2013)

John Gielgud 'Foreword' to Daviot, Gordon *Plays* (London: Peter Davies, 1953)

Gielgud, John, *Early Stages* (San Franciso: Mercury House, 1989)

Grime, Helen, *Gwen Ffrangcon-Davies: Twentieth-Century Actress* (Pickering and Chatto, 2013)

Grove, Valerie, *Dear Dodie: The Life of Dodie Smith* (Chatto & Windus, 1996)

Haddon, Elizabeth, 'Introduction', to Gordon Daviot: *Dickon* (Heinemann Educational Books, 1974)

Harben, Niloufer, *Twentieth-Century English History Plays: From Shaw to Bond* (Macmillan, 1988)

Hart, F. R. & J. B. Pick, *Neil M. Gunn: A Highland Life* (John Murray, 1981)

Henderson, Lesley, *Twentieth-Century Crime and Mystery Writers,* 3rd Edition (St James Press, 1991)

Huggett, Richard, *Binkie Beaumont: Éminence Grise of the West End Theatre 1933–1973* (Hodder & Stoughton, 1989)

Ibell, Paul, *Theatreland* (Continuum, 2009)

Lamb, John A. (ed.) *The FASTI of the United Free Church of Scotland* (1900–1929)

Low, Rachael, *Film Making in 1930s Britain* (George Allen & Unwin, 1985)

MacCormick, John, *The Flag in the Wind* (Edinburgh: Birlinn, 2008)

Val McDermid, 'The brilliant unconventional novels of Josephine Tey', *Daily Telegraph*, 15th November 2015

MacDonald, Mairi A. *The Banks of the Ness* (Edinburgh: Paul Harris Publishing, 1982)

MacEwen, Sir Alexander Malcolm, *The Thistle and the Rose: Scotland's Problem Today* (Edinburgh: Oliver and Boyd, 1932)

McIntosh, Hugh P. F., *A Soldier Looks at Beauty* (Simpkin Marshall, 1928)

410

Mackay, Sheila, *Inverness: Our Story* (Inverness Local History Forum, 2007)

The Malvern Festival Programme, 1949

Mangan, Richard (ed.) *Gielgud's Letters* (Phoenix, 2004)

Mann, Jessica, *Deadlier than the Male: An Investigation into Feminine Crime Writing* (David and Charles, 1981)

Martin, Christina R., 'A Mystery about this: justified sin and very private memoirs in the detective novels of Josephine Tey' (Unpublished doctoral thesis: University of Strathclyde, 2001)

Maurier, Angela du, *It's Only the Sister* (Cornwall: Truran Books, 2003)

Mavor, Ronald, *Dr Mavor and Mr Bridie: Memories of James Bridie* (Edinburgh: Canongate/N LS, 1988)

Mitchell, Gladys, *Laurels are Poison* (London: Vintage, 2014)

Morley, Sheridan, *John Gielgud: The Authorized Biography* (New York: Applause Theatre and Cinema Books, 2002)

Newton, Norman, *Inverness: Highland Town to Millennium City* (Breedon Books, 2003)

Pick, J. B. (ed.) *Neil M. Gunn: Selected Letters* (Edinburgh: Polygon, 1987)

Preece, Robert, *Song School, Town School, Comprehensive: A History of the Inverness Royal Academy* (Inverness: IRA, 2011)

Ramsden, Caroline, *A View from Primrose Hill* (Hutchinson Benham, 1984)

Reid, Robert A. (ed.) *Oban High school – the first 100 Years* (Oban: Oban High School, 1993)

Rose, Martial, *Forever Juliet: the life and letters of Gwen Ffrangcon-Davies* (Dereham: Larks Press, 2003)

Roy, Sandra, *Josephine Tey* (Boston: Twayne Publishers, 1980)

Sayers, Dorothy L. *Gaudy Night* (London: Hodder & Stoughton, 2003)

Smith, Dodie, *Look Back with Astonishment* (W. H. Allen, 1979)

— *Look Back with Gratitude* (Muller, Blond & White Ltd, 1985)

Smith, D.S.O, Vice-Admiral Humphrey Hugh, *A Yellow Admiral Remembers* (Edward Arnold & Co, 1932)

— *An Admiral Never Forgets* (Seeley, Service & Co, 1936)

Steen, Marguerite, *Looking Glass: an Autobiography* (Longmans, 1966)

Nancy Ellen Talburt, 'Josephine Tey' in Earl F. Bargainnier (ed.) *10 Women of Mystery* (Ohio: Bowling Green University Popular Press, 1987)

Taylor, Linda, *A Brief History of the First Hundred Years of St Andrews 1882–1982* (1982)

Sarah Waters, 'The lost girl', *The Guardian*, 30th May 2009

Watt, Patrick, *Steel and Tartan* (Gloucestershire: The History Press, 2012)

Webster, Margaret, *Don't Put Your Daughter on the Stage* (New York: Alfred A. Knopf, 1972)

— *The Same Only Different: five generations of a great theatre family* (Victor Gollancz, 1969)

Recordings
British Library NSA:
Margaret Harris interviewed by Alison Chitty (1992), C465/06/01-22; F3033-F3050 + F4730-F4733 C1 PLAYBACK – tape 4
Isolde Wigram, interviewed by Colin White, C1168/571/01-02

BBC:
Interview with Gwen Ffrangcon-Davies, *A Life in the Theatre* (BBC television, 1983)
Interviews with Gwen Ffrangcon-Davies: BBC *Desert Island Discs* (1962; 1988)
John Gielgud at the BBC, BBC radio collection audio cassette, released 2000.

Channel 4:
Richard III – The King in the Car Park, Wednesday 27 February 2013

Online Sources
Am Baile, Highland Council, history and culture website: http://www.ambaile.org.uk

Select Bibliography

The American Film Institute, *Catalog of Feature Films*: http://www.afi.com

British Broadcasting Corporation, Radio Times Archive [Genome Project]: http://genome.ch.bbc.co.uk

British Film Archive: http://www.bfi.org.uk/archive-collections

British Newspaper Archive: http://www.britishnewspaperarchive.co.uk

Commonwealth War Graves Commission: http://www.cwgc.org

Citizens Theatre Company: www.citz.co.uk

Internet Movie Database: www.imdb.com

National Library of Scotland: www.nls.uk

Neil Gunn Society: www.neilgunn.org.uk

Orlando: Women's Writing in the British Isles from the Beginnings to the Present: accessed via www.nls.uk

Pathe: http://www.britishpathe.com

Paterson Collection: http://www.patersoncollection.co.uk

Scotland's People: http://www.scotlandspeople.org

Times Archive: accessed via www.nls.uk

Index

Note: Titles of books and plays are shown in *italic*. Titles beginning with 'The' have been grouped under 'The' in the index. There are separate entries for Beth MacKintosh, Gordon Daviot and Josephine Tey but these are inevitably complementary with some overlap.

421